The Light Blue Lanyard

Fifty Years with
40 Commando Royal Marines

Major J. C. Beadle MBE MC RM

A Square One Publication

Published in 1992 by
Square One Publications
Saga House, Sansome Place, Worcester WR1 1UT

© 1992 J. Beadle
British Library Cataloguing in Publication Data
Beadle, Jeffrey Charles
    Light Blue Lanyard:
    Fifty Years with 40 Commando Royal Marines
I. Title
359.9
ISBN 1-872017-52-5

Typeset and Printed by Severnside Printers Limited, Upton-upon-Severn, England

"Raised in urgent, clouded days, the Commandos hardened them-selves for battle by sea, land or air, in which nothing was certain except the hazards they would have to face. To them, danger was a spur, and the unknown but a challenge".

Her Majesty Queen Elizabeth, The Queen Mother

Excerpt from Her Majesty's address to representatives of the war-time Commandos at the unveiling of the Commando Memorial.

Spean Bridge, Achnacarry
27 September, 1952.

CONTENTS

ACKNOWLEDGEMENTS

Today's events all too soon become the faded memories of the past and unless recorded, are lost forever. Various episodes appertaining to 40 Royal Marine Commando will be found piecemeal in other books and magazines, but I have endeavoured to fill in the omissions and correct a number of inaccuracies. My aim has been to produce a comprehensive account of the first Royal Marine Commando, from its auguration on 1942 into the post war period when 40 Commando Royal Marines extended its activities to the world beyond the Mediterranean.

To register every incident of the 50 year history would result in an impossibly long chronology. I have therefore compromised by covering all major activities and have included sufficient detail of a minor nature to give the reader a perception of life in this Commando in times of conflict and in peace.

This achievement has only been possible through the encouragement which I have received in full measure from former members of 40 Commando and personnel currently serving in the Royal Marines. In particular I wish to express my sincere appreciation to Major Alistair Donald for his advice and assistance with the research and to Bill Pook and my wife Gabrielene for editing the material.

I wish to thank the Director and staff of the Royal Marines Museum for providing facilities and access to records and photographs, the Editor, Globe and Laurel for permission to draw on material published in the journal relating to 40 Commando Royal Marines and 3 Commando Brigade Royal Marines; the Imperial War Museum for access to records and photographs and to all former and serving members of Her Majesty's Armed Services who have contributed to these pages.

Jeffrey C. Beadle

FOREWORD

by Lieutenant General Sir Henry Beverley KCB OBE
Commandant General Royal Marines

The story of 40 Commando Royal Marines is, in many ways, absolutely central to the recent history of our Corps and, in chronicling the history of this distinguished Unit, a major contribution to the preservation of our heritage has been achieved. St Valentine's Day 1942 did, indeed, mark the beginning of a new chapter in the annals of the Royal Marines, and one of absolutely critical importance to the high profile and reputation that the Corps enjoys today.

It was the injection of vitality provided by the Commando role that proved the inspiration and raised the profile of the Corps in the middle of the Second World War. Those volunteers from around the Corps, who responded to the cautionary order "Royal Marines Commando…' in the drill shed on that first parade at the Depot, Deal, from their Commanding Officer Lieutenant Colonel J P Phillipps were indeed making history.

The Commando characteristics of flair and initiative, fitness and intense professionalism when fused onto the traditional values emanating from our maritime heritage have resulted in fighting men of the very highest quality. That is quite evident from this work, which tells the story of the fifty years' history of the first of our Commando Units in great detail from its origins through the epic of Dieppe to the Northern Ireland tours, The Falklands and Operation HAVEN in Northern Iraq.

Major Beadle is eminently qualified to be the author; intimately involved as he was with the Unit from the early days, and blooded with them in battle. He has now made a further splendid contribution: not only those who have worn the Light Blue Lanyard but all associated with the family that is the Royal Marines, will read this book with great pride in our Corps – and no little nostalgia.

CHAPTER 1

14 February to 31 May 1942.

*The first volunteers – Weeding out and the early days of training – Scotland
and an introduction to the American Rangers – Formation of the ill-fated
T Company – The move south in preparation for the Dieppe raid.*

ST VALENTINE'S DAY, 14 February 1942, marked the beginning of a new
chapter in the history of the Royal Marines. The first of a steady stream of
volunteers for a special unit, known briefly as The Royal Marine Commando,
assembled at North Barracks, Deal. Introduced as a temporary wartime
expedient, this Commando was the forerunner of a further seven Royal
Marine Commandos. These units served in Commando Brigades alongside
Army Commandos in Europe, the Middle East and Far East in World War II.
On completion of hostilities the Army Commandos were disbanded and the
Royal Marines continued to keep alive the traditions and exacting standards
of that elite force.

Army Commandos were formed soon after the evacuation of the British
Expeditionary Force from Dunkirk in June 1940. It is questionable why The
Royal Marines, whose role is ideally suited to amphibious warfare, was not
involved with the formation of Commandos at an earlier date. In the Army
Bureau of Current Affairs pamphlet No 46 of 12 June 1943 it is stated that "Had
sufficient Marines been available when Commandos were first organised, it is
possible that all of them would have been based on Royal Marines personnel".
The fact is that the Corps was already fully committed at that time.

The first priority of the Royal Marines at the outbreak of hostilities in
September 1939 was to provide detachments in HM ships for manning the
guns in the war at sea. Approval was given towards the end of the year to form
the Royal Marine Brigade (RM Bde) and in January 1940 an additional
formation, known as the Royal Marine Group of the Mobile Naval Base
Defence Organization, was sanctioned.

Between the time of the German invasion of Norway on 9 April 1940 and the
surrender of France on 10 June nine weeks later the Royal Marines despatched
a contingent to occupy the Faeroes and a battalion strength force to occupy
Iceland. Detachments were also landed in Norway, Holland and France. In the
summer months following Dunkirk, while the British Army was absorbed
with the task of reorganising and rebuilding its depleted formations, the RM
Bde provided one of the few complete forces available in Britain to counter the
threat of German invasion. This Brigade was itself committed in August 1940
to land at Dakar, but a shortage of suitable landing craft led to the cancellation

of the operation.

Later the same month approval was given for the formation of the Royal Marine Division at a strength of three brigades, each of two battalions. The Division incorporated the RM Bde. In addition, the Corps provided the RM Siege Regiment, the 11th Searchlight Regiment and the 1st Anti-Aircraft Regiment, all deployed on the Channel coast. The Corps commitments relative to its size were considerable. In consequence it was not feasible to attempt the formation of additional specialist units until the major threat of invasion had diminished and sufficient men were available. This became possible towards the end of 1941.

"FOR THE ATTENTION OF ALL ROYAL MARINE TRAINED PERSON-NEL – VOLUNTEERS REQUIRED FOR SPECIAL DUTIES OF A HAZARD-OUS NATURE". The eye catching message was signalled to all Royal Navy ships, Royal Navy and Royal Marines shore establishments in late November 1941 and repeated in Admiralty Fleet Orders (AFOs) between that time and early February 1942.

The response was immediate. A contingent from Portsmouth Division assembled at Royal Marines Barracks Eastney to await instructions while the first Chatham Division volunteers were drafted to Deal. Their task was to open up the unoccupied North Barracks in preparation for the arrival of this new force. Further west, in the wartime Depot at Lympstone, all trained ranks assembled on the parade to hear the Adjutant proclaim the requirement for volunteers.

Marine J. Forbes, a 'hostilities only' volunteer with other similar young men, had until that moment been finding life rather dull. "This was an invitation not to be missed." he said, with the memories of that day still fresh in his mind. "We had to give our names in to our company offices. No details were revealed but it was an opportune moment to escape from the tedium of Depot duties and offered some prospect of excitement and adventure. The rumours were plentiful as we packed our kit and prepared to move the next day."

The invitation was also accepted by regular officers, NCOs and marines. Early morning on 14 February 1942 Lieutenant A.D.Comyn, with 100 other-ranks from the Non-Commissioned Officers' School at Thurlestone, joined forces with the Lympstone contingent and boarded a train at Exeter.

There was plenty to think about on the journey eastward. The war had not been going well. Almost each month of 1941 had seen a new setback for the Allies. A newspaper communique of the day reported that Rommel's Afrika Korps was poised ready to strike at the Libyan capital of Benghazi. Germany had occupied Yugoslavia, Albania, Greece and Crete and followed up these successes with an onslaught on Russia. Further west, the Americans found themselves pitched into the front-line with audacious attacks by the Japanese on Pearl Harbour and the Philippines. It would not be long before the flag of the rising sun was to be seen flying at mastheads in Malaya and Singapore.

Passing the time by contemplating the future, Forbes visualised a landing on the coastline of France or the formation of an independent raiding force for the South Pacific. Very soon, both would become reality which ended with tragic consequences. Meantime, thoughts of immediate action faded when the 'old soldiers', recognising familiar countryside, realised they were approaching the pre-war Royal Marine Depot at Deal. The West Country draft was not the only group travelling to Deal that day. Lieutenant-Colonel J.P. Phillipps, an officer dedicated to the Corps like his father Lieutenant-General P. Phillipps CB, CMC, MVO., arrived on the London train. The Colonel was no stranger to Deal, having served as Adjutant of the Depot between 1937 and 1940. Although known to his fellow officers as "Tigger", many young officers (YOs) and marines (Mnes) under training unashamedly referred to him as "Tiger Phillipps". He received news of his appointment to command the new formation while serving in the rank of brevet-Major at the Army Staff College, Camberley. On leaving Camberley he spent short periods at the Royal Marine Office and headquarters of Lord Louis Mountbatten, Commodore Combined Operations, organising staff requirements and arranging the war-establishment for the first Royal Marine Commando.

The Colonel was accompanied by Major R.D.Houghton, more familiarly referred to as "Tich" by the men who had served with him previously. Maj Houghton had transferred from the 15th Machine Gun Battalion to be second-in-command of this new force. He was to serve again as Commanding Officer of 40 Commando Royal Marines in 1944 and as Brigadier of the 3rd Commando Brigade Royal Marines between 1957 and 1959.

Corporal P.J.Churchill, also arriving from London, was surprised to see an officer step from the train carrying a long-bow and quiver of arrows. He had envisaged that more sophisticated weaponry would be available but had no cause to worry. Captain P.W.C.Hellings, awarded the Distiguished Service Cross for his actions during the withdrawal from Boulogne and Calais in September 1940, was an experienced and capable officer who had persuaded the best of the Bren-gunners from the 3rd Battalion Royal Marines to join him in this new venture. Soon to be a mainstay of the unit, he was in later years to become Commandant- General Royal Marines. Meanwhile he was to command A Company.

The following morning all ranks were mustered in the drill-shed behind the old Victorian accommodation block where Lt Col Phillipps brought the men to attention with the cautionary order, "Royal Marines Commando"!* From this moment there was no time for further speculation. A hard training programme had already been prepared and a stringent weeding-out process

---

* Ex members of the Commando have verified that the adjective 'Marines', i.e. Royal Marines Commando, was used on occasions between February and August 1942. The singular adjective 'Marine' was used officially throughout the Corps until January 1951 at which time it was changed to 'Marines'.

commenced immediately.

The pre-war Depot, with its extensive sick-bay facilities, had the benefit of an equally large Royal Navy medical staff. The move of Depot training to Lympstone had left them with a much reduced work-load, but now they were back in business! The Commando volunteers ran the gauntlet of tests devised by doctors who entered into the spirit of the occasion. The stringent medical standards took their toll and many good men were bitterly disappointed to find themselves rejected as medically unsuitable. Those who passed the medical were confronted with a series of searching questions by Lt Col Phillipps and Maj Houghton. All the NCOs were told bluntly that they would have to justify their rank or revert to marine, and this proved to be no idle threat. A number of marines, disillusioned to find no glamour, extra pay or relaxation of standards of dress or discipline, requested to return to their units (RTU). Their requests were immediately approved as they were of no value to the Commando.

At first it was thought best not to accept married men but this ruling was quickly modified and the final decision in all cases rested with the Colonel. The sifting process continued for some time, with border-line decisions mostly resolved during the vigorous training programme. A considerable number of men failed to make the grade and reluctantly accepted RTU. They were replaced by fresh batches of hopeful volunteers who arrived at Deal almost daily. The following extract from the unit war diary illustrates the breadth of the trawl:-

15 Feb '42
Lt D.E.M.B. Tod from Portsmouth Div. Lt H.O.Huntingdon-Whiteley from Chatham Div, join with 72 ORs from 101 RM Bde, Beach Engineers and RMTT Depot.

16 Feb '42
Lt M.J. Ephraums from HMS *Cumberland* with 25 ORs from RM Siege Regt, Plymouth Div. and 18(Mob) Bt.

17 Feb '42
39 ORs join from Por Div, 12 RM and Sussex Battery 2 CA Regt. Lt N.E.S Maude from Holding Battalion Deal. 40 ORs RTU at own request.

20 Feb '42
2/Lt I.C. McKellar and 10 ORs from Argyll and Sutherland Highlanders (102 RM Bde). Lt H.W.F. Grant-Dalton from Portsmouth Div. and 38 ORs from 102 Bde.

24 Feb '42
Ty/Lt E.W. Ecrepont from 9 RM. Lt J.E. Steibel from HMS *Nelson* and 100 ORs

from 104 (Trg) Bde, 12 RM and 103 Bde.

All ranks of the 8th Argyll and Sutherland Highlanders (8 A & SH) became eligible to volunteer for the RM Commando subsequent to the attachment of that Battalion to the 102nd RM Brigade. On the creation of the Royal Marine Division the existing RM Bde was divided to produce the 101st and 102nd RM Brigades and a new 103rd RM Brigade was formed. Towards the end of 1940 the brigade establishment was increased to three battalions and to help achieve the required numbers the Army sanctioned the loan of the 8 A & SH to the 102nd Brigade.

Training occupied the major part of each day and frequently cut into the precious hours usually devoted to sleeping. The skilful use of light weapons and fieldcraft was repeatedly tested and interspersed with close-quarter combat and the use of grenades. Swimming, running, physical training and 20 mile marches along the lanes and beaches in East Kent formed a regular feature of the programme. Life was not dull and the majority of men were only too happy at the end of an exhausting day to relax and clean their equipment.

The opportunity to rest was never guaranteed. Everyone took his turn at guards, fatigues and fire pickets. In addition to night exercises it was not unusual to find the Commando ordered to assemble in the early hours, quite possibly on the roof-tops of the barracks. On one occasion the Colonel ordered every access to the barracks to be closed for 48 hours and all personnel entering or leaving during this time had to shin over the eight-foot-high flint walls.

Improvisation and improvement were always encouraged and any suggestion or idea which could benefit the Commando was carefully considered. Modifications were made to uniform, although it must be emphasised that standards were rigorously maintained. Greatcoats were exchanged for sleeveless leather jerkins and a length of knitted woollen material, having the appearance of a sleeve stitched closed at both ends, was issued as an additional item of headdress. The cap-comforter, as it was known, gained immediate popularity. Not only was it warm and snug fitting but its versatility enabled it to be used as a scarf, waistband, foot-warmer or receptacle in which to carry eggs and other "live-off-the-land" commodities. Boots have always been of major importance to the infantry and the value of good boots was equally appreciated by the commandos. The rope-soled type proved most effective for silent movement in built-up areas but failed to give adequate support to the ankles when crossing rough country or marching long distances. The rubber-composition ridged sole SV boot proved very reliable when it became available a few months later* and was preferable to the leather-soled boot. The standard canvas webbing equipment continued to be used but short cloth puttees were provided in addition to the canvas gaiters. The puttees were found to give additional support to the ankles and also held the battledress or

---

* First issue of SV boots from Special Service Brigade received on 19 June.

denim trouser leg more securely than did the gaiters.

A sleeveless jacket of strong canvas material incorporating various pockets was provided for field tests. It was designed to replace the webbing equipment, but made the wearer uncomfortably hot during long periods of activity and was not accepted for general use. Two other accessories were provided for each man. The four-foot toggle-rope with an eye-splice at one end and wood-toggle at the other was carried around the waist while the fighting knife* was attached to the sleeve or trouser leg of the battle dress by a leather scabbard. A combined knife-knuckleduster was also supplied but it was not a popular weapon and the few that were issued were returned to store or eventually discarded.

The main weapons were:-

The short-magazine Lee-Enfield .303-inch rifle (SMLE) with open U-type backsight, sighted to 2,000 yds (1,829m) and 18-inch sword bayonet. This excellent weapon had changed little since its introduction to the British Army in 1907 and could produce an accurately aimed rate of fire of 15 rounds a minute.

The American Thompson .45-inch sub-machine-gun (SMG), developed by Colonel J.T. Thompson, was used during the 1930s depression by American law enforcement officers and criminals alike. It was fed by a 50 round drum or 20 round box magazine with a rate of 800 rounds a minute. Only box magazines were issued to the Commando units.

The Bren Light Machine Gun, (LMG) produced in 1938 from the Czechoslovakian prototype, had a range of 2,000 yds (1,829m) and fired 30 round magazines at 500 rounds a minute. It was a most adaptable, reliable and accurate weapon.

Three types of hand gun were available. The British Webley and Scott Mark VI revolver, mass produced for the British Army in 1915 and known as the "Webley 45". The American Smith and Wesson .44-inch calibre revolver – modified to take the British .455 and .38-inch cartridges – and the American Colt seven shot .45-inch automatic, were part of the lease-lend deal with America.

The primary hand grenades consisted of the Mills 36 fragmentation, the phosphorus smoke, the 77 anti-tank and the 69 stun grenade.

The support weapons within each company comprised the 2-inch mortar and the Boys .55-inch anti-tank rifle. The Support Platoon was equipped with the 3-inch mortar and the Vickers .303-inch water-cooled medium machine-gun (MMG) with a range of 3,800 yds(3,475m).

---

* The FS knife designed by Fairburn and Sykes (ex-Shanghai policemen who joined the Army Commandos) in conjunction with J. Wilkinson Latham of Wilkinson Sword.

Training areas were established in Deal and the surrounding countryside. Part of the town had been evacuated following severe damage to property by cross Channel shell-fire and bombing in the numerous air raids. This section was utilized for street fighting. Adjacent farmland and the Sandwich Golf Course echoed to the sound of platoon and company battle drills. Further west, live firing of the various weapons was a daily occurence on the range occupying the narrow strip of land between the cliffs and sea at Kingsdown.

All this activity produced roaring appetites and, having in mind the stringent food-rationing imposed on the civilian population, the quantity and variety of food available at mealtimes was embarrassingly plentiful. If there were any complaints about quality or quantity they were never recorded.

During March Lt N.S.E. Maude attended a demolition course run by the Royal Engineers. In addition to commanding the Demolition Platoon he was given command of Headquarter Company on return to the unit and duly promoted Captain. Sergeant A.F. Martin was promoted Acting QMSI on 27 March and appointed Commando Sergeant Major. The last Sunday of that month was declared a National Day of Prayer and the Commando paraded for a church service in South Barracks.

With the passing weeks, liberal rations, thorough training and sound leadership produced tangible results with all ranks merging into an exceptionally fit, well co-ordinated and self-reliant team. Even at this stage it was found necessary to RTU men who were unable to keep pace with the increasing physical demands. Lt Col Phillipps was well aware that his new unit, like many original ideas, would have to prove itself over a period of time. The Commando was not readily accepted by everyone in the Corps and a number of sea service veterans challenged its ability to do anything that was not within the scope of one or more Royal Marine ships' detachments. After all, they argued, the provision of landing- parties had been part of the Marines' stock-in-trade since 1664. However, by early 1944 three Royal Marine Commandos had proved their effectiveness in action and the sniping criticism from within the Corps ceased.

By the end of March 1942 the RM Commando had attained the full War Establishment strength of 446 all ranks (Appendix A). This number was slightly less than the Army Commando establishment of 460, but the requirements were identical and based on the following factors:-

(a) The Commando unit was designed to operate from a firm base against an enemy held coast, to act as a spearhead of a landing or to take on specific targets outside the main operational zone of the Army.

(b) The men were to be lightly equipped, requiring no transport once ashore, and to be able to cover short distances quickly to reach the objectives and to be self-sufficient for 24 hours or more relying only on the supporting arms which could be carried.

(c) The commando was not designed or equipped to hold a position for a long time or to form part of an organised infantry action requiring complicated equipment or support arms.

(d) The organisation had to be simple and flexible to permit the formation of raiding parties of any strength.

(e) Supporting arms such as heavy-weapons, wireless and headquarters had to be portable and transport had to be considered as non-essential.

The RM Commando did not immediately conform to the five-troop organisation. The reason is most likely associated with the fact that the Corps had found the battalion structure effective and could see no advantage in changing to an organisation of which senior staff lacked knowledge and experience. In consequence, a modified battalion organisation was adopted consisting of three companies, a signals platoon, demolition platoon and close support platoon.

The time had arrived to expand and sharpen the pace of training. Arrangements were made to move to Scotland where the wide open spaces and rugged coastline, rough terrain and sparsely-populated areas would provide more testing conditions. The Army had already established a Commando Basic Training Depot at Achnacarry, but Lt Col Phillipps, following an independent course of action, decided to form a base at HMS *Dorlin*, a wartime combined operations training centre three miles further west on the shores of Kentra Bay.

The Commando moved north by train on 5 April, spending part of the night marooned in a tunnel while the Germans bombed a Midlands town ahead of them. Eventually they arrived at Crianlarich in the early hours of the morning, where members of the Women's Voluntary Service revived flagging spirits with mugs of hot tea and doorstep-thick sandwiches. B Company changed trains and proceeded to Oban where it embarked in landing-craft for passage to Tobermory, on the island of Mull. For most of the young commandos this was the furthest point they had ever been from home and an interest in the unfamiliar landscape overcame their weariness from hours of travel.

The remainder of the unit continued on to Glen Finnan where, in the cold morning light, as Mne Forbes remembers it "The view of the mountains and forests and the crisp clean air contrasted sharply with the stuffy smoke-filled compartments of the previous night". An antiquated loch steamer carried the Commando the length of Loch Shiel to Acharacle, where it was sub-divided into three groups, two of which moved to training areas at Salem and Glen Borrodale. Commando Headquarters and X Company were based at Sheil Bridge Lodge, about three miles from Dorlin House.

Commando HQ personnel were accommodated in Nissen huts adjacent to the lodge where the CO had his office. The company accommodation was mostly under canvas. P Company had the added luxury of running water – received via a stand pipe from a nearby stream! Living conditions were by intention spartan and there were times when sleeping on the snowy ground, with a single blanket and gas-cape for cover, proved to be a real test of endurance.

A benefit of the Loch Shiel location was the ready availability of landing-craft. The companies exercised in turn with the wooden hulled Eureka assault boats which could carry 25 men. Powered by twin-screw petrol engines, their shallow draught and light construction made them ideally suitable for running inshore. A canvas cover could be drawn over the troop space to provide protection from the elements but they were extremely lively in rough weather and vunerable to enemy gunfire. Prior to landing, the assault troops had to climb out along the narrow walk-way either side of the troop-space. From this position they could jump over the bows – hopefully onto the beach but more often than not into three or more feet of water. There were no toilet facilities in this type of boat. On longish trips a call of nature could only be answered by hanging over the stern with the support of a helping hand.

During one of the many landing exercises a Eureka carrying A Company personnel went aground 15 yards from the shore. The first dozen men jumped into knee-deep water closely followed by the signaller, whose movements were restricted by the heavy No 18 wireless set on his back. Falling short of the ledge on which the others had landed he disappeared beneath the surface. There were other similar incidents but the involuntary submariners were invariably fished out none the worse for the immersion. Eventually some of them were to find themselves in similar predicaments on an enemy beach.

Much of the training programme was devoted to improving fieldcraft and acquiring the basic skills that would enable the men to live off the land. The boy scout practice of lighting a fire with a single match proved to be more difficult than expected, particularly when the kindling was saturated with rain. However, the ability to produce a fire and a hot mug of tea under such conditions was a splendid boost to morale. Edible flora and fauna were rather limited by the time of year. The fishy taste of seagulls eggs ruled them out of the daily diet other than as a last resort, but the occasional pieces of venison that "found their way" into the cooking pot improved the most basic menu. All ranks were aware that hunting deer was strictly illegal, the skill was not so much in the hunting but in avoiding being caught in the act. None went hungry and everyone became adept in the art of making a snug, dry shelter from sticks, bracken and anything else to hand.

Tactical exercises, field-firing, cliff-climbing, compass marches and hill-walking occupied the attention of all. Commando HQ was not exempt from these activities and its members found themselves one morning making an ascent of Ben Resipol in full marching order. The 2,775-ft summit culminated in a small wind-swept cairn. This rather precarious position was occupied by Maj Houghton, the Adjutant and a signaller who was conscious of the heavy set on his back. Their arrival at the top coincided with the receipt of a signal from Sheil Bridge Lodge which said "RM Office require to know immediately the number of pairs of SV boots held in store". The brief reply is best left unrecorded.

Recreation such as football played a minor part in the programme as there was little spare time or reserve energy for this form of activity. On one occasion Cpl F. Usher had a 'run ashore' from Acharacale, over the hills to Fort William. There he found that the beer was rationed to one pint per person, perhaps wisely. On the return journey to camp he fell over a cliff fortunately suffering nothing worse than a few bruises.

During this period the opportunity arose to carry out a more involved exercise to test the Commando against the local defences. Landing at night from raiding-craft on the west coast of Ross Cromarty, the commandos had to make their way across country unobserved to the Royal Air force Station at Dingwall, their objective on the east coast. The enemy forces were provided by Scottish Command and the RAF, who were only too pleased to participate.

Moving only by night, the Commando steered clear of the main populated areas and spent the daylight hours lying-up under cover. Sufficient rations, which included pemmican, a sun-dried meat once used by North American Indians, were carried for the entire exercise and there was no shortage of stream water. The unit managed to avoid all contact with the defenders until the objective was reached. At this stage a number of exaggerated reports about commandos sped around the RAF Station and it is said that some of the WAAFs barricaded themselves in their quarters to protect their honour!

While the Commando was in Scotland, elements from each company spent an "acquaint period" at the Army Commando Training Depot, first established in the castle and grounds at Achnacarry in December 1941. The approach to this frequently cold, wet and windy location, 14 miles from Fort William, was marked by a series of "graves". The white crosses were a daunting sight for anyone entering the Depot for the first time, particularly as it was rumoured that one death a month was an acceptable training risk. On closer inspection the graves proved to be realistic training aids with captions such as "This man showed himself on the skyline", and "These men bunched", printed on the crosses. The stark warnings were unlikely to be forgotten by the men reading them.

Lt Col C.E. Vaughan OBE., and his personally selected team of instructors had acquired a reputation for being hard but fair taskmasters. Training standards and tasks – like the obstacles on the assault course – were tough and numerous. The challenge was designed to extract the maximum effort and resourcefulness from each of the trainees. Only live ammunition was used on exercises and there were casualties, but the men who successfully completed the 12-week course knew they had achieved the highest standard of military training available in the British Army.

Royal Marine commandos made their first contact with the American rangers while they were at Achnacarry. They completed some of the training together, but the informal attitude shown by the rangers to their officers and NCOs was not readily appreciated by the marines. However, in the rare off-duty moments efforts were made to form a better understanding of each other over a few beers in the canteen.

During this training period Lt Col E. Brockman, Quartermaster General Royal Marines, called on Lt Col Phillipps to arrange for a small force to be made available for a special mission. Two officers and 36 other ranks were selected for this purpose and formed into an independent detachment known as T Company. Lt Tod was promoted to acting-captain on 14 April to assume command of the Company. Lt Grant-Dalton became second-in-command and A/Sgt A.W. Henderson, nearly 10 years senior in age to the remainder of the detachment, was appointed as senior NCO.

T Company had to undertake the full 12 week course at Achnarry. Towards the end of the training Capt Tod was severely incapacitated and ended his connection with the detachment. It would have seemed natural for Lt Grant-Dalton to assume command but Capt D. Wright, with no previous connection with the Commando, was appointed in his place and after a brief visit to the Company he returned south to the Isle of Wight to arrange accommodation for the detachment at Chale. It was in the village of Chale that the men were introduced to Cdr J. Langlais RN, the Captain of HMS *Fidelity*, and given an indication of their future task.

Jaques Langlais was the *nom de guerre* for Claud Peri, a Corsican agent of the French Cinquieme Bureau in the Far East who returned to France in 1940 and, with approval of the authority commandeered the cargo ship Le Rhin for clandestine operations in the Mediterranean. After a raid on Las Palmas he sailed to Gibraltar and presented his ship and himself for service in the Royal Navy. His offer was accepted by Adm Sir James Somerville who liked his reckless daring and both Langlais and Le Rhin, renamed HMS *Fidelity* were commissioned into the Royal Navy. Following Adm Somerville's appointment on 13 April 1942 to command the Eastern Fleet arrangements were made for Langlais to sail to the Far East to continue his raiding tactics.

Cdr Langlais's second in command was known as Madeleine Barclay. The wife of Mons Bayard, a rubber planter in Indo-China, she had been raped in front of her husband who was then killed by communist terrorists. Rescued by Claude Peri she became one of his agents and changed her name on being commissioned in the WRNS as a Third Officer after a two week crash course at Greenwich.

The First Lieutenant, Lt Cdr J.W.F. Milner-Gibson DSC,RN, was recalled for service in 1939 and had the distinction of being the RN Officer in command of the first offensive allied landing in France after Dunkirk when Maj R.J.F Tod's force of 200 men landed in four parties between Boulogne and Berck on 23/24 June 1940.

While the *"Fidelity"* carried out an extensive refit at Southampton, T Company, increased in strength to 51 NCOs and marines, pursued its own training programme in the area of Chale and Ventnor but had no contact with the Royal Marine Commando. Capt Wright relinquished command of the Company towards the end of August at which time Lt Grant-Dalton was promoted to Acting Captain and Lt W.A.N. Trask joined the detachment as second-in-command. The entire company moved to Ringway Aerodrome, Manchester, at the end of October for a two week parachute course and on completion joined *Fidelity* in Southampton. In addition to a considerable armament of guns and depth-charges the ship carried a motor-torpedo-boat (MTB 105), two landing-craft and two Kingfisher seaplanes. On 17 November *Fidelity* sailed north, first to Ullapool and then to Liverpool where she joined convoy ONS 154, outward bound for North America.

Meantime the Commando had completed a series of testing exercises and it was time to consider the future. Lt Col Phillips went to see the Adjutant-General on 25 April to discuss plans for the way ahead and replacements for T Company. Before the end of the month, 54 volunteer reinforcements had joined the Commando. They included Lt A.M. Berriff from the RM Div – he was to give sterling service as the unit Quartermaster – and Lt K. Smale from 2nd Battalion Royal Marines, who was to spend all but a few months of hostilities as a prisoner-of-war in Germany. Until the arrival of Lt Berriff the duties of Quartermaster, Imprest Holder and Training Officer were all undertaken by the 2 I/C Maj Houghton.

Following his visit to the Adjutant General the Colonel received instructions from Special Service Brigade Headquarters (SS Bde HQ) to move the unit to the Isle of Wight for attachment to the Special Service Brigade (SS Bde), working with but not under command of the 214th Independent Infantry Brigade, 2nd Canadian Division. All ranks were pleased to hear that they were moving closer to the scene of action. The Commando embarked in HMLSI *Princess Beatrix* at Greenock on 18 May and arrived at Ryde five days later. The advance party had done its job well and the companies were able to move immediately into lodgings (billets), in Sandown, Shanklin and Ventnor. There was no objection to the men finding their own billets and this became the custom. They were issued with ration cards and received a daily allowance of six shillings and eightpence, the rough equivalent of 32 pence at today's prices. With this modest sum they could choose their own standard of living and accommodation. The method worked well and had the advantage of streamlining the process of moving and administration. The landladies, many of whom had husbands or sons in the services, made them welcome. The daughters of landladies were equally pleased to see them and several struck up life-long partnerships.

Commando HQ occupied the Upper Chine Girls' School, Shanklin, left vacant when the pupils were evacuated to the West Country. It was centrally located to the companies and later in the war 46 Royal Marine Commando occupied the school for the same purpose. The company commanders utilised garages and garden sheds for offices and stores and side-streets were adopted as company parades. A few enterprising public house landlords provided spare rooms for meetings and assembly points knowing that this gesture would also bring extra business their way.

Settling into this new environment presented few problems and the training continued with renewed vigour. Mne G. Trafford, who was billeted in Sandown with other members of 6 Platoon, remembers the months of June and July as being gloriously hot. On one of these summer nights the platoon was ordered to muster outside Newport railway station at 2200 hours prior to the start of a night exercise. About eight of their number arranged to meet two hours earlier, inside the Stag Inn at Lake. "After a couple of pints we hitched a lift on a lorry as far as the Fighting Cocks at Arreton. Another pint and another lift took us to the Barley Mow at Shede from where, after a final pint, we marched through Newport to arrive at the station nearly 15 minutes late!"

They were not the only defaulters. Only half the platoon arrived at the correct time and the platoon commander, Lt Ecrepont, became increasingly annoyed as the stragglers appeared. It was almost 2230 hours before all were present. Lt Ecrepont marched them off at a brisk pace to Carisbrooke and on to Calbourne. At this stage the beer they had consumed was beginning to make its presence felt. "What about a halt then?" could be heard from the column, but the pleas fell on deaf ears. After a further very long 20 minutes they came alongside a quarry where Lt Ecrepont and Sgt Kerr roared out in unison "Take cover!". It is unlikely that a platoon ever moved as quickly as they did at that moment. Lt Ecrepont having made his point the march continued and the platoon was never again late.

The training programme assumed a new pattern with more time devoted to street fighting, house-clearing and demolitions. Also, swimming in fighting order with the aid of the Assault Life Jacket best known as the Mae West became a regular drill. The Mae West, aptly named after the well endowed film star of the '30s era, was a dark-blue canvas and rubber tube which could be tied round the chest with tapes. Once inflated it gave the wearer adequate support in the water. The value of this item of equipment was to be tested in battle before the end of the summer.

Platoon and company groups travelled to Portsmouth Dockyard where exercises with landing-craft were carried out inside the port installations. A number of men issued with long handled axes were told to practise cutting wire hawsers with as few strokes as possible. Others scaled quayside walls and crossed wire entanglements with the aid of bamboo ladders. The rope and rubber soled boots were tested during this period and the general concensus was that the former were preferable for this type of activity.

While they were in the dockyard arrangements were made for the commandos to familiarise themselves with HMS *Locust*, a shallow-draught gunboat which had seen service in China. Commander R.E.D. Ryder VC,RN. her captain, had won his laurels as naval commander of the daring and successful block-ship raid on the port of St Nazaire carried out by Lt Col A.C.Newman's 2 Commando on 27 March 1942.

The commandos were re-acquainted with the American rangers when Capt R.J. Batterson and two NCOs of the United States Marine Corps arrived on 20 June for temporary attachment to Commando HQ. Capt J. Aster, a public relations officer, also joined the unit the same week. There was no disguising the fact that some form of operation was imminent. While the men were aware that they were preparing for a raid across the Channel they had no idea when or where this would be. Lt Col Phillipps and members of the headquarters staff who had already been briefed, spent many hours at Upper Chine School, working on a detailed study of maps and plans for a raid on the port of Dieppe which had been given the code-name Operation Rutter.

Maj Gen Houghton, recalling this period of preparation when he was second-in-command said "There was a safe in the port offices at Dieppe that we were required to blow. We were told that if we could get the contents it could shorten the war by six months. I am pretty certain that it contained some vital piece of equipment. We had all the apparatus for doing this. We had the safe-blower, a little man who was in one of the companies. Someone came down from London and found out what equipment he wanted and within a couple of days this was brought to Upper Chine School by a naval officer. I sent for the marine who checked over the contents, and then I had to undertake that on no account was he to have access to the kit until we went on the raid. I had a fairly large safe in my office and put it in there with the Commando imprest!"

Honours and Awards
A Ty Sgt J. R. Odendall was awarded the MBE for rescuing a pilot from the wreckage of a burning aircraft. The 'plane had crashed in the vicinity of Commando personnel during field exercises on the Isle of Wight.

CHAPTER 2

1 June to 31 August 1942

Operations Rutter and Jubilee – The raid on the German fortified seaport town of Dieppe.

OVER 50 years have elapsed since the Dieppe raid gave a boost to the morale of the hard pressed British people. Even so, the military and psychological value of the operation balanced against the frightful loss of life, continues to be a controversial issue among military historians and others connected with the operation. Many years after the war, Field-Marshal Bernard Montgomery* referred to it as an action lacking adequate preparation, organisation and communication. Other senior officers assessed the raid as a lesson that had to be learned, even if the learning had to be achieved the hard way. Lord Louis Mountbatten said:- "The battle of Normandy was won on the beaches of Dieppe. For every one man who was killed at Dieppe at least 10 or more had their lives spared on the beaches of Normandy." Answering to a question in the House of Commons, Prime Minister Winston Churchill said "This raid, apart from the information and reconnaissance value, brought about an extremely satisfactory air battle in the west."

The men at the sharp end, particularly the hundreds of Canadians and the handful of Royal Marines commandos who landed in front of the town and returned to England later that fateful day, considered themselves very lucky to be alive. Many of them owed their lives to the selfless conduct of comrades who did not survive and to the steadfast support provided by the allied navy and air force.

This was not the first raid of the war on the mainland of Europe but it was the most ambitious. Limited resources ruled out any form of second front – repeatedly called for by Russia – but the idea of a raid in force across the Channel appealed to Churchill. It offered a solution to Stalin's demands by tempting Hitler to transfer troops from the Eastern Front to strengthen Channel coastal defences. It also gave encouragement to the home front that had endured months of intensive bombing.

The task was given to the Chief of Combined Operations, Vice Admiral Lord Louis Mountbatten, who decided that an attack should be made on the strongly fortified seaport town of Dieppe. The plan required the capture of coast-gun batteries on either side of Dieppe, followed by the capture of the town, port facilities and the destruction of all military installations. The

---

* Field-Marshal The Viscount Montgomery of Alamein KG,GCB,DSO.

15

German invasion barges in the harbour, prisoners and any information of intelligence value were to be brought back to England. Responsibility for the military phase of the operation was delegated to Lt Gen Montgomery, Commander-in-Chief, South-East Command. Vice Adml Mountbatten was very keen that the Royal Marines should be used for the main force and Lt Gen Montgomery was also of the opinion that experienced troops should be employed on an operation that could prove difficult and complex. However, higher authority decreed that the 2nd Canadian Division, champing at the bit after two long years of training, should be given a chance to prove themselves.

Dieppe has changed little since World War II. It is a large seaside town with a substantial harbour and dock installation at the mouth of the River D'Aques. An expanse of cultivated grass and a promenade – protected by a seawall about five feet high – spans a broad seafront. On either side of the town the ground rises sharply, culminating in cliffs with sheer chalk faces about 250 to 300ft high which overlook Dieppe and the shingle beach. In 1942, sections of the beach and promenade were covered with wire entanglements; the houses and casino on the seafront were fortified; pillbox and gun-emplacements, both in and on top of the cliffs, covered the beaches and harbour entrance. Some of the gun-emplacements are still visible. A mile further east at Puits and nearly the same distance west at Pourville the ground descends to sea- level, providing access inland. A further five miles to the east at Berneval and about four miles west at Varengeville headlands overlook the English Channel.

Operation Rutter was to take place on 4 July or as soon as weather conditions were favourable. Airborne troops were to drop at Berneval and Varengeville prior to the main landings to neutralise coast gun-batteries sited on these headlands. A battalion of the Royal Regiment of Canada would then land and capture Puits while the Queen's Own Cameron Highlanders of Canada and the South Saskatchewan Regiment would carry out a similar operation at Pourville. Both forces would move inland to connect with the main force which would have penetrated to the rear of Dieppe.

The main force, comprising the Royal Hamilton Light Infantry on the right flank, the Essex Scottish on the left flank, the 14th Canadian Army Tank Battalion (Calgary Regiment) in the centre and the Fusiliers Mount Royal in reserve, were to make a frontal assault, passing through the town to join up with the flank battalions. The Royal Marine Commando in the shallow draught gunboat HMS *Locust* was to force an entrance to the harbour. The commandos then had the task of capturing and destroying the dock installations, having first removed prisoners, intelligence material and any boats intended for use as invasion craft. The Commando rehearsed embarking and landing from HMS *Locust* and chasseurs (French gunboats) in Portsmouth Dockyard on 25 June.

The naval force of about 200 vessels included converted merchant ships acting as troop-carriers; tank-landing-craft (LCTs), infantry-landing-craft (LCIs), motor-gun-boats (MGBs), chasseurs, minesweepers and four British destroyers. No capital ships were made available for the operation. The air cover was provided by an international force consisting of bombers and fighters from the RAF, United States, Polish, Czechoslovak, Norwegian, Belgian and French air forces. In all, the total personnel committed to take part in this combined land, sea and air operation was estimated at 9,000 men. The main force embarked at Newhaven and in the Yarmouth Roads off the Isle of Wight on 2 and 3 July. The Royal Marine Commando – which had assembled in Upper Chine School on 26 June for security reasons – embarked in HMS *Locust* and three chasseurs at Ryde on 3 July.

Rapid deterioration of the weather ruled out any guarantee of adequate air-cover on 4 July and the operation was postponed for three days. The Royal Marine Commando and a number of troops in the smaller assault craft disembarked, but the main force remained aboard the larger troop-carriers waiting for an improvemant in conditions. At approximately the same time as the Royal Marines re-embarked at Ryde on 7 July, German fighter-bombers attacked the assault force at anchor off the Isle of Wight. Two of the transport carriers incurred serious damage and heavy casualties. These factors, coupled with the possibility that the German bomber force could have alerted their coastal defences, led to the cancellation of the operation.

Lt Gen Mongomery was aware that hundreds of men comprising the assault force were familiar with details of the raid and surmised that this information would soon become common knowledge. He was therefore surprised to find that Combined Operations had obtained the approval of the Chiefs of Staff to mount the operation again. He expressd his concern in a letter to Gen B. Paget, Commander-in-Chief Home Forces, recommending that "the raid on Dieppe should be cancelled for all time". Higher echelons decreed otherwise. Within two weeks preparations had commenced to mount Operation Jubilee. Maj Gen J.H.Roberts MC, was appointed to command the land forces. Lt Gen Montgomery had by this time arrived in the Middle East to take command of the Eighth Army at the then little known location of El Alamein.

On the Isle of Wight, Lt Col Phillipps imposed strict secrecy on everyone in the Commando. Planning details were restricted to HQ staff and company commanders only. Meanwhile an exercise was arranged on the mainland to keep the men fit and to cover the main intention. A warning order indicated that "Jubilee" could take place at any time between 18 and 23 August. Tanks of the 14th Canadian Army Tank Battalion were embarked in the LCTs on 17 August and an orders group (O group) for all unit commanders was held that morning to clear up final details. There were two major changes to the original plan. The dovetailing of the air- drops and sea-landings was considered too risky with the uncertain weather conditions prevailing. In consequence the airborne troops were replaced by 3 Commando, commanded by Lt Col J.F.D. Slater, and 4 Commando, commanded by Lt Col Lovat DSO,MC. It was also decided to dispense with the preliminary bombing of the enemy defences to avoid unnecessary French casualties.

Once again the Royal Marine Commando assembled at Upper Chine School for a briefing by the Colonel prior to embarking on 18 August. The Commando deployed as before, with Headquarters, Signals Platoon, A and X Companies and two demolition teams in HMS *Locust*. A third demolition team and B, P and Q Companies were allocated to three chasseurs. Some last minute instructions were given to the men after they embarked and Mne Forbes, on HMS *Locust*, finding himself without any specific task, sought the advice of Regimental Sergeant-Major F. Martin. "Well, son" he said, thrusting a folded Union Flag into his hands, "When we get to the fish market in Dieppe hoist this flag".

Preceded by minesweepers, the flotillas from the Isle of Wight and Newhaven set out across the Channel shortly before midnight. The passage was uneventful until 0330 hours when the Eureka raiding-craft carrying 3 Commando on course for Berneval crossed the path of a German cargo vessel and its escort of E-boats. The E-boats immediately attacked the plywood-hulled Eurekas, which scattered in all directions to avoid the cannon fire. In the ensuing gun battle one E-boat was sunk, but the British escort vessels received a hammering and all radio communication with the main force was knocked out.

Maj Gen Roberts in HMS *Kelpy* was unaware of 3 Commando's misfortune and to the possible danger that the German coast-defences might be alerted before the main force reached its destination. Of the 25 raiding craft carrying the unit only six were to reach the objective. One of the leading Eurekas had avoided the conflict with the E-boats and arrived at the appointed landing place five minutes ahead of time. The 18 commandos led by Maj P. Young landed unopposed, climbed the cliff and from the cover of a cornfield fired at the gun battery until their ammunition was expended. They withdrew to their raiding-craft without incurring any casualties. The other five raiding-craft which touched down much later met a prepared German defence. The commandos attacked courageously but stood no chance against the withering fire directed at them. The gun-battery remained intact and free to fire on the main assault force as it approached Dieppe.

Further west, on the right flank at Varengeville, 4 Commando crossed the Channel in HMS *Albert* and transferred to LCAs for the landings in two groups at 0430 and 0453 hours respectively. Group 2 led by Lt Col Lovat had to capture two pill-box positions before proceeding to the main objective. Group 1 led by Maj D. Mills-Roberts landed unopposed and moved forward to the battery defences. Both groups attacked according to plan and destroyed the coast gun-battery in copybook style. It was a first-class effort achieved against stiff opposition with comparatively few casualties.

Closer to Dieppe, on the east flank, the Royal Regiment of Canada landed at Puits just before dawn with the aim of capturing the headland to the east of the town and the port area. For some inexplicable reason the landing was delayed. By the time the assault craft touched down the German defences had been

Vice-Admiral Lord Louis Mountbatten addressing Canadian soldiers and British commandos, on board HMS Locust, 18 August 1942.
Photo: Imperial War Museum.

HMS Locust escorted by Chasseurs of the Free French Navy, approaching Dieppe.
Photo: Imperial War Museum.

alerted and had saturated the beach with gun-fire. The Canadians were unable to penetrate with any degree of success beyond the pillbox and heavy wire entanglements along the seawall. Three platoons of reinforcements from the Black Watch (Royal Highland Regiment) of Canada were also pinned on the beach by mortar and machine-gun fire. Evacuation was impossible in the face of concentrated German fire. Of those that landed 211 were killed and 20 died later of their wounds. Out of the 515 men who landed it was only possible to extricate 65 to safety. The German guns on the eastern headland remained intact and were ready to fire on the main assault force approaching Dieppe.

The South Saskatchewan Regiment achieved a partially unnopposed landing at Pourville. Unfortunately the major part of the unit was put ashore on the west side of the River Scie and the river became a natural obstacle between them and Dieppe. Deadly German gun-fire, sweeping across the only bridge and surrounding fields halted every attempt by the Canadians to gain a hold on the east bank. The Queen's Own Cameron Highlanders of Canada who followed them ashore, advanced about two miles towards their airfield objective before they also were forced to halt. Both units, suffering considerable casualties, withdrew. The German battery on the high ground immediately west of Dieppe was by then ranging on the landing craft of the main force approaching the beach in front of Dieppe. Nearly all the fully alerted German ground defences were intact and overhead the fighter bombers of the Luftwaffe were already pinpointing targets.

The Essex Scottish and the Royal Hamilton Light Infantry moved towards the shore at 0520 hours through a smoke-screen laid by chasseurs and supported by the guns of the four escort destroyers. Emerging from the smoke they were met by a hail of gun-fire from the fortified houses along the seafront and numerous concrete emplacements along the cliffs on both flanks. Immediately on landing at the east end of the beach the Essex Scottish advanced to the promenade wall. Thick barbed wire entanglements barred further movement to all except one small group which infiltrated the town. In those brief minutes 200 dead and wounded Canadians had marked their progress up the beach.

The Royal Hamiltons landed on the west shore and about 200 of their number managed to force a way through the wire defences to capture the casino and adjacent pillboxes. Small groups of men moved into the town, where they fought with German patrols. The Churchill tanks of the 14th Canadian Army Tank Regiment (Calgary Regiment), in action for the first time, should have been supporting the landing but, due to a navigational error, were 15 minutes late. When they eventually beached 14 tanks advanced onto the promenade but concrete road-blocks prevented any further progress. A further 15 remained stranded on the shingle beach.

It was broad daylight as HMS *Locust* approached the harbour. Mne Forbes, with the Union Flag tucked safely inside his battledress and lying 'head to tail' on the deck with other members of the landing party, was convinced by the sound of the ships gunfire and smell of cordite that *Locust* was making itself felt. Shaking the heels of the marine in front of him he made a remark to this effect but the reply was discouraging "It's us that's being hit, you clot!" From his vantage point on the bridge Capt Hellings could see that the concealed German guns along the cliffs to the east of the harbour had not been silenced. The *Locust's* armament was no match against these shore defences but all guns returned fire as Cdr Ryder manoeuvred the gun-boat towards the entrance. He called off the attempt after the ship had been repeatedly hit, deciding that it would be futile to continue while the German defences controlled the channel. His only option was to withdraw and resort to a bombardment of the batteries.

The crews of the destroyer escorts had their hands full, laying smoke while the main armament bombarded the shore batteries and the Oerlikon gun-crews engaged enemy aircraft attacking the landing force. Overhead German and Allied pilots fought their own battle for air supremacy. The situation on the beach was chaotic. Gun-crews in the Churchill tanks doggedly fought the German fortified positions but, bogged down in the shingle or immobilised with damaged tracks, they were sitting targets. The beach was littered with dead and wounded, many of them lying in the same formation as they had left the landing craft. Isolated groups seeking cover behind the seawall and stranded tanks fired at the Germans concealed in the pillboxes and fortified houses while others worked desperately to clear a way through the wire entanglements.

The beach was obscured from the view of HMS *Kelpy* by the smoke-screen. A brief wireless message received by Gen Roberts from one of the few Canadian groups to have reached the town led him to believe the east side of the beach had been cleared. Acting on this information he gave orders for the reserve battalion – Les Fusiliers Mont Royal – to land. They fared no better than the Essex Scottish and the casualties steadily mounted from the intense enemy fire into their exposed position. Cdr Ryder, who had attended an O-group in HMS *Kelpy,* returned to HMS *Locust* to inform Lt Col Phillipps that Red and White Beaches had been cleared and that Maj Gen Roberts required the Royal Marines to land on White Beach in support of the Essex Scottish. The Commando was to pass through the town and, after reforming, move south-west to attack the gun-batteries on the cliffs from the south. Lt Col Phillipps, transferred his headquarters with A and P Companies into two Landing-Craft-Mechanised (MLC's), while X and B Companies with one demolition section, under command of Maj Houghton, embarked into Landing-Craft-Assault (ALC's). The Mortar Platoon, Q Company and two demolition sections remained in HMS *Locust*.

The MLC carrying A Company started to move inshore at 0730 hours. In his report written after the raid Capt Hellings recorded "We proceeded under cover of smoke provided by a chasseur which accompanied us to within about 500 yards of the beach. All the while shellfire of about four-inch calibre in addition to three and four-inch mortar fire was directed at us from the cliffs to the east and the end basin of the mole. This increased in intensity with the addition of light machine-gun and rifle-fire as the range shortened".

Sgt J.Steedman had a clear view of Capt Hellings, who was sitting on top of the wheelhouse shouting instructions to the navy coxswain trying to control the rudder by hand. The steering and one engine had been damaged during the initial landings and the other engine was running hot. In recalling the event Sgt Steedman said "There were shells all around us and looking over the side I could see dead Canadian troops lying on the beach. We could hear someone shouting 'go back, go back' and then I saw that it was Col Phillipps, wearing white gloves, waving us back". Minutes later the MLC was hit close to the stern, rendering the steering-gear useless and a chasseur moved in to take them in tow.

The landing-craft carrying B Company followed Maj Houghton's ALC towards the beach but lost contact in the smoke-screen. In a report subsequent to the action the Company Commander, Capt J. Deveraux, wrote "When we emerged from the smoke I could see the CO in his MLC and he intimated that we were to land on White Beach some 300 hundred yards ahead. Fire was being directed at us from the cliff-defences and as we moved closer to the beach Mne T.Breen fired his LMG to good effect, neutralising a gun post near the casino. An MLC was lying broadside to the beach in front of us and I could see the CO standing at the stern, signalling to us to withdraw. We went half to starboard but collided with an MLC carrying part of A Company. Going about we went through fresh smoke and on the way out drew alongside MLC 125, which was sinking. We were able to take off Cpl Ryan and two wounded naval ratings, but it turned out that our own ALC was holed on the port side near the engines and taking water fast and so we moved towards chasseur 43, who took us aboard".

Earlier that morning Lt K. Smale and his platoon had transferred from chasseur 43 to an ALC and at 0730 hours proceeded under heavy shell and mortar-fire towards the beach. Mnes Carlan and Kettlewell were hit as soon as the ramp was lowered but the remainder moved clear of the landing-craft up the beach and took cover behind a Churchill tank. Although the tank was disabled the crew inside continued to fire at targets along the sea front. The tank was itself a target, drawing fire from many directions, but provided the only shelter available to the platoon who would otherwise have been annihilated.

By 1100 hours it became evident that there would be no further troop landings and Lt Smale gave orders to move back under cover of smoke from canisters which they had carried ashore. Cpl Harvey, who gave an account of this episode later, said that they became split up as they moved back to the shoreline carrying some of the wounded men. His last glimpse of Lt Smale was as he returned up the beach towards the tank. The remnants of the platoon were seen by the coxswain of an ALC lying close inshore looking for survivors and they were taken aboard.

Maj Houghton approached the shore in his ALC through a series of smoke-screens and shelling. Recounting that part of the action he said "Restricted visibility made it very difficult to maintain station and we found ourselves out on the flank where the Fusiliers Mont Royal were pinned down. The ALC then beached in shallow water, but with the terrific amount of bullets flying around it would have been impossible to land and it became necessary to pull out to make a new approach towards the centre of the beach. This was more successful and when the ramp dropped we moved quickly up the shingle beach. Almost immediately the ALC blew up behind us. It was probably caused by one of the many mortar bombs that were falling all round us hitting the demolition charges that had been left in the ALC."

"Ironically the doctor* was our first casualty, but further casualties quickly followed from rifle, machine-gun and mortar-fire directed at us from the houses along the seafront and the cliff defences. We advanced as far as the promenade wall where further progress was barred by thick wire-entanglements swept by enemy fire."

"Pinned in this position with practically no cover, unable to move forward and without any means of returning by sea, we concentrated our efforts on inflicting as much damage as possible on the enemy positions. Lacking any form of communication with our own forces we continued in this manner until the official time of withdrawal had passed. The beach was strafed by our own aircraft at 1400 hours as part of the planned withdrawal programme and it was just the luck of the draw that we found ourselves on the receiving end".

Lt Col Phillipps with his headquarters transferred into one of the MLCs that had already carried in some of the Canadians. Mne Forbes found a seat on a pile of discarded blankets-probably used during the night crossing-and was joined by various ranks from X Company and the Signals Platoon. Sgt J.F. Kruthoffer, platoon-sergeant of 10 Platoon, having seen one of his men killed and others wounded during the attempt to enter the harbour in HMS *Locust,* was relieved to see that a more suitable method of landing was being provided. In a personal account he wrote "Our spirits rose to create an almost cheerful atmosphere, but this happy interlude ended when we turned in for the final approach and started to receive the close attention of the shore batteries and dive bombers".

With the distance to the beach decreasing steadily the MLC became the target of concentrated machine-gun and rifle-fire. Not to be outdone, RSM Martin gave fire orders to Mnes M. Bradford and F. Singleton who aimed their Bren guns at the houses on the far side of the promenade. Although the landing-craft was repeatedly hit the two marines maintained a steady rate of fire, standing in an exposed position without thought for their own safety.

Lt Col Phillipps had by this time moved to a prominent position on the stern of the MLC to direct the other landing-craft towards the beach. As they moved

* Sur Lt H.E. Dunning-Gale RNVR.

clear of the smoke it became obvious to him that any attempt to reach the town over the beach covered by a scything crossfire would mean certain death for the majority of the Commando. Realising the futility of the situation he put on a pair of white signalling gloves so that his actions would be more clearly seen, and standing up, he shouted and indicated with his hands to the other landing-craft to turn out to sea. Presenting such an obvious target it was only a question of time before the enemy ranged on him and he fell with a fatal wound in the head.

It is possible that the Colonel's MLC hit an under-water obstruction, because it grounded about 20 yards from the beach. Mne Forbes knew that something was wrong and, writing about this action later said "We must have been at an angle to the beach because the enemy fire seemed to be concentrated on the port side and the machine-gun bullets were making a curious repetitive noise along the length of the armour plating. Someone shouted 'Let the ramp down' but nothing happenend. A young sub-lieutenant called out to the Colonel 'We'll get you off, sir', but he was hit and disappeared over the side. Some ratings working on the engines were also hit."

"It was then that I smelt and saw fuel oil seeping into the blankets from a damaged pipeline. I turned to say something about this to Capt Comyn, who was sitting directly behind me, but there was no reply.

"He was sitting bolt upright with his head leaning forward. Looking closer I could see that he had a severe wound in the back of the neck and appeared to be dead. Beyond him lay Lt Col Phillipps. A signaller and I crawled over to see what we could do to help. The Colonel was badly wounded and barely conscious. His last faint but clearly audible command before he died was "Fight on, fight on."

At the other end of the MLC Sgt Kruthoffer could see a number of things happening simultaneously "There was a group forward trying to kick the ramp down. The Colonel, engine-crew and others were hit and falling. A scrum at the stern end tried to dodge the small-arms fire coming from the cliffs and some, who were trying to climb over the portside were falling back hit. Two Bren gunners, one shouting for more magazines and the other firing from a sitting position which presented a threat to anyone who moved sideways, were firing at gun emplacements on the cliff".

RSM Martin gave the order for every man to fend for himself. Someone lit a smoke canister and suddenly the fuel soaked blankets along the port side erupted in a sheet of flame. Mne Forbes observed that "While conditions outside the landing-craft seemed daunting, they were infinitely preferable to those inside it. Anyone climbing over the side was picked off and the only answer was to try to vault over. This I did and almost landed on top of Cpl Tait, who was eventually taken prisoner".

"There were about 30 to 40 men in the water supported by Mae Wests, uncertain whether to head for the beach or to swim out to sea. I went to the assistance of Mne Singleton, who was swimming with one arm while towing

Colour-Sergeant Harwood out to sea. CSgt Harwood had been wounded and was floating on his back. Unfortunately the three of us together became a prominent target and the project had to be abandoned. The ping and splash of bullets round our heads was all too close and frequent and did not improve when a flight of Me 109s strafed us."

"I continued towards the ships, which appeared to be at least two miles out, and swimming, even with the assistance of a Mae West became difficult. I lost count of time and had just about given up hope when I was seen by a 'flak-ship'. A line was thrown, followed by a Carley float, and I was hauled aboard. Unable to walk, two ratings took me below where there were many Canadians, most of them wounded. Someone told me that the RSM had also been picked up. The noise became deafening as the Royal Marine gun-crews above our heads opened fire, and I seem to remember being told that a Ju 88 was shot down. Some time later the Royal Marine officer came to see me and asked me if I knew anything about his brother-in-law Capt Comyn. Conveying the sad news to him was not easy."

There were many others that day who had little option but to swim. About the same time that Maj Houghton's ALC blew up, Capt Manners quietly gave orders to the marines in his landing-craft to "Abandon ship." They had only minutes previously transferred from another craft, which had been holed. Now they had been hit again and a fire in the engine compartment was out of control.

Mne McConkey was among those who took to the sea, and after swimming a short distance looked back to see someone hanging on to the side of the boat. "So I shouted to my mate Cowan and we swam back to find that it was Willie McKnight, an Argyle and Sutherland Highlander and a great drinking man. I said :' What's the matter Willie, wounded ?' 'No, Mac', he said, 'I canna swim'. So I replied ' you canna sink either – you have a Mae West on'. This didn't convince Willie, but a bamboo scaling-ladder was floating past and we grabbed it, stuck him on one end and headed out to sea with him shouting 'You ....are going the wrong way!'"

HMS *Berkley* was heading in their direction but received a hit below the water-line and began to sink. Some time afterwards HMS *Brocklesby* closed in with rope ladders over the side to pick up survivors and they were rescued in company with Cpl C.White, who recalls swimming for about an hour. "The ship was under attack by dive-bombers as well as machine- gun and shell fire from the shore, and a shell passed clean through the funnel as I was being hauled aboard. A number of the gun-crews had become casualties and the captain asked if any of us could fire an Oerlikon. I said I could and had a go at the Stuka bombers and cliff positions."

"As the withdrawal time of 1400 hours approached the captain ran the ships stern nearly into the beach and picked up all the men he could while the ships guns blazed away giving covering fire. Eventually we had to shove off, with masses of shingle being flung into the air from our churning propellers. We were practically aground! Thankfully we made it, fighting off air-attacks until darkness brought some respite. We docked at Portsmouth about midnight where the Navy took us aboard the old HMS *Victory* and after a mug of rum we bedded down between decks. The following morning we made our way to the Isle of Wight and after checking in at company HQ returned to billets and a great welcome from our landladies".

The Commando assembled at Upper Chine School on 21 August, but this time many familiar faces were missing. Out of the 370 strong force that sailed to Dieppe, 75 officers and men were unable to muster on the tennis courts. The total RM Commando casualties including those taken prisoner were 23 all ranks killed and 76 wounded. The Royal Navy lost 75 all ranks killed and the Royal Air Force incurred 69 fatal casualties.

Details of the appallingly high casualties suffered by the Canadians only became known over a period of time. Many were taken prisoner. The Royal Hamilton Light Infantry embarked with 582 men of whom 217 returned. The Royal Regiment of Canada sailed with 554 and only 65 came back to England. Of the 553 strong Essex Scottish, 52 returned. These losses were hard to comprehend. Les Fusiliers Mont Royal embarked with 584 and returned with 125 men. The Queen's Own Cameron Highlanders of Canada sailed with 503 and came back with 268. The 523 strong South Saskatchewan Regiment returned with 353 and the 14th Canadian Army Tank Corps of 417 came back with 247 men. Other Canadian units suffered smaller losses. Over-all a total of 907 Canadians lost their lives.

The Dieppe raid was closely studied by those responsible for planning future amphibious operations. There had been numerous mishaps, some unavoidable but others were attributable to insufficient knowledge and information, lack of judgement and limited experience. Combined, they had produced overwhelming odds against which the raiding force was unable to compete. This costly enterprise made it clear that many lessons had still to be learned before a seaborne assault of similar magnitude and complexity could be launched with any certainty of success.

At the Commando HQ in Shanklin, Capt Manners, now the senior officer, directed that all ranks who could be spared from their duties should be given 10 days' leave. During this period the HQ staff concentrated on the urgent task of bringing the Commando up to strength. The time was also considered appropriate to adopt the Army Commando troop formation and preparations were made accordingly.

It so happened that a new batch of 'hostilities only' officers were on their way to the Commando from the Royal Marines Officers Training Wing, Thurlestone, and on 25 August, Temp 2nd Lts J.C.Beadle, R.S.Chiverall, D.Copsey, I.D.Laidlaw, T.D.Morgan, A.Neale, and J. O'Brien arrived. Further NCO and marine volunteer reinforcements joined the following week and the reorganisation and training commenced with new determination.

A few days before the Commando concentrated at Upper Chine School for

HMS Locust laying smoke in front of White Beach. Photo: Imperial War Museum

HMS Berkley holed below the water line. Photo: Imperial War Museum

the Dieppe raid, the local dance hall at Lake was placed out of bounds following a disagreement between some of the commandos and the men of the Duke of Cornwall's Light Infantry. A degree of rivalry was to be expected and the DCLI, who were accommodated in barracks, were envious of the financial benefits of the Commando billeting allowance which in turn attracted the girls. The eventual confrontation, according to Cpl G.Trafford "Was a wonderful fight, inside and outside the dance hall, but there were no particular victors". A truce was called after the Dieppe raid and Basil Bolwell, the owner of the dance hall, gave a dinner for the entire Commando. Placed at the side of each plate was a small card on which the following words were printed:

"One day, perhaps not so far ahead as we think, a monument will be raised in Dieppe. And this will be the sense of the inscription it will bear:
'Here it was, on this ground, that the Combined Forces of the Free Nations of the World first set foot in Europe after the German enslavement.
They stayed just one long heroic day,but they brought the first glimpse of the light of liberation. From the hour of their departure we lived for the hour of their return.' "

"Dieppe day will live not only in the history of Britain but in the history of Europe, long after those of us whose hearts lifted to the thrill of it have passed on. Measure it not as an achievement but as a portent. It was the shadow of the shape of things to come."

August 19th, 1942

Extract from The *Sunday Express* 23 August 1942 "John Gordon on the War"

The following awards were subsequently approved for distinguished service at Dieppe:

Maj. R. D. Houghton	MC	Lt K. W. R. Smale	MC
Mne G. R. Bevan	MM	Rne T. E. Breen	MM
Mne L. C. Bradshaw	MM		

CHAPTER 3

1 September 1942 to 30 June 1943

*A new CO, 2 IC and Adjutant appointed – Royal Marine Commando
renamed Royal Marine 'A' Commando – Weymouth and preparations for a
second cross-Channel raid – Reorganisation from company to troop
formation – RM 'A' Commando renamed 40 Royal Marine Commando –
Return to the Isle of Wight and Scotland.*

FIT YOUNG men are surprisingly resilient in moments of stress and their recuperative powers when combined with a high spirit of adventure are incredibly rapid. A newcomer to the ranks of the Commando in September 1942 would not have suspected that they had just survived a very tough battle indoctrination. The men were in good heart, their laughter spontaneous and their morale unshakeable.

An important factor that contributed to this happy situation was the Adjutant General's decision to fill some of the gaps caused by the Dieppe battle casualties from promotions within the Commando. A letter drafted by Lt D.L Barclay, who had been transferred from X Company to Headquarters as temporary Adjutant, may not have entirely influenced this decision, but the fact remains that his letter proposed this course of action and the reply received from the Royal Marines Office on 8 December 1942 approved the promotions as recommended :-

Capt J.C. Manners to be promoted to Act Lt Col and to take command of the R M Cdo.

Capt P.W.C. Hellings DSC, to be promoted Act Maj and appointed Second-in-Command.

Lt D. L. Barclay to be Act Capt and appointed Adjutant.

Other promotions made at the same time included Lts Bradley, Ephraums, McKellar and Steibel to be acting captains and these officers were appointed to command the companies. While no mention was made of Mne Forbes in the letter from the Royal Marines Office he was not forgotten in the euphoria of the moment. It was he who had typed the letter to the RMO setting everything in motion and it was Capt Barclay who directed him to sew on his first stripe.

Approval was now given for the Corps to form a second Commando from the 8th Battalion Royal Marines. In consequence, on 10 October 1942 the R M

Silent tanks, burning landing-craft and the dead tell their own story.
Photo: Imperial War Museum.

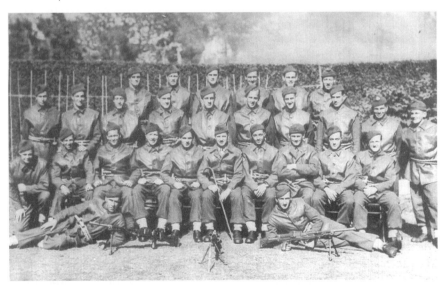

No. 10 Platoon, X Company, May 1942. Platoon Commander Lt I. C. McKeller
Argyll and Sutherland Highlanders. The men are wearing the standard training
dress of wool cap comforter, leather jerkin over battle dress or denims with toggle
rope around the waist.
Photo: Imperial War Museum.

Commando was re-named Royal Marine 'A' Commando and the new commando became Royal Marine 'B' Commando. The intention had been to use the second Commando as a training and holding unit to provide reinforcements for the original unit. However, there were calls for an increase in the number of Commandos and R M 'B' Commando became an operational unit.

While these deliberations and changes were proceeding, close attention was given to the improvement of fighting skills and efficiency of RM 'A' Commando. Each company was directed to develop, improve and perfect a specified military technique with the aim of passing on the lessons learned to others in the unit. The idea was sound and of considerable value although some of the presentations provided unplanned surprises. In the course of demonstrating beach assault techniques, an over zealous X Company demolition team, intent on impressing the observers with the effectiveness of a beach charge, added extra explosive for good measure to the main charge. The charge was intended to blow a hole in a large discarded metal boiler but, when detonated, the boiler and a hefty chunk of Shanklin beach ascended skyward. The observers, suitably impressed but a little shaken, scattered madly before gravity reversed the ascending mass of sand, shingle and metal in their direction.

Friendly but keen competition was used extensively at all levels as a means of striving for perfection. Speed marches became a daily ritual and platoons vied with each other to cover a set distance in the fastest time. Webbing straps were tied with string or boot laces to prevent the fighting order working loose while running. An even distribution of weapon loads was achieved with each man taking a turn at carrying the LMGs, mortars and anti-tank rifles. Occasionally the speed marches were routed to finish on one of the sea-front piers where the platoon would jump over the side and swim ashore. This procedure was unpopular with the landladies who objected to marines standing on their doorsteps in puddles of sea-water at lunchtime. The ability to negotiate cliff obstacles quietly and quickly was considered to be of primary importance and received special attention. At Dieppe, both 3 and 4 Commandos had to make cliff ascents. Future raiding parties across the Channel could expect to encounter similar obstacles. Particular emphasis was therefore applied to the study of cliff-climbing techniques. Each man was equipped with a toggle-rope and the eye splice at one end and a wooden toggle at the other provided simple and effective connections to construct a strong rope of variable length.

Cliff-climbing required a mixture of skill, strength, balance and a good head for heights. After numerous assaults on the chalk cliffs along the seashore and rocky outcrops in various quarries, the right and wrong way of ascending and descending the near vertical emerged. In due course a number of marines, obsessed by the challenge of scaling the impossible, became the natural cliff-leaders (CLs) of the day, finding footholds where none appeared to exist. The others were dependent on them to secure the ropes on which they, the less nimble, could haul themselves, their weapons and their equipment up the cliff-face. The CLs carried lengths of thin cod-line on their ascents, to which the main ropes could be attached and hauled to the cliff top. Sisal and hemp rope of various lengths procured from HM Dockyard were in general use by the summer of 1942.

Rarely were the sure footed seen to stumble, but one intrepid marine, playing a leading role in a demonstration near Shanklin, fell from half-way up the face of a quarry, landing with a resounding thud in front of the assembled company. Maj Hellings – a keen and capable cliff climber – was unruffled by this unrehearsed incident and continued with an ad lib of "Now that is a particularly good example of how not to do it".

With the means of ascent mastered, experiments were made with various methods of descent. The commandos were unfamiliar in 1942 with the art of abseiling, and unless careful control was maintained in descending the more vertical cliffs, the risk of rope burned hands was very real. The problem of hoisting and lowering ammunition, heavy weapons and stores also had to be resolved and resulted in the introduction of a rope, stretched taut and secured at an angle of about 45 degrees, from the top of the cliff and securely anchored at the base into the beach. The items to be hoisted or lowered were attached to a pulley on this rope with a spring clip, and then hoisted or lowered as required by means of a light line attached to the pulley.

The angled rope provided a fast means of descent for commando personnel. This method required the additional aids of a toggle rope slung over the inclined rope, strong hands to grasp each end of the toggle rope and a small prayer on the way down. The angle of the rope was fairly critical and if too acute the speed of descent could be excessively fast and dangerous. Although the most severe mishaps experienced in RM 'A' Commando were injuries to ankles this method of descent became known generally as the death slide. Experimental descents of notional wounded were made by volunteers strapped to or hanging on to the back of Sgt G. Swan, ginger haired giant. But not everyone possessed his strength or had sufficient faith in the strength of their fellow-men and the tests were discontinued.

Rope line or toggle ropes were also used for negotiating obstacles and consisted of three parallel lengths of rope stretched taut and secured over the gap or river to be crossed. The two outside ropes served as hand rails and were connected to a single centre strand (the foot rail) at six or eight feet intervals by toggle ropes. Negotiating this type of bridge required practice and confidence. If ropes were insufficiently taut the user could find himself either balancing on the centre strand with slack and useless hand ropes or conversely, hanging from the hand rails with the centre strand inches from his feet.

Particular attention was given to perfecting a 'set piece' attack on a coastal gun-battery. Detailed planning and endless rehearsing continued, by day and night before Lt Col Manners was satisfied. A mock-up of a gun-battery was constructed on Chillerton Down and after a number of dry-runs the Commando was ready to stage a demonstration of a night assault using live ammunition. To add a touch of realism to the scene a dozen marines were co-opted to act as German sentries and gun-crew, with clear instructions to move to a place of safety before the live firing commenced!

Mne G. Trafford, who was detailed to be one of the German sentries, faced the problem of travelling from his billet in Lake to Newport, where unit transport would meet him and take him the remainder of the way. Not wishing to be cluttered with additional clothing he dressed in the authentic German uniform and forage cap provided. Carrying a German helmet and Schmeisser sub-machine gun, he walked to the bus stop, boarded the vehicle and, having paid his fare, found himself completely disregarded by the conductor and other passengers throughout the journey!

Towards the end of September the Commando took part in a major exercise. Operation Sark was designed to test all ranks in night landings on enemy occupied territory, cross-country night navigation, lying -up discipline and battle procedures. By this time the men were extremely fit and just about ready for anything. The junior officers and section commanders thought they had done well during the exercise but the senior staff were not so easily satisfied and found enough points for comment and criticism to ensure that the young leaders didn't get too big for their boots.

The Commando moved to Weymouth on 2 October and occupied billets in the town. The period between 3 to 15 October was devoted entirely to troop and unit night exercises culminating in exercise Operation Blackmore. During this time the normal day and night routine was reversed. All ranks slept or rested during the afternoon and on completion of their evening meal mustered for a briefing on the programme of events for the night ahead. This would be followed by a stand down until it was time to parade at 2200 hours or later, depending on how far each troop had to travel to the assembly area. Troop parades were held again in the morning, followed by cleaning of weapons and equipment and a review of the previous night's activities. This routine, modified to suit the nature and scale of the training programme, was repeated every 24 hours. The local dance-hall was a favourite rendezvous and it was not unusual to see commandos dressed in combat rig with darkened 'Al Jolson' faces dancing until it was time to leave for the assembly area.

About the same time that RM 'A' Commando moved to Weymouth, 3 Commando moved into the town and commenced exercising in the area, and Polish troops also arrived in the locality. It became apparent that another raid across the Channel was imminent and the arrival of the *Princess Beatrix* (merchant vessel converted to assault ship) really set the tongues wagging. Rumours of a raid on Cherbourg started to circulate around the town and the feeling in RM 'A' Commando was one of disquiet at the lax security. This broadcasting of news to anyone at large seemed to be a sure way of inviting the enemy to prepare an unfriendly reception for them on the other side of the Channel.

The rumours were not far off the mark. Plans were prepared at Combined

Operations Headquarters for a landing on the Cherbourg Peninsula designed to provoke an air-battle similar to the engagement in the skies over Dieppe on 19 August. While the allied air forces would have welcomed the opportunity to challenge the Luftwaffe – and the commandos were certainly keen to strike again at a German target – no one looked forward to a repetition of the shambles on the beach at Dieppe. As events turned out the proposed raid was considered unnecessarily risky and the plan was shelved.

In the days that followed, two noteworthy events took place. The first, on 26 October, concerned the initial issue of the green beret. There were men in the unit who were reluctant at first to wear the new head-dress as they considered the colour to be effeminate. Their feelings soon changed and it was not long before the practical and prestigious value of the green beret out-weighed any colour prejudice. The green beret was worn with pride, in action or on parade, in preference to any other form of head-dress.

The second event occurred on 29 October. The anticipated reorganisation from company to troop formation was implemented, and concurrent with this reorganisation, the Commando was renamed 40 Royal Marine Commando. There is no documentary record to show who initiated the change of name or who selected "40" as the number. The decision, was more than likely, made at Combined Operations Headquarters and agreed by Royal Marine Office, but the number and change of name did not originate within the unit. It has been suggested that the number may have been chosen to link the new Commando with the 4th Battalion Royal Marines. The 4th Battalion holds a prominent place in Corps History for its daring and highly successful raid on the fortified harbour of Zeebrugge on 23 April 1918. The battalion, having suffered 353 casualties including the loss of its commanding officer, was disbanded and as a sign of respect it was never reformed. However, the more logical reason for the choice of "40" would have been to provide a numerical margin between Army and Royal Marine units to allow for the formation of additional Army Commandos. The renaming process included RM "B" Commando, which in turn became 41 RM Commando. On 30 October 40 RM Commando, operation-ally equipped including wireless sets, heavy weapons and first line ammuni-tion, marched out of Weymouth in torrential rain towards Southampton, en route to their former billets on the Isle of Wight. Winter training continued in much the same fashion as before but selected personnel were sent to the mainland to qualify as snipers, assault-engineers, drivers and signallers. Others attended courses specialising in the use of foreign weapons and explosives or trained as parachutists. Fitness was of major concern and the daily programme always included a period of physical training taken by a qualified instructor – if sub-units were fortunate enough to have them – or by platoon commanders, who copied the exercises from military pamphlets. Sports were mainly confined to soccer, boxing and tug-o-war. Given an open space, a leather ball, boxing gloves and a stout rope other equipment was of secondary importance. With its activities so closely related to the sea the

Commando availed itself of a whaler from the Navy. The 27 foot, clinker-built boat was moored in Bembridge Harbour and platoons took it in turn to use it for sailing or boat pulling (rowing).

There was no training on 25 December although a few stalwarts in Sandown had a quick dip in the sea to work up appetites for the landladies' Christmas dinners. Far out in the Atlantic, T Company in *Fidelity* could raise little enthusiasm for Christmas celebrations in their overcrowded living quarters, and similar conditions must have prevailed on other ships in Convoy ONS 154. In any event all thoughts of Christmas were forgotten when a large U-boat pack commenced to attack the convoy on 26 December. Within 48 hours 15 vessels had been sunk and the rescue ship *Toward* was unable to take on more survivors. The Commodore of the convoy, V Adm Egerton, signalled *Fidelity* to assume the rescue role and Cdr Langlais launched one of the Kingfishers to cover *Fidelity* while she recovered survivors. Unfortunately the seaplane capsized and sank in the rough sea during take-off. The plane's crew were rescued but the depth- charges carried in the plane exploded, causing considerable damage to the condenser pipes in *Fidelity*.

Unable to keep up with the convoy, on 29 December Cdr Langlais decided to launch the second Kingfisher and MTB 105 (without torpedos), to maintain an anti-submarine watch while repairs were made to the condensers. On the return of the seaplane the pilot reported sighting a submarine and two fully-laden lifeboats 16 miles from the ship. Cdr Langlais instructed MTB 105 to investigate and rescue the survivors but she developed a fault in the main engine and could not proceed. A landing-craft was launched to complete the task and rescued 41 survivors from the *Empire Shackleton* including V Adm Egerton. Shortly afterwards *Fidelity* was attacked by U-225, but the single torpedo missed and the submarine disengaged when Cdr Langlais replied with depth charges. Shortly before 2100 hours U-615, making a rearward sweep of the convoy, also sighted *Fidelity* and fired three torpedoes, but all missed the target or failed to detonate. Again Cdr Langlais ordered depth charges to be fired and the submarine withdrew.

Temporary repairs to the condenser pipes completed, Cdr Langlais decided to make course for the Azores, a distance of 170 miles, and signalled his intention to C-in-C Western Approaches. MTB 105, still dogged by main engine failure but running on her Ford V-8 auxiliary, maintained watch astern as *Fidelity* barely made headway. Communication between *Fidelity*, MTB 105 and the outside world broke down finally during the night and MTB 105 eventually lost visible contact with the ship.

The Admiralty signalled *Fidelity* to make for Gibraltar or the Azores and sent the tug *Eminent* to her assistance. The Admiralty received *Fidelity's* last communication requesting a repeat of two previous signals regarding the rescue tug at 1130 hours on 30 December. Five hours later U-435 attacked the *Fidelity* with three torpedoes. The first missed but the second and third found their target. Kapt Lt S.Strelow, the U-boat commander, reported on his return to St Nazaire that two depth charges were fired by the ship, which by this time was sinking rapidly with three to four hundred survivors on overcrowded rafts trying to escape to the Azores. His description of the ship, its armament and a seaplane were strong evidence that he was referring to *Fidelity*. The *Eminent* and an unspecified number of destroyers searched the last reported position of the ship and surrounding area but found no trace of survivors or floats. The crew of MTB 105, who had constructed a sail from blankets and canvas gun-covers with hopeful expectation of reaching the West of England, were picked up by HMCS *Woodstock* on 1 January 1943.

In mid-January 1943 on the Isle of Wight a quantity of dehydrated rations, prototype of the 24 hour K-ration pack, was delivered to the Commando for testing. The task was given to Y Troop and a composite section was detailed to act as guinea-pigs. The men were issued with a selection of the food blocks and a supply of ship's biscuits which were as hard as iron. With these items tucked inside their mess tins they were dispatched to the mainland for seven days to live under combat conditions, patrolling "behind enemy lines". To make conditions as realistic as possible a local infantry unit – only too happy to "have a go" at a handful of commandos – undertook to be the enemy!

The guinea-pigs were required to rendezvous with a team of doctors at predetermined points every 24 hours, to be weighed, to have their physical condition checked, and to receive the next 24 hour ration pack. Cpl P.J.Bone lost his dental plate shortly after the start of the exercise when the patrol made a hasty early morning exit from a farm, with the enemy hot on its heels. He was embarrassed at the loss, and the thought of chewing hard tack without the essential "gnashers" was a dismal prospect. However, he solved the problem at each rendezvous by placing pieces of hard tack inside a sock which he then placed in front of a wheel of the doctor's jeep. When the jeep moved on he had a suitably crushed edible mass!

Further tests on the K-rations were carried out by P and Q Troops on a seven-day march from Southampton to Chesterfield, a distance of 198 miles. One half of each troop consumed K-rations while the others fed on standard rations. It was not long before the march developed into a race, with P Troop finishing a day ahead of their rivals. The men, who were asked to voice their opinion on the value of the rations after the march, had no strong feelings about them . Their comments varied from "Some items are tasteless" and "They make you thirsty", to " They're nice and light to carry but don't fill you up". A general summing up described the rations as palatable and adequate if used according to instructions. The tendency while marching was to use some of the items as munch bars instead of reconstituting them with water. This led to a thirst problem. Noticeable weight losses were recorded but marines on the standard rations had also slimmed down. The latter reason could possibly have been the result of being deprived of landladies' steamed puddings during the seven-day march!

The Commando returned to Scotland in April and moved directly to the hilly and somewhat bleak area of Loch Doon for an intensive period of field training. Battle drills and field-firing occupied the days, with compass marches and patrols on most nights. Appetites were well-sharpened and the men slept soundly under blankets which by morning were covered with a layer of hoar-frost. The field training coincided with the lambing season and the ever-observant Maj Hellings made it clear that while rabbits were fair game it was close-season as far as the lambs were concerned. Nevertheless, some rabbits in cooking pots were unusually large and succulent!

Moving down to the coast on the last day of April the unit found billets in Kilwinning, Kilmarnock and Irvine. Commando HQ occupied Burnside House in Irvine, an impresive granite faced building standing in its own grounds and enhanced by the addition of a white flagpole "acquired" by Maj Hellings. A resourceful billeting team – CSgt K.C.Morris and Constable J.McGillvray – undertook their task with the utmost enthusiasm and unwittingly set the future course for LCpl Forbes by directing him to the comfortable home of a widow and her daughter. He eventually married the daughter and resides very happily in that locality today.

The billeting team also placed Mnes F.Shaw and D.Gee in a small dairy in Kilmarnock. There they spent off duty hours watching TSM R. Anderson training in preparation for a major professional boxing contest. Reg Anderson, who had specialised as a Royal Marine physical training instructor, had challenged the British heavy-weight Jack London for his Lonsdale Belt and the contest was to be held in London. Anderson's two loyal supporters travelled with him to the capital city on the big night. The Royal Marine challenger lost the contest on a points decision but his splendid performance was a topic of conversation for a long time.

There was no quick access to open spaces in the unit's new location and training had to be adapted to the restrictions of town environment. Rope climbing and cliff haulage was practised on tall buildings, while small plots of waste ground were utilised for close-quarter combat, fitness- training and the never ending cycle of weapon proficiency tests.

During this period the Boys anti-tank rifle, which had become ineffective against improved tank armour, was replaced with the Projector Infantry Anti-Tank. The PIAT soon gained a reputation for its devastating effect upon tanks and its awkward loading and firing characteristics. The compression of a powerful spring before the weapon could be fired – equivalent to lifting a 200lb weight – and a powerful recoil action simulated the restraint of a bucking mule!

The Commando moved to Dunmore in early May to take part in exercise Slipshod. This was an unfortunate choice of code-name as the night-landing to capture and destroy a coast gun-battery was faultless in every detail. A few days later the Chief of Combined Operations visited Lt Col Manners and hinted that something was in the wind. This was substantiated when all ranks were ordered to report to the medical officer for inoculation against yellow fever and other tropical diseases. A warning order to move at 24 hours notice was announced on 12 June and, with excitement mounting, precautionary measures were taken to send home civilian clothing and other unessential kit.

P Troop faced the problem of what to do with Bob the Airedale. Bob had been their mascot since the formation of the Commando at Deal and was a friend to all. It was decided to have a whip-round for his train fare to the Isle of Wight. A telephone call to one of the landladies established that he would be well cared for and with label firmly attached to his collar he was drafted south. A collection was taken every pay day for his upkeep and he lived on to a ripe old age.

40 RM Commando embarked in TSMV *Derbyshire* at Gourock in early June 1942, with the task of acquainting themselves with the layout of the ship and the assault craft it carried. Each troop exercised with the landing-craft and the training culminated in a night-landing on the Isle of Arran to attack a coast gun-battery. On completion, the *Derbyshire* returned to Gourock, the Commando disembarked and the men returned to their former billets to stand-by for the word go.

The order arrived on 16 June and the Commando rejoined *Derbyshire* together with the Special Service Brigade Headquarters, elements of the 1st Canadian Division, British Army personnel and contingents of the Royal Air Force. V Adm R. Gowan visited the ship on 24 June and he intimated that action was imminent. Not far away 41 RM Commando embarked in the *Durban Castle*, also converted to carry landing-craft. Numerous other merchant ships were busily completing the loading of troops, stores, vehicles, ammunition and the thousand-and-one items required for war. Towards nightfall on 28 June the *Derbyshire* and *Durban Castle* sailed in convoy through the Firth of Clyde, heading for the Atlantic.

CHAPTER 4

1 July to 9 September 1943

The assault on Sicily – Augusta, bombing of the "Princess Emma" – Toe-hold on the foot of Italy. The landing at San Venere and advance to Pizzo.

EVERY inch of accommodation and storage-space aboard the *Derbyshire* contained service personnel, baggage and equipment, reserve supplies and ammunition. With so many members of HM Forces crammed together the atmosphere below decks was hot and claustrophobic, especially at night when port-holes and doors were closed to lessen the risk of an unshielded light acting as a beacon to a marauding U-boat. The galley staff did their best to cope in kitchens designed for a more leisurely service, but the other ranks meals were frequently cold and unappetising. Thankfully the weather remained good and the majority found their sea legs quickly.

The outward appearance of the peace-time cruise-ship had been radically changed. Her former colours were covered with drab grey paint and the graceful lines were broken by the addition of single 6-inch gun mountings fore and aft. Twenty LCAs were slung in two flights either side of the upper deck and, to complete the transformation, the mizzenmast was shortened to provide a clear field of fire for an anti- aircraft gun.

The first night at sea presented a few problems when the time came to sling hammocks. Those fortunate enough to find themselves alongside a Royal Marine with sea-service experience gratefully accepted a quick lesson in the correct way to tie knots, fold blankets and hoist themselves in and out of the suspended canvas bed. The less adventurous spent a restless night on the inflexible iron deck. With the exception of the traditional daily issue of rum to navy and marine personnel the *Derbyshire* was a dry ship*. Regulations forbade the sharing of rum tots, but there is no doubt that Army and Air Force personnel would have been offered a sip of "Nelson's blood".

The daily ship routine was quickly established and attention focused on the maintenance of weapons and equipment, the checking of stores and general activities designed to keep mind and body active. All deck spaces were used for exercising and inspections. It was not long before the Royal Marines discovered that many of the Canadians were unfamiliar with the mechanics of the Bren gun and Thompson sub machine-gun. Instruction in the handling of these weapons was soon arranged, culminating in live-firing at tin cans thrown over the stern of the *Derbyshire*.

---

* No alcoholic drink available.

TSMV Derbyshire Bibby Line. 11,600 tons launched 1935. Converted to a troop transport ship with two flights of landing craft. Photo: Bibby Line

Part of Allied invasion force on the approach to Sicily. Photo: Imperial War Museum.

On 1 July orders for Operation *Husky** were issued to Commanding Officers and Orders of the Day, by Gen Montgomery commander of the British Eighth Army, Gen A.G.L. McNaughton the GOC-in-C First Canadian Army (in England) and Lt-Gen G.G. Simonds commanding the 1st Canadian Division, were read over the ship's broadcast system. The troops knew they were heading for the Mediterranean but details of the destination were confined at this stage to planning staff only. The concept for the role of the Commandos in the Italian campaign had first been considered in January 1943 at the Allied Conference in Casablanca. Many variations for an overall plan were studied before final agreement was reached on 3 May by Commander in Chief Gen Dwight D. Eisenhower and his deputy Gen Sir Harold Alexander. The British Eighth Army was given the task of landing between a point just south of Syracuse and the Pachino peninsula. The Seventh United States Army would land on either side of the Gulf of Gela, with both armies pushing quickly northwards to cut the island in half. It was Gen Montgomery's intention to land his divisions simultaneously, with 1st Canadian Division, 51st Division and 231st Brigade securing the southern tip and the 5th and 50th Divisions the eastern sector. The 1st Canadian Division, consisting of the 2nd Canadian Infantry Brigade on the left and 1st Canadian Infantry Brigade on the right, were to land in the area south of Pachino. The task of securing the coastal defence batteries on 2nd Canadian Infantry Brigade's front was given to 40 and 41 RM Commandos. On the eastern flank, 3 Commando in the *Prince Albert*, sailing in convoy with other elements of the Eighth Army from North Africa, had the task of capturing a coast battery near Cassibile.

The officers assembled in the smoking-room on 3 July for a briefing by Brig R. Laycock. He outlined the main plan for the assault on Sicily and the part that each unit of the Special Service Brigade would play in the overall plan. 40 and 41 RM Commandos were to land in two successive waves on a stretch of beach to the west of Cape Passero to be known as Commando Cove. 41 RM Commando had the task of establishing a beach-head through which 40 RM Commando would pass, rolling up the enemy defences to the west. Alternative plans were prepared in the event of the *Derbyshire* or *Durban Castle* being sunk before the assault craft could be launched.

For the assault, 40 RM Commando was divided into two forces. Force One on the left under command of Lt Col Manners, and Force Two on the right under Maj Hellings. The Commando's task was to destroy one or possibly two coast-defence batteries and other enemy defences, and then to move inland to high ground and re-organise.

During the days which followed detailed briefing was carried out at all levels, every scrap of information was assimilated and orders committed to memory. Maps and air photos presented a picture of a flat sandy beach with the ground rising gradually to the west side of the bay. Immediately inland the

---

* Page one of the Operation Order is reproduced at Appendix B

fine sandy soil was cultivated with grapevines, tomato plants and clusters of olive trees. An occasional cart-track bordered by roughly constructed dry-stone walls led to small white-washed single-storey houses and farm build-ings. Close to the beach stretches of barren ground were thought to be salt pans.

Air-photographs revealed camouflaged positions indicating concrete ma-chine-gun emplacements and other coast-defence works. The Intelligence Section translated this information into a scale mock-up of the coast sector which helped to give a realistic picture of the area to be attacked. Landing drills were interspersed with the briefings and the movement from the assembly points between decks to landing-craft stations and embarkation into the LCAs was rehearsed until it could be achieved with eyes closed. Nothing was left to chance.

There was a flurry of movement in the convoy on 4 July when a Royal Navy escort reported the sighting of a submarine. The moment passed without incident and on 5 July, while it was still dark, the convoy passed through the Straits of Gibraltar into the Mediterranean. The convoy became more vunerable to enemy attack by submarine and a U-boat was sunk by one of the destroyers. Although this action was not visible to anyone in *Derbyshire* Adm P. Vian signalled the information to all ships in the convoy.

The Administrative Order issued on 7 July contained details of dress, rations and ammunition, landing serials and other relevant information. The order directed that marching boots were to be worn from that day, to accustom feet for the foot-slog ahead and, since the 48 hour ration pack would be too bulky to carry during the assault the contents were to be divided so that the second half could be dumped ashore with the packs. Mepacrine tablets (anti-malaria), mosquito cream and water-sterilisation tablets were to be carried as the water was suspect and malaria was known to exist in the area. These items shared valuable space with mess-tins, spare socks and hand-grenades.

Ammunition was issued on 8 July and, to ensure that an adequate supply was available, the initial allocation of reserve ammunition and mortar bombs to be carried in the landing-craft was increased. Hand-grenades were primed with detonators and all weapons were given a final inspection. Escape packages were issued, each consisting of a transparent plastic envelope contained 5,000 lire in paper money, a metal button magnetised to act as a compass when placed on a smooth surface and a small wafer-thin file which could be sewn into the seam of a jacket or trousers. Little thought was given to the potential value of the escape pack except for the money, used for the most part to augment the rations during the advance to Messina.

After breakfast on 9 July large packs were stacked at specified points between decks ready for landing after the beach-head had been established. (A hundred or more of these packs continued on to India in the *Derbyshire* and were eventually re-united with the Commando in Italy!) During the morning convoys of ships from Haifa, Tripoli, Sfax, Gourock and Liverpool converged on a course for the south of Sicily. Soon after mid-day the fair weather that had accompanied the convoy from Britain deteriorated rapidly and storm-force winds whipped up the sea into an ugly grey mass of broken waves which threatened to engulf the smaller landing craft.

The problems of launching LCAs into those churned-up waters would have been immense. Thankfully, by the time the final briefing was completed shortly after 2100 hours the wind had abated, leaving a moderate swell in its wake. The officers of 40 Commando, in combat rig and with blackened faces, assembled in the smoking room at 2245 hours for a final word by Lt Col Manners after which, having tipped the ship's stewards, they proceeded to their landing stations. All passage- way illumination, with the exception of red police-lights, had been extinguished to allow eyes to adjust to night vision. At 0030 hours 10 July the convoy of assault ships and landing-craft, troop-ships and supply-ships, shielded by their Royal Navy escort, set course on the final leg for the southern tip of Sicily.

Immediately the canvas retaining-stays holding the LCAs firm in the launching davits were cast loose the assault craft began to swing with the sideways roll of the *Derbyshire*. This swing increased as they were lowered down the side of the ship's hull. The first flight was launched without incident and as the LCAs moved clear the second flight on its descent passed the heavy steel blocks of the first flight which were swinging wildly on their cables. Heads were hastily lowered as one LCA received a hefty clout which damaged the landing ramp.

Flotilla 127, with 40 RM Commando and Brigade HQ embarked, joined the LCAs from *Durban Castle* carrying 41 RM Commando and set course for the coast of Sicily. Although out of sight, the coast-line was indicated by distant flares dropped by RAF bombers. There was a heavy swell running and the occupants of the landing-craft were drenched in the spray that showered over the landing ramps. Pulses quickened in anticipation as the assault craft closed the distance to Commando Cove. This was the moment for which the Royal Marines had long been training. For many, this would be the first encounter with the enemy. Their feelings were of buoyant optimism and blissful ignorance of reality. Some of the men who remembered the beaches at Dieppe were a little pensive but determined to even the score.

The coxswain of the LCA with the damaged ramp had a problem keeping station. Each time the boat dipped into the swell sea-water poured through gaps at either side of the ramp flooding the well. The bilge pump proved ineffective and to overcome the problem half the occupants of the LCA moved onto the side-walks and all stores and ammunition were stacked as far aft as possible. This accomplished the men in the well used their steel-helmets to bail out water. While the bailing was in progress Mne S. Udakis, attendant and runner to Lt Beadle, felt it appropriate to remind the platoon that 10 July 1943 was not only a memorable day for the Allied Forces, it was also his 21st birthday. Under the circumstances the contents of the platoon commanders hip flask, reserved for emergencies, served an immediate and worthy purpose.

Locating Commando Cove should not have proved difficult but neither Commando touched down on the correct beach. 41 RM Commando, nearly 30 minutes behind the scheduled time of 0230 hours, beached to the west of the intended landing point and 40 RM Commando, too far to the east, had to move 500 yards or more towards the objectives. A number of LCAs grounded on sand bars short of the beach and the men had to wade ashore. Q Troop landed among the Canadians and it was 0530 hours before they joined the remainder of the force.

In the words of Mne R. Jaques of X Troop "It was a relief to get ashore even if it was a wet landing and on the wrong beach." LCpl Forbes found the landing almost a carbon copy of an exercise carried out in Scotland. As he recalled "We had a wet landing near Irvine and after drying out in Gaules Golf Club we pulled a handcart supporting a heavy machine-gun through the sand dunes to join the main force at Irvine harbour. The major difference in Sicily was that when we found the Commando they popped off a few rounds in our direction under the impression that we were the enemy!"

In the event the Italian opposition was faint-hearted and offered little resistance. The coast-gun batteries were in reality machine-gun emplacements and these were captured with few casualties. Some of the 40 RM Commando objectives were taken by 41 RM Commando, their landing having overlapped into that sector. 40 RM Commando moved inland at soon after 0800 hours to establish a defence position at Point 23. Patrols were sent out and a considerable number of prisoners were rounded up during a relatively quiet morning. Mnes Jaques and Gray, who were escorting 30 Italian soldiers to a barbed-wire compound on the beach, found others voluntarily joining them on the way and eventually accumulated a few hundred prisoners !

Towards noon both Commando units were mortared and sustained casualties. A counter bombardment silenced the enemy mortars and the results were seen when the commandos, advancing to take up new positions, passed dead and wounded Italians with their dead horses still harnessed to upturned gun limbers. On reaching the final objective on the high ground, the Commando units consolidated their defence positions, digging into the dry dusty soil among the vines and olive trees. Patrols were sent forward but made no contact with the enemy. The only sign of opposition was from the air and this was directed at the shipping off-shore.

After the heat of the day the contrastingly cold night was keenly felt by the troops clad in khaki drill. Patrols were active throughout the hours of darkness but there was no sign of enemy movement or a dawn counter attack. Once again the two Commandos moved forward to establish a new line of defence and it became apparent that the opposition in this area had ceased. Towards the end of the day both Commandos were moved into divisional reserve. 40 RM Commando had suffered nineteen casualties, two of whom subsequently died. Lord Louis Mountbatten visited the unit on 13 July and shortly

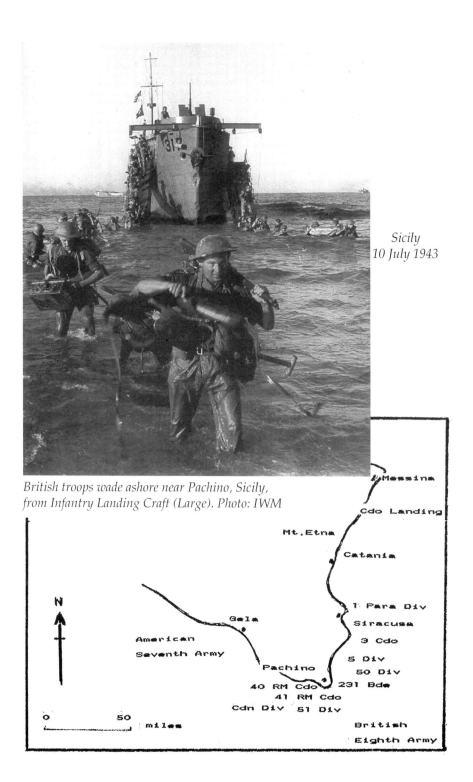

Sicily
10 July 1943

British troops wade ashore near Pachino, Sicily,
from Infantry Landing Craft (Large). Photo: IWM

Messina

Cdo Landing

Mt.Etna

Catania

N

1 Para Div

Gela

Siracusa

American
Seventh Army

3 Cdo

5 Div

Pachino

50 Div

40 RM Cdo
41 RM Cdo
Cdn Div

231 Bde

51 Div

0   50   miles

British
Eighth Army

afterwards Lt Col Manners received orders from Brig Laycock to be ready for a quick move.

Further east, 3 Commando, having captured the coast battery was called upon almost immediately to land near Agnoni with the object of capturing a road bridge at Ponte dei Malti. The 1st Parachute Division was to drop further north to seize a bridge at Primosole. Both operations were entirely successful but the cost in casualties was considerable. The actions were designed to open the route for a speedy advance by the Eighth Army through Catania to Messina but Gen Dempsey's 13th Corps met strong German resistance on the high ground west of Catania.

Brig Laycock was called to a meeting with Gen Dempsey and Adm McGregor where it was decided that 40 and 41 RM Commandos would land six miles north of Catania, move into the town and form a beach-head around the harbour. This would enable the 17th Infantry Brigade commanded by Brig Tarlton, to land unopposed in the beach-head and attack the German defences from the flank. Orders were sent to both Royal Marine Commandos to proceed immediately by LCIs to Syracuse. In the meantime planning for the operation was undertaken by Brig Laycock and Lt Col T.Churchill aboard *Price Albert*.

Arriving on 15 July the two Commandos moved into fields on the perimeter of the town to await developments. There was a succession of air raids on the shipping in the harbour throughout the night and the barrage from the anti-aircraft guns produced a hail of shrapnel which discouraged attempts to stretch out on the ground and sleep. Details of the forthcoming operation had not been officially announced but word passed around that the two Commandos were to make a landing north of Catania. This rumour gained strength when the motor-vessels *Princess Beatrix* and *Princess Emma* joined the *Prince Albert* in the harbour next morning.

Brig Layock, Lt Col Churchill and Adm McGregor held a further meeting to finalise details for the operation to take place that night. The Commandos embarked but no specific orders were issued before the ships sailed for Augusta. By the time they arrived in Augusta Harbour Brig Laycock had co-ordinated plans with Brig Tarlton but as time was running short – it was then 1800 hours – he issued verbal orders to the commanding officers. The basic plan required 40 RM Commando to land and form a beach-head through which 41 RM Commando and the Special Raiding Section would pass into Catania to capture the harbour. Before the orders group had dispersed a message was received from 13th Corps cancelling the operation because the Germans had reinforced their positions. In the event, it was decided to keep the Commandos embarked in readiness for any new commitment.

Almost as soon as it was dark German aircraft attacked Augusta. The air raids continued intermittently through the night concentrating on the ship-ping in the harbour. Shortly before dawn on 17 July, four anti-personnel bombs exploded around the forward part of the *Princess Emma*. The shrapnel penetrated the ships side adjacent to the marines mess deck and detonated a box of primed 36 grenades. The shrapnel from the bombs and grenades wreacked havoc in the confined deck space occupied by B and P Troops, killing 13 men including P Troop commander Capt J.Steibel and the Commando Medical Officer Lt Cdr W. Pride. A further 58 men of 40 RM Commando were wounded. The ships company also suffered grievous losses. In one swift moment of misfortune two fighting troops had been put out of action. In this dreadful shambles Cpl W. Ainsworth worked quickly to apply shell dressings and directed others to attend to the wounded. His calm and quick reaction helped considerably to reduce the loss of life and subsequently he received the BEM for his endeavours.

There is no doubt that this immediate reduction in the effective fighting strength of 40 RM Commando contributed to the three week period of frustrating inactivity that followed in make-shift camps in the dusty vineyards of Brucoli. It was here that Surg Lt J. Littlewood RNVR joined the unit. A further period of delay followed at Lentini where strafing by German fighters was a daily irritation and a working party suffered further casualties when captured ammunition they were loading into trucks exploded.

The stubborn defence by the German forces in the area of Catania led Gen Montgomery to change the axis of advance to by-pass the massive feature of Mount Etna on the inland side. Here the terrain was more suited to infantry activity and in consequence the Commando Brigade used the time to prepare for the forthcoming landings in Italy. The Commando units had an opportunity to plan their days more constructively and a further move took 40 RM Commando to Acireale, where it was possible to enjoy a brief period camping in lemon groves and exploring the slopes of Mount Etna. The Commando Brigade was reinforced on 22 July with the arrival of 2 Commando from Gibraltar. This Army Commando, led by Lt Col J.M.T.F. Churchill, brother of Lt Col T.B.L. Churchill, joined forces with the 4th Armoured Brigade to land a few miles south of Messina to block the German withdrawal to Italy. By the time they landed on 16 August the German rear-guard had already crossed the Straits of Messina to Italy, leaving behind the remnants of Italian infantry units who were eager to surrender.

Although the stretch of water between Messina and San Giovani is only a fraction over two miles wide Gen Montgomery had a very clear idea of the problems which lay ahead. He expressed his concern to Gen Alexander about the standard of preparations that had been made for the campaign and, in his memoirs "Montgomery of Alamein", said "The decision precisely where to land in Italy was not firm till 17 August, the day on which the campaign in Sicily ended. So far as the Eighth Army was concerned I was to launch it across the Straights of Messina on the 30 August, but was given no "object". On the 19 August I insisted I must be told what I was to do in Italy. My object was given to me on the 20 August, ten days before we were to land in Italy."

The original intention was for the invasion of Italy to be carried out entirely

Italian air defence warning system near Pachino

Italian infantry captured in the area of Pachino. Photos: Imperial War Museum.

by the Eighth Army on a two-corps front. There would be two landings made simultaneously – Operation Baytown – directly across the Straights of Messina and – Operation Buttress – on the north coast of the toe in the area of Gioia Taura. Two main factors led to changes in the original concept. The first was the introduction of an additional plan – Operation Avalanche – to land the fifth US Army at Salerno. The second was a need to consider the implications of negotiations with the Italian Government who were seeking an armistice and who were thought to be willing to join the Allies.

The Italians actually signed armistice terms on 3 September but this was not made common knowledge. The revised invasion plans provided for an announcement to be made at 1800 hours on 8 September, declaring the unconditional surrender of Italy. At 2100 hours on that day, American airborne troops would land near Rome while Italian divisions occupied the city. Also, the Italian army would seize Bari, Brindisi, Naples and Taranto. Finally, at 0430 hours 9 September, the Fifth US Army would land at Salerno and the 5th British Corps would land at Taranto.

Gen Montgomery was very sceptical about placing any reliance on the Italian army and made this known to Gen Alexander. However, by 17 August it had been agreed that the Eighth Army would make the landings across the Straights of Messina, while the 10th Corps – who were to have carried out Baytown – would now join the Fifth US Army in Avalanche.

When the armistice was announced, F M Rommel, with 20 German divisions at his disposal in Italy, quickly disarmed the Italian forces in the German occupied areas. Operation Baytown was originally planned for 30 August but a shortage of landing-craft and naval planning staff arising from demands for Avalanche resulted in delay. These resources were eventually provided and Baytown was re-programmed for the night of 2-3 September while the Salerno landing was planned for 9-10 September.

On 1 September, 40 RM Commando and 3 Commando were placed under the command of Brig R.E.Urquhart's 231st Infantry Brigade. The two Commandos embarked in LCIs and lay off Messina as a floating reserve for the latter stages of the 13th Corp's initial landings in the toe of Italy. Small reconnaisance parties were provided by 3 Commando in the area of Bova Marina and the SRS landed at Bagnara to hold the town until forward elements of the 15th Infantry Brigade arrived on 4 September. The initial landings met little opposition and Gen Dempsey's 13th Corps continued the momentum with a left hook from the sea on 8 September directed at Pizzo. The place chosen for the landing was the small harbour of San Venere, nearly three miles south-east of the town. 40 RM Commando and two reinforced troops of 3 Commando had the task of landing 30 minutes ahead of the 231st Infantry Brigade to secure the beaches and capture San Venere. The landing – Operation Ferdy – was timed for 0230 hours.

The Commando Force, carried in three LCIs each towing two LCAs, sailed from Messina shortly before midnight 7 September. The LCA release position was reached at 0200 hours but a heavy swell hindered the transfer of stores and men to the LCAs throwing the programme an hour behind schedule. Further time was lost while the captain of the leading landing-craft cruised up and down looking for a prominent harbour wall. This was eventually identified as a small stone quay. Force One of 40 RM Commando (Maj Hellings), comprising A and B Troop and a platoon of X Troop, landed with the two troops of 3 Commando at 0417 hours, half a mile to the right of the intended landing point at Green Beach. By good fortune they were unobserved and pushed inland to establish a bridgehead on the railway line to cover Amber Beach where the Brigade would land.

Force Two of the Commando (Lt Col Manners), consisting of Tactical HQ, Q and P Troops, landed on Red Beach (the quay) at 0500 hours. The first glimmer of daylight gave warning that the landing-craft would soon be visible to enemy observation posts and, before Force Two was clear of the quayside mortar bombs and shells, fired from positions on the hillside overlooking the harbour, exploded around the commandos. Moving rapidly out of the built-up area Force Two turned south-east along the coast road to take up positions on the right flank of Force One and adjacent to 3 Commando's positions between a road bridge and the shoreline.

Y Troop stepped ashore from an LCI at 0540 hours. Unable to make W/T contact with Commando HQ the troop moved out of the village to establish defence positions on a bridge and road junction to the left of the built-up area. A patrol moving forward from this position encountered mortar and machine-gun fire from the high ground. One of the enemy machine-gun posts, manned by Italians, was clearly visible among the trees and well directed rifle fire put this gun out of action. Mobile 88mm guns, screened by the trees on the high ground were now shelling the LCTs bringing the Brigade ashore. A second patrol attempted to locate the guns but was recalled when the troop, having established wireless communication with HQ, was ordered to join Force One. Force One made contact with the 1st Hampshires at 0830 hours 8 September and moved into Brigade reserve on the outskirts of San Venere. By this time the 1st Dorsets had landed and strengthened the line between P and Q Troops and the two troops of 3 Commando. While this reorganisation was proceeding the enemy began a systematic pounding of the beach-head with 88mm guns, mortars and machine-guns. P and Q Troops caught the main concentration of fire and incurred 40 casualties, including Lt Chiverall who was killed by a mortar bomb.

At 1000 hours Lt Col Manners received a message from Brig Urquhart to silence the 88s. Two batteries were involved. B Troop was ordered to deal with the one in front of the Dorsets while A Troop attacked the battery in front of the Devons. A call was made to support the attacks with an air strike. B Troop's fighting patrol moved forward through mortar fire and, in a quick skirmish overran the battery, taking nine prisoners. The patrol then withdrew to allow the Kittihawk bombers to finish the job. The fighting patrol from A Troop

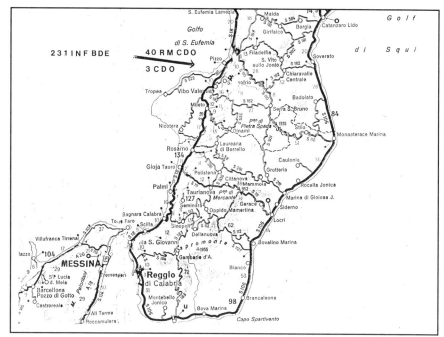

Operation Ferdy. 8 September 1943.
The landing at Porto di San Venere and advance to Pizzo

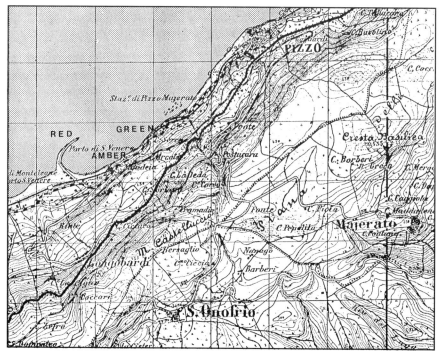

51

completed an almost identical attack with the Kittihawks delivering the coup de grace.

At 1115 hours X and Y Troops were ordered to advance along the coast road towards Pizzo to assist a company of the Hampshires who were holding the left flank of the bridge-head. Arriving at the location both troops came under machine-gun and mortar-fire from the high ground to the right of the town. X Troop, on the seaward side, was ordered to send a patrol forward to reconnoitre Pizzo. Lt Morgan, who led the patrol, decided to make the approach along the railway line and in the process came face to face with a German patrol in the vicinity of the station. The leading sections of both patrols immediately became involved in close quarter fighting.

Mne R. Jaques, who was on that patrol, remembers walking very quietly through a long tunnel in total darkness "When we emerged into the daylight we came under fire and some of us took cover behind the wheels of the railway trucks. We had a little 'set to' with Jerry in the station and were eventually told to get back to our lines under our own steam. Later that night Cpl 'Pusser' Hill led our section back to the station to look for Pete Jaggard, who did not return from the afternoon encounter. Although it was bright moonlight we found no trace of him".

When the patrol came under fire, Lt Morgan moved his rear section to the right, behind the cover of a stack of bricks, from where they could attack the main group of Germans in the station. Grenades were thrown and the Germans withdrew through the shrubbery and trees into Pizzo leaving behind one officer and six infantrymen who had been killed. Two of Lt Morgan's patrol had been wounded and a third was missing. This foray was hardly over when the patrol was subjected to machine-gun fire from the high ground beyond the station. To avoid unnecessary casualties Lt Morgan gave instructions for the men to withdraw. The body of Mne P. Jaggard was found in the vicinity of the station. Lt Morgan received the Military Cross for his determined leadership in this action.

Mid afternoon enemy mortar and machine-gun fire intensified on the left flank and was immediately followed by a German counter-attack on that sector. Four armoured cars with machine-guns firing, approached the forward positions along the coast road. Meanwhile, about 130 infantry, under cover of the trees on the hillside, attempted to infiltrate between B and D Companies of the 1st Hampshires. These two companies were forced to pull back to avoid encirclement. The Royal Navy came to their assistance with a ship to shore bombardment which initially hammered X and Y Troops positions but when corrected, broke up the German attack. A Troop was brought forward to strengthen the line and, apart from spasmodic mortaring and shelling during the remainder of the day, there were no more attacks on the beach-head positions.

At 2100 hours 8 September, news filtered through that the Italians had signed an armistice. The announcement of their unconditional surrender was

Pizzo railway station

Shell damaged tank landing craft at Porto di San Venere.
Photos: Imperial War Museum.

actually broadcast at 1800 hours by Marshal Badoglio from Rome, and Gen Eisenhower from Algiers, but for the men in the front line this information was not verified until the next morning. Y Troop patrols were active as far as Pizzo throughout the bright moon-lit night and a patrol from X troop entered the outskirts of the town at first light without making contact with the enemy. 40 RM Commando moved forward at 0800 hours 9 September to form a perimeter round Pizzo while the 2nd Battalion Devonshire Regiment passed through the town. The Commando then returned to San Venere and remained in that area until contact was made with the 5th Division at 1930 hours. The Eighth Army was now established in Italy and further north 41 RM Commando and 2 Commando were in the vanguard of a large amphibious force preparing to land with the 10th British Corps and the Fifth US Army at Salerno.

Honours and Awards
For distinguished service in Sicily and Italy:

| Cpl W. A. Ainsworth | BEM | Capt M. J. Ephraums | MC |
| Lt T. D. Morgan | MC | | |

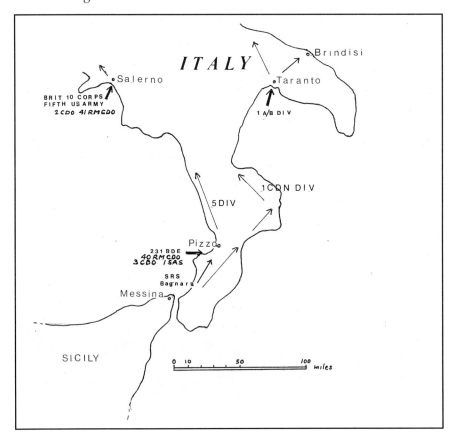

54

CHAPTER 5

1 September to 7 October 1943

The Battle For Termoli.

ON completion of Operation Ferdi, 40 RM Commando, 3 Commando and the 2nd Special Service Brigade Detachment Headquarters remained in the area of Vibo Valentia awaiting the next move. Rations were plentiful, the grapes were in season and living conditions, while spartan, were an improvement on previous weeks. The Sicilian campaign, in-so-far as 40 RM Commando was concerned, had been frustrating and negative. In comparison the Vibo landing produced positive results and the men, in buoyant mood, were keen to keep the pot on the boil.

Lt Col J. Durnford Slater DSO, the deputy commander of the 2nd Special Service Brigade, received orders on 11 September to land six reconnaissance patrols along the west coast of Italy to acquire all possible information about the enemy. Planning was nearing completion when it became evident that the British 5th Division of 13th Corps was continuing to advance rapidly and patrols were no longer required.

News of the Salerno landing, in which 41 RM Commando and 2 Commando were to play a prominent role, was announced by the BBC a few hours after the 5th U S Army and British 10th Corps carried out landings on 10 September. By this time 13th Corps had lost contact with the German forces who had withdrawn rapidly to contain the bridgehead at Salerno and to form a new line of defence following the Italian armistice.

It was assumed that the Germans would do everything possible to prevent a link up between British 8th Army and the 5th US Army. With this in mind plans were made to land the 2 SS Bde Detachment at Veri Scarbi, mid-point between Salerno and the existing 13th Corps forward positions, with the aim of holding a major road junction on the north-south route until the arrival of the 5th Army from the north and 13th Corps from the south. This landing was cancelled as 13th Corps continued to advance without opposition and the link-up was completed unaided in the area of Auletta on 16 September.

41 RM Commando and 2 Commando, under command of Lt Col T. Churchill, returned to Sicily for a well deserved rest while Brig Laycock flew to England for discussions on the Commando reorganisation and to badger his superiors for reinforcements. Shortly after his arrival in UK it was announced that he was to succeed Adm Mounbatten as Chief of Combined Operations.

Meanwhile Lt-Col Durnford Slater was informed that the 8th Army was moving to the north-east coast of Italy and the 2 SS Brigade Detachment and

Special Raiding Squadron, consisting of 1st Special Air Service, were to go with 13th Corps to the Adriatic coast. The existing location of 13th Corps made it more expedient for 5th Division and 1st Canadian Division to proceed overland. The Commando units and SS Bde Detachment, travelling by sea, avoided the dust and ruts of poor roads but experienced instead a slow sea trip in the claustrophobic troop spaces of Landing Craft Infantry (Large) which had limited galley and toilet facilities.

The detachment sailed from Scalea on 22 September, calling at Messina and Catania, where they remained for three days before proceeding to Taranto and Bari. Lt Col Durnford Slater met them on 30 September having travelled overland with the Brigade Intelligence Officer, Capt A.Peile, arriving in Bari on the day the Germans vacated the town. Bari would have been a good place for a "run ashore". Instead the men were informed that action was imminent and spent their stay of a few hours replenishing ammunition and regrouping in the landing-craft.

The force sailed for Manfredonia where they were briefed for a landing – Operation Devon – that was to take place in the area of Termoli on the night of 1-2 October. The intention to make a right hook from the sea behind the German front line had already been decided by Gen Montgomery while the Commandos and SRS were on their way to Bari. The 8th Army had made good progress following the initial landings in Italy and on the right flank the 78th Division was pushing towards Serracapriola as fast as the terrain, enemy mines and demolition obstructions permitted. In the mountainous region on the left flank the 1st Canadian Division was fighting its way through Riccia.

However, the German 10th Army was strong enough for Field Marshal(FM) Kesselring to conduct an orderly withdrawal along the north-eastern slopes of the Appenines. It could therefore be expected that he would endeavour to use any natural barrier to hinder the allied advance and, given the opportunity, could establish a strong line of defence on the River Bifurno which flows into the Adriatic about two miles east of the seaport town of Termoli.

Gen Dempsey's plan required the 2 SS Bde Detachment to land without supporting arms west of Termoli and, having captured the town and port area, to make contact with 11th Brigade of 78th Division who were moving up from the south-east. The success of this operation would force the enemy to continue to withdraw to the north-west and gain a very useful harbour and important lateral road to Capobasso for the allies

In planning the assault Lt Col Durnford Slater and his staff-officer Maj B. Franks were aware that 40 RM Commando were 100 men under strength while 3 Cdo, under command of Capt A.G. Komrower in the absence of Lt Col P. Young who was unwell, had been reduced to four troops.

Termoli is a small coastal town and fishing port 120 miles from Bari. The older buildings and church stand on a small promontory with the houses on the northern side overlooking the harbour. The east side of the town is bordered by a cultivated valley which extends inland beyond the built up area

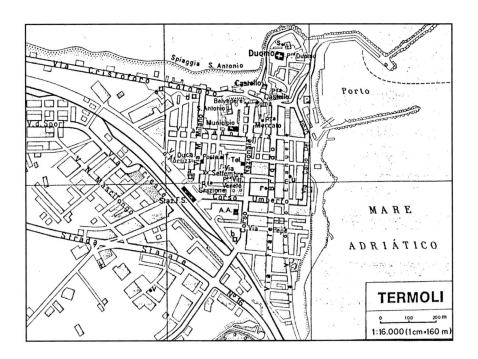

TERMOLI

0   100   200 m

1:16.000 (1 cm = 160 m)

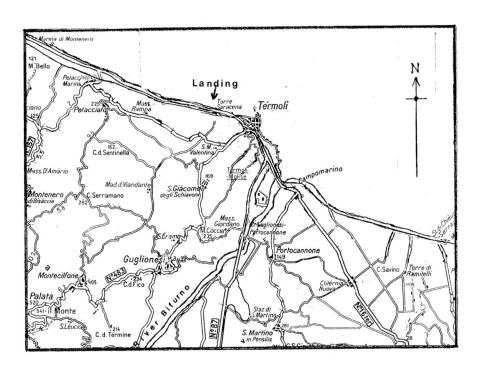

Termoli 1987: Beach Huts and Hotels now stand on the 1943 beach-head

Via Carlo Del Croix, leading to the South Side of Termoli. Photos: Author

and to the west the ground falls away gradually to sea level. A minor road follows the line of a narrow plateau southward and inclines gently to a moderate crestline (Pt 169) before descending again to Guglionesi, a large village about 10 miles inland.

Information regarding the enemy in the vicinity of Termoli was limited and no aerial photographs were available. Details gleaned from intelligence reports indicated that the German 1st Parachute Division was in action against the British 78th Division and a counter attack from this direction was a possibility. The primary routes of communication in 1943 were the railway, which followed the line of the coast and marked the inland boundary of the town at that time and Highway 16, the coastal road from which the winding Highway 87 connects with Naples.

It was decided to land the force on the night of 1/2 October, about a mile west of the town. 3 Commando would land in six LCAs and establish a small beach-head. Lt Col Durnford Slater's HQ would follow them ashore in a seventh LCA and 40 RM Commando and 1st SAS would land from four LCI(L)s. The task of 40 RM Commando was to pass through the beach-head and capture the town and harbour. The 1st SAS would establish a defensive position to cover the approaches from Vasto and reconnoitre eastwards along Route 16. If the road and rail bridges over the River Bifurno were still intact they were to guard these until contact was made with 11th Bde.

After a postponement of 24 hours for an improvement in the sea conditions the detachment sailed from Manfredonia at noon on 2 October in LCIs of the 22nd Landing-craft Flotilla, under the command of Lt Cdr R.Lammert RNVR. The weather was settled, the sea conditions were good and the LCIs, with the LCAs in tow, made steady headway until LCI 136 grounded on a sandbank about a mile off-shore and four miles short of the objective.

The LCAs had to be slipped to enable LCI 136 to go astern and clear the obstacle but due to good seamanship, a cloudy sky and a lack of enemy surveillance, the flotilla arrived at the LCA release-position undetected and on time at 0115 hours 3 October. Transferring 3 Commando to the LCAs proved a tricky operation as the sea had developed a moderate swell. However it was accomplished without incident and the LCAs led the flotilla on the final approach to the landing point.

The LCAs motored quietly inshore to lower their ramps unchallenged onto a sandy beach. 3 Commando moved quickly about the task of establishing the beach-head while Lt Col Durnford Slater and his HQ proceeded ashore. The leading troop of 3 Commando, climbed the railway embankment 150 yards inland and saw a steam locomotive facing the direction of Vasto. Attached was a passenger-coach and a flat based truck with a large metal hook at the rear end designed to tear up the railway sleepers as the train moved forward.

The reaction of the commandos was swifter than that of the Italian train driver and fireman. Sign language was sufficient to persuade them to step down from the cab and together with 12 German passengers who were found asleep in the coach, were held in the beach-head where they could not jeopardize the landing.

LCIs 181 and 136 with 40 RM Commando and 1st SAS aboard were now close in-shore preparing to beach at 0230 hours. A sandbank brought both landing-craft to a halt 50 yards short of the shoreline and it soon became evident that the intervening depth of water at this point was about six feet. The steep angle of the ramps pre-warned the commandos that they were likely to get more than their feet wet. Mne S.Shorrock of 9 Platoon disappeared with his Bren gun below the surface but was hauled up by Cpl F. Usher who, although six-feet tall, found it difficult to keep his nose above water.

The landing continued with the occasional splash of water and squelch of saturated boots to mark the arrival ashore. A major mishap was the immersion of the wireless sets with a consequential delay in communication as all information had to be passed by runner. It was also found impracticable to carry the medium machine-guns ashore and they were sorely missed later on.

It had started to drizzle by the time 40 RM Commando had formed up on the railway and every one was thankful when Q Troop set off along the line at 0300 hours towards the town, followed by Y and P Troops and Advance HQ. The second half of the Commando, A,B and X Troops under command of Maj Hellings followed a short distance behind, ready to peel off to their objectives at the appropriate time.

Q Troop had the task of capturing the east side of the town and holding the bridge over the railway. Y Troop would capture the west side of the town with P Troop backing up as required. A Troop, with the Mortar Platoon attached, would clear the harbour area and protect the left flank while B and X Troops moved inland to form road-blocks on the routes leading to Vasto and Guglionesi.

The locomotive was soon left behind and the commandos, moving in single file on both sides of the track, maintained a steady pace in the still night air. The distant barking of a dog was suddenly answered by another just ahead of the forward scouts shattering the silence. The leading sections were now entering the built-up area and while Q Troop continued along the railway line Y and P Troops fanned out along the unlit roads using the dark shadows of the houses as cover.

The first shot was fired soon after a Y Troop scout came face to face with an Italian civilian. The encounter was unfortunate. His reaction at the sight of the black-faced commando in the early hours of the morning was to scream loudly and run. Within minutes a battle royal had developed in and around the approaches to the station. A group of German soldiers aroused by the noise attempted to drive away an army truck, but a short burst from a Bren gun brought it to a halt. Near the station another truck, hit by tracer, was burning furiously and its load of ammunition and flares added an impressive but lethal "Brocks fireworks" display to the proceedings. German infantry with automatic weapons became active from the cover of buildings and side streets and it required a concentrated effort to winkle them out. In the general melee and darkness a shadowy figure just feet away could be friend or enemy.

P Troop took on the task of clearing two large buildings behind the station from which enemy automatic fire was proving particularly troublesome. In clearing this area two of the enemy were killed and 20 were taken prisoner. Interrogation of the prisoners by the Intelligence Officer, Lt Neal, revealed that some of them had been part of a demolition team with orders to blow up the station and water-tower. The charges had already been placed in position and were ready for firing by match fuses. As the morning light strengthened boxes of the explosive could be seen on the station platforms and there were a few anxious moments while the fuses were located and disconnected. Until this was achieved it was thought prudent to keep the captured demolition team in the station!

Meantime Q Troop had reached the railway-bridge, where automatic fire was directed at the leading section from a building adjacent to the bridge. Lt B.P.Hill ordered a platoon attack and brisk close quarter fighting developed with both side throwing grenades. During this initial encounter Lt Hill was wounded. The building, apparently being used as the garrison headquarters was well defended and in the process of clearing it 20 Germans were killed and another 30, mainly parachutists were taken prisoner. Maj Rau, the senior of the three officers among the prisoners, was identified as the local battle-group commander.

On the seaward side of Termoli A Troop had secured the area around the church and No 1 Platoon proceeded to check that the harbour was clear. Cpl J. Humphrey, with Mnes C.T. Ockwell and F.R. Hastings scouting ahead, led the platoon to the stone quay and finding the area unoccupied, moved eastward along the beach. Meanwhile No 2 Platoon – on their right flank – cleared the houses which bordered the road running parallel to the shore. This road ascended at a sharp incline from the harbour to the east side of the town.

Advancing along the foreshore No 1 Platoon came under fire from the town above them. Cpl Humphrey, having seen the path of tracer bullets, reported the approximate location of the enemy position to Capt Ephraums who decided to reconnoitre. Taking Cpl Humphrey as guide and his runner and Sgt J. Haslett of No 2 Platoon to make up the reconnaisance party, he led the way up the Via Carlo Del Croix. Anticipating that the enemy were located somewhere near the top, he turned into a side street with the intention of working round behind the German position. As the reconnaisance party entered the Corso Umberto, they were fired on at close range. Capt Ephraums gave orders to return fire and indicated his intention to bring up No 2 Platoon, but when he attempted to extricate himself from his very exposed position he was killed instantly.

Sgt Haslett, also attempting to move back, was shot in the forearm but kept going to make contact with his platoon. They moved up and quickly overpowered the enemy, taking two prisoners in the process. The German position, consisting of a deep trench, had been invisible in the darkness and this had cost

A Troop dearly. Maj Hellings was out of touch with Lt Col Manners and therefore unable to inform him of recent events in the port area.

At 0530 hours Lt Col Manners established his headquarters in one of the station buildings and with first light rapidly approaching gave orders for Q, Y and P Troops to consolidate in and around the buildings on the east and south-east perimeter of the town bordering on the Strada Statale (Highway 16). Lt Col Durnford Slater had also established his HQ near 40 Commando's HQ and gave instructions for one troop from 3 Commando to reinforce the perimeter south of the railway line. While they were in this position the 3-inch mortars of 3 Commando neutralised a 75-mm gun which had started to shell the station area.

It was at this stage that Q and Y Troops came under fire from mortars and artillery which wounded Capt J. Bradley and TSM W. Lees of Q Troop and Lt C. Laidlaw of Y Troop. The bombardment heralded the start of the first German counter-attack. This was launched from the valley on the left flank where a group of 30 German paratroops advanced under cover of bushes and trees as far as the rear gardens of the houses. They were repulsed with a loss of 12 killed and a further eight were wounded and taken prisoner.

Less than half an hour later a second German attack was made from the same direction. It lacked the strength and impetus of the former assault and six of its number, attempting to infiltrate between the houses, were killed by commandos who had established themselves in some of the buildings. The remaining Germans withdrew quickly.

Shortly before 0800 hours a runner reported to Lt Col Manners that X Troop was in position astride the junction of the route to Guglionesi and branch road to Vasto. Mne R. Jaques found himself a suitable viewing point behind a well in the forecourt of a farmhouse and in recalling those early morning hours he said "A total of seven lorries and a staff car came along the Vasto road and we captured them all and kept the prisoners in the farmer's barn. We heard the sound of a motorcycle approaching and the rider stopped and raised his hands when challenged but the sidecar passenger jumped out and ran off across a field with bullets all around him. He was wounded in his attempt to escape and found later by a patrol searching the area."

Lt Col Manners, in his report of the operation written on 10 October, recorded "It was quite apparent that the presence of the Commando was completely unsuspected. One lorry contained the mail and the equivalent of our NAAFI ration for the troops in the vicinity of Termoli". Needless to say the commandos were well supplied with cigarettes during the operation.

The Colonel also received a message from Capt Ecrepont of B Troop indicating that they had established a road-block near the brickworks at Point 169, approximately two miles from the town. The troop had captured an officer and one other rank of the paratroops who had been walking along the road towards Termoli. The troop had also ambushed two lorries and two motorcycles which had driven into their position, accounting for six enemy killed and six prisoners. A patrol sent to reconnoitre the area of San Giacomo reported that Germans were holding the village in some strength

The 1st SAS, led by Maj P. Mayne, had also been active from the time of landing. One group covered the approaches to the town from the direction of Vasto and stopped attempts by the enemy to infiltrate along the beach. A second group set off eastward along Route 16 to check the road and rail links crossing the Bifurno River. They found these demolished, but made contact with Lancashire Fusiliers who informed them that the battalion was preparing to cross the river at 1400 hours with the aim of linking up with 40 RM Commando.

The 1st SAS had a run of bad luck that morning. Two sections, preparing an ambush on Route 16, were encircled by the enemy and were themselves killed or captured. Another SAS group, making its way from Bari to Termoli in a captured German Lancia, picked up Sgt Forbes of 40 RM Commando – on his way to rejoin the unit from hospital – near the pontoon bridge over the Bifurno. The bridge had been damaged by shell-fire and he had been waiting in a convoy of trucks while sappers carried out repairs. The SAS in their truck dodged the German shelling and having crossed the pontoon bridge hared off across country to drop Sgt Forbes in the town. Minutes later a random shell hit the truck killing all the occupants.

The question of the disposal of prisoners presented the commandos with a steadily increasing problem. The situation in the beach-head was still fluid and it was decided that the best solution would be to hand them over to the Navy. The task of taking them to the harbour was given to 12 Platoon and Lt Beadle detached one section for this purpose. The prisoners, mainly paratroops and numbering well over 150, had not been thoroughly searched and it was with some relief that the guard arrived at the quay to find one of the LCIs lying alongside. The embarkation of the Germans had just commenced when Stuka aircraft dive-bombed the LCI. The bombs, with the exception of one which knocked the bottom out of an old fishing-boat, landed in the sea on either side of the landing-craft and the prisoners, plus one magnificent Alsatian dog belonging to Maj Rau, were safely embarked.

With the main area of the town cleared by 0800 hours, Lt Col Manners received orders to form a strong perimeter in the vicinity of the the X Troop road block and B Troop's position at Point 169. Retaining Q and A Troops in their existing locations to protect the left flank he proceeded to move P and Y Troops with HQ to join B and X Troops. Almost immediately the leading sections of P Troop came under fire from the direction of the valley on the left flank. The troop commander, Capt L.G.B. Marshall, instructed P Troop to continue the advance while he moved with two sections towards the valley. Nearing the ridge he came up against a force of about 40 Germans armed with two light machine guns and numerous other automatic weapons.

Initially surprised by the superior strength and fire power of the enemy, he deployed the two sections in line, gave the order to fix bayonets and advanced with all weapons firing from the hip. Without doubt the initiative and leadership displayed by Capt Marshall, combined with the courage and determination of the outnumbered marines, shattered the morale of the Germans. While the marines miraculously suffered no casualties in this encounter the enemy lost 10 killed, eight wounded and a further 20 were taken prisoner. With the opposition removed, the two troops and Commando HQ reached the new location without further incident.

At 1100 hours, A and Q Troops with the Mortar Platoon, received orders to join the remainder of the unit. 40 RM Commando was now deployed with B and P Troops plus one detachment of mortars occupying the area of Point 169. The road junction was covered by Q and X Troops while A Troop, a mortar detachment and Y Troop covered the right and left flanks.

Soon after midday elements of 56th Reconnaisance Regiment entered the town in their armoured cars and carriers. Their arrival was a welcome sign of a link-up with 11th Bde. Lt Col Durnford Slater arranged for them to take over the positions held by 3 Commando and 1st SAS, and these units were withdrawn into Termoli to get some rest.

The situation in 40 Commando's area became quiet around midday and it appeared that the Germans were withdrawing towards Guglionesi. However, at 1500 hours B Troop became the target of machine-gun fire from a house in San Giacomo. The 3-inch Mortar detachment attached to the troop partially demolished the building and nothing more was heard from that direction. During the late afternoon small groups of Italian civilians walking through 40 Commando's positions from the direction of Guglionesi reported that the Germans were assembling there in strength. This information was passed to Lt Col Durnford Slater who signalled 13th Corps for an artillery bombardment to be targeted on the area.

A short distance along the road to Vasto a section of X Troop led by Cpl Usher had just completed clearing an area of woodland to the south-west of the town. In recounting the episode Fred Usher said "We met two Italians who told me that the Germans were about to blow up a railway-bridge over the river. I called on our Bren gunner to give us covering fire while we crossed the river on the seaward side and from this position we attacked the Germans, killing one and taking another, who was wounded, prisoner. The others withdrew. After removing the demolition charge we returned to the troop". Cpl Usher was subsequently awarded the Military Medal for his initiative.

To the east of Termoli the Lancashire Fusiliers, supported by four Sherman tanks manned by crews of the 3rd Canadian Light Yeomanry, had also managed to cross the river in the afternoon but were still a considerable distance from Point 169 and unable to make contact with 40 RM Commando by the end of the day. In consequence, just before last light Lt Col Manners withdrew B and P Troops from their exposed positions in the area of Point 169 and closed the Commando into a lager for the night. Almost as soon as it was dark the Germans sent up white flares around the perimeter to mark their forward positions.

It was to prove a long night of aggressive patrolling for the men of 40 RM Commando. Most of them had been without sleep since leaving Bari and prospect of resting in the immediate future was doubtful. The patrols brought in a number of prisoners during the night, mainly stragglers from units that had occupied Termoli when the commandos arrived.

Towards midnight further reinforcements from 78th Div arrived by sea in the form of the 36th Brigade HQ with 8th Battalion Argyle and Sutherland Highlanders, 6th Battalion Royal West Kents and elements of 11th Brigade HQ. The units disembarked in the harbour and because of the lateness of the hour were billeted in the town for the night.

Early morning of 4 October, Lt Col Durnford Slater was informed that the 2nd SS Bde Det would be relieved of its commitments by 0830 hours. The wireless message was welcome news but somewhat premature. Elements of 56th Recce Regt passed through 40 RM Commando's positions at 0800 hours on the Vasto road followed an hour later by the 8th Bn A and SH along the Guglionesi road. The Argyles dug in on the seaward side of Point 169, the Germans having occupied the latter feature during the night. The Royal West Kents also moved out of Termoli to take up defensive positions to the south-west of the town.

A few minutes before 1100 hours a German mortar bombarded on 40 RM Commando's positions preceeded a Germans attack on the 8th A and SH's from the direction of Point 169. About 50 German infantry supported by three tanks could be seen advancing from the far ridge. A counter bombardment by the Commando mortars, concentrating on the German infantry was effective in breaking up the attack. When the general situation had quietened down 40 RM Commando was able to move into Termoli where billets were found for some very weary men. Lt Col Manners was informed that the Commando would have to remain at two hours notice to return to the perimeter, and in circumstances it seemed a reasonable request. The Luftwaffe straffed the town and harbour during the afternoon, but by that time most of the men were in a deep sleep, oblivious of the outside world.

The reaction of the townspeople following the landing was varied. Many welcomed the arrival of the British and were soon providing the men with thick sandwiches of bread and eggs. Others were openly hostile and gave the appearance of wishing to continue their association with the Germans. Sniping from within the town resulted in a number of casualties and Lt B.A. Cooper, who joined 40 RM Commando a short time before the Termoli landing, was killed leaving the house where Lt Col Manners had established his HQ. Four Italian youths were found with rifles in their possession and taken into custody. Orders were immediately given by Lt Col Durnford Slater for all Italian youths to be rounded up, and he threatened them with drastic reprisal action if the sniping continued. This had the desired effect.

Shortly after 40 RM Commando's return to the town, Lt Col Durnford-Slater

Station approach from the Corso Umberto. Photo: Author

received a request from 36th Bde for reinforcements to secure the right flank of the 8th A and SH where enemy activity threatened its position. Lt Col Durnford Slater complied by sending 3 Commando to occupy the area to the north-west of the road junction previously held by X Troop, 40 RM Commando. Two hours later, in response to a call for help from 11th Bde, he despatched one troop from the 1st SAS to hold a position on the railway-line about one mile to the west of Termoli. This troop was placed under command of Capt Komrower and given the task of covering the approaches along the coastline.

By 1430 hours 3 Commando was in position at a farm half-a-mile west of road junction, with Cdo HQ and 2 Troop occupying buildings south of the road and 4, 5 and 6 Troops dug in on the forward edge of an olive grove overlooking the River Sinaca. The troop from 1st SAS took up positions on its right covering the railway line and the beach. To the left of 3 Commando the 8th A and SH took up defensive positions in and around a church and brickworks.

The weather had steadily deteriorated as the morning progressed and by early afternoon heavy rain was making conditions unpleasant for the men on the perimeter. The effect of the stormy weather was to have serious consequences for the men holding Termoli. Flood-water from the mountains tore into the pontoon bridge across the River Bifurno, sweeping part of it towards the sea. Abruptly the flow of reinforcements to Termoli by road ceased.

During the afternoon Col Chevasse, commanding 56th Recce Regt, moved his HQ into the olive grove in rear of 3 Commando's HQ and the Commando was placed under his command. The Regiment relieved the 8th A and SH in the area of the brickworks and took over the right hand sector of 36 Bde's front. 3 Commando's position was reinforced with four six-pounder and one 17-pounder anti-tank guns and a section of three medium machine-guns from the Kensingtons. Two forward observation officers (FOOs) from 78th Division Artillery set up their OP at the forward edge of the trees and four Sherman tanks moved up to support the Argylls. Apart from a few shells landing in the area of the farm the hours passed fairly quietly.

Towards late afternoon it became evident that the Germans intended to increase pressure on the predominately British force when a patrol from the Recce Regt, returning from Route 16 near Ciata, brought in a prisoner from the 26th Panzer Division. Enemy activity for most of the night was deceptively quiet, but soon after 0400 hours on 5 October the noise of tanks approaching from the south could be heard. Shortly after dawn 12 German aircraft bombed and machine-gunned the town causing a number of casualties among the civilian population and British service personnel.

At 0800 hours 40 RM Commando was called out to form a defensive perimeter on the immediate outskirts of the town. The Lancashire Fusiliers had by this time moved up and were covering the approaches from the east and south. 40 RM Commando took up positions on their right flank with P and

X Troops and a detachment of 3-inch mortars adjacent to the right hand company of the Fusiliers. Y and B Troops covered the approaches from the south and west while A and Q Troops were held in reserve.

The commander 11th Bde made contact with Lt Col Durnford Slater about 0920 hours and told him that the situation had deteriorated and asked for the Commando force to assume responsibility for the immediate defence of Termoli. It was not long before mortar fire descended on 3 Commando's positions and the Sherman tanks became the target for German armour's gunfire.

Intermittent and accurate shelling of the town developed and the 2nd SS Bde HQ in a building near the convent was hit, resulting in some casualties to its staff. It was discovered later that this artillery fire was being directed onto targets by a German paratrooper who had established an observation post inside the clocktower of the town church. He was in wireless contact with his own troops and it must be assumed that he had hidden himself in the tower fairly soon after the landing on 3 October. When eventually discovered he refused to surrender and was shot.

Towards noon the Argylls lost their grip on the church south of Termoli and some of their number filtered down the road through 40 RM Commando's positions. Shortly afterwards the troop of the 56th Recce Regt in the area of the brickworks was overrun and 40 RM Commando's positions were shelled and mortared throughout the afternoon. Repeated attempts by the enemy to penetrate along the railway and shoreline from the direction of Vasto prompted Lt Col Manners to move Q and A Troops over to the right flank to support 1st SAS. They were ordered to hold the high ground by the cemetery and to prevent the enemy occupying any buildings on that side of town.

It was about this time that the Germans launched an attack with Mk IV Tiger tanks and infantry along the valley towards the right flank. Just as the pressure on this flank was increasing a Bren-carrier platoon on the town perimeter withdrew, leaving this sector undefended.

Lt Col Manners took the Bren-carriers under his command and re-established them in positions to cover the approaches to the town from the direction of the railway and the beach. The Kensingtons machine-gunners, on the left flank of 3 Commando, had a field day. The German infantry offered them an excellent target and were eventually forced to abandon their advance. It was not however all one-sided and 5 Troop of 3 Commando was forced to withdraw to the far side of the olive grove.

German tanks approaching from the direction of the church turned towards the olive grove, from where they were engaged by the anti-tank guns. The gunners, firing at extreme range, missed their targets and German tanks in retaliation knocked out one of the six-pounders. Col Chevasse sent an urgent wireless message to 78th Div for an artillery barrage to be directed onto the German armour. The barrage and an air strike produced the desired result and the Germans discontinued the attack.

At 1700 hours 11 German Mark IV Tiger tanks with infantry support, assembled among the trees opposite 40 RM Commando and the troop positions were mortared and shelled for the next hour. Lt Col Manners had been given command of two six-pounder anti-tank gun detachments for the immediate defence of the town, but after being subjected to the intense mortaring the gun crews abandoned their guns. These were taken over by marines from B Troop under the supervision of TSM K. Hawkins and Cpl R. Moffat. Writing about this incident Bob Moffat said "The first round we fired hit the ground a few feet in front of us but after the third attempt we hit a farmhouse from where the Germans had been firing a Spandau. That seemed to quieten things for a while."

Mid-afternoon two Bofors-gun detachments arrived in company with a detachment from 2nd Special Air Service led by Maj S. Scratchley. Although few in number they were valuable reinforcements. The 2nd SAS were sent immediately to reinforce the right flank where the Germans were exerting considerable pressure on A Troop and 1st SAS. By 1830 hours German infantry had infiltrated along the railway and the SAS and Royal West Kents fell back to join up with 40 RM Commando on the right of A Troop's position. A German prisoner taken at this time disclosed that his regiment was part of 16th Panzer Division. For some inexplicable reason the German armour failed to press home the attack. It may have been that the Kensingtons' machine-gunners had harassed the German infantry to the extent that they would not support the tanks, or because the tank crews were reluctant to advance further in the failing light. Whatever the cause it was a thankful reprieve for the hard-pressed defenders of Termoli.

Although the enemy activity diminished after dark Lt Col Durnford-Slater, concerned about the exposed position of 3 Commando, gave orders for their withdrawal and at 0145 hours 6 October the unit commenced to move back into the town, accompanied by the 56th Recce Regt HQ, the Kensingtons and the remainder of 8th A & SH. While this reorganisation was proceeding the London Irish made a welcome appearance in Termoli. At 0200 hours Lt Col Manners toured the forward positions of 40 RM Commando with Lt Col Butler of the Irish Fusiliers and Lt Col Mckenzie of the Lancashire Fusiliers in preparation for an attack that was to be launched by the two battalions at 0800 hours.

Fighting flared up again at 0530 hours, when German artillery shelled the town. This was closely followed by German infantry trying to penetrate the defences along the railway line on the right flank. Enemy aircraft made a low level attack over the forward positions at 0655 hours and all the signs signalled a busy day.

The Germans pre-empted the Fusilier's attack by starting one of their own at 0700 hours, with Tiger tanks and infantry from the valley, directed towards P Troop. Fortunately, two six-pounder anti-tank guns attached to the troop were well sited and knocked out the two leading tanks, one of which finished

Gen Montgomery congratulating 40 RM Commando on a job well done. The 7 October 1943, the day after the battle. L to R: Lt. Col Manners, Capt Maude, Gen Dempsey, Lt Morgan. Photo: Illustrated London News

Lt Col Wray receiving a 'Town Crest' presented by the Mayor of Termoli, on the occasion of 40 Commando RM 'revisiting' the town in 1990. The photograph is taken from approximately the same position as the 1943 photograph. Photo: RN

up among some trees in P Troop's positions. The remaining tanks withdrew and the infantry, lacking the armoured support, were pushed back.

The enemy now switched its attention to the centre and right flank, attacking across the valley and along the railway line and beach. A and Q Troops and the SAS were subjected to intense mortar and machine-gun fire but held their ground and fought back with every weapon available. The attack wilted under this firepower and the Germans withdrew leaving behind a considerable number of casualties.

The north end of the cemetery occupied by 7 Platoon of Q Troop was also the target of intense mortar fire and it was forced to vacate the position until the fire slackened. The platoon returned to the cemetery, only to be driven out again. This manoeuvre was repeated twice more before it was able to clear and hold the position. Members of the platoon found that a German mortar detachment had dug itself in between some graves on the far side of the cemetery.

Y Troop had dug-in on the level ground to the left of the cemetery and could observe 7 Platoons movements as well as that of German tanks and infantry approaching on the other side of the valley. A number of armour piercing shells came in the troops direction but ricocheted off the ground without causing any damage. Two Sherman tanks sent to reinforce the troop moved into 12 Platoon's area. While briefing one of the Canadian tank-commanders, the platoon commander stood alongside one of the tanks feeling comfortably secure, but the moment was short lived. Armour piercing shot whirring past uncomfortably close was accompanied by the roar of revving engines and the tank commander's parting words "Those goddam things go through these cans like a knife through butter". There was obviously no point in offering a sitting target to the German panzers and it must be emphasised that the Canadian tank crews performed a magnificent job, reinforcing positions where the pressure was greatest, and eventually forced the enemy back beyond the cemetery to the far side of the valley.

With the left flank quiet Lt Col Manners moved X Troop over to reinforce Q and A Troops positions. The supporting company of the Lancashire Fusiliers was withdrawn at the same time, to prepare for the two battalion attack which had been re-programmed to start at 1400 hours. Vigorous exchanges of fire continued until about midday when there were indications that the enemy was starting to withdraw. The air attacks were no longer evident and the shelling stopped.

At 1355 hours the leading companies of the Fusiliers, supported by the four Sherman tanks, moved up through B and Y Troops positions to start the attack. A and Q Troops, with 1st and 2nd SAS, gave them fire support with every weapon available and the 3-inch mortars and two six-pounders, still manned by the B Troop marines, joined in for good measure. The advancing Fusiliers encountered little opposition as the enemy, having decided to call it a day, had already commenced to withdraw westward. At 1630 hours, 40 RM Commando and the SAS were able to return to Termoli.

Next morning 40 RM Commando, 3 Commando and the 1st and 2nd Special Air Service paraded on a weed-covered stretch of ground by the harbour where Gen Montgomery, accompanied by Gen Dempsey, carried out an informal inspection of the 2 SS Bde Detachment. Gen Montgomery congratulated the men on "a job well done" and for having "saved the situation". He is reported to have told Lt Col Durnford Slater to take the Brigade to Bari, where there were girls and wine in plenty.

The Termoli landing was a classic Commando operation. The Royal Navy having accomplished a long sea trip undetected by the enemy, landed the men at precisely the right time and place. There is no doubt that the complete surprise obtained contributed largely to the early successes. The over all achievment was considerable, although the cost in Brigade casualties, 45 all ranks killed and missing and 85 all ranks wounded, was high.

In an operation spanning five days they overcame all attempts by a force vastly superior in numbers and armament to dislodge them and in so doing won a valuable harbour, caused the enemy to withdraw from the natural line of the Bifurno and denied them the use of the important lateral road from Naples, thereby forcing them to retreat further northwards.

The following awards were approved for distinguished service during the battle for Termoli:

Lt Col J.C. Manners	DSO	Maj P.W.C. Hellings	MC
Capt L.G.B.Marshall	MC	Capt J.W.E. Bradley	MC
CSM J.J.Convery	DCM	Cpl F.G. Usher	MM
Mne F.P. Tyman	MM		

CHAPTER 6

8 October 1943 to 21 February 1944

*Molfetta, the Commando base – Formation of Special Service Brigades –
Return to the south-west coast and assault crossing of the Garigliano River.*

IMMEDIATELY after the capture of Termoli, 3 Commando moved south to the seaport town of Molfetta to rest and reorganise. Meanwhile 5th Corps assumed responsibility for the north-east coastal sector of Italy and 40 RM Commando and the SRS were placed under command 5th Corps for operations. Lt Gen Dempsey made an informal visit to 40 RM Commando and the SRS in Termoli and 3 Commando in Molfetta, to say farewell to the men of 2 SS Bde who had impressed him with their very high professional skill and determination.

Lt Gen C. Alfrey, commanding 5th Corps, was sympathetic to the administrative problems facing the Commando units. Most of their heavy stores were still in Sicily. They lacked the benefit of the second-line services normally provided for infantry battalions and any long distance movement, including the collection of ammunition, equipment and rations, was mostly accomplished with captured vehicles. He recognised that there was an urgent need for them to have a base in Italy where stores could be maintained and where they could rest, train and re-organise between operations.

Molfetta was chosen for this purpose with Termoli serving as an advanced base from which to launch future operations. 40 RM Commando, less Y Troop which remained forward for any immediate commitments, moved to the new base on 10 October. Arrangements were made for the rear party of 2 SS Bde to join them from Sicily and shortly after their arrival the entire brigade was transferred from the 8th Army to 15th Army Group.

About this time important decisions were taken in London which were to reflect in major changes to the Commando organisation. The existing brigades were to be re-designated as the Special Service Group – more or less equivalent to the Army divisional organisation – to be commanded by a Major-General. Within the group the Commandos were to be organised into Special Service Brigades, each consisting of two Royal Marine and two Army Commandos with a brigade headquarters consisting of Royal Marines and Army personnel. In the event the 1st SS Bde (UK) was formed from three Army and one Royal Marines Commandos while the 4th SS Bde (UK) consisted initially of three Royal Marine and one Inter-Allied Commando.

In the Mediterranean, Lt Col T.B.L.Churchill was promoted Brigadier and assumed command of 2 SS Bde, comprising 40 RM Commando, 2 and 9 Army

Commandos and the recently formed 43 RM Commando. The SRS, 3 Commando and 41 RM Commando returned to UK where 3 Commando joined 1 SS Bde and 41 RM Commando formed part of 4 SS Bde.

Molfetta proved to be a good base for 2 SS Bde. Only 15 miles north-west of Bari, the town with its substantial harbour showed little sign of war damage and by the time the Commandos arrived life in the local community was rapidly returning to normal. There were plenty of billets and the householders were happy to provide accommodation with the prospect of army rations in the offing.

The billeting routine was similar to that on the Isle of Wight with each troop selecting a suitable place to muster for daily inspections and briefings. General administration, lectures, discussion groups and similar instructional activities were held in the general locality where platoons were billeted. Other forms of training requiring more space were carried out on farmland on the outskirts of the town. A firing range constructed by P Troop was used extensively by all personnel who were keen to maintain a sharp edge on their marksmanship. Signals and tactical exercises without troops (TEWTS) were conducted by HQ staff while physical training instructors arranged inter-troop soccer matches and a boxing competition. The padre, not to be outdone, staged a concert party which had its opening and closing night in the local cinema on 20 November.

The majority of men in the unit had learned to speak a little Italian and good relations were established with the local families. During off-duty hours the ice cream parlours and wine bars made popular meeting places and the barbers were only too happy to enjoy the increased trade provided by their new customers. While fraternisation with the new allies was firmly discouraged it would have been unnatural to ignore the very attractive Italian girls. Social behaviour was still rather Victorian and if a girl had a meeting with a commando she was normally chaperoned by a sister or girl-friends to ensure that correct proprieties were observed. A Sunday walk was customary for the residents and on these occasions the main street would be thronged with young and old. For a while the commandos were able to enjoy this peaceful interlude in their more warlike activities. In Termoli, Y Troop made the most of their less salubrious surroundings. Here also conditions were returning to normal but the town and the people, who had only recently been part of the front line, were taking longer to recover. Lt Col Manners arrived in Termoli on the morning of 4 December with instructions for Capt McKellar to provide a group to carry out a reconnaissance of Pelagosa, a small island 70 miles out in the Adriatic and approximately midway between Italy and Yugoslavia. The intention was to find out if the island was occupied and, if so, by whom. Arrangements were made with the senior British Naval officer to provide a suitable vessel and the recce party of 20 men embarked in LCI 361 which sailed shortly before midnight.

By 0900 hours the following morning Pelagosa was clearly visible and it was possible to distinguish a cluster of buildings with a lighthouse close to the line

Molfetta. The base for the 2nd Special Service Brigade

Molfetta. The author's billet in December 1943. Photos : Author

of approach. It also became apparent that there were no beaches and a heavy surf breaking over the rocky shoreline presented a tricky operation for the landing parties. The task was eventually accomplished without mishap in two inflatable dinghies.

There had been no sign of life on the island up to this point but, as if on a given signal, a group of 15 Italian servicemen, in a mixture of army and naval uniforms, appeared from the buildings. They were unarmed and it was soon established that they were responsible for maintaining the lighthouse and a radio and cable relay station. However, they had lost all communication with the mainland and adjacent islands, the lighthouse had been machine-gunned by German aircraft and provisions from Brindisi were well overdue. In fact they were unaware that Italy had surrendered!

The decision having been taken to evacuate them to the mainland all serviceable equipment was dismantled and ferried to the LCI, which had moved around to the north of the island where the dinghies were less vunerable to the heavy surf. Their weapons, rusty and quite useless were destroyed and as soon as their personal effects were collected, they were embarked and the LCI returned to Termoli.

A week before Christmas Y Troop was called upon to provide a small reconnaissance party to land at Rimini. The intention was to invite the enemy to believe that a landing in that area was under consideration. The recce party of five men led by Lt Beadle was to complete the round trip of 400 miles in an Italian MTB, carrying additional cans of fuel on the upper deck for the extended journey. There were no air photos of the intended landing point or information about enemy defences.

The plan involved paddling ashore in an inflatable dinghy, carrying a second dinghy with a tear in the casing. This dinghy, with an Ordnance Survey map of the locality and a tommy-gun magazine of ammunition were to be partially hidden where they would eventually be found. Having located and attracted the attention of a guard or patrol the recce party would then withdraw to the beach and to the MTB. The volunteers were aware that returning to the MTB might prove difficult and prepared for an alternative walk back through Italy.

In the event, on the night of the operation the Italian MTB commander lost precious time finding a way around an extensive minefield between Ancona and Pesaro. With daylight very close and fuel running short he turned for home without the mission being accomplished. It was a frustrating anti-climax for the recce party who were reliant on the Italian crew for getting them to the starting point. Shortly after this episode Y Troop moved to Molfetta to rejoin 40 RM Commando for Christmas. They found that a number of changes had taken place, notably that Capt Barclay had been promoted and that he and Maj Hellings had returned to England to take up new appointments. Capt Maude was promoted Major and became second-in-command of the unit.

Malaria and jaundice had taken their toll since the unit's action at Termoli and a number of personnel were confined to their billets or removed to hospital for treatment. It was ironic that within the space of two weeks of Y Troop moving to Molfetta, Capt McKellar was invalided to UK after a jeep accident and Lt N. Longand, a replacement for Lt Laidlaw who had been wounded at Termoli, contracted hepatitis from which he failed to recover.

In late December No 2 Belgian Troop and No 6 Polish Troop of the 10th Inter-Allied Commando arrived in Molfetta and were placed under command of 2 SS Bde. In order to give the men some experience of the way in which the Brigade worked, Brig Churchill arranged for their attachment to the Commando units. The language barrier, particularly with Polish commandos, sometimes caused misunderstanding. On one occasion, when a troop parade was dismissed, it took three days to locate the Poles who had failed to comprehend that the parade was a daily occurence! Nevertheless these men proved to be very resourceful and rock steady in action.

Shortly after Christmas 15th Army Group received a request from 10th Corps, operating with the Fifth US Army, to assist in the advance north of the Garigliano River. The task was given to 2 SS Bde and Brig Churchill moved 9 Commando to the south-west coast where the unit carried out a raid on the coast near the mouth of the Garigliano River on the night of 29 December. Shortly afterwards 40 RM Commando received orders to join 9 Commando in the Naples area. Y Troop, temporarily with one officer, remained in Molfetta to collect personnel released from hospital, then rejoined the unit in the locality of Castellamare.

Transport for 40 RM Commando was provided by the US Army and the move westward across Italy commenced on 31 December. The tortuous route over the mountains was not designed for heavy vehicles. The roads had broken up with the excessive traffic and ruts and potholes hidden by snow and patches of ice, added to the problem of maintaining a grip on the slippery surface. The situation was not improved when the convoy was forced to make a lengthy diversion around Potenza, where an outbreak of typhoid had been reported.

Night-halts were a welcome relief from the interminable bouncing, jolting and intense cold. At Tolve a group of HQ staff were invited to join villagers in a stone-flagged room heated by a fire of brushwood. The smoke-filled space soon caused prolonged coughing and smarting eyes, but the friendly gesture and the opportunity to thaw out outweighed all discomforts. Arriving at Vico Equense on 6 January, the two Commando units were joined soon after by 43 RM Commando, who arrived from UK via North Africa. The three Commandos were soon to find themselves heavily involved. 40 RM Commando was given the task of supporting the 56th London Division in crossing the Garigliano River while 43 RM Commando and 9 Commando were to land at Anzio. During these preparations Brig Churchill was informed that 2 Commando was to be placed under command of Special Operations Executive and sent to the Adriatic island of Vis.

Above: The Garigliano River. Crossing point of 40 RM Commando 17 January 1944.
Below: Garigliano, looking towards Castlelforte. Photos: Author

40 RM Commando moved to Villa Liturno, a small village on the Volturno River roughly 10 miles from Capua, where the unit was divided into two forces for the Garigliano operation. Force One, commanded by Capt Ecrepont, comprising B and Q Troops and a forward observation detachment from the Royal Artillery, was placed under command of the 169th Brigade. Force Two commanded by Capt Marshall consisted of A, P and X Troops placed under command of the 167th Brigade. The aim of both forces was to exploit the initial successes of the leading battalions by penetrating through and behind the German positions where they could disrupt communications and generally create as much havoc as possible.

The terrain over which they were to operate was vastly different from that experienced on the low and flatter regions of the 8th Army front. Massive hills and mountains running parallel to the coast presented a formidable obstacle, with roads, railway lines, bridges and tunnels mined, blocked or destroyed by the retreating enemy. The Germans also took full advantage of the natural obstacles provided by the ravines and gulleys now treacherous with deep mud and fast-flowing rivers.

The crossing of the Garigliano commenced on 17 January, Force One left the forming-up position at 1830 hours and crossed the start-line on time at 2030 hours. The final approach and crossing, in light collapsible canvas-covered boats, were accomplished without difficulty. On the north side of the river the 2nd/6th Battalion Queen's Royal Regiment had marked the way forward through barbed-wire entanglements and mines with white tape. The tape was easily followed for 700 yards until it abruptly ended near an orchard.

Capt Ecrepont decided to skirt round the trees to reach the first checkpoint consisting of a track crossing their front about 300 yards further on. The leading scout had only moved a few paces when a mine exploded beneath him. Switching direction to the left of the trees the force made better progress but two more commandos stepped on mines before the track was found. During this time the only response from the Germans had been spasmodic shelling and machine-gun fire at long range, but now a machine-gun post on the high ground immediately before them fired directly at the commandos. The leading sections attacked the position and one prisoner was taken.

With first light less than an hour away Capt Ecrepont ordered the men to dig in where they were and sent a patrol to contact the 2/6 QRs who were located on their right flank. Both units co-ordinated their defences in preparation for any counter-attack, but none developed. The only visible sign of enemy activity was a small group of infantrymen descending the hill slightly to the left front. Athough some distance away, the target was worth a burst of Bren gun fire and the commandos had the satisfaction of seeing the Germans scatter. As the day progressed Force One was itself subjected to close observation and any movement on their part was quickly answered with heavy shelling and mortar fire.

Towards dusk a patrol led by TSM K.S.Hawkins went forward to reconnoitre

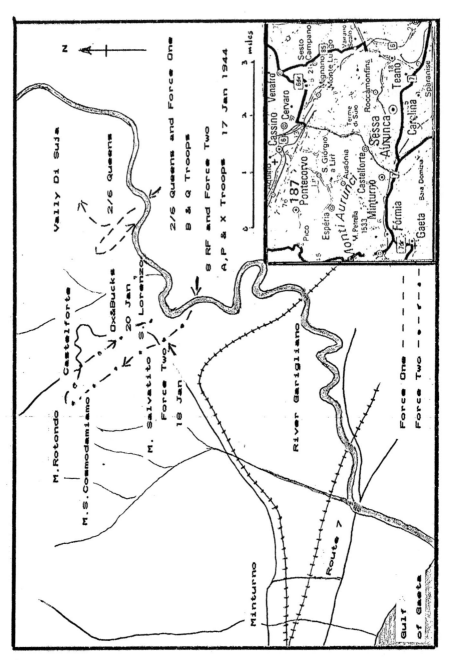

The Garigliano River Crossing 17 January 1944.

the Di Suja Valley. They heard a group of Germans talking and laughing and were so successful with their stalking that all 12 were taken by surprise and captured. Pursuing the motto of reinforcing success, TSM Hawkins returned to the same area later that night with another patrol and bagged another 18 prisoners!

Just before first light Lt Hill took a small patrol to the rear to meet a supply party bringing rations up to Force One. The first attempt to locate the supply party was unsuccessful but they found two Germans who were taken prisoner. A second reconnaissance led by Sgt W.Ainsworth was more rewarding. Not only was the ration party found but on the return leg a further six Germans were netted without any loss to themselves.

Force Two had a more involved crossing of the Garigliano. The three troops negotiated the river at 2015 hours, following closely in the wake of the 8th Battalion Royal Fusiliers who were keeping well up with a creeping artillery barrage. The Germans had opened fire with artillery, mortars and machine-guns almost as soon as the British force crossed the start-line. Movement once the river had been crossed was made more hazardous by mines.

According to Cpl Usher of X Troop "The German machine-gunners appeared to be firing on fixed lines and thankfully the crossing was accomplished without too many casualties. My section (No 9), was ordered to clear a machine-gun post and in the process I took a bullet in my right thigh and grenade splinters in the shoulder. My main concern was the cold. I was picked up the next day and taken to hospital in Castellmare, where they discovered that I had frostbite!"

Cpl Humphrey of A Troop also recalls the night vividly. "We crossed the river alright," he said "but not long afterwards the man in front of Sgt Bill Shea stepped on a mine which killed him and blinded Bill, who was thrown backwards by the blast. As senior corporal of No 1 Platoon I took over from Bill and we continued up the hillside. Later that night a hand-grenade fell close to the fellow alongside me and when I tried to kick it away there was a big yellow flash and that was it."* A Troop incurred further casualties climbing the hill, including Lt Copsey who received a severe leg wound.

Force Two continued for a further 1,000 yards to the Minturno- Castelforte road, where it established a defensive position with the Fusiliers to the north of the road. At first light Capt Marshall ordered A Troop and No 6 Platoon P Troop to clear a hill feature to their front while No 5 Platoon P Troop was tasked to clear the eastern slope of Mount Salvatito and place an OP in that locality. The OP position was held for the next three days, during which time the forward-observation-officer (FOO) was able to direct artillery fire on to a number of German positions.

At 0800 hours No 6 Platoon mounted an attack on a enemy post dug in on

---

* Joe Humphrey lost his sight and was wounded in the shoulder. Both he and Bill Shea are St Dunstan's men and made successful careers as physiotherapists.

an adjacent spur which had been giving considerable trouble. The Germans were not prepared to give in without a hard fight and it was only after eight of their number had been killed that they withdrew. Lt T.A. Smith and four of his platoon were wounded in this action. X Troop, dug in alongside a cemetery near the road, sent out a patrol led by Cpl J.Morton to deal with a machine-gun post which had been firing into their positions. It accomplished this task, killing one German and taking seven prisoners without any loss to itself. Towards the end of the morning Capt Marshall sent A Troop to reinforce the Fusiliers who were dug in on Monte San Como. The Germans had a good view of their positions and the commandos were shelled and mortared throughout the day.

Under cover of darkness Force One moved forward 2,000 yards to occupy the position they should have reached the previous night. Capt Ecrepont had received instructions during the day to take, if possible, Point 320, a hill feature about 300 yards beyond the original objective. He decided to split his force into two patrols, the first to take the original objective and the second Point 230. The first patrol, nearing the objective, encountered a machine-gun post which it destroyed with the loss of one marine. The second patrol occupied Point 320 without any opposition. Both patrols consolidated in these positions where they were subjected to shelling and mortar fire. At 0200 hours another patrol led by Lt Neale was sent out to reconnoitre a small valley where it encountered a well defended machine-gun position. An unsuccessful attempt to capture it resulted in one casualty.

The King's Own Yorkshire Light Infantry relieved Force One at 0930 hours on 21 January and the commandos returned to a position close to the point where the river had been crossed to become Brigade reserve. Even here shelling and mortaring on 23 January resulted in a further three casualties. In this period Force One had captured 46 prisoners and accounted for 20 enemy killed. Their own casualties amounted to one killed, five missing and 10 wounded.

Approximately 1,200 yards inland the British infantry were preparing to advance to Monte San Cosmodamiano. This high feature was overlooked by the higher peaks of Monte Rotondo which, if held by the enemy, could be a serious threat to the advancing units. It was therefore decided to send Capt Marshall's force to infiltrate through the German positions, to clear the mountain and interrupt traffic on the roads running north-west from Castelforte which were still firmly in enemy hands. As soon as it was dark the force, less 5 Platoon, split into section strength patrols and set out at 30-minute intervals to make the descent into the valley before climbing the mountain on the other side. Progress through the outcrops of rough and precipitious rock, keeping direction and avoiding enemy posts, was slow and tiring and dawn was not far off when Capt Marshall gathered a depleted force together for a brief halt.

He assumed that Capt O'Brien was somewhere in the vicinity with another group of the force but was unable to establish contact with them. There had been no exceptional activity during the night and he could only guess that the intended infantry attack had been delayed or cancelled. Without sufficient numbers immediately available to hold Monte Rotondo he decided to continue with the second part of his instructions. Scouting patrols were sent out to reconnoitre the area and one of these returned with two Italians who were able to provide useful information about the location of the German positions and local topography. With this assistance the force was able to work its way through to a point on the Castelforte road about 1,000 yards from the town.

Keeping a wary eye open for any movement on the road, Capt Marshall organised his sections to cover the approaches from both directions. Other groups were detailed to prepare a road-block and cut telephone wires, while one section reconnoitred along the line of the road. Before work could be started on the road-block a German motorcycle combination approached from the town followed by a motorcyclist and armoured-car. The commandos made a quick scramble for cover and fired at the group as the vehicles neared their position. Both motorcyclists were hit and crashed into the road-side but the armoured car accelerated out of range.

The reconnaisance party returned soon afterwards to report that they had seen a gun-site further down the road. Preparations were quickly made to attack this position and the Germans, caught by surprise abandoned the guns after a short fire-fight. The site contained two small field-guns which had already been prepared for demolition and it did not take the commandos long to complete the job. During this time a mopping-up party came across a column of motorcycles, staff cars, two armoured cars and other vehicles parked under cover of trees and bushes near the road.

A group of Germans was in the process of driving these vehicles on to the road as the commandos closed in through the trees and scrub. There was a brisk exchange of small arms fire and one of the armoured cars was put out of action when Cpl Mne. Patrick, who had worked his way towards the armoured vehicle, lobbed a 77 grenade between its wheels. A Red Cross ambulance, distinguishable by the markings on its sides, drove away with one of the occupants spraying bursts of bullets from an automatic weapon but this fire was not returned. One of Capt Marshall's force was lightly wounded in this encounter.

A further attempt was made to establish a road block but this was cut short by the arrival of a Mark IV tank. Once again a 77 grenade proved effective, setting fire to the tank which withdrew towards Castel Forte. Much to the concern of the commandos three more Tiger tanks appeared, firing as they approached and wounding two of the group. The tank crews, apparently confident that they had the commandos out-gunned, halted a short distance from them. A German officer climbed out of his tank and, speaking in English, said "Come here, I have orders for you." The response from Capt Marshall's force was a sharp burst of Bren gun fire.

The only line of withdrawal for the commandos was across the road to the shelter of a gulley, but this required crossing in front of one of the tanks. Capt Marshall worked his way round to the rear of the tank and armed only with his Colt automatic pistol, jumped onto the armoured casing to fire at the crew inside through the open hatch. This courageous action provided a diversion which gave the commandos time to slip across the road into the tree-filled gulley, taking their three wounded with them. Capt Marshall was quick to follow. With ammunition running low and the wounded mounting, it was decided to remain under cover until nightfall. Force Two then made the two-mile trek back to its own lines where, just before dawn on 20 January, it was greeted by an artillery stonk from the British guns. After a brief rest during the morning they moved to the south-east of Castelforte to reinforce the Oxford-shire and Buckinghamshire Light Infantry.

The same afternoon, Lt Atkinson led a 12-man patrol to attack a German position of about company strength. The enemy put up a fierce resistance and four of the commandos were wounded in the first clash. One Spandau was silenced, but the patrol was eventually forced to withdraw under heavy fire. At 0300 hours 21 January, the Ox and Bucks were relieved by the Royal Berkshires and Force Two moved to Point 411 where it dug in adjacent to the Fusiliers to cover the ground down to the river. Three men were wounded during repeated shelling of the positions that morning but attempts by the Germans to infiltrate the line were driven off without further casualties.

Heavy shelling on 22 January inflicted a further three casualties among Force Two's number and it was suspected that the Germans were preparing to attack. Towards midnight a patrol led by Capt O'Brien set out to reconnoitre a likely enemy forming up position in a valley to the east of Lorenzo. The night was very dark and the patrol's progress was hampered by mist and fine rain. Apart from a brief encounter with a small German patrol on the outward leg no sign of enemy activity was found in the valley.

Returning to its own lines by a different route the patrol cut across a field of tall grass and unknowingly entered a minefield. The explosion of an S-mine killed TSM G.Malcom instantly. Mne Frost had a leg severed and a further six men were wounded, including the medical orderly Sgt C.A. Sirrister MM, RAMC. The explosion alerted the Germans who made numerous attempts to close in and destroy the patrol but Mne N. Patrick skilfully used his Bren gun to hold them at a distance until help arrived. Capt O'Brien was also wounded but insisted on seeing that his patrol was withdrawn safely before walking two miles to Commando HQ to make his report.

Arnold Sirrister had landed with 2 Commando at Salerno where he was in the thick of the action attending to the wounded. He was seconded to 40 RM Commando after the battle for Termoli when 2 Commando commenced a recruiting tour of the Middle East to replace losses.

Towards evening on 23 January Forces One and Two received orders to re-group. The Commando moved into Corps reserve to the south-east of Mont Salvatito where, for the first time in many days, the men were able to enjoy hot food and a change of clothing.

The task of supplying the front-line troops was not without problems, and according to RQMS K. Frost, more familiarly known to the men as 'Freezer', "It seemed to rain for weeks". He had established his team in a gutted house where, he said " there had been some dead Germans among the rubble and the rats were everywhere. There was a sharp bend on the road to Advance HQ, a favourite target for the German artillery who stonked it at methodical intervals. One night we were waiting on the road near this bend for some of our men and gradually became aware of odd sounds and shadows passing us on either side. It was a heck of a shock to find that it was a supply-party of black Americans moving up to the forward positions!"

Between 23 January and 21 February, 40 RM Commando was employed as an infantry battalion under command of 167th Brigade, 6th Division. Subsequently the unit was transferred to 13th Brigade, 5th Division in the Lorenzo area to carry out extensive patrolling. The Commando was not equipped or constituted for the infantry role but acted with considerable spirit in carrying out this task. During the time which elapsed since crossing the Garigliano River on 17 January to the final day in the line on 21 February, 40 RM Commando casualties amounted to 12 killed and 65 wounded.

The following awards were approved for distinguished service during operations immediately following the crossing of the River Garigliano:

Capt E.W.Ecrepont	MC	Cpl J.J.Gorman	MM
CSM K.S.Hawkins	MM	Cpl G.A.T.Johnson	MM
CSM G. Malcom	MM	Mne N. Patrick	MM
Capt L.G.B.Marshall MC	bar to MC	Capt J.P.O'Brien	MC

CHAPTER 7

22 February to 31 March 1944

The Anzio beach-head. A continuation of the role of infantry in the line.

ON leaving the Garigliano sector 40 RM Commando occupied billets in Vico Equense to enjoy for a brief moment the luxury of a roof overhead, hot baths and a few nights of uninterrupted sleep. Y Troop, with a number of reinforcements who had been discharged from various hospitals in Sicily and Italy, travelled overland from Molfetta to rejoin the unit on 22 February. The Allied landing further up the coast at Anzio was by then a month old but little news of developments in the beach-head had filtered through to personnel at Vico Equense.

The intention to land an Allied force at Anzio was a joint decision taken by Winston Churchill, Gen Eisenhower and Gen Alexander at Tunis in December 1943. The German winter line based on the Rapido and Garigliano Rivers, Cassino, the Appennines and the Sangro River was a formidable obstacle against which the American 5th Army and British 8th Army were making little headway and an amphibious operation appeared to be the best solution. Churchill accepted that a landing would not be without risk, but decided that it was necessary to circumvent the German defences to remove the stalemate situation. A successful outcome would open the road to Rome. Gen Alexander planned to use one American and one British division under an American corps commander for the landing, code-name Shingle – initially programmed for 20 January.

The prelude to the landing commenced on 17 January with a thrust by the British 10th Corps across the Garigliano river, the crossing of which 40 RM Commando had taken part. This was followed by a crossing of the Rapido River five miles south of Cassino on 20 January by the American 2nd Corps. Further inland, on the right flank, the Free French Expeditionary Corps continued to probe forward through very difficult terrain in the mountains.

While 40 RM Commando patrolled the area of Castel Forte, 43 RM Commando and 9 Commando, in company with the American 1st, 3rd and 4th Rangers, led the landings of the 1st British and 3rd American Divisions at Anzio on the night of 21/22 January. The two Commandos encountered negligible enemy opposition and on the completion of their objective – the capture of the high ground on the perimeter of the town – they were withdrawn to Naples.

The initial landing force with attached troops forming the American 6th Corps, under the command of General Lucas, were all ashore by last light on

23 January. The build-up of the beach-head continued at a tremendous pace and by 25 January was substantial in men, vehicles, stores and guns. Even so, Gen Alexander and Gen Mark Clark were dissatisfied with the proportionately slow rate of advance by the beach-head force and became increasingly aware that the initial advantage gained from the element of surprise was fast disappearing.

FM Kesselring reacted quickly to the landing and produced a local force to contain the Allies until a stronger mobile reserve, already briefed for such an eventuality, could be directed to the beach-head. At no time was it necessary for the Field Marshal to withdraw troops from the front line. The German resistance stiffened and Gen McCreery found it necessary to order 43 RM Commando and 9 Commando to return to the beach-head to support 46th Division in the advance from the Garigliano. The Commando objectives were the high features of Point 711 and Mount Ornito. This time they faced increasing opposition in gaining their objectives, particularly 9 Commando which suffered many casualties. Shortly after their return to Naples Brig Churchill sent 43 RM Commando to the Dalmatian island of Vis to reinforce 2 Commando, with the task of defending the island and giving the Partisans commanded by Tito a helping hand.

The build-up of the Anzio beach-head continued round the clock and by the end of the first week the Allies had landed four divisions and a massive number of vehicles and supplies. However, within the same period FM Kesselring had ringed the eight mile deep and 15 mile wide beach-head with eight divisions and was able to concentrate artillery fire on any part of this sector. As each day passed the initiative slipped steadily from the grasp of Gen Lucas.

The American 1st and 3rd Rangers incurred heavy losses in a gallant attempt to capture Cisterna. The British also suffered many casualties in taking Campoleone, where they were finally held at the foot of the Albani Hills. As time progressed the 56th (London) Infantry Division and American 45th Infantry Division found themselves up against mounting pressure from the Germans who were intent on pushing them back into the sea.

Headquarters 15th Army Group called on Brig T. Churchill for Commando assistance to bolster the flagging spirits of the exhausted troops in the British sector. This task was given to 40 RM Commando and 9 Commando, who received their orders on 28 February and embarked the following day. It proved a busy time for Lt P.J. McColl of 40 RM Commando, who was promoted Captain, appointed Adjutant and given the task of drafting the movement order all within the space of a few hours.

In the short interval before sailing from Pozzuoli Harbour a group of enterprising marines paid a courtesy call on an American store ship and pursuaded the supply officer to supplement their rations with canned fruit and chocolate bars. These luxury items were rarely obtainable at the best of times and the generosity of the Americans was much appreciated. Towards evening the landing craft with the Commando units embarked cast off from the quay-side and set course for Anzio.

In the grey light of the following morning the marines observed the scene from the deck of the landing-craft as they moved slowly towards Anzio Harbour. "I could see an assortment of American and British warships and supply ships," said Mne Shaw "and beyond them were the beaches, cluttered with stores, vehicles and dumps of equipment. There was some heavy enemy shelling going on and it looked as if every shell was finding a target."

Immediately it had landed 9 Commando was placed under command 167th Brigade and 36th United States Combat Engineers. The scene must have been particularly galling to the men of this unit when they realised that their earlier successes had not been exploited. 40 RM Commando was placed under command 169th Brigade and while Lt Col Manners and Maj Maude were attending a briefing session at Brigade Tactical HQ the Commando moved to a thickly wooded area on the fringe of the town. Deep pits dug between the pine trees had been covered with tarpaulins supported by metal frames taken from three ton trucks and these provided a dry shelter for the first night. An adjacent RASC unit also provided the commandos with a hot meal.

Early next morning 40 RM Commando was transported forward to a position 10 miles north and one mile west of the Anzio – Aprilia road. The ground in this area was flat, marshy scrubland, almost devoid of trees and overlooked the German positions on the forward slopes of the Albani Hills. Although the scrub provided some cover from view, almost any movement during daylight invited a swift mortar or shell-fire response from the enemy. Attempts to dig more than a few inches into the marshy ground were futile, as any hole quickly flooded. The only effective cover had to be a compromise of a shell-scrape and earthwork about three feet high. This was covered with a groundsheet and any available foliage was added for camouflage.

The Commando Tac HQ was an enlarged version of one of these defence works. CO's briefings in this confined and claustrophobic shelter required those taking part to behave more like contortionists than combat equipped commandos. A degree of patience was required while the cheek by jowl fitting-in process was pursued – and the clumsy-footed soon knew who their friends were. Y Troop officers experienced this situation when they attended a briefing on 3 March. There was an immediate need to obtain up-to-date information regarding enemy strength and dispositions and to help ease the pressure on a sector of the front-line. The task was given to Y Troop to provide a fighting patrol that night, with orders to sweep and clear an area of ground and farm buildings in front of the forward company of The Queens and, if possible, to take prisoners.

The weather on 3 March was stormy, and deteriorated further towards nightfall. Y Troop, in single file, moved forward in almost total darkness and incessant rain through gulleys knee deep in mud. Progress to the start line was a slow, tedious process. H Hour had been set for 0230 hrs but Capt Laidlaw decided to defer this by five minutes to ensure that the tail end of the troop had time to get in position on the start line, recognisable as a low bank of earth at the forward edge of The Queens' positions.

At 0235 hours, as Y Troop began the attack, sheet-lightning directly overhead illuminated the entire scene as clearly as if the men had been standing in the centre of a flood-lit arena. The sudden blaze of light was followed by a deafening clap of thunder and torrential rain signalling a thunderstorm. Momentarily blinded by the flash and aware that enemy foxholes were only yards away the men surged forward to retain the initiative. Maintaining control over the slippery churned-up ground in the cloudburst and inky darkness was nigh on impossible, but instinctively the men moved in the right direction.

12 Platoon (Lt Beadle) had the task of clearing the area to the immediate front. There were no wire entanglements but the shellholes were a nuisance obstacle into which the men pitched waist deep in mud and water. Having crawled out of one hole they stumbled into another a few steps further on. Gradually the German entrenchments were located and dealt with and the all-important prisoner taken. 11 Platoon (Capt Laidlaw) found the derelict farm buildings held by a section of Germans supported by a Spandau machine-gun. Clearance of the buildings was carried out briskly and the enemy lost at least a third of its strength before the remainder withdrew into the darkness. The men of Y Troop then returned to their own lines in section groups carrying two of their number who had been wounded. Ironically, while the men were shaving, cleaning weapons and preparing breakfast Mne J.Towers, 12 Platoon's point scout, was killed by a random mortar bomb. The loss of this gentle and likeable young man was keenly felt by everyone.

The following night 2 Platoon (Lt Brockbank) of A Troop was given the task of patrolling to the right of Y Troop's action. A farm building overlooking the start line should have been cleared by Army troops but as the patrol approached this point it suddenly came under fire from Germans in the building. Two Germans were shot by members of the patrol but as the enemy fire intensified they were forced to withdraw having themselves incurred three casualties, one of whom died of wounds.

On 5 March 40 RM Commando, forming part of the 56th Division, moved into the line to the east of the Anzio-Aprilia road and close to the southern bank of Moletta River. Taking over from the 2nd Battalion Sherwood Foresters and 2nd Battalion Duke of Wellington's Regiments in torrential rain the unit occupied an area of gulleys which branched into two arms pointing towards the German positions. Y Troop occupied the left gully, B Troop the right gully and Q Troop the stem. Commando officers making a reconnaissance of the front line positions the day before the changeover noted that the soldiers were exhausted. Incessant mortaring and other enemy activity had deprived them of sleep. Mne Udakis, a runner with the recce party, endeavoured to liven things up with a tune on his mouth-organ but the soldiers were too tired and dispirited to appreciate his efforts.

The changeover was carried out during the hours of darkness to avoid being seen by German observation-posts on the high ground behind their front-line positions. Any activity above the cover of the gulleys in this sector during daylight, except by stretcher-bearers, was an immediate invitation to a sniper's bullet or mortar-bomb. Movement by night also had its problems. The communication lanes between the rear and forward positions were restricted in number and width by numerous minefields. Ration or ammunition parties, the wounded, reinforcements and reliefs all had to use these routes, which became known to the Germans and were shelled and mortared. Mne Shaw was severely wounded in one of these stonks while carrying rations forward to Y Troop and had to be evacuated under a Red Cross flag the following morning. Americans, British and Germans moved their wounded in daylight under the protection of this flag and for the most part the medical teams and orderlies doing this job were greatly respected. However, it was suspected that a German stretcher-team in the sector occupied by 40 RM Commando was being used as cover for a "spotter" to observe its forward positions. The stretcher-party would come very close to the front-line trenches, normally between 1500 and 1600 hours daily. Almost as soon as the Germans had returned to their own lines, the Commando forward positions adjacent to where the stretcher party had been working were very accurately mortared. TSM Hawkins of X Troop imprudently decided to tackle the Germans regarding their abuse of the Red Cross flag and in the process was taken prisoner.

Even in the shelter of the gullies any movement outside the trenches was performed with a sense of urgency. A call of nature took the form of a quick scurry to a corner of the gully as random mortar-stonks were not uncommon at any time. Sgt B. Moffat of B Troop has vivid memories of the mortaring which, he recalls "Seemed to go on for ever. Some of the German mortars were mounted so close to the Commando positions that you could hear the 'ping' as the bomb hit the firing pin. When you heard that noise you counted to 10 and then put your head well down". It was in one of these bombardments on Y Troop's positions that Capt Laidlaw and Mnes Selfridge, Chapman and Wallace were wounded. Mne Wallace subsequently died and Mne Chapman, having lost a foot, was invalided from the service.*

The men in the forward positions lived in slit-trenches cut into the tops of the banks or dugouts constructed along the sides of the gullys. Daylight hours were spent cleaning weapons, bailing-out, repairing and improving the trenches and drainage. It rained frequently and the gully beds were mostly covered in water. Ammunition and rations were distributed and between attending to their personal toilets the men made the best of the 24-hour ration packs, taking it in turn to rest. It was difficult to relax at any time, particularly when one sensed the presence of the enemy but could not see him. Day

---

* Letter from Capt Laidlaw to Mne Chapman 5 April 1944 Appendix C.

patrolling was carried out along the gullies but no Germans were netted during this period.

Apart from daylight reconnaissance along the wadis, patrolling was mainly confined to the hours of darkness and a high degree of alertness was maintained at all times to combat enemy raiding-parties or major attack. German patrols were also active and frequently used smoke, shelling and mortaring to cover their movements or to simulate the start of an assault. However, they did not attempt an infantry attack in strength on 40 RM Commando's positions.

In addition to the combat duties the need to provide carrying parties for ammunition, water, rations, wireless batteries, sandbags duck-boards and other forward-line necessities left little time for sleep. The Commando held this forward position for five days during which German intelligence stepped up its propaganda broadcasts on the local radio network. The honeyed tones of a female known as "Anzio Lil" could be heard at intervals each day persuasively appealing to the commandos to give-up the useless fight against overwhelming numbers.

On the night of 8 March Capt J.Wakeling, who succeeded Capt Ephraums as OC A Troop, received orders to take a fighting patrol to the left of the Commando front to silence a machine-gun post and to assess the enemy strength. H-Hour was to have been 2300 hours, with a smoke and high-explosive support fire programmed for 2345 hours to cover the withdrawal. In the event an unexpected heavy bombardment by the enemy delayed H-hour. Although the commandos did not set out until midnight the timing of the support-fire was not adjusted. In consequence the patrol moved forward through the remnants of the smoke. This actually turned out to their advantage as the Germans had taken shelter in their dug-outs and only one sentry remained on watch. He was quickly silenced and the commandos moved from dug-out to dug-out lobbing No 36 grenades into the entrances and shooting any of the enemy who appeared above ground. The Germans were quick to recover from the initial surprise and a Spandau opened fire on the patrol from the left flank. At this point Captain Wakeling was wounded and having accounted for at least 10 of the enemy he considered it prudent to withdraw.

Two days later a small reconnaissance patrol commanded by Lt Hill worked its way along a small gully to the north-west of the Commando position to test the strength of the German defences. Approaching the end of the gully the patrol came under heavy Spandau and rifle-fire and, assessing that the enemy was entrenched in strength, withdrew without incurring any casualties.

The 14th Battalion Sherwood Foresters relieved the Commando on the night of 11 March, at which time the unit came under command of 18th Infantry Brigade, 1st Division. Moving to a rest area 40 Commando spent 48 hours in close proximity to a 25-pounder gun battery engaged in a long range duel with German heavy artillery. The locality was by no stretch of the imagination relaxing. The Commando moved to its original position on 13 March and commenced to send out patrols with the aim of obtaining prisoners for interrogation.

THE ANZIO BEACH-HEAD

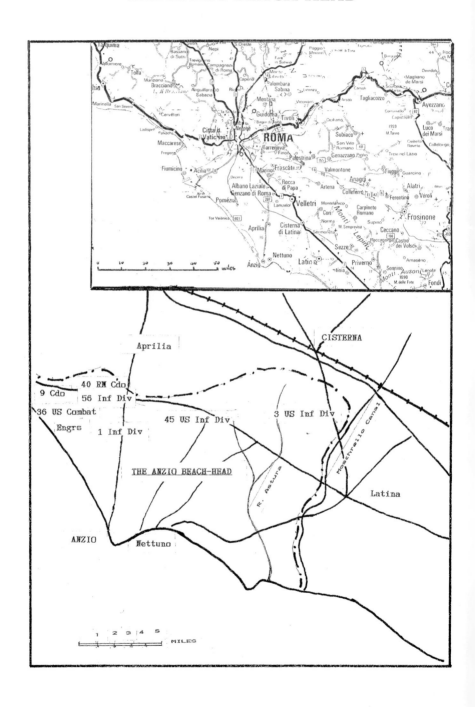

The build-up of the beach-head Photo: Imperial War Museum

Lt Hill's patrol reconnoitered an area in front of the Yorkshire Dragoons on 14 March but were unsuccessful. On the following night a patrol led by Lt Smith was silhouetted by trip flares and with the Germans alerted to its location was forced to withdraw under intense fire. A third patrol tried again on 16 March and with more positive results. Led by Lt C.L. Dutton the patrol charged a Spandau position, shooting one of the machine-gun team. In the general commotion Lt Dutton knocked out another German with a blow to the jaw and the patrol withdrew unscathed carrying the prisoner who subsequently provided some useful information. A diversionary patrol taken out on the same night by Lt J.Tarry accomplished its task successfully but five of its men were wounded in the process.

The Commando returned to the front line the next day to relieve the 1st Buffs. There was no major activity during the five days the unit was holding the position but intermittent shelling and mortar fire resulted in a number of casualties and Lt Col Manners' command-post was partially demolished. The 1st Buffs took over again on 22 March and 40 RM Commando was withdrawn to Anzio where on 24 March it was joined by 9 Commando, also depleted by casualties. Both Commandos embarked in LCI's and sailed out of the harbour to the accompaniment of some desultory shell-fire. Arriving at Pozzuoli on 26 March they found that Mount Vesuvius had erupted in their absence and was continuing to spew out thick clouds of smoke and dust. The Commandos moved into 159 Transit Camp and after a night's rest entrained at Naples en route for Molfetta. On arrival Lt R. Neale and four NCOs were temporarily detached to provide training teams in Corsica.

The casualties, 12 all ranks killed and 63 wounded, were mainly attributed to artillery and mortar fire. Three commandos were taken prisoner.

CHAPTER 8

1 April to 31 July 1944

40 RM Commando move to the Dalmation Coast – Introduction to Tito's Partisans on Vis – Boarding parties operate with Coastal Forces to intercept German supply ships- Partisan and Commando raiding forces attack the German garrison on Brac.

APRIL proved to be a fairly quiet month and an opportune moment to concentrate on unit administration. Uniform, equipment and weapon inspections assumed priority over other activities. The Rev R. Briggs introduced his relief the Rev R.Hook RNVR, to the men in the sub units advising them that his own time under the Mediterranean sun had come to an end.

In the temporary absence of Lt Neale, the role of Adjutant was taken over by Lt J.Tarry, who found himself acting as peacemaker between the Military Police and a handful of commando hotheads. A small group of marines had over imbibed the local vino and imprudently accused the "red-caps" of being illegitimate, or words to that effect. Ruffled feathers were eventually smoothed and the Adjutant gave orders for the ringleaders to "cool it". Before this could be put into practice further friction developed between commandos and army personnel in Molfetta and it was decided to move the unit to a secluded locality on the outskirts of the town!

The Commando quickly established itself under canvas and a training programme coupled with sports and entertainment was in full swing in a matter of days. The officers, having acquired a marquee for use as a mess, arranged a guest-night and in the absence of an orchestra a signaller with a fine tenor voice was invited to sing arias from Italian opera. He accompanied himself on an accordian and received a tremendous ovation from the assembled company, which included doctors and nursing sisters from the New Zealand Base Hospital near Bari.

Events changed again during the evening of 2 May when Lt Col Manners received a warning order to have the Commando ready to move at a moment's notice. By noon the next day the unit had passed through 197 Transit Camp at Bari and with all stores, ammunition and weapons embarked was on its way to Vis, the only Partisan held island off the Dalmation Coast.

Vis is one of hundreds of islands, some not much bigger than large outcrops of rock, which extend along this coast. Formed after the last ice-age when the coastal region was partly submerged, the islands consist mainly of rough limestone ridges which climb steeply from the sea. Vis, with its numerous coves and rocky shoreline, is nine miles long and four miles wide. The population is mainly centred on the two natural harbours of Vis and Komiza and the remains of five stone forts are a reminder of five years of British occupation following capture of the island by Admiral Sir William Hoste in 1811.

In May 1944 Vis was the only Dalmatian island free of German domination. Garrisons had been placed on Korcula and Hvar as late as 24 December 1943 and records indicate that the German Naval War Staff planned to occupy Vis – operation Freischutz – between 20 February and 1 March 1944. The plan was postponed indefinitely when it became known that Allied reinforcements had arrived from Italy to bolster the Partisan forces. Although only 27 miles from the mainland port of Split and in close proximity to the larger, German-occupied islands of Brac, Hvar and Korcula, this Partisan stronghold had become a thorn in the side of the Axis forces and a beacon of freedom for the many Yugoslavs on the mainland suffering from the atrocities of the invaders.

Immediately after the invasion of Yugoslavia by German, Italian, Hungarian and Bulgarian forces in April 1941, large numbers of Yugoslavs moved into the hills and mountains. The rugged terrain and dense forests gave them cover from air attack and restricted the movement of Axis ground forces. In Serbia the pro-royalists united for mutual protection and together fought the Germans and pro-German Serbs and Croats. Throughout the country there was considerable upheaval with local conflict and political rivalry merging into a common hatred of the invading enemy.

From this very confused issue two leaders emerged. The first was General Draza Mihailovic, a former army general and anti communist who had the support of a large number of his pro-royalist army officers and men as well as the royal government-in-exile in London. Gen Mihailovic organised Serbian detachments, traditionaly known as Cetniks, (from the Serbian 'ceta' meaning military company), to fight the invaders. There were about 5,000 Serbs in the Cetnik movement by September 1941 but a number of these defected to the Germans before the end of the year. Mihailovic made contact with the quisling government in Belgrade and there was growing evidence of collaboration between the Cetnik movement and the Axis powers. In response to a request by Mihailovic for British aid Captain D.H. Hudson was sent to Yugoslavia to contact patriotic groups and met Mihailovic. By this time fighting between Cetniks and Partisans was a frequent occurrence.

The second leader was Josip Broz, more widely known as Tito, the name he adopted in 1933 after his release from five years of captivity for political activities in the Communist Party. Tito assumed leadership of the country's communists in 1937, forming a central committee and reinforcing the political independence of the Yugoslav Communist Party. After the capitulation of the regime and army in April 1941, Tito organised a nation-wide struggle for national liberation and two months later, as commander of the Supreme Headquarters, developed the tactics of guerilla warfare. Fighting spread over the country and about one fifth of the territory was liberated. In December of that year he formed the First Proletarian Brigade consisting of 80,000 Partisan fighters, which became the core of the National Liberation Army. The enemy at that time consisted of 510,000 Axis troops and 150,000 pro-Axis Serbian sympathisers.

By early 1942 Marshal Tito's Partisans were fighting for survival. A request to Russia for arms and ammunition met with a negative reply and in the summer Tito was forced to withdraw his main army from Bosnia 200 miles north to Croatia. During the first half of 1943 the Germans mounted two major operations with the intention of annihilating his main army and freeing the Axis line of communication through Yugoslavia from Greece to Italy. Nearly 18,000 Cetniks were mobilized to assist in this operation. The Partisans carried out a fighting retreat into the highlands of Montenegro, routing the Cetnik forces in the process.

Between the summer of 1941 and beginning of 1943 Britain sent eight missions and several liaison officers to Yugoslavia and delivered 23 tons of supplies to Gen Mihailovic. None of the equipment was received by Tito's Partisans. Eventually, on 27 May 1943, a six man mission including Maj W.F.Deakin, a friend of Winston Churchill, was sent to see Marshal Tito. The Partisan military situation had once again deteriorated and Tito's HQ and the mission narrowly escaped into east Bosnia. Maj Deakin made clear to UK the urgent need for material support and in June 1943 Winston Churchill directed that all possible help should be given to Tito's Partisans.

Italy had the best part of 16 divisions in Yugoslavia at the time of Italy's surrender on 8 September 1943. Marshal Tito's Partisans immediately assumed control of the area the Italians had occupied as well as their armaments. The Germans, concerned that an Allied landing on the Dalmatian coast was still possible, regained control of most of the coastline and islands with the exception of Vis.

Allied Force HQ Cairo assumed a closer interest in the Balkans after Italy's surrender. Brig Miles of Force 133, an organisation which maintained a liaison with all the Partisan groups fighting the Germans, arranged for an Allied mission headed by Brig Fitzroy Maclean to visit Marshal Tito in December 1943. On his return Brig Maclean recommended that a small Allied force should be sent to help the Partisans retain a presence on the Dalmatian islands. Vis would be used as a depot for the supply of arms and equipment – collected from the Sicilian battlefields – to Partisan forces on other islands and the mainland. Also, the island would provide a possible spring-board for a strategic landing in Yugoslavia if the Allied Forces were unable to make progress in Italy. The latter idea was abandoned when it was realised that land communications in Yugoslavia were inadequate for any large-scale advance on the eastern side of the Adriatic.

Lt Cdr M.C. Morgan-Giles OBE, GM* moved to Vis as senior naval officer

* Later, Rear Admiral Sir M.C. Morgan-Giles DSO,OBE,GM,MP. Awarded the George Medal for gallantry during an air raid on Bari when a US Liberty ship carrying mustard gas was sunk and the harbour contaminated.

Vis (SNOVIS) in January 1944, organising the anti-invasion patrols and attacks against small ship-convoys, carried out by the MGBs and MTBs of the Coastal Forces. A small group from 2 Commando landed on Vis with the agreement of Col Millu, leader of the Partisans, and Cdr Cerni the Partisan naval commander and, by mid-February 1944, the remainder of 2 Commando, under the command of Lt Col Churchill were established on the island with a detachment of Bofors and 4-pdr guns. Further Allied reinforcements followed.

43 RM Commando joined 2 Commando on 20 February and was closely followed by 2 SS Bde HQ. Brig Churchill had not seen much of his brother, Lt Col Churchill, since leaving England and was pleased to have this opportunity of exchanging news. A series of small exploratory and nuisance raids carried out on adjacent islands by 2 Commando, 43 RM Commando and Partisans between February and the end of March enabled Brig Churchill to gauge the strength of the German garrisons on Solta, Hvar and Brac.

40 RM Commando arrived on Vis during the early morning of 5 May. Two troops, A and Y, disembarked at Komica where they established camps on the hillside overlooking the town. The remainder of the Commando proceeded to the east side of the island, sailing between the promontories of Fort George and Fort Wellington to tie up alongside the quay in Vis Harbour. Having landed they climbed the sharply ascending hillside to make camp in and around the village of Podselje.

Commando HQ overlooked one of the few cultivated areas on the island in the centre of which the all important airstrip was visible as a patch of fairly level, hard-packed earth. This had been cleared and graded by the Partisans earlier in the year and accommodated the island air force of three over-worked Canadian Mustangs. The airstrip provided a macabre point of interest for those in the vicinity. Its length, restricted by rising ground at one end, a sharp drop at the other and surrounded by vines, made landings a dicey business. It was not unusual to see a Mustang bouncing along the runway in a series of hops before coming to rest uncomfortably close to the vines. Frequently the pilots had no alternative but to open the throttle and try again. The gamblers among the onlookers, both Partisan and Commando, would then lay bets on whether or not the pilot would "make it" the next time round !

American Liberators returning to Italy from raids over Rumania and Hungary used the strip for emergencies but, lacking the length and surface required for heavy bombers the chances of their making a good landing were slim. On one occasion the crew of a damaged bomber bailed out over the island but the plane continued to circle the island until the fuel ran out and it exploded into a hillside.

It took some time to become familiar with the ways of the Partisans. This band of brothers and their female comrades in arms had been drawn together from all corners of Yugoslavia. Although they conversed in different dialects and languages they shared an intense hatred of the Germans and all who sided with them. Many had seen members of their families ill-treated, tortured and killed and they were not in the mood to give or seek quarter.

A youth who could have been in his early teens attached himself to 12 Platoon a few days after the commandos had arrived on the island. Dressed in oddments of clothing, with bare feet, unkempt hair and a German pistol tucked into his trousers, he looked a wild, sorry sight. The platoon cook put him to work in the field kitchen and the platoon Sergeant organised a bivouac,bedding and clothing. It was not long before this young man was presentably dressed, well scrubbed and sporting a green beret on a close cropped head.

The 26th Dalmatian Udarna Divizija (Division) was the main Partisan force on Vis and consisted of the 1st, 11th and 12th Dalmatian Brigades and the 3rd Overseas Brigade. The Division was supported by artillery, engineering and other logistical units and comprised a total force of 13,500 Partisans, that is, approximately 150 Partisans for each square kilometre of island!

The officers were for the most part from the non professional class but earned their promotion on leadership and ability in action. The women had equal status with the men and also achieved promotion to NCO or officer rank on ability. They dressed in a variety of Yugoslav, Italian and British uniforms. Their own uniform consisted of a grey-green serge jacket and trousers with leather belt and braces, a glengarry-type cap with a red cloth star set in the front, and wellington-type boots. The weapons were mainly of Italian or German origin.

Partisan discipline was strict and practical. The conditions and facilities on the island did not permit much privacy between male and female rank and file yet they had little choice other than to live in close proximity. However, any closer relationship between the sexes was strictly taboo. Pregnant Partisan women were an encumbrance and punishment was harsh for anyone breaking the rules. This message was made very clear to the commandos.

An early task undertaken by all 40 RM Commando personnel was to learn the Yugoslav words and phrases essential for day to day contact with their new allies, in particular the essential words required when confronted by a Partisan sentry at night. They had their own ideas about guard duties and would sometimes challenge and shoot simultaneously for good measure. One quickly adapted to this behaviour, and also to the sight of women carrying weapons and grenades. The marines were always ready to dub an individual with a nickname, and two of the more robust Partisan females became known as Beretta Bessy and Luger Lil, characterised by the make of hand-gun they carried.

V Adm Sir Walter Cowan Bt,KCB,DSO,MVO, aged 74, one of the island's colourful characters, was a familiar figure among the commandos. With the special consent of the Admiralty he had rejoined the Navy in 1939 in the rank of Commander and persuaded Adm Sir Roger Keyes, then Director of Combined Operations, to allow him to serve with the Commandos. He was captured at Tobruk and exchanged – much to his distaste – for an Italian

Vis: Partisans and commando personnel on Vis in May 1944.
Photo: V. Bibicic, Vis Museum

General. On his return to the Mediterranean, the C-in-C, Adm Sir John Cunningham, asked Brig Churchill if he would accept him as a liaison officer and this was agreed. Sir Walter carried out a valuable task organising the Partisan shipping and spent his spare time walking about the island in tropical rig, wearing a Royal Navy cap and carrying a shepherd's crook, encouraging the Partisans to salute 'Navy fashion' instead of holding up the clenched fist.

Field training in the close confines of the island had its problems but a directive from Commando HQ gave Y Troop the task of preparing a demonstration troop attack. This was carried out on 16 May with a critical Commando and informal Partisan audience observing from a hillside. When it was completed the Partisans politely applauded, but what they were actually thinking they never revealed. Their own tactics were not to be found in any military manual!

40 Commando's first involvement with boarding party sorties took place on the night of 18/19 May. The intention was to intercept, capture or sink shipping that was supplying and reinforcing the German garrisons on the islands within a range of 50 miles. The supply ships were mainly cargo schooners sailing from Split and Makarska. The usual technique for intercepting a supply ship was for the Coastal Forces boats to lie in wait near the shore of one of the islands and close in from astern when the ship had passed.

The Coastal Forces had considerable success during April 1944 when the ships' companies of the Motor Torpedo Boats(MTBs) and Motor Gun Boats

(MGBs), under the leadership of Lt Cdr T.Fuller*, captured a number of German controlled schooners. In consequence the Germans commenced to escort the merchant ships with R-Boats and heavily armed F- lighters. On 18 May, A and Y Troops each provided a boarding party of one officer, two corporals and four marines. The A Troop detachment (Lt Copsey), embarked in MGB 661 (Lt Cole) and Y Troop's boarding party (Lt Beadle), was allocated to MTB 667 (Lt Jerram). The boarding party personnel had been advised to wear pullovers or other warm clothing under their battledress, and gym shoes replaced boots. Each man was armed with a TSMG, five magazines of ammunition and a No 36 grenade.

The two boat flotilla, commanded by Lt Cdr Fuller in MGB 661, left Komica at 1945 hours on a course which would take it to the end of the Peljesac Peninsula extending between the islands of Hvar and Korcula. Speed was reduced at 2330 hours when the dark outline of the peninsula could be seen silhouetted against the sky. Cruising forward quietly Lt Cdr Fuller gave orders for the boats to heave-to with engines idling about 10 feet from the cliff.

After 50 minutes of seeing and hearing nothing the patrol eased gently round the point to the Korcula side of the peninsula where, after a further wait of 30 minutes, the dark shadows of two small ships could be seen moving south-west from Cape Loviste (Hvar). Estimating the distance was not easy, but they were thought to be at about 1200 yards range. Lt Cdr Fuller signalled to Lt Jerram and moved off north-east at 10 knots to engage from the port side. As speed increased to 17 knots the boarding parties took up positions kneeling on the decks forward of the bridge while the boarding party officers observed from the bridges of their respective boats.

The range had closed to 600 yards when the enemy opened fire and the convoy dispersed. It was now possible to distinguish a 700 ton schooner followed by a lighter and three armed escorts, identified as two I-boats and one R-boat. The MGB and MTB returned fire, concentrating mainly on the armed escorts as the range closed to 50 yards. MGB 661 raked the R-boat while MTB 667, on the port side of the MGB, directed its fire- power at the schooner, which caught fire, and the nearest I-boat. Tracer shells cut a curved path through the darkness in both directions and almost immediately the port .5-inch turret on the MGB was hit by incendiary ammunition and caught fire. The illumination attracted the German gunners and the MGB received further hits admidships. Fuel in the engine room exploded in a ball of fire and a subsequent explosion jammed the steering gear.

MGB 661, out of control, with fire extinguishers expended and numerous casualties aboard, headed for the cliffs of Korcula at 14 knots. The MTB skipper, alerted to the situation by a flash-light signal, discontinued the engagement and set off in pursuit. Lt Jerram closed 667 alongside 661 and while two of the boarding party jumped across with the wash-deck hose to

---

* Lt Cdr T. Fuller DSC and two bars RCNVR.

Komiza harbour, Vis. In the foreground, Motor Gun Boat 658 commanded by Lt L Reynolds DSC, RNVR. Astern, a typical schooner used by the Partisans, A and Y Troops camped on the lower slopes of Mount Hume behind the town.

MGB 166 undergoing commissioning trials before proceeding to the Adriatic. Photos: L. Reynolds

extinguish the flames the crews lashed the boats together and transferred the wounded to 667.

Returning to Vis was a slow business. Motor Mech J.A. Lacey was able to enter the 661 engine room to shut down the engines but attempts to repair the severely damaged rudder controls proved ineffective and the two boats had to remain lashed together. At about 0330 hours the speed was reduced still further so that repairs could be made to lines that had parted with the constant friction. Throughout the night the boarding party on 667 attended to the wounded, applying tourniquets and giving morphine to those with the most severe injuries. Eventually the boats entered Komica harbour at 0530 hours. It was a depressing moment when one of the seriously wounded crew members who had survived the long trip to Vis died as he was being taken ashore.

An air reconnaisance carried out later in the morning located the schooner and one of the I boats beached on the Peljesac peninsula, where they were straffed and set on fire. Further attempts were made during May to bring home a prize, and a second A and Y troop sortie, using a similar combination of boats, intercepted a small schooner hugging the island coast of Korcula. Lt L. Dutton, the boarding party officer from A Troop, recorded in his report "It returned our fire with a machine-gun before running ashore with enough steel thrown at it to sink a cruiser." Attention now turned to operations of a different nature. The precise strength and locations of the German forces on the island of Brac had not been assessed and it was decided to land a reconnaisance force in the south-east corner of the island to check that area. The force, consisting of S and Q Troops of 40 RM Commando and C Company of the 2nd Highland Light Infantry (HLI) under a composite headquarters from the Special Service Brigade, sailed in LCI 133 from Komica on 22 May.

Landing at 0115 hours on a small beach, Q Troop climbed a precipitous path up the cliff to establish a bridge-head. The remainder of the force followed and moved inland over extremely rocky ground to a ridge overlooking Smrka. Shortly after its arrival at 0550 hours a pre-arranged straffing and bombing attack was made on the village by Spitfires from Italy.

Patrols reconnoitred the surrounding area during the day but no contact was made with the enemy and the entire force returned to the bridge-head shortly after 0110 hours the next morning. Re-embarkation from the original beach was found impossible and although there was a short delay while an alternative beach was found the force returned to Vis in time to have the boats well-camouflaged and screened before daylight. Although little had been achieved, the coping with problems of landing and moving over the difficult terrain helped in the planning of future operations.

Towards the end of May, 2 Commando and 43 Commando landed on Mljet with the aim of attacking the German garrison. After a long climb into the hills they found the enemy had moved to alternative positions and the operation had to be abandoned. A few days after the raid Brig Churchill was recalled to London to take part in discussions and pass on information and experience of combined operations in the Mediterranean area. Prior to his departure he handed over command to his brother.

An unfortunate accident occurred on 28 May resulting in the death of Lt Hill. It was particularly ironic that he survived the dangers of Pizzo, Termoli, Garigliano and Anzio only to succumb to an encounter with a mine forming part of the Vis defences. He was buried in the old British Naval cemetery beside a Sub Lt of HMS *Victorious* who died of wounds received in action with the French ship *Rivola* of 74 guns on 23 February 1812.

On 29 May, AHQ in Bari and Cdr Cerni on Vis, were alerted to a major German offensive which had commenced on 25 May against Marshal Tito's forces in central Bosnia. Armoured and infantry columns had closed in on his headquarters at Drvar and he and his staff narrowly escaped capture by German parachutists. Tito asked for a large scale diversion to be made immediately in Dalmatia. Col Pearson, representing Force 266 (previously Force 133), flew to Vis to discuss the situation with Col Millu and Lt Col Churchill. They decided that a combined Partisan and British attack should be made against the German garrison on Brac.

A further meeting was held on 31 May at which most of the planning difficulties for the operation – codename Flounced – were resolved. Information obtained from various sources following the reconnaisance landing on 22 May indicated that an attack on the German garrison would not be easy. The 738th Regiment of the 118th Jaeger Division, less one company located on the eastern tip of Hvar, was supported by two batteries of the 668th Artillery Regiment and about 150 pioneers. Their main position, manned by 500 Germans, was in the centre of the island south-east of Nerezisce and consisted of a series of hilltop strong-points which could give fire support to each other. They were also protected by four 105mm guns. The approaches to these positions had been cleared of cover and were reported to have been mined.

About 2,000 yards south-west of this position a fortified observation post overlooked the entire south coast of Brac and the Hvar Channel. The OP was manned by 20 men and an artillery officer whose job was to direct the fire of the main position against any force attempting to land. The Germans also had strong-points at Selca and Sumartin defended by a force of 400 men and supported by a battery of four 105mm guns. A further 280 Germans were at Supetar supported by three 75mm guns.

In planning the attack, the senior representatives of 2 SS Bde and 26th Dalmatian Udarna Division decided that four separate forces would be required to deal with the four German strong-points. "North Force", consisting of 500 Partisans, would cut the Nerezisce-Supetar road and eliminate the Germans in Supetar. " OP Force" comprised of one company of 2nd HLI and a platoon of Partisans, would attack and destroy the OP prior to the main Partisan / British force landing. "North Force" and "OP Force" would land from schooners the night before the main landing, lie up during the day and close in on their objectives after last light.

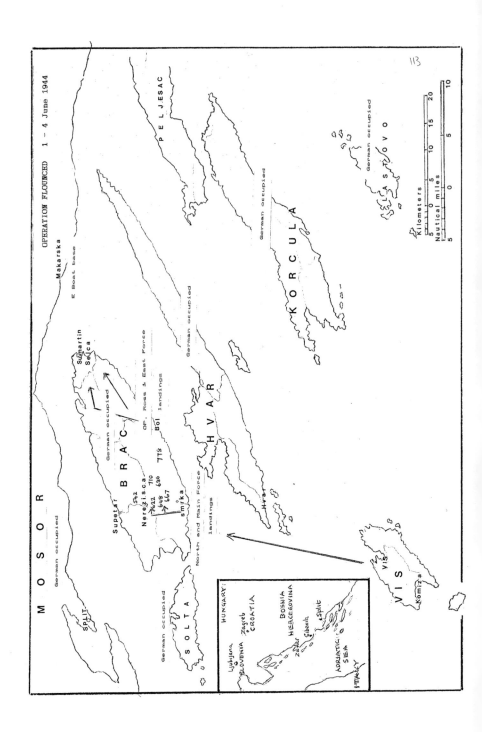

OPERATION FLOUNCED   1 - 4 June 1944

MOSOR

SPLIT
German occupied

E Boat base

Makarska

SOLTA
German occupied

Supetar
Sumartin
Selca

BRAC
German occupied

Nerezisca
542
710
622
636
648
667
779
smrka

Op. Ross & East Force
Bol landings

North and Main Force landings
German occupied

HVAR

Hvar

PELJESAC
German occupied

KORCULA

VIS
Komiza

LASTOVO
German occupied

HUNGARY
SLOVENIA
Ljubljana
Zagreb
CROATIA
BOSNIA
HERCEGOVINA
Zadar
Sibenik
Split
ITALY
ADRIATIC SEA

Kilometers
Nautical miles

"East Force", a total of 1,400 Partisans from the 1st Overseas Brigade, would land at Bol to cut the Nerezisce – Selca road and destroy the German forces in the eastern end of Brac.

"Main Force", under joint command of Lt Col Churchill and Cdr Cerni and consisting of 1,300 Partisans of the 13th Brigade, 43 RM Commando, P and S Troops of 40 RM Commando and No 3 Section of 10 Troop Raiding Support Regiment with two field-guns, would land over three beaches about five miles south-west of Bol and move inland to surround and destroy the main German position. A, Q and Y Troops* of 40 RM Commando and 2 Commando were held in reserve.

The mountainous nature of Brac made the provision of artillery support very difficult, but it was decided to back "Main Force" with one troop of Partisan manned 75mm guns and one battery of 25-pdr guns of 111th Fd Regt RA based at Bol. Protection from air attack was to be provided by six Browning guns of C Battery RSR. "East Force" was given similar support and was the only "Force" to be provided with jeep and trailer transport for gun-haulage.

The RAF was to start the ball rolling with an attack by 242nd Group on the main German defences at 0600 hours 1 June, using rocket-firing Hurricanes. From then on the RAF agreed to have fighters on call from the Vis air-strip, ready to attack any position or to intercept enemy shipping or aircraft. Brig Miles also enlisted the assistance of the US Army Air Force to attack Split and Makarska as soon as the operation had commenced.

The Royal Navy, in conjunction with the Partisan navy, agreed to transport all troops and to escort and supervise the landing and unloading of ships. Lt K.J.Webb was appointed Naval Force Commander while Lt Cdr Morgan Giles, remained on Vis to supervise the loading and turn-round of the vessels. In addition to the Coastal Forces MTBs and MGBs based at Vis the Navy had the support of two destroyers and several MLs, all of which were to be deployed at night to protect the shipping-lanes. The Partisan navy provided 20 schooners and caiques and one coaster.

The preliminary landings of "North Force" and "OP Force" proceeded as planned. All the vessels returning to Vis were camouflaged so that by first light there was no signs of any unusual activity. "Main Force" embarked at Vis in an assortment of 40 vessels the first of which sailed for Brac at 2100 hours, 2 June. The passage was uneventful and the landings were made at the designated beaches between 0030 hours and 0430 hours. During that time 4,500 Partisan and British troops, 16 field guns and 20 jeeps with a considerable quantity of ammunition and supplies were put ashore.

The "OP Force", attacking the OP at midnight 1/2 June, met stiff resistance from the Germans entrenched in concrete emplacements. The HLI and Parti-sans suffered many casualties from small arms, mortars and grenades while trying to breach a complicated minefield protected by barbed-wire entangle-

---

* X Troop were on detached duties in Italy.

ments. Eventually they had to wait for daylight and reinforcements before overcoming the opposition.

"North Force" formed a perimeter around Supetar and although they overran one of the 75mm guns they were unable to capture the town. By dawn, "East Force" was on their way to Selca, the Partisan 75mm guns at Bol had commenced to fire on the main German positions and the German gunners had started to retaliate with a counter bombardment.

RAF Hurricanes opened the attack on the main German defences at 0610 hours 2 June, scoring hits on the gun-emplacements and reducing their firepower. The Partisans, who were now in a semicircle facing the hill features 622, 648 and 667, commenced to attack their objectives while 43 RM Commando attacked hill feature 542. A heavy concentration of enemy fire and mine fields prevented the Partisans from penetrating the defences and they withdrew. 43 RM Commando was also held up by heavy fire and mines and Lt Col R.W.B. Simmonds called off the attack at 0800 hours.

It became apparent that a more co-ordinated attack and a concentration of artillery support was required. The outcome was that the Partisans agreed to attack Points 648 and 622 during the morning while 43 RM Commando and one Partisan battalion attacked Point 542 in the afternoon. The morning attack over-ran two outposts but failed to penetrate the main defences. The afternoon attack commenced at 1600 hours with a 30 minute artillery barrage. Fifteen minutes later the Partisan commander operating with 43 Commando informed Lt Col Simmonds that his battalion would not be able to take part in the attack. The Commando continued with the attack and made some progress into the defences but again encountered heavy fire. Little further headway had been made by 1700 hours and Lt Col Simmonds gave orders to withdraw under cover of artillery fire and smoke.

With nightfall imminent a hurried conference was held to decide further action. "North Force" had not been able to penetrate into Supetar and the only real success appeared to have been the capture of Selca by "East Force", which had overwhelmed the German defences in that area. The "Main Force" Partisans agreed to make a further attack that night, but this also proved unsuccessful. Meanwhile Lt Col Churchill made a wireless signal to Vis for the remainder of 40 RM Commando and all available Partisan reserves to proceed to Brac.

Shortly before midnight A, Q and Y Troops, under command of Lt Col Manners, with 300 Partisans and two 25 pdr guns, embarked in schooners and MLs at Komiza. They were all in fine spirits and the Partisans passed the time singing patriotic songs. While the voices of the Partisans were unlikely to merit recognition alongside a Welsh choir their enthusiasm and fervour more than compensated for any discord in the improvised harmony.

The reinforcements landed at Planica beach at 0345 hours and commenced a long uphill haul with replenishment ammunition to an assembly area near Nerezisce. Following a lengthy reconnaisance of the area during the morning,

Lt Col Churchill and Cdr Cerni agreed a plan that 40 and 43 RM Commandos would attack Point 622 at dusk while the Partisans harrassed Points 542 and 648. The Partisans were reluctant to commit themselves to capturing the hilltop defences and it was only after a lengthy discussion that they agreed to harass their designated objectives.

In consequence it was 1715 hours before orders for the attack, timed to start at 2115 hours, were issued from Brigade HQ. Lt Col Simmonds received these orders at 1730 hours. Atmospheric disturbance prevented any wireless contact with 40 RM Commando. Lt Col Churchill instructed Capt E.R. Wakefield to take a copy of the orders to the unit but he and his Partisan guide – who was assumed to know the locality – became hopelessly lost.

Lt Col Manners had received a "stand-by to move" order at 1800 hours. Concerned at hearing nothing further he set out at 1930 hours to contact Brigade HQ, to find the reason for the delay. On the way he met Lt Col Churchill who, anxious at the non return of Capt Wakefield, was personally attempting to contact 40 RM Commando. Because of the lateness of the hour he quickly outlined the plan to Lt Col Manners and accompanied the three troops to the start line with all possible speed. On the way they met Capt Wakefield and his guide, who were by this time completely exhausted.

Meanwhile 43 RM Commando had moved forward under cover of an artillery barrage ranged on Point 622 and attacked at the appointed time. They found a way through the mines and reached the top of the hill, but at 2215 hours were counter attacked and in the process lost contact with B Troop. Unable to communicate with 2 SS Brigade HQ Lt Col Simmonds withdrew the Commando at 2230 hrs.

40 RM Commando, minus half its striking force, arrived at the start line at 2130 hours. To save time Lt Col Churchill decided to brief the three troops himself. Standing on a outcrop of rock with Lt Col Manners beside him, he pointed towards a number of small brushwood fires clearly visible on the hillside to be attacked. The fires were the result of the earlier shelling. He said that it had not been possible to contact 43 RM Commando by wireless but he thought it likely they had already taken the hill. He also thought that in any event the Germans would be tired and short of water, and an attack made with plenty of noise and vigour would overcome any resistance.

Lt Col Manners' supplementary orders took less than a minute. 12 Platoon (Y Troop) would be advance guard to the foot of the hill at which point Y and A Troop were to extend in line, with Y Troop on the left and A Troop on the right. Commando HQ would position itself in the centre with Q Troop forming a second line behind the two forward troops. Two green Verey lights were to be fired to indicate that the hilltop had been cleared.

On the approach across a shallow valley a machine-gun which appeared to be firing on fixed lines from the left flank caused three casualties in A Troop. On arrival at the foot of the hill Lt Beadle made contact with Capt R.G. Schooley, B Troop Commander of 43 RM Commando. He said they had been held up by wire and mines, and had incurred some casualties. A two strand barbed wire fence crossed the line of advance and Capt Pirrie, a Royal Engineers officer on Lt Col Churchill's staff, made a quick inspection of the ground immediately ahead. He reported that the front was clear and Lt Col Manners ordered the assault to start. The night, which up to this point had been moderately quiet, was suddenly shattered by the shouts of the men of 40 RM Commando as they advanced up the hill with bayonets fixed and firing from the hip. The harsh crack and whine of exploding grenades was accompanied by the sound of bagpipes played by Lt Col Churchill as he and Lt Col Manners urged the men forward.

Someone in Y Troop shouted "Mines"! but in the general noise one explosion sounded very much like another. Mnes J. Meiners and D.Gee of 12 Platoon with Pte D. Bissendon, 11 Platoon, were working their way up the hill clearing trenches when a stick grenade exploded blinding Bissendon. Soon afterwards Mne Gee was shot in the head. In the fire-fight to capture the first line of defences Troop Commander, Capt Laidlaw and Mne G. Bates of 11 Platoon were killed. Ian Laidlaw, wounded at Termoli and again at Anzio, had jocularly remarked before leaving Vis that "It is someone else's turn to catch a packet this time"!

Continuing the assault up the hill Cpl J.Bone and Mne A.L.Woods of 12 Platoon were wounded and Lt L. Dutton commanding 11 Platoon was killed, further reducing their numbers. OC 12 Platoon could see no sign of the other troops of 43 RM Commando as he approached the crest with his runner Mne S. Udakis and a small group of Y Troop. Almost immediately a cluster of mortar-bombs and rifle-grenades exploding around them preceding a German counter-attack from the exposed left flank. Cpl L.G Harvey was killed and Lt Beadle, knocked unconscious by the blast and shrapnel was assumed by Mne Udakis to have been killed. As the counter attack developed Cpl C.E. White was wounded in the neck and in company with Mnes Woods, Muscroft and Meiners, and Mne D. Fletcher the troop signaller, was overrun by the enemy and taken prisoner. Mne Udakis, miraculously unscathed, managed to contact TSM Gordon, who rallied the remainder of Y Troop and consolidated their position.

On the right flank A Troop had fought their way up the hill, capturing six prisoners in the process, but Lt L.Cross, 2 Platoon commander, was killed and the troop incurred a number of other casualties. Consolidating on the far side of the hill, Capt J. Wakeling ordered the pre-arranged two green Verey lights to be fired to indicate success. This signal coincided with the start of the German counter-attack on the left flank. To avoid being encircled TSM Gordon moved Y Troop closer to A Troop where their combined efforts repulsed the attack and a further six German prisoners were taken.

Immediately Lt Col Manners and Lt Col Churchill arrived at the top of the hill it became evident that 40 RM Commando was very thin on the ground. The headquarter group had also suffered casualties on the way up. Capt Pirrie had been killed and Capt Wakefield, critically wounded, was put in the shelter of an outcrop of rock. There was no sign of 43 RM Commando and no visual signals from the Partisans to indicate that they had reached their objectives. A considerable amount of small arms fire was coming from the direction of the left flank and as Lt Col Manners moved towards Q Troop to confirm the defensive positions, he was severely wounded in his left arm. Lt Col Churchill applied a handkerchief tourniquet to the arm and placed him by the side of Capt Wakefield.

Mortar bombs and rifle grenades were now falling around their position and a heavier concentration of machine-gun fire indicated that a counter-attack was imminent. Lt Col Churchill ordered Cpl A. Verri, the Brigade HQ signaller, to move to a more sheltered position down the hill. His instructions were to contact Brigade Headquarters for artillery fire to be put down on the far side of the hill and to locate 43 RM Commando. The Colonel then sent a marine to bring Q Troop forward and another runner was despatched to locate 43 RM Commando.

Although disabled and weak from loss of blood, Lt Col Manners prepared to fire his revolver at the approaching enemy and Lt Col Churchill had his American carbine ready to hand. It was at this point that a mortar bomb exploded in the middle of their six man group killing Capt Wakefield and wounding a marine. Seconds later Lt Col Manners received a further wound in the right shoulder. Mne R.F.Wood had just joined the group and went to the assistance of Lt Col Churchill who was removing Lt Col Manners equipment. While doing so Mne Wood was killed.

A group of Germans, about 30 strong, advancing towards the position were stopped by rapid fire from Y and Q Troops but other German infantry started to infiltrate round the right flank. Lt Col Churchill tried once again to contact 43 RM Commando by playing " Will ye no'come back again" on his bag pipes. The call was apparently heard by Capt A. Blake, who arrived on top of the hill with D Troop, but they lacked sufficient strength to hold the Germans and were forced to fall back. More grenades fell in Lt Col Churchill's position and he was stunned by one of the splinters. Shortly afterwards their position was overrun by the enemy.

Maj Maude established a defence position in one of the captured trenches. He was joined by Capt Schooley, who had reinforced Q Troop with some of his men from B Troop (43 RM Commando). They were all engaged in trying to contain the German attack on the left flank, but as the men of B Troop were almost out of ammunition Maj Maude ordered Capt Schooley to establish a firm base with his troop at the foot of the hill. Before this order could be implemented Capt Schooley was killed and the task was taken over by Lt Odenham.

Maj Maude had also received reports from A and Y Troops that ammunition was running low and, aware that the flanks were insecure, he ordered both Troops to return to the start line while Q Troop covered them. When this was completed Q Troop was withdrawn from the hill at 0200 hours 4 June. No further attempts were made to engage the enemy and the process of returning to Vis commenced before dawn. 40 RM Commando and 43 RM Commando withdrew to the beach at 0830 hours. The move was greatly assisted by a detachment of Partisan nurses from the First Field Hospital who worked untiringly to care for the wounded and by Padre Hook, who organised and assisted with carrying-parties for the evacuation of the wounded.

The return to Vis was carried out in full view of enemy positions on the mainland at the eastern end of the Hvar Channel. The Navy, operating under the constant threat of attack from German E-Boats 12 of which were known to be at Makarska, lifted the two Commando units and Partisans with their guns,vehicles, ammunition and stores from the various beaches without interference from the enemy. The situation may have been different if the Germans had known that the Navy could only muster four MGBs against an E-Boat attack. The RAF maintained a constant patrol and the pilots of two ME 109s, mistakenly assuming the sea-borne force would be an easy target, were shot down by two Spitfires. The Spitfires were also used to harass the German positions on Brac during and after the withdrawal programme.

A small force from 2 Commando covered the final stage of withdrawal from the beach head and a group of its men remained on the island for some time in the hope of finding personnel, injured or otherwise, who may have evaded the Germans. The following night a 40 RM Commando patrol led by Lt A. Smith returned to Brac on a similar mission and three MGBs lay off Supetar Harbour in the hope of intercepting the transfer of Germans or their prisoners to the mainland. Both the patrol and the MGBs returned to Vis empty handed.

Immediately following the night attack the Germans re-camouflaged their trenches with gorse and scrub and collected the dead and wounded. Lt Col Churchill and the other Commando prisoners were kept in a stone hut on Hill 122 until later that morning when the unwounded prisoners were taken out to collect further casualties, including Lt Beadle and Cpl Bone. Cpl Verri was brought to join them at noon, having evaded capture until dawn. Cpl Bone died in the early morning of 4 June and Lt Col Manners, who had been moved to a first-aid tent, died that afternoon. At dawn on Monday 5 June Lt Col Churchill with the other commando prisoners held a burial service with all possible military ceremony, and filled in the single trench grave. Lt Beadle was taken to Supetar with the German stretcher wounded and later transferred to hospital in Belgrade. Lt Col Churchill was flown to Germany, where he was followed in due course by the other Commando prisoners. The casualties incurred by the 2nd SS Bde amounted to eight officers and six other ranks killed and 40 other ranks wounded. Two officers and 12 other ranks, seven of whom were wounded, were taken prisoner.

The following awards were approved for distinguished service during operations in the Adriatic:

Maj J.D.Wakeling   MC   Lt J.C.Beadle   MC

CHAPTER 9

6 June 1944 to 27 February 1945

A new commanding officer and second in command – Reorganisation and training in Italy and Malta – Albania and the battle for Sarande – Corfu and the provision of military support to the Greek authority.

A dispirited 40 RM Commando returned to Vis. The raid, from the unit point of view had been unsuccessful. The German defences, well-sited and prepared in the area of Nerezisca, were proof against the piecemeal and, in some instances, hasty attacks by the Partisans and Commandos. It was accepted that there was little similarity between the strategy of the Partisans and the British. It was not unknown for them to undertake an operation without fully assessing all the factors and to abandon the action if they felt there was little to be gained in pursuing the objective. Nevertheless the Partisans were extremely courageous and fought well. The Brac operation achieved the purpose of drawing German reinforcements on the mainland to Split which in turn eased the pressure on Tito's forces. The hard lesson – eventually employed in Albania – was that in a combined operation the Partisans task should not directly affect the Commando task.

In addition to suffering considerable manpower casualties the men of 40 RM Commando had lost their respected leader. Lt Col Manners, affectionately known as "Pops", had been held in high esteem by all ranks and they found it difficult to accept that someone else would take the helm.

The majority of wounded received treatment on Vis where Capt Rickett RAMC had converted two houses into wards with an operating theatre the lighting of which was improvised from biscuit tins. The First Base Hospital lacked major equipment and some of the more serious cases were moved to Italy. Maj Maude was also hospitalised and in his absence Capt Wakeling – promoted acting temporary major on 16 June – assumed command of the unit. During this period Lt Neale's detachment rejoined the unit from Corsica and the first leave party sailed to Bari for seven days rest and recreation.

Brig Churchill was recalled to Vis immediately after the raid on Brac and set about the task of obtaining replacements for the Brigade. Meanwhile Col V. Street, second in command to Brig Maclean, organised Marshal Tito's flight from Bosnia to Italy in an RAF Dakota on 3/4 June. The Partisan leader was then taken to Vis in HMS *Blackmore,* commanded by Lt Cdr D. Carson RN. Having lived a nomadic existence for many months Marshal Tito established his HQ in a cave near Podselje on Mount Hume, where he lived until the liberation of Belgrade in September 1944. The cave eventually became a shrine to the Marshal. Access to the island of Vis, post World War II was, until June 1990, confined to residents of Vis, members of SUBNOR*, 2 SS Brigade and Coastal Forces who served with the Partisans during 1944-45.

A further attempt was made by Coastal Forces to disrupt enemy shipping on the night of 9/10 June 1944. On this occasion the boarding party led by Lt Copsey embarked on MGB 647 (Lt Mountstephens) and, in company with an MTB they idled along the channel between the island of Mljet and the Peljesac peninsula in good visibility provided by a full moon. Observing nothing they turned to go back but as they did so the MTB signalled the sighting of an enemy vessel astern.

Returning to the original course they increased speed and continued for about six miles without further sight of enemy boats. There were numerous channels between a group of small islands in the vicinity and it had to be assumed that the enemy had taken refuge somewhere among them. The channels were too shallow for the MGB to navigate and so the search was discontinued. Nearing the point where they had originally turned they came under fire from a shore battery, but this did not distract them from seeing a lighter with an R-boat escort sailing southwards very close to the shore. The MGB and R-boat opened fire simultaneously. The enemy's aim was accurate and lethal. The MGB's two pounder pom-pom, the starboard twin 0.5-inch turret and twin Lewis mountings were all put out of action.

However, the MGB had the last word and, although repeatedly hit, accurate shooting by its six-pounder crew sank the R-boat. A loud explosion was also heard from the direction of the lighter. Aware that the shore defences on Mljet were alerted and could contact the E-boat base at Makarska it was thought prudent to head for Vis. In this engagement the Coastal Forces lost three sailors killed and three wounded. Mne W. Bryce of the boarding party was killed and Mnes Bothe and Marshall were wounded.

On Vis, there was considerable speculation within the unit as to who would be appointed commanding officer. Maj Maude's chances were ruled out when he received a posting to UK. While it seemed unlikely that a third CO would be promoted from within the Commando few, if any, relished the thought of a newcomer taking over. Such was the general mood of the Commando when Lt Col R. W.Sankey DSC, the new CO, and Maj P.R. Matters, the unit's new second-in-command arrived at Podselje on 1 July.

Lt Col Sankey was an impressive figure who had been Corps heavy- weight boxing champion in his earlier days and still looked capable of winning a bout or two. He enlisted in the Royal Marines in 1932 and was awarded the Kings Badge on completion of recruit training. Although over age for a Corps Commission he served as an NCO until 1935 and then decided to try his hand at a civilian career. Re-enlisting on the outbreak of hostilities he was commissioned in 1940 and posted to 11th Battalion RM. The unit which he was

---

* SUBNOR : The Federation of Veterans Association of the People's Liberation War.

eventually to command.

Both newcomers had a chance to meet the men informally on the following day at a garrison cross-country race, the first of its kind on Vis, which 40 RM Commando won. The unit was not fully represented at the cross country meeting. A small raiding force of 15 men under the command of Capt Marshall was otherwise occupied preparing for a fighting reconnaisance on Mljet.

Capt Marshall's advance force landed on the eastern end of the island on 3 July and proceeded to Mihogska, where it contacted known local residents who recommended suitable areas for a base. The main force landed on 5 July and reconnaisance patrols covered most of the island during the subsequent two days, observing enemy movement. They observed that the enemy had concentrated on high ground near Soura. Local people reported that the Germans' morale was low but that their considerable superiority in numbers and well prepared wire and mine defences made an attack on their position by a raiding force an impractical proposition.

The commandos considered cutting the water supply to the garrison but the Germans had warned the villagers that if they did not comply with instructions they would mortar their houses. The commando force attempted to ambush German patrols and on two occasions opened fire to provoke an attack but without success. Before leaving Mljet on 13 July Capt Marshall's force provided the villagers with chocolate, cigarettes and a number of propaganda leaflets, the last to be delivered to the Germans with the next consignment of water!

On their return to Vis they found that Maj Gen R.G.Sturges CB, DSO, had visited the Commando units and discussed future movements with Brig Churchill and the COs. Also, Lt Col Sankey had already commenced the task of rebuilding the unit and a number of officers and other ranks had left the unit to return to UK. Capt P. Delap, the army medical officer, could view the CO's approach to the problems impartially. Writing on that subject in later years he recorded "It required tremendous moral courage and stamina to recreate 40 RM Commando. The first superb vitality had been shot out of it and a few splendid chaps who could not re-adjust from the magnificent free-wheeling days were returned to UK. Others gave him their full support. Capt Marshall, with newcomers Capts W.J.Hiles and M. Macpherson, played a prominent role in the re-training programme".

Lt Col Sankey made arrangements to move the Commando to Italy and the main body sailed from Vis in the SS *Lubljana* on 15 July. The vessel was escorted for some distance by two Yugoslav schooners packed with singing Partisans. In the short period that the commandos had been on the island a strong feeling of comradeship had developed between them and their Yugoslav comrades.*

The Commando, under canvas south of Bari near Monopoli, pursued a

---

* This relationship has continued to the present day. Members of the Coastal Forces Veterans Association and Commando Associations have made regular visits to the island and in 1991 presented a computer to the Vis primary school.

programme of administration and training until 17 August. On that day the unit sailed to Malta in SS *Timslemvis* where the accommodation at the RN Rest Camp, Ghain Tuffieha, was comparatively luxurious compared to that experienced in recent months. During the initial stages of a progressive training programme seven officers and 160 other-ranks joined the unit. The reinforcements looked slightly out of place with pale limbs protruding from khaki shirts and shorts. Nevertheless, the majority were not lacking experience and most had served with Lt Col Sankey in 11th Battalion RM.

While 40 RM Commando reorganised in Malta, control of Allied land operations in Dalmatia was transferred to Land Forces Adriatic. This new formation, commanded by Brig G.M.O Davey, also absorbed 2 SS Brigade. During July, 2 Commando sailed from Vis to establish a bridgehead on the Albanian coast at Spialje and 9 Commando established a base on the Greek island of Kithera. Brig Churchill visited 40 RM Commando in Malta on 10 September and a few days later Lt Col Sankey received orders to move the unit to Monopoli to prepare for an operation involving the capture of an airfield on the Greek mainland. Although the plan was scrapped, another took its place and the Commando embarked in LCIs on 24 September, bound for a place in Albania roughly midway between Lukove and Sarande, known as 'Sugar Beach'.

Following a series of Russian successes on the eastern front the Axis forces in Greece, Albania and Yugoslavia were at risk of being separated from their main forces in central Europe. The withdrawal of German forces from the Greek islands had already commenced and preparations were in hand to evacuate the 2,500 strong German garrison on Corfu via the port of Sarande. Alerted to this situation Brig Davey gave orders for the Commandos to capture Sarande.

The initial plan required 2 Commando to land at Sugar Beach with four .75mm guns plus additional machine guns and mortars of the Raiding Support Regiment, advance inland through a valley (Commando Valley) to connect with the north-south road, follow the road south and capture the port of Sarande. This plan was abandoned when a reconnaissance patrol reported that a considerable amount of German artillery positioned between Delvine and Sarande shelled everything that moved in the vicinity of the road. However, according to Albanian Partisan sources of information, Borsh had been evacuated by the enemy and the coastline between that locality and Sugar Beach was in Partisan hands. In consequence action was taken to land 2 Commando at Sugar Beach on 22 September when the unit established a bridge-head there.

In the meantime Brig Churchill reviewed his plan and assessed that a stronger force would be required to take Sarande. Patrols estimated the strength of the German force at Delvine to be in the region of 500 men and the garrison at Sarande at 1,200 men. A reconnaissance of the Sarande defences established that the Germans did not anticipate an attack on their positions from the rugged hill country north of the town. An assault from this direction would most likely achieve surprise, although the logistics required for such an operation would be considerable. Having assessed the pros and cons Brig Churchill decided to plan accordingly. The troops selected to take part were to be known as Houndforce and the operation was given the codename 'Mercerised'.

The logistics required careful study as the inhospitable terrain presented a major problem. The mountains, ascending sharply from the shore-line to 2,000 feet, were intersected by thickly wooded valleys with no definite paths and no easy way of keeping direction. Extensive areas were covered by spikes of rock up to nine inches high and less than a foot length apart. Walking on this surface was extremely uncomfortable and difficult. Mules could not traverse this type of terrain and every item from ammunition to water would have to be man-packed forward to the point from which the attack would be launched.

The only approach to the hills from Sugar Beach was along a valley, soon to be become all too familiar to the humpers travelling its seemingly interminable length as Commando Valley. In addition to the problems already described, Commando Valley was blocked half-way along its length by a massive 400 ft high outcrop of rock. Beyond this barrier there were two more outcrops to be negotiated before reaching the plain, and the land between Sarande and Delvine was a mass of small hillocks!

Disembarking at Sugar Beach 40 RM Commando established a base camp within the bridge-head. Q Troop took over part of the perimeter defence from 2 Commando, Y Troop was despatched on a reconnaissance of the approaches to Sarande and in the days that followed the other rifle troops established observation posts on the high ground to the north overlooking the town. Action was also taken to mine the road between the bridge-head and Borsh. Attempts to ambush enemy traffic on the Sarande- Delvine road met with little success, mainly because daylight movement was easily observed by the enemy and met with artillery and mortar fire.

Contact was made with the Partisans to the north of Commando Valley and a permanent liaison was established with their HQ at Shen-Vasil. A troop of the RSR, with four 75mm guns, 40mm Bofors and 4.2-inch mortars, was moved from Sugar Beach to Shen Vasil in an attempt to neutralise enemy gun positions but found that most of the German artillery was out of range. On 28 September Q Battery of the 111 Field Regiment RA arrived from Italy with eight 25-pounder guns and moved into position to strengthen the RSR at Shen Vasil. Maj R. Daniells took command of all guns and established a programme of harassing fire on Sarande and the Sarande-Delvine road.

This was the start of a major artillery duel, with the Germans counter bombarding, first with 75mm guns and 105mm guns, concentrating mainly on Q Battery. The Q Battery guns replied with superior accuracy and unlimited reserves of ammunition. The Germans then responded with 88mm and 150mm guns from Delvine. The German 150mm coast batteries on Corfu also joined in with harassing fire on Shen Vasil, Sugar Beach and Commando

THE BATTLE FOR SARANDE

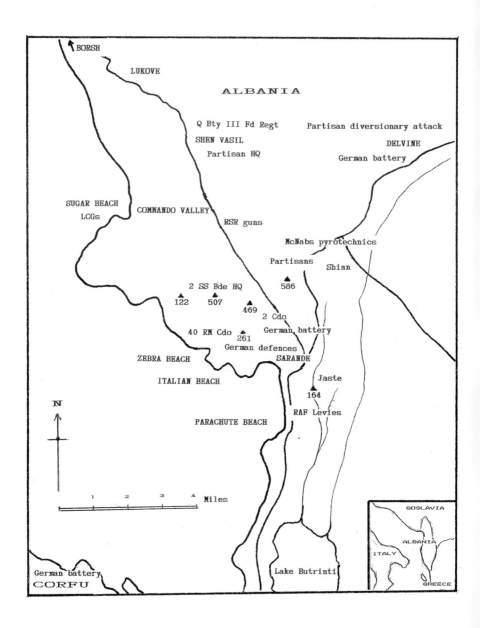

Landing Craft Gun at Sugar Beach. Two of these craft provided artillery support during the battle for Sarande. Photo: RM Museum

Gunners of the Raiding Support Regiment manhandling a 75mm gun into position on Sugar Beach. Photo: RM Museum

Valley but, lacking observation positions and firing at extreme range the shelling, although unpleasant, was inaccurate and there were few casualties.

The first few days after the arrival of 40 RM Commando were fine and warm but rain fell on 27 September and continued non-stop for the next eight days. While solving the shortage of drinking water it saturated the ground and parts of Commando Valley were converted into a raging torrent. The men were soaked to the skin for days on end and the continued exposure took its toll, particularly among the humping parties. Groundsheets were sent from Italy but it was impossible to keep dry and the number of men from both Commando units incapacitated by trench foot steadily mounted. Over 150 were evacuated to Italy and a further 200, with feet too swollen to wear boots, were treated in the base camp at Sugar Beach.

Taking a calculated risk that the enemy would not attack in such appalling weather, Brig Churchill gave orders for the manpower in the observation posts to be reduced to about eight men in each post. Lt Cdr Usherwood commanding the Naval force, provided four LCIs offshore in which troops were able to spend 24 hours drying out, resting and fortifying themselves with hot meals. This had an immediate beneficial effect and the sick rate reduced rapidly. Eventually the weather improved and by 6 October Houndforce was again manning the observation posts in full strength and on the offensive.

Further reinforcements arrived from Italy on 7 October, increasing the force at Brig Churchill's disposal to 400 men of 40 RM Commando. 350 men of 2 Commando. 500 Albanian Partisans and 130 men of the 1st Paratroop Company RAF Levies. There were also sufficient supporting arms to give equality of fire power. With the German evacuation of Corfu proceeding rapidly, Brig Churchill decided to attack Sarande on the morning of 9 October.

The plan required 40 RM Commando to advance from Point 122 to clear Zebra Beach and Italian Beach and then capture the enemy positions in the area of Point 261. The Commando would then proceed eastward along the coast to undertake the primary task of clearing Sarande. On 40 Commando's left flank 2 Commando would advance southwards from Point 469 to attack a strongpoint midway along the ridge and then capture a coast defence battery at the far end of the same feature. One Partisan force of 200 men would be deployed on its left flank to capture enemy positions along the Sarande-Delvine road. Meantime, the RAF Parachute Levies would make a landing at Parachute Beach – south of Sarande – to attack and clear Point 164.

A second force of 350 Partisans would carry out a diversionary attack on Delvine from the north during the night of 8/9 October and at the same time Lt D.G.McNab of the New Zealand Engineers and a team of 10 men with pyrotechnics would simulate a brigade attack in the area of Shian. Their intention would be to draw the attention of the Delvine garrison away from events in the Sarande area.

The plan was not without risk as the entire left flank of the attacking force, with the exception of Point 586 held by a troop of 2 Commando, would be undefended. This troop was also the only available reserve. If intelligence reports of the enemy strength were incorrect it was possible that Houndforce would be outnumbered.

Houndforce deployed on 8 October. Brig Churchill established his HQ on Point 507 while 2 Commando and 40 RM Commando, less A Troop providing the Brigade HQ guard, moved to their start lines on Points 469 and 122 respectively. These positions were already occupied by Houndforce observation posts. During the afternoon of 8 October a Royal Navy destroyer commenced shelling enemy positions around Sarande while the Raiding Support Regiment moved its guns forward, positioning one troop at the end of Commando Valley and the other at Yoke Beach. This phase was followed by the Partisans diversionary attacks and McNab's fireworks, both evolutions proceeding according to plan.

Precisely at 0400 hours on 9 October 1944 the guns of Houndforce began a preliminary 30-minute bombardment to cover the advance of both Commandos. At 0430 hours Q Troop of 40 RM Commando launched an assault on Point 261 while P, X and Y Troops, supported by the mortars and guns of S Troop and the RSR, advanced towards Sarande. Almost immediately the advancing troops were confronted with cross-fire from a series of Spandau machine-gun positions which inflicted casualties and prevented further progress until each obstacle had been eliminated by a local attack. X Troop commander Capt W.J.Hiles was killed in one of these encounters. It was hard, close-quarter fighting in darkness pierced frequently by incendiary ammunition and star-shell chandeliers which illuminated the ugly reality on the ground.

Q Troop, having gained possession of Point 261 prepared for a predictable counter-attack which commenced at 0630 hours. Hanging on tenaciously to the ground they had won the commandos forced the Germans to keep their distance and after an hour of hard fighting the pressure on the hilltop position ceased. In this struggle troop commander Capt M.S.MacPherson was killed and both platoon commanders were wounded. A Troop moved up in support of Q Troop with Maj Wakeling taking command of both.

It was 0955 hours by the time X Troop had started to clear paths through the mines on Zebra and Italian Beaches. This action was essential to the operation as the beaches were required for early use as forward ammunition supply points. During the mine clearing operations Capt P. Whitehouse RE of Brigade HQ was killed.

Further inland on the left flank 2 Commando completed a difficult approach to its objective and after a short sharp fight in which Capt G.A. Parsons MC and Lt J Coyle were killed, reported the capture of the gun battery. About noon Brig Churchill was informed that Jaste, a village to the south-east of Sarande, was in Partisan hands and the RAF Levies, after an unopposed landing south of Sarande, had caught the German defence post at Point 164 off-guard and taken 30 prisoners.

P, X and Y Troops had advanced through a series of anti-personnel minefields and wire entanglements towards the western outskirts of Sarande. Their approach, hampered by mortar fire and machine-guns firing on fixed lines, was held up shortly before noon by Spandaus in windows and doors of houses on the perimeter of Sarande and the hillside overlooking the town. Machine-gun fire was also directed at them from the hospital about 400 yards to their front. P troop incurred a number of casualties including Capt Marshall who was seriously wounded in the head. Medical officer Capt Delap was also hit by mortar bomb fragments. According to Mne F. Shaw, who was Capt Marshall's runner/orderly "Capt Delap continued attending the wounded with blood running down his face. He just would not sit down".

Lt Col Sankey called for support fire and this was provided by a Navy frigate five miles off shore and S Troop's 3-inch mortars. At 1500 hours P, X and Y Troops advanced again for the final onslaught with covering fire from Q and A Troops and the MMGs of S Troop. With two of his Troop commanders dead and a third gravely wounded Lt Col Sankey was actively to the forefront ascertaining the exact location of the enemy and organising a series of local attacks, of which three were led by himself, in order to gain ground.

After four hours of savage street fighting the German resistance was finally broken and the garrison of 750 men surrendered. According to a report in The Sunday Times of 8 April 1945 "Major Stusser made a most graceful surrender, offering his official residence, his radio and his excellent stock of wines to Brig Churchill". Further prisoners were taken when four schooners carrying German troops arrived from Corfu during the evening. Their number included the garrison commander of Corfu, who suddenly found himself without a job!

In this action 40 RM Commando suffered nine killed and 48 wounded. The losses would undoubtedly have been heavier but for the excellent leadership of the officers and NCOs and the professional skill of the men. Lt Col Sankey was awarded the DSO for leadership and determination.

Immediately 40 RM Commando had taken over the German defences a start was made to find billets for the remainder of Houndforce in Sarande. Most of the houses had been expertly booby trapped and Lt McNab, who had assumed the duties of Capt Whitehouse, organised demolition teams to dismantle these devices. It was a long and dangerous operation and in the process McNab was himself wounded. Nevertheless he continued with the tricky task and the following morning, while working in the shopping centre of the town, found a container that had held time delay fuses. Although a thorough search was made neither fuses or charges could be found, leading him to believe that they had been buried beneath the paving stones in the shopping quarter of the town.

Brigade HQ was alerted and Brig Churchill, deciding to play safe, ordered an evacuation of the area. This proved to be a wise precaution as the town centre blew up the next day ! Lt McNab had an uneasy feeling that there were still more time delay charges hidden in the undamaged buildings and with this in mind it was decided to move Houndforce temporarily to Sugar Beach. McNab's assumption was correct. There was a second explosion which considerably dwarfed the former blast and caused extensive damage in Sarande.

The attention of Houndforce was now directed at Corfu and arrangements were made for aircraft from the Balkan airforce to drop leaflets over Corfu town on 11 October. These contained details of the fall of Sarande and called on the German garrison to surrender. The garrison had already thinned-out to a fraction of its former size and required no further prompting. A pilot on a reconnaisance flight the next day observed white flags flying from a number of buildings in Corfu town and a troop from 40 RM Commando was sent to the island on 13 October to accept their surrender. News of civil unrest on the island prompted Brig Chuchill to instruct Lt Col Sankey to take the remainder of the Commando to Corfu with instructions to prevent any civil disturbances and to give military support to the Greek authority until such time as the government could manage its own affairs unaided.

The people of Corfu town welcomed the men of 40 RM Commando with open arms. There was singing and dancing in the streets and drinking of wine to celebrate the end of the German occupation. The islanders were not only pleased to be rid of the Germans but hoped the British would provide them with a lifeline to help them out of their troubles. The two major political groups, known as EDES and ELAS, each with a force of Andartes (armed supporters) were jostling for power. Both Andartes considered themselves to be the stronger force. There was considerable friction and 'sabre rattling' between the rival groups and their strong- arm men blatantly patrolled the streets with bandoliers of ammunition slung across their shoulders and weapons at the ready. The EDES party had received both the approval of the Allies (Caserta Agreement) and the support of the Greek Orthodox Church to control the island until it was possible to form a Greek government. However, the ELAS party also had a large following of supporters and there were fears among the less politically motivated populace that civil war could erupt at any moment.

Both the EDES and ELAS political organizations had their origins in the formation of guerilla forces subsequent to the attack on Greece by Italian forces in October 1940 and eventual German occupation of the country and dependent islands in April 1941. The National Liberation Front, or EAM, formed in September 1941 under Communist leadership, was linked with the National Popular Liberation Army, or ELAS, led by Gen Sarafis, which became active mid-1942. The National Republican Greek League, or EDES, was formed in September 1941 under the command of Col Napoleon Zervas. This party recognised the authority of Gen Plastiras the Republican leader, exiled in France. A group of less importance, the National and Social Liberation, or EKKA party – a mixture of Liberal and Republican led by Col Dimitros Psaros – came into being in 1943. With the exception of the EDES party there were no

ALBANIA
Capt L. G. B. Marshall
MC and Bar. Officer
commanding P Troop.
Died of wounds received
in the battle for Sarande.
Photo: Capt P DeLap.

Lt Col Sankey (left), OC 40 RM Commando and Lt Col Fynn OC 2 Commando, at Sarande prior to 40 Commando's departure to Corfu, Greece. Photo: Imperial War Museum

Albania. Partisans of the 12th Brigade after the capture of Delvine. Battle for Sarande 9 October 1944. Photo RM Museum.

Royalist groups, the senior army officers having either left the country or distanced themselves from politics after the flight of King George II of Greece to England.

The British government accepted that it was necessary to make use of the Communist and Republican led resistance forces in Albania and Greece against the Axis forces, but its primary concern was to ensure that Greece in particular did not succumb to the control of a predominately Communist led group that would willingly accept Soviet direction. Anticipating that the British Government would attempt to reinstate a post war Royalist regime the EAM strove to gain full control of Greece with the EDES group their main target. ELAS opened its attack on the rival groups in October 1943 but despite superiority in manpower and weapons little impact was made on the EDES force and an armistice was called in February 1944.

To add to the problems confronting the Corfu people in October 1944, the indiscriminate issue of paper deutschmarks during the German occupation had led to rampant inflation and the Greek drachma was almost worthless. The hospital, mental home and orphanage were desperately short of food and it was known that some of the patients in the mental home had died of starvation. The Swedish Red Cross had established a small organisation on the island and despite the Germans' commandeering part of their food stocks, and hampered by a lack of transport, they managed to distribute food to the most needy and provide fuel to keep the electricity supply to the hospital working.

The police did little to stop the activities of racketeers involved in a thriving black market. They were generally unhelpful and many were accused of corruption and co-operation with the Germans. This was the scenario that greeted Lt Col Sankey on his arrival in Corfu town. While the commandos took part in the victory parades and the civilians attended services of thanksgiving, the Colonel and HQ staff established themselves in the royal villa of Mon Repos, overlooking the sea, to concentrate on the task of formulating a plan for maintaining the peace.

According to Philip Matters, "When we arrived in Corfu we were absolutely whacked and we hadn't taken our clothes off since leaving Italy for Sugar Beach! The NAAFI rations arrived about a week later and we celebrated by having a dance in the Royal Villa. It was attended by Gen Zervas, his regimental priest the Archbishop of Paramytrhra, and his liaison officer Col Barnes NZ Army. The dance was a great success, although a few of the civilian guests were critical of some of the girls who were there saying that they had been too friendly with the German soldiers. This was understandable as we had sent jeeps into the town with instructions to the drivers to bring back the prettiest girls they could find. A local band played for us but half-way through the lights went out and we had to telephone the power station to tell them to put them on again".

Sgt Forbes had remained with the rear party in Italy during the Sarande action but rejoined Commando HQ in time to sail with them to Corfu. One of his memories of that period was moving into "Mon Repos". This beautiful villa had been the birthplace of Prince Philip, now Duke of Edinburgh and Captain General Royal Marines. The building, which had been used as the German HQ, had escaped the ravages of war and the interior had been well maintained by a household staff, who were retained by Lt Col Sankey.

One of the more lowly members of the villa staff, odd job boy Linos Tsringagi, was very pro-British. He had distributed transcripts of the BBC news around the cafes during the Italian-German occupation and after the arrival of 40 RM Commando his one ambition was to become a commando. Approaching Sgt Forbes on this point he emphasised that he was British through some unknown forebears by writing on his arm with red stencil-correcting fluid 'Me Blood the British'. Deciding to extend the charade Sgt Forbes had a word with Capt E. Cooper, the Adjutant, who agreed to see the keen volunteer. Linos promptly went into the villa garden and returned with a bunch of flowers. Before marching Linos into the Adjutant's office Sgt Forbes warned him to "call the Captain sir". Linos marched into the room and came to a smart halt. Saluting with one hand and presenting the flowers with the other he thrust his arm forward, saying "Sir Cooper, me blood the British "!

Captain Cooper was a good sport and said " Kit him out, we'll get the stuff back later". Since Linos never had occasion to leave the villa grounds the order seemed legitimate enough.

The task confronting Lt Col Sankey, of safeguarding the peace of the island, was not an easy one. To show favour to EDES would destroy the faith of the ELAS supporters and, more seriously, those who supported neither party. Following the early euphoria of peaceful celebrations the political rallies brought about a feeling of unrest. Gen Zervas reinforced his Andartes with the 65th Regiment from the mainland. The regiment, wearing British battledress, was well disciplined and it was decided to retain this force until a formal Greek national army could be organised. Another smaller but very useful formation that came to the island was an Allied Military Mission under the command of Capt A.E.Rogers US Army, who worked tirelessly to assist Lt Col Sankey.

The first step to establish law and order throughout the island and gain the confidence of the people was taken immediately. To implement this the island was divided into four sectors comprising north-east, north-west, southern and Corfu town. Each sector was garrisoned by a small commando force of about 100 men. Their job was to show the flag and prevent any incidents of unrest. Small mobile patrols in Jeeps made daily excursions round the sectors gaining the confidence of the villagers who knew that they could call on them quickly in case of need. It was not long before there were occasions where the villagers, finding it necessary to travel to a distant village, would entrust their valuables and key to their houses with the "Commando Corporal" rather than anyone else in the village!

A number of German deserters were rounded up and minefields and booby traps removed. The state of roads, bridges, houses and telephone communications was noted and passed to Commando HQ where a maintenance programme was initiated. Calls for assistance from members of the local community were numerous. "The Germans took my mules. Will the Commandant please get them back"? "The Germans took my son to Albania. Please find him"!

Many requests were dealt with satisfactorarily but occasionally the end result was unexpected. Capt Delap established a very efficient medical service on the island as stores were, for once, plentiful. Following the death of Capt Marshall, his MOA Mne Shaw, was attached to one of the RAMC medical teams and became familiar with the sight of local villagers asking the staff for medicines and drugs. On one occasion he saw a distraught woman attempting to explain something to an RAMC Lance-Corporal. Unfamiliar with the language he assumed that a member of the family was ill with a temperature or malaria. In consequence he gave her a small quantity of mepacrine, the yellow tablets issued to service personnel in areas where there was a risk of malaria. Two days later she returned with a happy smile and took the Lance-Corporal to her house, where her daughter had given birth to a fine healthy baby. He noticed that the daughter's stomach was bright yellow where apparently, her mother had rubbed in the crushed tablets!

The people steadily gained confidence when they observed that the commandos were intent on assisting them to maintain law and order. The marines based in the town of Corfu invariably walked about unarmed. Lt Col Sankey sent for the Prefect of Police and after some very straight talking told him to go and put his house in order. Whatever was said had the desired effect. From then on the police were noticeably more reliable. There was still the major problem of how to lower the tension and maintain peace while the Andarte and many civilians walked around armed to the teeth. Minor incidents forewarned that real trouble could flare up at any time and the obvious solution was to disarm the Andarte and all civilians. To set this in motion Lt Col Sankey arranged a meeting of all the political leaders and the commanders of the Andartes and OC 65th Regiment.

This meeting, the first of many held at the Allied Military Mission, was apparently very stormy and adjourned when the commamnder of the ELAS Andarte refused to allow his troops to be disarmed without the consent of a higher authority. Eventually, after a number of inneffectual meetings of which some were attended by an official representative of the Greek government, the ELAS commander finally consented to abide by the Caserta Agreement and conform to the orders from Gen Zervas.

Gen Zervas had doubts about the ELAS troops complying peacefully and, not wishing to be instrumental in provoking civil war, was reluctant to commit himself to a date and time for the disarmament. Lt Col Sankey therefore decided to go ahead and disarm the Andartes and civilians without waiting for this order. He called all the Greek political and military leaders and the Prefect of Police together at Commando HQ on 26 October to explain the details. On being told that the disarmament would go ahead with or without their help they reluctantly agreed to co-operate.

The plan required the formation of a number of groups of British and Greek personnel, with each group consisting of two officers and 12 commandos from 40 RM Commando, one Greek officer and 12 soldiers from the 65th Regiment, one political leader, one policeman and one interpreter. The groups were provided with transport and details of the the Andarte locations. In each location the Andarte were assembled and the situation explained to them by both political and military representatives while the Greek soldiers were kept discreetly in the background.

Maj Matters commanded the group that went south to disarm the Andarte near the towns of Levkimmi and Strogili. Nearly 200 troops were on parade at Levkimmi with an enormous amount of weaponry and ammunition. Recalling the incident Philip Matters said "My interpreter Van Dapergolas and I harangued the parade telling them that for them the war was over unless they opted to join the Greek forces in Italy. I ended by shouting something like 'Soldiers of Greece lay down your arms'. There was an uncomfortable pause until one of the Andarte either laid down his rifle – or possibly dropped it by accident – and the others were so surprised that they all conformed. The commandos and Greek troops then swept onto the parade in three tonners and scooped up all the booty. We then drove as quickly as possible to Strogili, hoping to arrive before news should reach that Andarte as to what we were about to do to them. They hadn't heard and our total collection amounted to about 10 tons of weapons and ammunition".

The arms were taken to Corfu Town where they were kept under a strong commando guard. By 2000 hours the same day all the Andarte had been disarmed without incident. A proclamation followed which called for the surrender of all arms held by civilians and these were handed in over a period of a few days.

A considerable effort was made to control the black market but as the 56th Regiment received British rations much of it found its way onto the black market at inflated prices. Working on the principal that "If you can't beat them join them" Lt Col Sankey issued a proclamation fixing the price of all British rations being sold. This did much to regain the confidence of the population and as a result all the black market prices fell considerably. During this period the Commando donated liberal stocks of food to the hospital, mental home and orphanage.

Lack of food and soaring inflation provided little incentive for the lower paid classes to work and in consequence bomb damage, maintenance and the restoration of public services had been neglected. This problem was overcome by providing 50 meals a day from British rations to a civilian work-force, and a soup kitchen was organised by one of the SNCO's. Gradually the clearance of the docks and repair work proceeded.

The education of the children had suffered through a lack of teachers and when the schools reopened at the end of October the classes were so over-crowded that it was impossible to give due attention to the pupils' work. The Commando stepped into the breach once again with the provision of selected NCOs and marines to teach English. The fact that the commando instructors had little knowledge of the Greek language did not appear to matter! They were popular with the pupils and were able to keep groups occupied while the teachers concentrated on the curriculum.

Although the drachma was maintained as the unit of currency on Corfu long after it had collapsed on the mainland uncontrollable inflation was a major worry. New currency from Athens was promised almost daily but the weeks rolled by without any tangible results. The Commando incurred its own financial problems when the BMA currency failed to arrive from Italy. Within a short period of time trade on Corfu faded away as the old drachma became worthless. A banknote printing press was located in Corfu Town and, according to Philip Matters, "We ended up producing notes to the value of two million drachma. My brother Geoffrey* used these in a bar and every time he bought a drink the manager crossed off one of the noughts on the note and gave it back! Sgt Forbes, who received his weekly pay in millions of drachma, sympathised with a Greek neighbour who stood on an upper balcony tearing up the 'paper' money, watching hopelessly as the pieces fell into the street below. A further aggravation for the commandos developed when the mail and NAAFI supplies failed to arrive from Italy and commodities such as razor blades, soap and toothpaste became impossible to obtain.

Lt Col Sankey called a meeting of all the bank directors and leading business men, together with the Mayor and Prefect of Police, to decide on a course of action. The outcome was an embargo on the import of all food supplies as this source was a primary cause of the inflation. In addition, arrangements were made for the Swedish Red Cross to provide essential food supplies for eight successive days and to issue food on every third day thereafter until the circumstances improved. Finally, a representative committee was sent to Athens to clarify the monetary situation.

Relief supplies began to arrive from UNRRA at the beginning of November. Although many problems remained to be solved, life became easier as local authority and the National Greek Government in Athens began to function more effectively. On 23 November the Bank of Greece on Corfu took receipt of £5,000 worth of the new drachma which, at the UK exchange rate, was worth two billion drachma to the pound. Anyone wishing to exchange old drachma for new notes had to produce 5,000,000,000,000 for one new drachma. Few were able to take advantage of this offer as most of the old notes had been used for more basic purposes.

The Commando's task in Corfu was now considered to have been achieved

---

* Lt J.G.Matters, unit Intelligence Officer.

128

and with the grateful thanks and good wishes of many of the citizens the main body embarked for Italy on 10 November. A rearguard of two troops under command of Maj Matters was to remain on Corfu until such time as the Andarte on the mainland were disarmed or a relief force arrived to take their place. Lt Matters returned to Corfu to assist with the admistration and he also organized the cricket! The Corfiots have a tradition of playing proper cricket and at that time used equipment left behind by ships on pre-war visits to the island. The commandos played several games with a Corfu team on grassland near the town perimeter. Under Corfu cricket rules there are no boundaries and on one occasion Lt Matters drove the ball to mid-off and it went down Nikiforou Street where it was eventually found in the Tsirigotis Bar. By this time Lt Matters and his partner had stopped for a breather after scoring 25 runs!

In December the rearguard found itself involved in an incident which could have developed adversely. The 3/40th Regiment, under the command of Gen Zervas, found itself hemmed in by ELAS troops near the mainland port of Preveza. To avoid open conflict Gen Zervas decided to evacuate the regiment to Corfu and the British agreed to assist with the evacuation. Maj Matters provided covering patrols from the rearguard on the nights of 25 and 26 December while the Royal Navy ferried the troops to the island. Fortunately the entire operation was completed without a shot being fired. Thereafter conditions stabilised sufficiently to enable the rearguard to leave for Italy on 2 January 1945.

The Corfu administration was now taken over by the Allied Military Mission headed by Lt Col Barnes. Within a few days increasing friction between the political parties severely hindered the mission in carrying out its administrative tasks and the distribution of supplies. Conditions on the island rapidly deteriorated and incidents of looting, ill treatment and unrest became more prevalent. Furthermore, discipline in the Greek National Guard, in the early stages of re-forming, overshadowed by a strong force of ELAS in the Preveza area and a concentration of Albanian troops in Sarande, showed visible signs of collapse. As a result Lt Col Barnes signalled to the authorities in Italy for the return of a British presence on the island.

The task was given to 40 RM Commando, who returned to Corfu with orders to defend the island against attack or infiltration by ELAS or Albanian forces; to assist the Greek government in maintaining law and order and to aid in the distribution of UNRRA supplies. Once again the island was divided into four sectors each with its own sub-unit force. Patrols made irregular searches of likely landing areas and boarding parties, working with the Royal Navy, maintained a check on all shipping in the vicinity of Corfu. Various incidents of civil disobedience in Corfu town were dealt with by combined EDES and Commando patrols, and pickets guarded against the recurrence of minor disturbances. Dockers were pursuaded to recommence the unloading of food supplies in return for payment in BMA money and gradually the situation in

Lt Col R. W. Sankey and Mr Makaas, a representative of the Greek government, shake hands on the occasion of the transference of authority from the military to the cival power. November 1944. Photo: R. Sankey.

Capt W. Pook driving the only Bren carrier on Corfu. The passengers L to R are: Lt R. Thompson, Gen Zervas (less beard) and a senior EDES officer. Photo: W. Pook

CORFU, GREECE.
*Translation of text on photograph: "To my exceptional friend and comrade,
commander of the 40th Commandos, Lt Col Sankey DSO, DSC, RM. In order to
show my absolute respect, admiration and love to a heroic son of Great Britain.*

Corfu 3 – 2 – 1945
W. Zervas

Photo: R. Sankey.

Corfu Town returned to normal.

Further afield the situation was less settled and various sources of information indicated that EDES troops were terrorising the villagers at Eno Koravkiana. A Commando patrol sent to investigate found that a number of the villagers had been roughed-up and looting on an extensive scale had occured. The EDES brigade commander was warned that such actions would not be tolerated and the village was placed under Commando protection.

Lt Col Sankey arranged a meeting of the local leaders of all the political parties who recognised and accepted that law and order could only be maintained with the aid of a non political, well-disciplined and suitably armed National Guard while at the same time disbanding the politically biased Andartes.

The Greek Military Mission arrived from Athens and the call up of the National Guard and disbandment of the EDES troops on Corfu commenced simultaneously. Gen Zervas arrived on the island on 25 January and received a very warm welcome by the islanders. By mid-February the National Guard was sufficiently well-organised to take control from the former Andarte and the island authority was able to attend to its own administration. Confidence restored and with signs of stability having returned to the economy of the island, the unit's task on Corfu was finally completed.

The achievements of 40 RM Commando in Albania and on the Greek island of Corfu were of an exceptionally high standard. After the bitter fighting for Sarande the unit undertook the difficult and sensitive task of helping a subjected and impoverished people, embittered and divided by conflicting political factions, to work together to produce a more stable economy and peaceful future. Decisions taken by Lt Col Sankey to reduce tension between rival factions were not made without risk to those involved. He was aware that much depended on the conduct, determination and diplomacy of all his men and that they would be outnumbered if things went wrong. However, his judgement was sound and his officers, NCOs and marines proved themselves to be excellent ambassadors in implementing his decisions in the cause of law, order and stability. These actions did not go unnoticed and letters of appreciation were received from senior staff in Italy and as far away as England.

While 40 RM Commando was deployed in Corfu, Brig Churchill returned to England. Lt Col Tod of 2 Commando was promoted Brigadier and assumed command of 2 SS Brigade. During this period the Brigade was renamed 2 Commando Brigade to avoid any association with or similarity between the Commando organisation and the infamous German SS units. Towards the end of February 1945, 2 Commando Brigade HQ, 43 RM Commando and 2 Commando in Italy, moved into the line north of Ravenna while 9 Commando and 40 RM Commando were placed under command Headquarters Adriatic Brigade for training and operations.

Shortly before 40 RM Commando returned to Italy on 27 February, Lt Col Sankey received a letter from Brig Davey informing him that "It would be necessary to prepare for another battle". He intimated that the unit would require two months intensive training on their return to Italy and held out hopes of some reinforcements being available.

The following awards were approved for distinguished service during operations in the Italian theatre, Sarande and Corfu:

Lt Col R.W.Sankey	DSO	Capt D.G.Angus	MC
Capt P. Delap	MC	Cpl E.E.Palmer	MM
RQMS K.G.Frost	BEM		

Mentioned in Despatches:

Cpl C. Cooper MM, CSM K.S.Hawkins MM, Sgt H.W.Hill, Mne F.C.H.Jockham, Sgt E.A.Kinnear, CSM G. Malcom MM, Maj N.S.E.Maude, Lt R.Neale, Lt J.A.Smith, Mne C.G.Strong.

CHAPTER 10

27 February 1945 to 12 February 1946

40 RM Commando returns to Italy and moves north to Ravenna – Front line activity at the River Reno – 2 Commando Brigade attacks the 'Spit'- The assault crossing of the Menate Canal – Porto Cosini, reorganization, – Guards for prisoners of war and leave – Unconditional surrender of the German Army in Northern Italy – Return to England – Demobilisation and disbandment.

THE return to Italy was uneventful and the disembarkation at Bari was followed by a 15 mile truck journey south to the camp at Turi. Preparations for a two months training session were soon forgotten when it was announced that the Commando's stay at Turi had been cut to 18 days. Most of that time was absorbed by administration and local leave. A number of reinforcements joined the unit including Capt G.C.Belbin, Lt R. Wilkie and the Rev H.R. Grey RNVR.

Eleven months had passed since 40 Commando moved to the Adriatic. At that time F M Kesselring's 1943 Winter Line spanning the Garigliano and Rapido rivers – the Cassino stronghold – the mountains and Sangro river had hardly been dented and continued to serve as an effective barrier to Allied progress until Gen Alexander's spring offensive in May 1944. Polish troops entered Cassino on 18 May; the break-out from Anzio followed eight days later and the Americans motored into Rome on 4 June. The limelight was then switched from Italy to the Normandy beaches for the D-Day landings on 6 June. Seven Allied divisions were transferred from Italy to UK in December 1943 to prepare for the D-Day landings and a further six divisions were withdrawn in August 1944 for Operation Anvil/Dragoon (landings in the south of France).

While 2 Commando Brigade was committed to operations on the eastern side of the Adriatic, F M Kesselring prepared a new main line of defence between Pisa and Rimini. The Gothic Line, as it became known, proved to be as equally difficult to break through as the 1943 Winter Line. Gen Leese, commanding the Eighth Army, launched the 1st Armoured Division through the Rimini Gap on 25 August 1944. Further west, the Fifth Army attempted to force a way forward along the road routes by Il Giogo and the Futa Pass. Little progress was made and in the process the British 1st Armoured Division received a terrible hammering. By October, with Bologna still in German hands, it became apparent that another winter would be spent astride the Appennines. Once again F M Kesselring had skilfully utilised the natural defences of Italy to his advantage.

After desperate fighting on the east of the line to capture Rimini, Coriano and San Arcangelo di Romagna, the Eighth Army came up against strong German defences along the River Savio in the area of Cesena. By this time command of the Eighth Army had passed to Gen Mc Creery. A further hard slog established the Eighth Army on the River Senio, a tributary of the River Reno which enters the sea south of Lake Commachio. In the centre the Fifth Army had dug in south of Bologna and their defences ran south-west to a point a few miles north of Pisa. This line was held throughout the winter of 1944 and into the early spring of 1945. 40 RM Commando moved north to Ravenna on 20 March to relieve 2 Commando who were holding a section of the front line on the south bank of the River Reno. The terrain was in marked contrast to that experienced by the men in Albania. Here, the country-side was low-lying, flat and open. Slow-moving rivers, canals and dykes intersected the farmland on their way to the Gulf of Venice and occasional small clumps of trees, which cut the line of the horizon, provided limited cover from enemy eyes. North of the Reno a spit of land just over a mile wide extended along the coast for about eight miles to Porto Garibaldi. Westward of the spit the water-covered Valli di Commachio extended over an area of 40 square miles, ranging in depth from a few muddy inches to a fathom or more.

The enemy, occupying the 'Spit' on 40 RM Commando's immediate front, comprised the 1st Battalion 236th Regiment and Reconnaisance Squadron of the 162nd Division Turcomans (of Russian origin). In reserve, between the front line and Porto Garibaldi, the ground was held by 2nd Battalion 236th Regiment. They were supported by rocket projectors and multi-barrelled mortars (mebelwerfers), but there was no sign of heavy artillery or the Luftwaffe. The forward positions of 40 RM Commando were dug in along the river bank where the connecting bridge between the north and south bank and the ferry had been demolished some time previously. X Troop was located in one of these positions and the following notes written by Cpl Fisher, who was attached to X Troop from the Intelligence Section, describes the scene.

"Capt Belbin, the troop commander, took me to a farmhouse about 200 yards from the river from where it was possible to see the enemy positions similar to our own on the other bank. There were several dead horses in the area which were very smelly, particularly when the enemy lobbed mortars in amongst them. I moved forward to the river bank after dark and joined Sgt Mitchell's section who were living in trenches and dugouts in the near side of the bank. A tunnel had been dug through the bank to a slit trench on the waters edge and my task was to man the trench during the hours of darkness to observe any movement on the other side. Almost opposite my trench was a well-fortified machine-gun post. About 300 yards further back was a farmhouse from which I could occasionaly see the glint of binoculars."

"After some days I was recalled to X Troop HQ to meet two Sergeants from the Intelligence Corps. They represented the Psychological Warfare Bureau

Northern Italy. The Gothic Line December 1944.

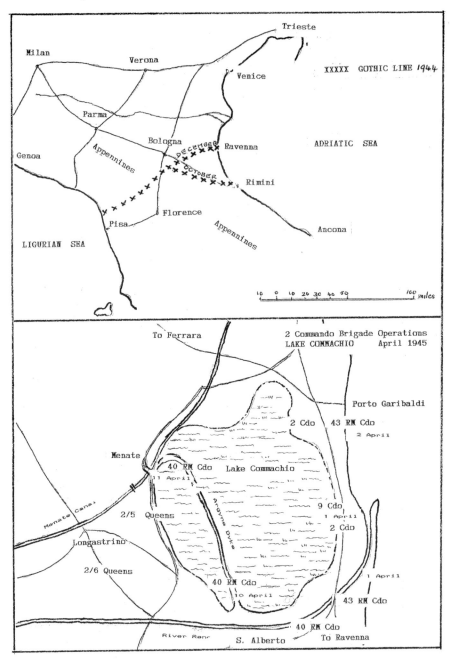

2 Commando Brigade unit dispositions April 1945

and wanted me to play four gramophone records to the Germans from my forward position. The records contained the sound of approaching tanks which then stopped and a voice relayed different messages in German to the enemy, concluding with the sound of tanks departing. I played the records every night but have no idea if they did any good. They brought some mortar retaliation and probably kept the Germans awake".

The major part of the nine days, from 22 to 31 March, was occupied with manning observation posts and being alert to any enemy movement. A major attack by the Germans was not anticipated but one could never be sure. Most of the time was spent maintaining a low profile during daylight hours – a tedious waiting game – and patrolling at night. Rations were brought forward after dark and one of the more pleasant duties undertaken by RQMS Frost was the night-time drive along the shell-pocked road to deliver the rum ration to the forward troops.

Towards the end of March, Brig Tod received orders from Gen McCreery, which gave 2 Commando Brigade the task of clearing the enemy from the 'Spit', the area of land between the sea and Lake Commachio. It was to be an extensive operation programmed over two days and involving the entire Brigade. The plan was known as Operation Roast and the codenames for the sixteen objectives to be captured were chosen from the books of the Bible. 40 RM Commando had a relatively minor role in this operation, a decision that probably stemmed from the short period of preparation available to the unit following its return to Italy.

The Commando was given three tasks. The first consisting of a diversionary assault crossing of the River Reno, to synchronize with an attack to be delivered by 9 Commando on two gun emplacements. The second was the provision of an immediate mobile reserve for the Brigade and to hold the existing line. The third consisted of a troop-strength assault force supported by two troops of tanks from the North Irish Horse, to clear enemy positions on the north bank of the Reno where it joins the western edge of the Spit.

43 RM Commando's task was to attack along the tongue on the seaward side of the Spit to secure a bridgehead over the Reno before continuing northwards up the Spit to a point 400 yards south of the Valetta Canal. 2 and 9 Commandos were to land on the west shore of the Spit with 2 Commando turning north to capture two bridges over the Bellocchio Canal and 9 Commando turning south to capture the previously mentioned gun emplacements. Both Army Commandos would then proceed north on the west side of the Spit to protect the left flank.

Lt Col Sankey moved his HQ forward at 2000 hours 1 April, into dugouts close to the pumping station by the Reno and 30 minutes later 40 RM Commando 'stood to'. The diversionary assault force was comprised of X and S Troops. P Troop provided the line holding party. A Troop would join forces with the North Irish Horse to clear part of the north bank of the river and Q and Y Troops, under the command of Capt F.Bristowe, formed the mobile reserve.

One section of MMGs from 43 RM Commando and the 3-inch mortars from 9 Commando were placed under command of Lt G. Russell.

Covering fire was provided by R Troop. This composite troop commanded by Capt Pook was formed specifically for the occasion and had the task of covering any noise created by X Troop while they were driving stakes into the river bank in preparation for the diversionary attack. The enemy retaliated with mortar fire which fell mainly in a small area of woodland occupied by Q Troop.

At 0455 hours, 43 RM Commando passed through Y Troop's positions for the start of the attack. The front remained relatively quiet until the enemy again retaliated with a bombardment of rockets and shelling, which lasted from 0520 to 0645 hours. Spandau fire was directed at the forward troop positions from the opposite river bank and the enemy shelling was concentrated on the seaward side of the line. Instinctively Lt Col Sankey ordered number six section to vacate its well sand-bagged position in this sector. Moments later the post was demolished and that alongside it severely damaged by a 88mm shell or missile of similar destructive force!

It was now time for X Troop to carry out the diversionary attack. The men commenced to haul the assault boats over the top of the river bank with the aid of ropes fastened to the prow of each boat and passed round the stakes at the waters edge. Some of the boats foundered on obstructions and did not reach the water. However, rifles secured to dummy figures in the other assault boats were fired by the simple process of pulling on lengths of cord attached to the triggers. Supported by Bren gun and mortar fire from positions along the bank and 3-inch mortars and artillery further back the ruse proved effective in drawing a heavy concentration of enemy fire onto this forward area.

Five miles up river A Troop, commanded by Lt L.Marsh, had crossed to the north bank of the Reno in Fantails* and storm boats and moved off at 0730 hours to attack "Mark". Arriving at the first dyke they discovered that it was wider and deeper than expected. Sappers and commandos covered the bottom of the dyke with fascines to provide a firm base for the tanks. These proved ineffective. The leading tank, attempting to climb the further bank, bogged down in the loose crumbly soil. Additional fascines had to be carried forward and plugged into the gap before the metal tracks of the tanks could obtain sufficient purchase to climb out of the ditch.

It was almost 1330 hours before A Troop was able to move forward again. Working in two-section groups the commandos cleared the enemy fox-holes along the bank of the river while the Fantails provided cover on the left flank and a tank shelled a nearby house as a precautionary measure. Enemy rifle and machine-gun fire from this direction increased in intensity and the forward group, who were fully exposed and in the line of fire, suffered three casualties. It became necessary to put down 2-inch mortar smoke and HE to cover them

---

* Amphibious armoured personnel carriers.

while they moved the wounded to the protection of the Fantails. Mne Williamson helped to neutralise the enemy fire during this time by standing in full view of the enemy while firing at their positions with his Bren gun.

After a further pounding from the tanks and A Troop's weapons, a group of the enemy in this locality decided to surrender. They came forward through the minefields under cover of a white flag but a few had the misfortune to be shot by their own men. Those who managed to find a way through the mine-field were taken prisoner. Shortly after this encounter Lt Marsh was wounded and Lt E.Seales assumed command of the troop.

Attempts to communicate with Commando HQ by wireless proved very difficult and any messages received were mostly unintelligible over the noise of the tank engines. Contact with HQ was eventually established on the 38 set in the leading tank. The commandos found that the most effective way of directing the tank gunners onto the enemy was to fire a round of tracer by rifle in the appropriate direction. The enemy was still very active and in an exchange of small arms fire Mne P.Griffen was killed. Lt Seales divided A Troop into three fresh groups and continued the advance parallel to the river towards their objective. The leading Fantail became bogged and there was a pause while the second Fantail found a better approach closer to the bank. Shortly after this incident the third Fantail was put out of action by a Tellermine. They were now very close to "Mark" where, in the final assault to secure this objective Mnes P.L.Coombes and W.I. Gorrie were killed and a further six marines were wounded. Towards late evening A Troop made contact with E Troop of 43 RM Commando.

The reserve troops were not required during this phase of the operation apart from escorting prisoners to the rear. R Troop usefully employed their PIAT teams against an enemy OP but were unable to assist A Troop with observed support fire as the enemy entrenched on the opposite bank, would have dealt swiftly with anyone showing themselves above ground. S Troop MMGs finally ceased firing at 0540 hours, each gun having used 16 belts while the 3-inch mortars ceased fire at 0610 hours having fired 400 rounds per gun. The mortar base plates required re-bedding twice during the shoot. All the Commando units accomplished their tasks successfully but not without difficulty or loss. Both 2 and 9 Commandos had to combat the glutinous mud and water of Lake Commachio, dragging storm-boats and wading through the clinging liquid to reach their landing points on the Spit. Approaching their objectives from the rear they took the enemy by surprise.

On day two 2 April, the clearance of the Spit continued with 43 RM Commando, on the right flank, moving over open ground towards the Valetta Canal. C Troop leading the advance was brought to a halt by the fire of a number of enemy machine-guns. Cpl T.Hunter worked his way closer to the German Spandau positions and, firing his Bren gun from the hip, climbed onto a mound of rubble from where he continued to harass the enemy. His courageous action held the attention of the enemy long enough to enable

A forward position on the bank of the River Reno. Long periods of watching and waiting. Photo: R. Jaques.

X Troop unloading ammunition prior to the assault on the "Spit".
Photo: RM Museum

Storm boat, used for crossing the River Reno and negotiating parts of Lake Commachio. Photo: RM Museum

C Troop to move to a more secure position but he did not survive those precious minutes. Cpl Hunter was awarded a posthumous Victoria Cross for his selfless action.

By nightfall on 3 April the Brigade had secured its objectives and established forward positions a short distance south of the Valetta Canal. In the days that followed patrols probed forward to the west of the Brigade's positions and four small islands within Lake Commachio were cleared by the Special Boat Section. Although 2 Commando Brigade now held the "Spit", the Germans continued to hold the ground to the left of Lake Commachio, at Menate and Longastrino. The task of capturing the two strong-points was given to the 169th Infantry Brigade with 40 RM Commando temporarily attached to lead the assault across the Argine Dyke and Menate Canal. Operation Impact as the assault was known, was programmed to commence on the night of 10 April 1945.

The plan required 40 RM Commando to capture the bridge and pumping station at Menate and, having secured these objectives, to exploit along the Strada della Pioppa. Troops of the 2nd/5th, the 2nd/6th and 2nd/7th Queens were to move up in Fantails at first light. The 2nd/5th were to move over the bridge previously secured by 40 RM Commando and capture Menate while the 2nd/6th were to capture Longastrino. The 2nd/7th Queens were held in reserve. The Germans had flooded the area to the east of Menate and Longastrino by blowing a gap in the bank of the Argine Dyke. The dyke actually followed a line to the north-west, converging on the Menate Canal very close to Menate and 40 RM Commando's objectives. Lt Col Sankey decided that the dyke would form the best line of approach to the objectives. The Commando would move forward under cover of darkness, crossing the gap in the dyke and the canal in six-man rubber assault boats. The boats would be carried by the leading troop.

During the afternoon of 10 April the Commando moved to the assembly area where the troops were joined by a section of Field Company Royal Engineers, two Forward Observation Officers and two Little Johns. The FOOs would direct the artillery and air support and, if Italian Partisan information was correct, the Engineers would have the task of clearing mines from the gap in the dyke.

The column moved forward at 2330 hours, led by the Royal Engineers and three Bren groups from Y Troop who, in addition to being the advance guard, would assist with the lifting of mines. P Troop were next in line, having the Menate bridge as their objective. They were followed by X Troop who were to secure the pumping station. Tac HQ with A Troop in reserve were a short distance behind followed by Main HQ with the RAP. Q Troop, carrying the assault boats, and S Troop in the rear.

The night was dry and clear and the moon, screened by a thin layer of cloud provided sufficient diffused light in which to move without stumbling over unseen hazards. Crossing the River Reno had taken longer than expected and it became necessary to push forward along the dyke at a pace which at times resembled a speed march. Arrangements had been made for the RAF to provide a diversion at this time with a bombing run over Menate and Longastrino. The marker-flares also illuminated the men on the dyke and their only hope of avoiding the attention of enemy observation posts was to remain perfectly still until the flares were extinguished. It was an uncomfortable feeling and the seconds dragged interminably knowing that it only required one observant sentry to catch them well and truly in the open.

The critical moment passed, the column continued its progress and Y Troop reached the gap in the dyke at approximately 0130 hours. A combination of thick mud and water defeated all attempts at wading and a call was made for Q Troop to bring the assault boats forward. The boats were laid side by side in the bottom of the gap to form a pontoon type bridge. One of the Bren groups, led by Lt Atkinson crossed first to provide cover for the remainder. About half of Y Troop had crossed the gap when a mine exploded, wounding Capt D. Thomson, Lt Atkinson and the entire Bren group, a further six marines and one Engineer.

Sick Berth Attendants removed the wounded while the sappers prodded a path forward along the top of the bank. They found numerous mines but questioned the advisability of lifting these in the dark. Lt Park, who had taken command of the troop, gave instructions to cut the trip-wires, leaving the mines undisturbed in order to save time. Surprisingly the mine explosion did not draw any fire or flares from the enemy positions. Eventually a narrow lane was cleared but it had turned 0300 hours before Y, P, Tac HQ and X Troops could continue with all possible speed towards the bridge. The dyke now turned sharply south-west with the Menate Canal running along the right hand side. An enemy sentry shouted a challenge across the flooded ground. Small arms fire started to crack through the air overhead and soon afterwards Lt J.D.G.Pegrum was killed. Arriving in view of the bridge Lt Park ordered Y Troop to take up fire positions along the dyke and P Troop moved up on their left. Maj N.M.Porter,commanding the troop, carried out a quick reconnaissance and notified his intention to Lt Park that he intended to cross the canal assisted by Q Troop.

The German defences now wide awake had opened up with 88mm and 75 mm guns, 81mm mortars and Spandaus. Maj Porter called Lt Wedgewood and Lt Sanford forward for a final briefing and impressed on them the importance of crossing the canal. Enemy rifle and machine-gun fire intensified as Maj Porter accompanied by his Troop HQ, Lt Wedgewood and 3 Section moved down the bank. Lt Wedgewood attempted to cross but found it too deep and moved further left where the group were able to wade and swim to the other side. Dawn was approaching.

Y troop engaged in a vigorous exchange of fire with the enemy in an effort to divert their attention away from P Troop. Grenades were thrown across the canal and 2-inch mortar fire was put down along the opposite bank. About 12 Germans ran to the far side of the bridge and the cover of some buildings as P Troop fought their way towards the bridge. Enemy small-arms fire from positions south of the canal inflicted casualties amongst P Troop support groups including Lt Wedgewood, but the ferocity of the enemy fire made it impossible to approach the wounded despite Bren fire and mortar smoke being laid. Lt Park of Y Troop made a wireless call to TAC HQ for a Red Cross flag and medical orderly. Pte Calder walked along the canal bank fully exposed to enemy fire. He called across the canal to a German NCO not to shoot and then waved a stretcher party forward to evacuate the casualties. Shots were fired in their direction and Cpl Whickstead was hit in the shoulder.

Gradually the enemy targets became more discernible as the morning light strengthened. A German machine-gun in a farm house on the left flank, which had been particularly bothersome, was silenced but casualties in Y Troop increased as they continued the fire fight and the 38 set (wireless), which had already been damaged by shrapnel, was finally rendered useless.

Maj Porter had placed his P Troop support group forward as far as possible to cover the assault but they and another group led by Sgt Hill, now found themselves exposed to a group of Germans entrenched to their rear. One by one they were 'picked off'. Lt Wedgewood, although wounded a second time, continued to retaliate with his Colt automatic.

On the far side of the canal, CSgt W.J.A.Harvey moved his assault group to cover L/Cpl Vickers' section while they attacked across the bridge. Vickers was wounded by small arms fire before reaching the west side and almost immediately the Germans counter attacked with infantry and a self propelled gun to regain the bridge. It was discovered later that the bridge had been prepared for demolition but small arms fire had sheared through the wires. Y Troop was close enough to the armoured gun to have engaged it with PIAT's but both projectors had been hit by shrapnel and were useless. The assault party continued firing until, with ammunition expended, CSgt Harvey attempted to withdraw. The severity of the enemy fire made this impossible and both he and Sgt W.Scott were killed. The remainder of the assault group were wounded and Mnes Harwood and Mullins were taken prisoner.

A group of German infantry moved with the SP gun to the pumping station. About this time the Fantails of the 2nd/5th Queens appeared and the Germans on the bridge panicked. Harwood and Mullins were quick to react and picking up rifles demanded the Germans surrender. The support groups of P and Q Troops were still engaged in the difficult task of providing covering fire for the assault group and trying to neutralise the enemy positions to their rear. No 4 Section moved up to reinforce Maj Porter's group but a shell exploded close to the section killing Cpl J.W.Woodall. Two more of the section were wounded. Shortly afterwards Maj Porter and Lt Wedgewood were both killed.

X Troop had extreme difficulty in moving through accurate enfilade spandau fire to the point where they were to cross the canal. According to Cpl Fisher "The German machine-gun emplacements were right on the canal edge and in a house about half a mile further on. Capt Belbin decided we needed assistance to make the crossing but HQ could not be contacted on the W/T. All that could be heard was a call from a marine in P Troop to say that his section had crossed the canal, he was wounded and the rest had been taken prisoner! I was sent back to find HQ to ask for some air or artillery support. I ran along the edge of the flooded area – the going was easier – got blasted over twice – found Maj Matters and told him what was wanted. Had only time to tell Capt Belbin on return that the request had been passed when the RAF came over and blasted the house".

The air strike, ordered by Lt Col Sankey on the house and pumping station, was delivered by four Spitfires at approximately 0930 hours. Under cover of this diversion Capt Belbin swam across the canal towing a line constructed out of X Troop's toggle ropes. Cpl Fisher, aided by one of the men in his section, helped to support the rope while the remainder of the troop hauled themselves across to the other side. This was the first occasion that 40 RM Commando made practical use of toggle ropes in action. Assault groups moved along the canal winkling out the Spandau posts while Capt Belbin led the main assault, first on the house and then on the pumping station. The commandos accounted for 19 prisoners including three German officers, and the SP gun which they used to good purpose against the German positions!

Q Troop was now ordered forward to take over the bridge and power house. There was still considerable opposition and the troop incurred 12 casualties in the process. A Troop was brought forward to secure the position, with the remnants of P and Y Troops – who had combined forces – and the Fantails

X Troop Commander, Capt G. C. Belbin wearing his trophy – a German officer's cap – after the capture of the Menate pumping station.

Lt Col Sankey and his Command Post team on the Argyne Dyke following the capture of the bridges and pumping station at Menate. Photos: Imperial War Museum

carrying the 2nd/5th Queens. X Troop patrolled westward towards noon, capturing a fortified house and taking 14 prisoners. Later in the afternoon the troop dug-in around another building and track junction to provide fire support to the 2nd/5th Queens who were about to attack the second bridge. While they were establishing their position a German SP gun shelled the house, knocked out one of the 2-pounder Little Johns and wounded Cpl R. Laisham

Intermittent fire continued until 2100 hours by which time the Queens had cleared the last of the enemy from Menate and were mopping up in Longastrino. Shortly after dark, Capt Belbin, his MOA "gunman" and Capt Pook were on their way to a house near the pumping station to attend a CO's O Group. They had unknowlingly entered a minefield, tripped a mine and all three were wounded. A stretcher party attempting to pick them up detonated another mine, resulting in further casualties. Subsequently Cpl E. A. Pitt died of wounds. The Commando losses at the end of the day were 27 all ranks killed and 45 wounded.

On 13 April, the Commando moved to Porto Corsini*, a small village on the coast near Ravenna to clean up, sort out arms and equipment and catch up on lost sleep. The battle had been hard and bloody but the objectives had been achieved. Both P and Y Troops were severely depleted by casualties and Lt Col Sankey decided as a temporary measure to reorganize the unit into three fighting troops and a heavy weapons troop. A small group of reinforcements who joined the unit at Porto Corsini included Lt I. J. Pook, whose brother Bill had by this time been evacuated to hospital.

The capture of Menate and Longstrino formed part of the opening stages of the final offensive in which the Eighth Army forced a way through the flooded areas to Argenta. Then on to Ferrara with Padua and Venice as the next objectives. On the left flank, the Fifth Army mounted a major offensive between Pistoia and Bologna towards Modena and Parma. After many months the tenacious German defence of the Gothic Line, first by FM Kesselring and then by Gen von Vientinghoff, had finally been broken. The German divisions which evade capture fell back rapidly to the River Po and beyond as the Allied advance gained momentum.

Lt Col Sankey said farewell to the unit on 19 April on his departure, under the Python Scheme†, to UK where he was to take command of the Infantry Training Centre Royal Marines (ITCRM), Lympstone. During his one year in command of the unit he re-built and led 40 RM Commando in two major actions. The unit had suffered a considerable number of casualties. There had been few opportunities for rest or relaxation and living conditions were, at the best, rough and ready. Even so the morale of the men had remained steadfastly

---

* Known also as Marina di Ravenna

† Python Scheme. To repatriate married men who had been overseas for over three years four months. Lt Col Sankey had been away from the UK since early 1941.

high.

Shortly after Lt Col Sankey arrived at ITCRM he met Sgt Forbes, who was passing through the camp on his way to join the Officer Cadet Training Unit at Thurlestone. After three years service with 40 RM Commando in the successive ranks of LCpl to Sgt, John Forbes had been recommended for a Commission.

Lt Col De'ath DSO arrived in Italy on 1 July 1944 to take command. He implemented a new training programme and reduced the paper work which had accumulated while the unit was in the line at Commachio. Maj J. R. Rushforth, a recent reinforcement, assumed the post of second in command and Maj Manners returned to the UK.

The war in Italy had now reached its conclusion. The operations of 2 Commando Brigade along the Spit at Lake Commachio and 40 Commando's assault crossing of the Menate Canal had helped pave the way for the advance of 78th Division and 56th Division through the Argenta Gap. This valuable contribution by the Commando in the final phase of the war in Italy was duly recognised by Gen McCreery who, on 1 May, signalled Brig Tod – "Well done the Commandos".

Gen von Vietinghoff agreed to the terms of unconditional surrender required by F.M. Alexander and these became effective in Italy on 2 May. Hundreds of thousands of Germans became prisoners of war. The announcement was greeted with delight in Porto Cosini amid the sound of ships' sirens and car horns. In a more relaxed atmosphere leave parties went to Florence and Rome while others on duty in Porto Corsini were detailed as guards on prisoner-of-war compounds. The area was flooded with German prisoners and practically every unit had to take some responsibility for looking after them. The Commando moved to Ballaria on 23 May and assumed the custody of 1,000 German SS prisoners held in No 60 POW Cage. Further numbers of light wounded rejoined the unit from hospital, Y Troop was reformed and the last of the Python Scheme personnel departed for England.

Lt Col De'ath received instructions to make preparations for the Commando to move to Naples on 15 June. It did not take long for the news to reach all ranks and the realisation that the unit would be returning home gave impetus to the packing and loading of stores and equipment. Vehicles and tentage were returned to supply depots and an effort was made to dispose of foreign pistols and other illegal souvenirs that had been acquired over two years of travelling. Even the interminable train journey in cattle trucks to the Torre-Annunziata rest camp at Naples, could not dampen the high spirits. On 19 June the unit embussed for Naples harbour to embark on the Carnarvon Castle. By chance the authors father Lt Col C.W Beadle MC, MM, who had served in France, North Africa and Italy, was returning home on the same ship. A number of the unit wounded were in hospital in Naples, among them Mne Shaw who was recovering from a gun-shot wound received at the Menate Canal. Capt Delap made a tour of the wards to ensure that he and others who could be moved safely, were taken to the sick berth in the Carnarvon Castle.

Arriving at Southampton on 26 June, the unit moved to the Commando Group Reception Camp at Basingstoke where elements of other Commando units were already established. A few days later 40 RM Commando paraded for inspection and a "Welcome Home" address by Maj Gen G.E. Wildman-Lushington CBE, General Officer Commanding the Commando Group. Leave was then given to all ranks.

Maj W. D. Read assumed command on 15 July and a gradual thinning-out of the unit commenced with the dispersal of officers and other ranks to 45 and 46 RM Commandos and the Holding Operations Commando at Wrexham. Brig D. Mills-Roberts DSO, MC, who succeeded Brig Tod as Commander of 2 Commando Brigade, visited 40 RM Commando shortly before Maj Read carried out a final reorganization into B, C, D and HQ Troops.

The final parade of 2 Commando Brigade took place in Winchester on Thursday 1 September 1945. On that day 40 and 43 RM Commandos with 2 and 9 Commandos assembled together and, after marching through the city, attended a 'service of thanksgiving for victory and dedication for the future', at the Cathedral. A special order of service was used with the Rev R. Hook, Chaplain to 43 RM Commando and the Rev R. Thomas, Chaplain to 2 Commando, officiating.

According to an item in The Hampshire Chronicle of 1 September 1945 "The salute was taken by Lt Gen Sir Robert Sturges KBE CB DSO., who was General Officer Commando Group when the Brigade was overseas. At their head was the band of the Royal Marines Eastney under the direction of Capt F.V.Dunn MVO, ARAM., Director of Music, Portsmouth. The white helmets of the bandsmen striking a bright and somewhat unfamiliar note, but one typifying the return of peace. They were loudly cheered by the very considerable crowd which had gathered in the streets. Among those accompanying Gen Sturgess were Brig R.J.F. Tod DSO, Brig T.H. Jameson DSO (Commander Portsmouth Division RM), Brig T.F. Durnford-Slater DSO, Brig D.Mills-Roberts DSO,MC, and Brig T.B.L. Churchill MC (the first Commander of the Brigade)".

The unit moved to Tichbourne House, Alresford where the amalgamation of 40 and 43 RM Commandos took place on 12 September. A representative troop from this combined force took part in the Thanksgiving Parade in London on 17 September. Now the wheel had turned almost full circle. On 24 September 1945 the new formation became the Royal Marines Commando (2 Commando Brigade). Countless events and changes had taken place since the first morning parade at Deal when Lt Col Phillips called the Royal Marines Commando to attention. The unit had seen active service in France, Sicily, Italy, Yugoslavia, Albania and Greece. Victory had been won at great cost. Between 19 August 1942 and the end of hostilities 40 RM Commando lost 203 all ranks killed. This total includes 52 all ranks of T Company who were lost at sea in HMS *Fidelity*. The names of these young men are recorded on memorials set in tranquil surroundings overlooking the former battle-fields and the sea. Their graves, maintained by the Commonwealth War Graves Commission, are bordered by British flowers and roses, to keep a link with home.

Details of Honours and Awards are listed at Appendix D.

Details of casualties 1942–45 are listed in Appendix E.

A total of 421 all ranks required hospital treatment for wounds.

Further reductions in the size of the unit continued and the remnants moved to Wrexham towards the end of 1945. CSgt Morris, the last of the original unit, left Wrexham on 12 February 1946 to return to civilian life. Thirteen months later a new 40 RM Commando emerged, to serve in a wider role covering a greater range of activities in most regions of the world.

The veterans of 40 RM Commando are members of a thriving old comrades association. Details may be obtained from the Secretary Mr A. W. Saunders c/o Royal Marines, Eastney, Hampshire.

CHAPTER 11

13 February 1946 to 30 June 1948

The post war period – Demobilisation of Army Commandos – Redesignation of 44 Royal Marine Commando to 40 Commando Royal Marines – Internal Security duties in Hong Kong – Termination of the British mandate in Palestine.

THE 3rd Commando Brigade, comprising 1 and 5 Army Commandos, 42 R M Commando and 44 R M Commando, deployed from India to Hong Kong and the New Territories mid September 1945. 44 R M Commando, under the command of Lt Col D.B. Drysdale MBE, was to spend the first four months in Kowloon where the under-strength police force was fighting a losing battle to maintain law and order. The town was in chaos and robbery, gambling and drug trafficking were rife. The unit's primary tasks were to stem the gambling and drug trafficking and to provide guards for the Japanese prisoner of war compounds. These duties contrasted sharply with the battle-training under-taken only weeks previously during Brigade preparations to launch an assault against the Japanese occupied coast of Malaya.

The Brigade, under the command of Brig C.R.Hardy DSO,OBE., had moved to India after successful operations in the Arakan to prepare for landings on the coast of Malaya. These preparations were short lived. The uranium bomb annihilated Hiroshima on 6 August; the start of the Russian offensive into Manchuria on 8 August and the plutonium bomb, which devastated Nagasaki on 9 August, culminated in the surrender of the Japanese.

Hostilities in Europe and the Far East at an end, the British armed forces commenced the process of demobilisation and a return to peace-time strength. The Army Commandos and other specialist units were among the first to stand down. The Royal Marines also reduced their commando establishment but retained 3 Commando Brigade. The Brigade was strengthened by the arrival of 45 Royal Marine Commando from UK in the spring of 1946 and it was not until the following October that numbers 1 and 5 Commandos were eventually disbanded. A decision was taken at this time to change the name of the Brigade to the 3rd Commando Brigade Royal Marines and the commando units were renamed 42, 44 and 45 Commando Royal Marines*.

The Corps war-time strength of nearly 74,000 men had by 1946 shrunk to a little over 13,000 including the Commando Brigade. Government pressure to reduce armed forces expenditure still further, led in due course to the Harwell

---

* normally referred to as 3 Commando Brigade (3 Cdo Bde RM), 44 Commando (44 Cdo RM) etc.

Committee – engaged on the task of examining the structure of the Services – to recommend a guillotining of the entire Corps. This drastic step was opposed by the Admiralty, who in turn made a counter proposal for a proportional reduction of the Royal Marines based on sea service requirements and the disbandment of the Commando Brigade.

The survival of the Brigade was due in no small measure to the resourcefulness of Lt Gen Sir Leslie Hollis. Shortly after taking office as CGRM in 1949, he negotiated with the Admiralty for the retention of the Brigade, while ceding a reduction of Corps manpower to 10,300 with the closure of Chatham Division.

On 7 February 1946, the Supreme Allied Commander South-East Asia, Adm Lord Louis Mountbatten GCVO, KCB, DSO, visited Hong Kong and inspected 3 Commando Brigade. A week later 44 Commando moved inland to the Kowloon frontier, where each troop was self contained in its own location. Primary tasks were to apprehend bandits and prevent smuggling across the border. The Troops also maintained a watchful eye on Chinese units moving through the colony for shipment to Manchuria, where they were to fight the Chinese Nationalists. Whenever possible the commandos assisted the local people, particularly the sick, and provided basic medicines and dressings. Mepacrine tablets and gentian violet, the marines panacea for all ills, were particularly popular!

Returning to Hong Kong island the Commando was quartered in Murray Barracks, providing guards and escorts for VIPs. This move of short duration was followed by a two month stay in Stanley Fort on the southern side of the island. Sgt C. White, who had last seen action with 40 Commando in Yugoslavia, joined the unit and was posted to A Troop. His primary duty was looking after the Japanese prisoners of war in Stanley prison while they were facing trial at the Supreme Court in Victoria. Having experienced the rigours of being a prisoner of war in Germany he was able to appreciate the situation and make comparisons with his own confinement behind the wire. In a letter describing his duties he wrote "We gave the Japanese prisoners a session of drill each day and found that they were quick on the uptake and soon drilling like a King's Squad. Every evening after exercise they were grouped together – about a hundred of them – and sang in English 'There'll always be an England'. They had strong voices and it sounded good. Those accused of minor crimes were allowed out to our billets where they cooked and repaired the plumbing and wiring. Some of them were quite skilled tradesmen. Of course there were a number who were found guilty of major war crimes and they were hung!"

" A few weeks later I was posted to S Troop and sent with a detachment to the border for anti smuggling patrols. We occupied a pre-war American Missionary School at Clearwater Bay where we rounded up six Japanese cavalry horses. As I was TQMS I put the animals on our ration indent and drew fodder for them. A marine who was an ex blacksmith, found some horseshoes and, having rigged up a forge, soon had them shod. The next task was to make

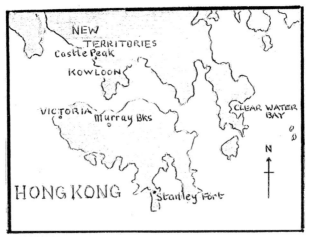

Castle Peak Hong Kong 16 March 1947. The flag of 44 RM Commando is lowered and the unit becomes 40 Commando RM, under the command of Lt Col Houghton MC. Photo: G. Fryer

some pack-saddles. On these we strapped a Vickers machine-gun, a three inch mortar and ammunition. Then off we would go for a week at a time into the hills. I enjoyed this period. It was a great life."

42 and 45 Commandos performed similar duties to those carried out by 44 Commando. By the time 44 Commando moved to Castle Peak in the west corner of the New Territories in October, Lt Col P.R. Matters, second in command of 40 RM Commando in 1944-45, had assumed command of the unit and Brig J.N.G. Wills OBE, of the Brigade.

Security arrangements were intensified during the Chinese New Year celebrations, when every Chinaman is honour-bound to pay his debts and carry more cash than usual. However there were no excessive disturbances or incidents and as the months passed the civilian authorities gradually resumed their pre-war strength and assumed greater responsibility for law and order.

On 16 March 1947, Lt Col R.D.Houghton OBE, MC, who, it will be remembered, was second-in-command of 40 Commando in 1942 assumed command of 44 Commando. This was considered an appropriate time to revive 40 Commando, a decision that was confirmed by the CGRM before Lt Col Houghton left UK. The intention was to perpetuate a Commando, representative of the Dieppe Raid and the Italian theatre-of-war, in addition to recognising 40 Commando's major contribution towards the Allied victory in Europe. In a simple but striking ceremony at Castle Peak, in the presence of Brig Wills and the officers and men of 44 Commando, a resumé of the history of the unit and its valuable contribution to the Arakan battle was read to the assembled company. On conclusion the flag of 44 Commando was lowered and the colours of 40 Commando were hoisted to the masthead.

The Brigade had been in the colony for nearly two years when all units received orders to make preparations for a move to the Mediterranean. Part of the farewell proceedings included a party for 500 Chinese children from poor families. The Naval C-in-C, V Adm Sir Dennis Boyd visited each unit, calling on 40 Commando on 7 May. This was the first time that the Commando had paraded since March but by all accounts the drill and steadiness in the intense heat would have impressed a Kings Squad. As if to match the mood of the many who were leaving Hong Kong, embarkation in the SS.*Strathnaver* on 17 May was carried out in heavy rain. However the dampened spirits of the morning were brightened in the afternoon by the band of the West Yorks Regiment, accompanied by impromptu singing and the farewells of a large crowd on the wharf as the ship cast off. The Brigade was on its way to Malta.

The island of Malta is familiar to many marines who served with the Commando Brigade in the fifties, but prior to that it had mainly been a port of call for 'big ship' marines. The following extract from a news item in the 'Times of Malta' published prior to its arrival, summarises the Brigade's commitments on the George Cross island: "For the first time, Royal Marines are taking over the garrison duties in their entirety, replacing British infantry who, along with the Royal Navy, had come to be regarded as 'Britains Ambassadors-at-

Lt Col R. D. Houghton MC, on assuming command of 40 Commando Royal Marines, 16 March 1947.

Brig J. N. G. Wills OBE, presenting a 3 Cdo Bde shield to the Commissioner of Police for Hong Kong, to commemorate the transfer of authority from the military to the civil power. Photos: R. D. Houghton.

large'. The 3rd Commando Brigade will form an integral part of the Malta Command, under Major General K.C.Davidson, General Officer Commanding Malta".

On arrival 40 Commando occupied Imtarfa Barracks, 42 Commando moved into St Andrew Barracks at St Julians and 45 Commando was located at Gdhira. Brigade HQ personnel were housed first at St Patricks Barracks but it proved too large for its numbers and they moved to more suitable premises in St George's Bay. Ceremonial parades loomed close on the horizon, and the first of these was provided for Maj Gen Davidson on 26 June by 40 and 45 Commandos. On completion the GOC commented favourably on a first class display and appeared well satisfied with what he had seen.

Almost before the brasswork on the equipment had a chance to tarnish, preparations were in hand for a parade of special significance. Maj Gen R.E. Laycock CB, DSO., visited Malta to say farewell to the Brigade on relinquishing his command as Chief of Combined Operations. Laycock was the epitome of the commando spirit. He had raised 8 Commando in 1940, in which one officer and 12 ORs of the Royal Marines had served. Also, 'Layforce' was prominent in actions at Bardia, North Africa and Suda Bay, Crete, in 1941. Perhaps his most prominent exploit was the unsuccessful but nonetheless daring attempt to capture or kill General Rommel in his HQ at Beda Littoria, in North Africa.

Maj Gen Laycock visited each of the Commandos between 2 and 5 July and dined with the officers in 40 Commando's Officers Mess before returning to England. In a letter to the CGRM, Lt Gen R.A.D. Brooks CB, CMG, DSO., he wrote "I can only say that the happiest memories of my three years with the Commandos and my three and a half years as Chief of Combined Operations were those concerning my relations with the Royal Marines, a Corps for which I have ever felt unbounding admiration".

The weather during August and September was glorious and the happy smiles of the married men announced the arrival of their families. But life was not entirely idyllic. Malta, referred to in a poem as "This silver isle set in a silver sea", was more familiarly known to service personnel as the island of "Bells,yells and smells". Only a few services quarters were available. The cost of rented accommodation and food was high and drinking water was rationed. Nevertheless the commando fraternity intended to make the most of the conditions prevailing and social functions were arranged to welcome the wives and children.

The Pembroke ranges were used extensively for small arms courses and all troops worked hard at fieldcraft and battle drills in preparation for a joint services two-day defence exercise in September. The all important ceremonial duties necessitated regular periods of parade drill each week but there were opportunities for those who used their initiative to escape for a while to exercise their talents at more challenging pursuits. Sgts Miles and Hollingsworth, lucky men, set forth for a mountaineering course in Austria.

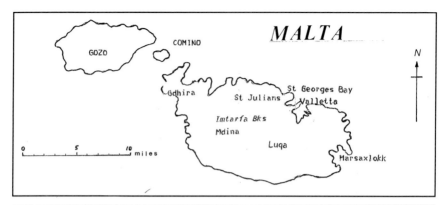

The Old Capital of Mdina

Valletta, Capital of Malta, looking across Marsamxett Harbour. Photos: Author

156

Training areas were restricted by the limited space on Malta and Lt Col Houghton in company with the COs of 42 and 45 Commandos visited Tripolitania to assess alternative facilities.

The CGRM, Lt Gen Sir Dallas Brooks, visited Malta in November at the personal invitation of Adm Sir Algernon-Willis, C-in-C Mediterranean, to inspect the Royal Marines of the Fleet and 3 Commando Brigade. 40 Commando was in Tripoli and after lunching with the officers of 45 Commando on 26 November he flew from Luqua airport to Castel-Benito to watch the unit exercising in the desert. The Commando had established a base camp in an old Italian barracks in Tarhuna but spent most of the deployment living in the sand practising the various elements of desert warfare. The men soon discovered that the heat of the day changed to extreme cold at night and most slept in their two-man bivouacs fully clothed and covered by two blankets.

Returning to Malta in LST HMS *Dieppe*, preparations were made to take over the duties of Governor's Palace Guard from 45 Commando. Time was also found for sport and Christmas festivities. The latter were hardly over when Ex Rumpus – an emergency embarkation of the Brigade was activated on 28 December. HMS *Triumph, Ajax* and *Dieppe* sailed within 10 hours and the exercise was considerd to be wholly successful. It proved to be a useful preparation for the men of 40 Commando who, in late January, were alerted to an operational requirement at the eastern end of the Mediterranean. Within hours the advance party was sailing towards Palestine in HMS *Cheviot* and the main body followed in HMS *Phoebe* and LST *Striker*.

In Palestine the political unrest that had existed for years between Jews and Arabs was marked with acts of violence by extremist groups. Animosity towards the British had intensified, accompanied by looting and pilfering of British Army stores and equipment on a large scale. On 27 September 1947 Britain informed the United Nations that it would terminate the Palestine Mandate and complete the withdrawal of British Forces by 1 July 1948. The withdrawal had begun but increasing acts of hostility called for stronger security measures. In particular it was essential to safeguard the port of Haifa through which the withdrawal by sea was programmed and the final stages of evacuation would take place. Responsibility for this task was given to 40 Commando.

The many historical and political events, policy decisions and other factors that influenced the Labour cabinet of the day to announce an early termination of the mandate would fill many pages, but these are the salient points:

Historically both Jews and Arabs are able to claim roots in Palestine. The forefathers of todays Jews populated the hill region known as Eretz Israel as long ago as 1,100 BC while the Philistines, from whom the word Palestine derives, inhabited the coastal region. The Arabs invaded Palestine in the 6th century and tilled Palestinian soil for 1,400 years.

British involvement with Palestine stemmed from 1917, with the need to enlist the influential support of Jews in Russia and America at a critical period

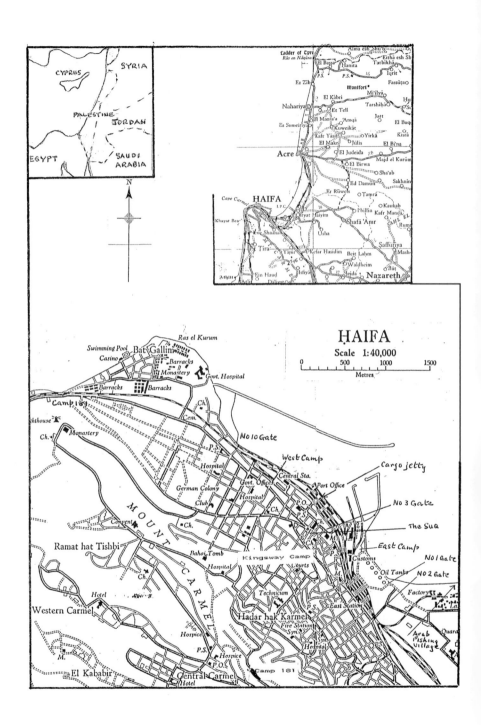

in World War I, and to protect her oil fuel outlet at Haifa. The end result was the occupation of Palestine by British forces and the Balfour Declaration promising a national home for Jews in Palestine. For political reasons backing was also given to Arab and Armenian claims for independence.

Allied victory was followed by a distribution of mandates on occupied territories. Ratified by the League of Nations in 1920, Britain received mandatory rights in Palestine and Iraq. Between 1920 and the outbreak of World War II Arab concern at the increasing influx of Jewish immigrants and their acquisition of Arab land in Palestine ended in riots. A government commission recommending partition was rejected by the Arabs because the most fertile land would have been allocated to the Jews and thousands of Arabs would have been uprooted. Widespread Arab revolt in 1938 was quelled by British troops aided by the Haganah (Jewish defence force carrying arms with Britain's approval). Efforts by the Labour government to curb Jewish immigration met with strong Jewish opposition in Britain, while in Palestine, Arab and Jewish underground organisations commenced to stockpile arms and ammunition. New plans for partition were shelved by Churchill when extremist Jewish elements (Stern Gang) assassinated Lord Moyne in 1943.

World War II brought new prosperity to Palestine, a revival of Arab leaders and the formation of the Palestine Arab Party. American and European Jews called for unrestricted Jewish immigration to Palestine and part of the Anglo American Committee's report of 1946 called for the immediate admission of 100,000 Jews. Mr Ernest Bevin's response was to continue a monthly immigration of 1,500. Embittered at the continued restriction, Jewish extremists in Palestine committed a series of atrocities causing considerable loss of life. In 1947 Britain submitted the Palestine issue to the United Nations and a special committeee, formed to investigate, recommended the end of the British mandate and the creation of an independent Palestine. Britain did not wait for the issue to be debated but made a declaration that it would withdraw from Palestine, ending the mandate unilaterally and hand responsibility over to the United Nations.

Arriving at Haifa on 28 January, 40 Commando was housed in a former transit camp (Camp 181), on the southern outskirts of the town before deploying in troop and sub-unit groups to Kingsway Camp, about one mile from the dockyard, and to East and West Camps within the dockyard. Tac HQ was established in the Port and Marine Police Station. While in this location the unit carried out cordon and search operations until assuming responsibility for the port area on 3 February. Lt Col Houghton was informed that the Commando's main task was to keep the port operational to enable the evacuation of some 10,000 British troops and other personnel to be carried out efficiently and as quickly as possible. The majority of wives and children had already been evacuated.

To achieve this purpose it was essential to reduce the communal strife between the Jews and Arabs in the port to a minimum and to improve security.

159

The existing pass system was totally inadequate with the result that unauthorised persons could gain access to the dockyard with ease and pilfering and looting were rife. Sand-bagged posts and slit trenches were established around the perimeter and guards were mounted at all vunerable points. One of the first tasks was to reinforce the Palestine Police on all the dockyard gates, where the sight of the green beret aroused a certain amount of curiosity. The presence of two man patrols in the dockyard also acted as a deterrent to would-be looters and helped to calm the Jewish and Arab workforce.

By all accounts 3 February developed into a turbulent day. At 1415 hours the Jews detonated a large bomb which shook the town and demolished an Arab house that was used as a strong point. A number of Arabs were killed and a soldier with a patrol of the 8/9 Parachute Battalion was wounded while trying to restore order. At 1515 hours Arab dissidents who were mingling with a large crowd of Arabs demonstrating outside 3 Gate shot and killed two former Royal Marine Policemen. Their bodies were recovered and the gates secured by commando personnel. Later that night a Commando patrol in the east section of the docks arrested two Jews in illegal possession of weapons and moved the body of a dead Jew shot earlier by a police patrol, to the mortuary.

The first few days and nights were particularly exhausting with everyone working nonstop to establish maximum security and order. Sandbag protected guard posts and slit trenches were prepared at all vulnerable points while patrols covered the dockyard and its perimeter.

It was during this period that distinctive coloured lanyards, worn on the right shoulder, and hose-tabs of identical colour were introduced to 3 Commando Brigade. These items of dress had been the subject of discussion by a Brigade working group prior to the Palestine issue. Capt W. Robinson, 40 Commando's Assistant-Adjutant and representative on the working party, has always assumed that the light blue lanyard worn by 40 Commando was chosen because it matched the colour of his eyes! The other distinguishing lanyards worn in the Commando Brigade are Maroon – HQ Commando Forces, Green – HQ 3 Commando Brigade, White – 42 Commando, Red – 45 Commando, Navy Blue – Commando Logistic Regiment and Old Gold and Red – Commachio Group.

Extreme vigilance was essential at all times to combat the nefarious activities of the terrorist organisations. Petty pilfering by Arab thieves was a daily occurrence but the Jews were particularly resourceful at larceny on a grand scale. Before the Commando arrived large quantities of stolen goods were removed from the port area by train through 2 Gate. A strong commando guard was mounted on the Gate to curtail this activity, but it was not always easy to ascertain the contents of the trucks. One train leaving the port with an unsealed wagon of goods aroused suspicion. While the guard was checking the contents someone quietly uncoupled the engine which moved off in the direction of the town. Prompt action led to the arrest of the driver and fireman who susequently admitted that they had intended making off with the engine, wagon and contents.

Before the security pass system was improved a team of Jewish workmen arrived at the dockside with a steam crane and began unloading steel sheets from a lighter onto a 10 ton truck. A wandering patrol became suspicious as only a short time previously the lighter had been loading similar steel sheets onto a War Department ship in mid-stream. The workmen, who had no authority to be in the dockyard, were arrested. Had the patrol been less alert this bold daylight attempt at stealing military stores would have succeeded.

Arabs and Jews were engaged in gun running and to combat the smuggling of arms the Commando provided a boarding party of section strength each night to patrol off shore in a Royal Navy launch. A patrol led by Sgt J. Docherty stopped an unidentified boat manned by Palestinian police. In the absence of a satisfactory explanation, the marines searched the boat, uncovering a large quantity of weapons and ammunition. On the way into harbour a futile attempt was made to bribe Sgt Docherty with £600 cash.

The majority of offenders were tried at the Law Courts adjacent to Camp 181 on the main Jerusalem road. CSgt R.S. Dobbs, the Commando small arms armourer, describing those days at the camp said "Very often we heard gunfire pass overhead as Jews or Arabs poked a weapon out of a window and fired at each other. The weapons were of a great variety. We knew this because while the courts were in session we would comb through the long grass and confiscate weapons hidden there by people attending the courts. Some of the weapons appeared to be homemade and would have been more dangerous to the firer than anyone else".

Lt P.R. Thomas, who was in command of the Mortar Group at Kingsway Camp was badly blasted by one of the many bomb attacks between the Arabs and the Jews. As a result, the wooden huts were reinforced with steel sheets and sandbags and it was decided to provide some form of pill-boxes for the defence of the camp. In refering to those days Lt Col Thomas said "It was in order to produce the pillboxes to defend Kingsway Camp that a couple of old Staghound armoured cars were collected from the Returned Stores section of the Ordnance Depot. They were very big American armoured cars, each fitted with two engines. While towing the vehicles back to camp one of the engines, which must have been left in gear, coughed in to life. It was only a matter of days before both cars were fully operational and allocated to one of the mortar sections".

"The Staghounds, each equipped with one 2-pounder and three Browning machine-guns, were painted, and we named one 'Dieppe',after the 40 Commando battle honour and the other 'Kangaw', after the 44 Commando Arakan battle honour. Cpl J.J. Maill was placed in charge of 'Kangaw' while Cpl D. Dennis was made responsible for 'Dieppe'. The armoured cars provided a very effective mobile reserve for the unit and were usefully employed as escorts for a number of VIPs and convoys".

An Emergency Section, provided by the fighting troops on a roster basis,

Guard of Honour for Gen Cunningham on 14 May 1948, led by Lt Musto and C/Sgt Pedrick. Photo: J. A. C. Uniacke

Guards on No 10 Gate searching Arab workers for weapons. Photo: G. Self

Staghound Armoured Car manned by a section of the 3-inch Mortar Group on patrol in Haifa. Photo: G. Self

Check point manned by member of the Jewish Haganah armed with Sten gun. Photo: G. Self

163

was kept on permanent stand by. The aim was to be able to deal quickly with minor outbreaks of trouble before events escalated. On one call-out the section was required to quell a disturbance between Arabs and Jews aboard the Greek ship *Cyrenia*, shortly after it had docked at Haifa. On other occasions it assisted the Army in searching for weapons in a camp of troublesome Arabs and was required to restore order when fighting broke between members of the Haganah and Jewish emigrants who were defying the Haganah ban on Jews of military age leaving the country.

Tension in the town increased with Jews and Arabs each accusing the other with good reason of hoarding weapons. As the two nationalities shared a financial interest in the port in addition to the export of oranges – both essential factors in Palestine's economy – it could be assumed that the situation would not deteriorate drastically until after mid-April when the citrus season would be over. However the bombing and sniping continued in varying degrees of intensity. An Arab worker, having finished his coffee in a Jewish cafe by 5 Gate, left a long fused 36 grenade at his table as a parting gift. His clumsy attempt at notoriety was noticed immediately, whereupon there was a quick exodus of Jews from the cafe as they chased the Arab and his accomplice towards 5 Gate. The anger of the Jews intensified when the grenade exploded, although no injuries were sustained. The guards arrested the Arabs and then tried to calm the Jews.

There were four bomb attacks and considerable sniping activity during the first week in March. On 3 March a bomb carried in a stolen military vehicle exploded near a large block of flats at the junction of Stanton Street and Allenby Road, killing 17 Arabs. The following day the Arabs retaliated with an oil bomb that was carried in a truck towards the New Business Centre. Members of the Haganah opened fire on the truck as it turned to enter Bank Street. The driver lost control and it crashed through a shop front where the bomb exploded killing one Jew and injuring two others. The Jews replied the next morning by throwing a grenade into the open window of a house in Iraq Street, killing five Arabs. Before the day was over the Arabs attempted another car-bomb attack but it ended in failure and the death of the driver when the stolen Post Office van came under fire from a Jewish road block.

A 're-housing' of the Commando took place in early March. Tac HQ moved to East Camp and the two fighting troops, already there under canvas, transferred to 10 Shed. The pace of the evacuation of British forces increased and there was considerable activity in the port as large numbers of troops, civilians, stores, equipment and baggage arrived from the interior. The Commando's responsibilities increased accordingly with patrols and guards constantly on the lookout for anti British activity and looting.

The Commando was equally involved with the security of ships off-loading supplies and stores. Towards the end of March, a cargo of agricultural tractors arrived in the SS *Flying Arrow*, destined for Jewish settlements. On inspection, the tractors 'materialised' as armoured half tracks. An attempt had been made to paint these to resemble tractors but the role of the machines was death not agriculture. The half tracks were impounded and taken under escort to 614 Army Ordnance Depot following an unsuccessful attempt by the ship's captain to have them towed ashore in lighters.

There was an increase in sniping towards the end of the month, following the arrival of Arab Liberation Army soldiers who camped to the east of Haifa. A bomb carried in a 15 cwt military truck, exploded in Harbour Street killing five Jews including a boy. The explosion set fire to 12 Jewish trucks and caused extensive damage to 6 Shed and nearby Jewish buildings. The Jews retaliated with a bombing attack, using a 3 ton vehicle carrying Airborne markings. The driver, who was dressed as an Airborne officer, stopped the truck in Iraq Street and was driven away in a jeep. The truck blew up, killing 11 Arabs, and a further 31 were injured. Continuing their terrorist activities the Jews fired mortar bombs from Mount Carmel into the Suq,(the Arab quarter of Haifa). The first exploded 50 yards from Commando Tac HQ, slightly wounding a British soldier. There were further British Army casualties that night and the following morning.

April started badly for the Arabs. The C-in-C Arab forces was killed in a Jewish attack on an arms convoy on its way to Haifa. His deputy was unpopular and their true leader had departed to join the Arab Liberation Army. New port-passes were issued by 40 Commando in April to eliminate the use of many suspect passes. The new passes were mainly taken up by Jews as the rapidly dwindling dockyard Arab labour force had almost disappeared by the end of the month.

Jewish snipers intensified their activities against the Arabs. Workers at the Consolidated Oil Refinery east of the port, and civilians in the village opposite No 1 Gate, were subjected to daily attack. Refinery workers, objecting to being shot at, went on strike. The villagers attacked trucks carrying aviation spirit from the refineries and all lorries driven by Jews were fair game. To deter these attacks the Commando armoured car detachments, alternated in protecting the lorries passing through the village. The unit also deployed OPs on the high ground to the south, to deal with Jewish snipers in that area and ironically, the preventive measures taken to stop the Arabs retaliating against the Jews led to the villagers venting their anger against the commandos. Great tact and diplomacy were required to regain their confidence.

While no apparent deliberate action was taken by the snipers against the commandos, Cpl Dennis, who was on patrol with Staghound 'Dieppe', stopped a ricochet in his rump while standing beside the armoured car. Mne Parkin's offer to remove the bullet with a pair of pliers was hastily declined! Although Cpl Dennis survived the incident he was killed by an Egyptian sniper during the Suez Operation in November 1956,

Cpl Maill vividly remembers a sunny Saturday morning when on duty in the village with his crew, he counted 12 unarmed Arabs, including a girl, shot by snipers, who could have been in any one of the numerous buildings with open windows overlooking the village. Spotting the marksmen was an impossible task. Returning to the dockyard shortly after midday Cpl Maill and his signalman heard a crack-thump overhead and looking towards the direction of the shot saw an Arab fisherman who had been folding his nets, keel over. Thirteen unarmed Arab civilians had been the deliberate targets of Jewish snipers.

On 14 April the Commando HQ moved from Camp 181 into Kingsway Camp to shorten the lines of communication and lessen the risk of isolation in the event of real trouble in the town. Tac HQ in West Camp, had access to Kingsway Camp by road over the railway line. The situation in Haifa town steadily deteriorated. Arabs and Jews in the areas of the New Business Centre and Jaffa Road sniped at each other continuously. Indiscriminate firing of mortar-bombs by the Jews started several fires and one of the bombs landed very close to East Camp.

As predicted, when the citrus season ended and oranges had been exported, there were signs that open conflict between Jews and Arabs was imminent. The British were informed that the Haganah had announced its intention to gain control of Haifa "in an attempt to restore peace and order". During the morning of 20 April the 1st Coldstream Guards withdrew from the town centre to the west of Haifa, leaving only the evacuation routes under the control of British troops. The Commando stood ready in fighting order for any eventuality and at 2000 hours all troops in Kingsway Camp, less a small security guard, moved into the dockyard.

Shortly before dawn on 21 April 40 Commando moved out to predetermined locations in the town. Defence posts were constructed in the Central Railway Station, Barclays Bank and other main buildings from where the approaches to the dockyard could be protected. Road blocks were set up in Harbour Street and between Nos 3 and 10 Gates in Kingsway. By 0515 hours the re-deployment was complete and the people in the town awakened to find the commandos firmly established among them.

The Haganah moved into action that morning from the direction of Mount Carmel. Shortly before 1000 hours mini-battles were being fought between Jews and Arabs in the vicinity of the Arab village near No 1 Gate and adjacent areas. Close to 1100 hours the OC Mortar Platoon received a request from one of the troop commanders, to deal with a Jewish sniper in Bank Street. Cpl Maill, patrolling in Staghound 'Kangaw' was sent to the area where two British policemen had been shot. Describing the incident Cpl Maill said "The sniper was firing from behind a metal shuttered window in a house a short distance from the road. I stopped the Staghound and fired three 37mm shells which removed the shutter, window and fittings, and I followed up with one 37mm HE shell for good measure. There was no further sniping from that building".

Short bursts of Bren fire, from a window position in Kingsway at noon, caused confusion among the traffic and sent civilians in the area scattering for cover. The firer, who was protected by a thick glass window and could have been Jew or Arab, was eventually silenced by PIAT bombs fired by Sgt R.R.Dodds. Nearby a Jewish Bren-gunner, on the roof of a building adjacent to the dockyard, deliberately fired at one of B Troop's roof-top positions in Kingsway. Lt A.H.W.Seed was hit twice but fortunately received only minor flesh wounds. Cpl D.R. Earp and two marines retaliated quickly. Making their way through a maze of streets with the crack of bullets whipping overhead they located the building and disposed of the two Jews manning the Bren-gun position. Lt Seed was evacuated to the British Military Hospital.

Rifle and machine-gun fire, punctuated by the crack of grenades and the heavier thump of larger bombs, intensified as night approached. The sky glowed with flares and the flame of burning vehicles and buildings. At 0522 hours on 22 April the Jews commenced firing mortar bombs at the Arab Quarter and surrounding area. Some of the bombs landed in the dockyard around East Camp, resulting in 20 casualties among the Mauritian Pioneers in a camp nearby. Lt R.M.Grant and his Section provided valuable assistance to them.

Recalling that morning, Lt Col Thomas said "The Arab population broke and ran. Most of the many thousand people came clammering to be let into the dockyard and congregated at 3 Gate. I will never forget that the Jews, who had undoubtedly won hands down at this stage, could not resist the opportunity of firing into this mass of humanity".

The gates were opened and the Arabs were escorted to the cargo jetty where they were out of the line of fire. Lt P.J.Pitman was shot through both knees while trying to make way for the women and children. During this time Jewish snipers continued to shoot into the struggling mass. While attending the wounded Arabs together with SBA A. McGlen, the Commando Medical Officer, Lt M.J.Cox RNVR, was shot in the thigh.

Marines in one of the commando positions on the roof of the British Sailors' Society's Club near No 3 Gate silenced three of the snipers and Lt Col Houghton ordered the Mortar Group Commander to provide fire- support and covering fire from the Staghounds. Refering to this incident Lt Col Thomas said "I looked through the scope on the 37mm gun at one of the dominant buildings halfway up Mount Carmel and could see a row of binoculars looking at me over a sandbagged wall. The 37mm was so beautifully accurate I remember knocking the sandbags one by one off the top of the wall, and presumably the people behind them as well. This stopped the sniping in the direction of No 3 Gate."

The mortaring continued for some time and one of the road block sections, which seemed to be the subject of attention, was withdrawn into the dockyard. By 0845 hours the following morning the Arabs had lost the will to fight. A meeting was arranged between Gen Stockwell, commanding North Palestine District, and Arab leaders who had not already fled, to discuss the evacuation of 37,000 Arabs from Haifa. The difficult task of controlling the thousands trying to seek safety in the dockyard and administering to the equally large numbers already in that sanctuary was to continue for several days. Schooners were brought to Haifa to ferry them across the bay to Acre and trucks carried others to the Lebanon border. Blankets,food and medical attention were provided by 40 Commando and efforts were made to cope with the almost-impossible task of sanitation. These actions earned the official gratitude of the Arabs.

A special Order of the Day issued by Lt Col Houghton to the Commando, read *"All ranks are to be congratulated on their bearing and efforts during the past very difficult period. It is probable that many days of hard work and trying circum-stances lie before us, but it is obvious from your performance today that 40 Commando will not fail, and is as good as ever."*

By the evening of 23 April the shooting had almost ceased and a truce had been arranged between the Arabs and the Jews. The main terms of the truce were that the Arab forces in Haifa were to be disarmed and the weapons were to be held in trust by the British until 15 May. In addition, all non Palestinian male Arabs were to leave the country. The full terms of the Haganah Com-mand' are listed at Appendix F.

The Commando was involved in the evacuation programme of moving 12,000 Arabs by road to the Syrian frontier or by sea to Acre. Medical assistance was provided for those in need and trucks were made available to help families take their possessions from the town to the docks. During a period of stormy weather a marine from the 3-inch Mortar Group, who preferred to remain anonymous, jumped into the sea at Acre to rescue an Arab woman and child. They had fallen into the water while transferring to a smaller boat that would take them ashore.

Eventually the evacuation programme ended and only 2,500 Arabs re-mained in Haifa. The Jews lost no time in trying to re-establish trading and commerce but the complete lack of Arab labour produced problems for the British military and Jewish port authorities. The British solution was to bring in the 1261 Docks Operating Squadron, who were assisted by 200 Mauritian Pioneers already in Haifa. The Jews for their part produced a temporary work force from their factories and workshops which was given the task of unload-ing civilian cargoes.

The 15 May, the day on which the mandate was to end, was approaching fast and all 40 Commando's resources were concentrated on the security of the dockyard and final phase of the evacuation of the British forces. The antici-pated unification of the Irgun Zvai Leumi with the Haganah had not materi-alised and there had been evidence of open clashes between these organisations during the recent conflict with the Arabs. The risk of extremist groups intensifying their attacks against the British forces in the final phase of the withdrawal was considered real enough for the GOC British Forces to call for the remainder of 3 Commando Brigade to proceed to Palestine. The Brigade Tac HQ and 42 Commando sailed from Malta in HMS *Striker* on 28 April while 45 Commando, training flew from Benina Airport on 30 April.

Guard under the command of Capt W. E. Robinson paraded for Gen Sir Alan Cunningham, High Commissioner for Palestine, prior to his departure from Haifa in the termination of the Mandate, on 15 May 1948. Photo: A. Pugh.

Z-Day. 30 June 1948. LST Striker with bow doors open, ready to embark 40 Commando. The last British unit to leave Palestine. Photo: A. Pugh.

Much to the chagrin of 42 Commando, 45 Commando arrived first. Equipped with stores and transport supplied by the 1st Guards Brigade, the unit relieved 40 Commando's road blocks in Kingsway and provided patrols in the southern sector of the town. 42 Commando arrived on Sunday night 2 May and was met by representatives of 40 Commando who set up a canteen in the LST tank space and supplied bag rations for the following day. Early the next morning 42 Commando departed in a vehicle convoy for Jerusalem, where they were to cover the evacuation of the High Commissioner, Gen Sir Alan Cunningham and the last of the British garrison. On 14 May Gen Cunningham left Jerusalem and travelled the short journey by air to Haifa where he announced the termination of the mandate. 42 Commando, adopting the role of rearguard, returned to Haifa by road.

In Haifa 40 Commando, entrusted with the personal security of the High Commissioner while he was in port, completed a sweep of the area and guarded all routes. Tension in the town had eased and 45 Commando had been able to return to Benghazi on 12 May. A Guard of Honour mounted by 40 Commando and 1st Battalion Grenadier Guards paraded for General Cunningham on the quay-side and, by all accounts, the standard of ceremonial drill performed by the "Royals" and the "Grenadiers" on 14 May, was of a very high standard. The pipes of the Irish Guards helped to enliven proceedings as Gen Cunningham inspected the guard prior to his embarkation in HMS *Euryalus*. At 0001 hours 15 May 1948, HMS *Euryalus* sailed into the darkness and Palestine became the Jewish State of Israel.

Although Haifa was now part of the Jewish State, the port installation was still under British control. This tended to complicate matters. One incident concerned the American ship *Marine Carp*, which had been boarded by armed Arabs in Beirut and all Jewish males of military age had been forced to disembark. The American Consul in Beirut advised the ship's captain that under International Law the Arabs were acting within their rights. The Jews, angered at this decision, made plans for the forced disembarkation of all Arab passengers when the vessel arrived in Haifa. As the dockyard was still under British control the proposed Jewish action would have been illegal and was prevented by Commando personnel.

The evacuation of British troops and stores continued rapidly. Many tons of stores were loaded and several thousand men passed through the dockyard each week. The Jews assisted by providing a Jewish Port Authority Police Force who worked under the command of 40 Commando. Recalling the lighter side of that busy period years later, Maj Gen Houghton said " A large lorry arrived in the dockyard weighed down by an enormous quantity of bottled beer, NAAFI stock no longer required in Palestine. There was no room for it in any of the ships and in consequence Maj Norcock purchased the consignment and the crates of beer were transferred to the Commando canteen. Apparently a severe shortage of bottles existed in Haifa and when the beer had been consumed he re-couped his outlay from a Jewish contractor in exchange for the empties!"

Brig J. N. Wills, arrived by troopship on 18 May, and divided his one-day visit between 40 Commando in the port area and 42 Commando in the town. Various changes were noticeable in the town, one of the most obvious being a reduction in the Jewish population. Between three and four thousand men and hundreds of women had been conscripted for the newly formed Jewish Army (originally the Haganah), and had been drafted to the north. A constant flow of Jewish troops arrived in Haifa for short periods of rest from the fighting zones around Jerusalem and Latrun, and air-raid precautions were strictly enforced by air raid wardens.

By early June additional resources to combat theft and sabotage were available to 40 Commando. Four small launches were acquired for patrolling the harbour and Sgt Dodds improvised a frogman section which successfully foiled attempts by the Jews to attach limpet mines to British ships. Military Police with dog handlers were placed under command to patrol the port area. The commandos had already enlisted some of the local dogs to work with their patrols and found these useful in deterring pilferers. Nevertheless two British Army half tracks were stolen. Drivers in British army uniform with apparently authentic identity cards and documents reported to the guardroom and drove the vehicles away. The theft was discovered when drivers of the 17/21 Lancers arrived later in the day to collect the vehicles. Attempts were made to bribe British personnel and Lt Thomas received an offer of £8000 on the understanding that he would leave a Staghound unattended at a certain street corner! Suffice to say that both armoured cars accompanied the Commando to Malta.

Time was found to celebrate the King's Birthday on 10 June. Those who could be spared from duties assembled in Kingsway Camp and marched the length of the dockyard to East Camp where Lt Col Houghton took the salute. On completion of the parade the troops were treated to free beer, provided by the Jewish contractor of dockyard labour! The following day the truce negotiated by the United Nations mediator, Count Folke Bernadotte, between the Arabs and the Jews became effective. The task that had been carried out with considerable success by 40 Commando was nearing completion.

Gen Crocker* visited the unit on 16 June, the day that the unit advance party embarked on the troopship *Samaria* en passage to Malta via Greece. During the week American marines and communication vehicles – forming part of the United Nations mediating team – arrived, and the last of the Arab refugees left the port under British arrangements.

The duties of the Palestine Police Force ended on 19 June. This force of British and Palestinian personnel provided valuable assistance to the Commando when the unit first arrived in Haifa. Numbering 16,000 at their peak, their strength had steadily declined as personnel were repatriated.

On 23 June, HQ Garrison Palestine and Commodore Palestine moved their

---

* General Sir John Crocker KCB,KBE,DSO,MC,ADC., C-in-C Middle East Land Forces.

respective HQs into HMS *Phoebe* and *Dieppe*, thereby easing the workload of the sub units responsible for their security. Z Day – 30 June – was to be the final day of evacuation and the loading of ships intensified as the deadline approached. From 1900 hours on Z-1, all Jews, with the exception of a few well known officials, were denied access to the dockyard. By this time only a small rearguard of British troops remained in the town of Haifa. Y Troop, with 3-inch Mortar Group under command, guarded the sector between Nos 1 and 3 Gates, East Camp and the Lee Breakwater. B Troop was responsible for the area around 5 Shed, the lighter wharf and jetty where a dozen war department ships were berthed. A Troop covered the main wharf, post office and 5 Gate while X Troop guarded Kingsway Camp and No 10 Gate. H and Q Troops were held in reserve.

Reveille on 30 June was at 0400 hours. The first of the rearguard units commenced to withdraw at 0550 hours, with 2 Company 1st Coldstream Guards entering through No 10 Gate while 2 Company Grenadier Guards marched through No 1 Gate. Four tanks of the 4/7 Dragoon Guards providing cover at Nos 3 and 4 Gates were then withdrawn and embarked. At 0710 hours the first sub units of 42 Commando entered the dockyard and completed embarkation shortly after 0900 hours.

Tac HQ of 40 Commando then moved from Kingsway Camp into the "military zone" which had established a small perimeter around HMS *Striker*. At 1115 hours, the Brigade Commander of 1st Guards Brigade handed over command of all British troops ashore in Palestine to Lt Col Houghton. Then, with the exception of HMS *Striker*, all British ships put to sea.

After a short interval of time Lt Col Houghton signalled for the withdrawal of the forward troops of 40 Commando. When they had embarked the Mortar Group took up positions on the forecastle of the LST.

Finally Lt Col Houghton reported to the GOC, Lt Gen G.H.A.McMillan and said "Withdrawal of British Troops in Palestine completed. 40 Commando Royal Marines, the last unit to leave, is now embarked."

The following Honours and Awards were approved for distiguished service in Palestine:-

Lt Col R.D.Houghton MC	OBE	Capt D.L.S.St.M.Aldridge	MBE
SBA A.McGlen	BEM	Sgt R.Dodds	MM
Cpl D.R.Earp	MM		

Mention in Despatches

Maj P.L. Norcock, Lt R.M. Grant, Lt P.R.Thomas, CSgt H.C.R.H.Bedborough, CSgt H.L.Cornish, Sgt R.J.McCleave, Cpl P.E.G.Pollard, Mne K.G.Dando, Mne J.T.Watlow and Mne R.A.Whapham.

CHAPTER 12

1 July 1948 to 30 May 1950.

*Malta – ceremonial and amphibious exercises. Cyprus – confinement of
illegal Jewish immigrants. Malta – a return to ceremonial and amphibious
training. Hong Kong – the threat of Communist expansion.*

RETURNING to Malta after six months in Palestine 40 Commando rapidly
adjusted to the peacetime routine of the Island garrison. In addition to
entertaining a steady stream of visitors the unit paraded for Adm Power,* the
new C-in-C Mediterranean. The United States Marine Corps 21st Landing
Team called at Malta in September with the American Task Force and were
shown the Ghain Tuffieha training area and a demonstration of a cliff assault
from dories by X Troop.

In addition to ceremonial and displays the unit was committed to a work up
programme and a series of amphibious exercises that culminated with a show-
piece landing in Mellieha Bay for senior officers of the three services. In
conclusion the sub-units demonstrated their prowess at dory landings, canoeing, swimming and climbing.

The swimmers, following a more peaceful pursuit after the exercises,
competed against a number of well trained local teams, and were successful
in winning the annual Malta Command Aquatics meeting.

There were a number of personnel changes in the Commando as tours of
duty came to an end. Capt W.E.Robinson assumed the duties of Adjutant from
Capt Harris and RSM R.J.Mather relieved RSM Travers. Lt Orpen, who had
been with the Commando for three and a half years, returned to UK in
company with the Rev D.J.W.L.Arter RN.

It was anticipated that a relatively quiet period would follow the exercises.
Instead Lt Col Houghton was informed that the unit was to make ready to
move to Cyprus. Crates and panniers appeared from troop stores and packing
became the order of the day. On 20 September, 40 Commando sailed out of
Grand Harbour, once more on its way towards the eastern end of the Mediterranean.

Disembarking at Famagusta, a small harbour on the eastern sea-board of
Cyprus, the Commando deployed to the base camp at Dhekelia and a smaller
camp adjacent to the Jewish internment camp complex at Xylotymbou. Dhekelia
Camp had been constructed a short distance from the rocky shoreline where
a large number of wooden huts, mostly with verandahs, looked out over the

---

* Adm Sir Arthur J.Power KCB,CBE,CVO.

173

sea and adjacent playing fields. Xylotymbou, a collection of Nissen huts a mile to the north of Dhekelia and close to a densely wooded area, stood on higher ground marked by rocky outcrops and ravines. The huts occupied by the Jewish internees were contained within three wire fenced compounds while the off duty guards occupied similar accommodation outside their perimeters.

The unit relieved the 1st Battalion Duke of York Light Infantry and assumed responsibility for guarding 8,000 Jews who, at one time or another, had been intercepted and apprehended by the Royal Navy while attempting to enter Palestine illegally. It was probable that some of the more recent arrivals had been escorted to Cyprus from Haifa by members of 40 Commando.

Every effort was made to relieve monotony and maintain standards. A reduction in the number of internees in one of the compounds enabled the troop responsible for that sector to allocate one day in four for section training. However, guard commitments at the other two compounds remained intensive and training was confined to a daily session of PT and weapon drills.

A welcome diversion arose with the arrival of 3 Commando Brigade Band on a five day visit to Cyprus. 40 Commando provided a Ceremonial Guard and joined forces with the Band to Beat Retreat in Larnaca, where the display had an impressive effect upon the intensely pro-Communist local populace. During the service held on Remembrance Day at Larnaca, the Communists, whose club was situated on the main square, erected a large portrait of Stalin and displayed a red flag and anti-capitalist slogans on placards. These were ignored by the British forces on parade. Mr Aldridge, the District Commissioner, commented that the arrival of 40 Commando; the fine performance of the Band and Guard and the general conduct and smartness of the men, both on parade and off-duty, had made his job considerably easier.

During the time that a troop was at Dhekelia the men were able to follow a more relaxed routine, take a few days leave and make use of the sports and recreational facilities. The programme included a five day initiative march, in which all personnel took part, covering distances up to 150 miles and ascending peaks as high as 6,400 feet. The men, working in groups of two or four, were given a time limit in which to visit specified places of their own choice. They were required to find or provide their own transport and make provision for accommodation and food. The more popular locations, such as Kyrenia, Platres and Paphos were not far away but some groups were prepared to travel as far as Cape Andreas, situated in the north-east corner of the island. Most slept in the open or in barns during the fine weather but a nights lodging could always be found in a monastery where the monks provided green chai (strong milkless tea), bread and tomatoes.

Arnold Hadwin OBE., a national service marine who became Group Editor of the Linconshire Standard Group PLC, participated in one of these light-hearted tests. The following article, describing his memories of that expedition was first published in the Evening Despatch on 14 November 1969, the twenty first anniversary of the birth of Prince Charles–

"I'm not likely to forget the day Prince Charles was born. The day afterwards I lived like a king. Twenty-one years ago today plus one, two rather weary members of 40 Commando Royal Marines descended out of the mountains to a foothill village west of Kyrenia in Cyprus. We had been 'doing' Cyprus – not like American tourists, but like Royal Marines. The hard way. On foot, on 'borrowed' mule, on abandoned cycle, on springless lorry – but mostly on foot. We had spent the night in a monastery and had had a breakfast of black bread, grapes and coffee (strangely enough a most pleasant breakfast). The November sun is not all that hot even at the eastern end of the Mediterranean, but sunny it was. Some of those foothill villages have an almost fairy-tale quality about them in the early morning light. So it was with the one we were approaching.

"I'm a bit hazy about this, but I think it was Monday. Certainly it was a week-day; hence our surprise when we got close to the village to find all the school children shouting and waving flags and the whole population excited to the point of non-alcoholic inebriation.(It was later that alcohol was introduced to the celebration). Now, we had been away from our unit for many days, cut off from normal civilisation; Commando initiative tests either involved robbing a bank or roughing it in the wilds, and we certainly hadn't been robbing a bank. We were pretty broke.

"At first Tom and I thought Enosis – union with Greece – had been declared in our absence. (Those were the days when it involved words rather than bullets). And when we were surrounded by the entire populace and hustled into the local hostelry we just thought it was their way of saying all was forgiven. They were flabbergasted that we didn't know. "Elizabeth – she has a son," said one rather prosperous looking gent, who might have been a Soho restaurant keeper (Come to think, I believe he did say in rather inarticulate fashion much later in the evening that he'd been in Soho). "Who's Elizabeth?" asked Tom, not because, even in those far off days, he was a Scottish Nationalist, but because we were both completely mystified.

"Princess Elizabeth! She and the Prince now have a son – an heir to the throne." Such wide constitutional knowledge! Such enthusiasm! That entire village celebrated the birth as if it were one of the most important things that had ever happened in it. There was poignancy as well as joy when they trotted out for us the village half-wit, proudly proclaiming that he received a pension from King George VI for having been shell-shocked in the war that had not long since ended. To cut a long story short, we stayed in that village till the next day. They gave us a hero's welcome; nothing was too good for us. You would have thought we'd had a hand in it. Our closest drinking buddy was the village policeman.

"I will never forget the day after Prince Charles was born. Nor will I ever forget reading in a small newspaper paragraph some years later that our drinking companion had been gunned down by EOKA terrorists".

By mid December the weather had changed considerably. Storm clouds darkened the skies and ice cold winds from the direction of Turkey cut through the protective denison smocks worn by the guards in the watch-towers. The Jews, who were of military age, spent hours drilling and exercising in the open spaces between the huts. Many were openly hostile towards the guards and made numerous plans to escape. The perimeter lighting, powered by worn out generators, failed frequently but the cold weather deterred the Jews from putting their escape plans into action. Eventually new diesel generators were installed to replace the overworked Ford V8 engines. As the months passed the commandos found the never ending perimeter patrols and gate guards tedious with little of interest at Xylotymbou to enliven the off duty hours. The numerous guard commitments prevented any form of shared Christmas celebrations but a choir, formed by the Rev L. Davies, broadcast a concert of carols over the rediffusion network at Dhekelia Camp on Christmas Eve and a considerable amount of beer and local brandy – both the same price – was consumed by the off-duty personnel

On 3 December 1948, Brig Wills handed over command of 3 Commando Brigade to Brig C.R.Hardy DSO+, OBE,. The Brigade was at the time fairly wide spread, with 40 Commando in Cyprus, 42 Commando in Egypt and 45 Commando in Malta. At no time had any of the units been static for very long and keeping a grip on this type of situation would have presented a challenge to any commander. A member of the Brigade staff referring to Brig Wills said– "Under his steady if sometimes strict guidance the Brigade surmounted its first two years of peace-time soldiering."

Brig Hardy was no stranger to the commandos, many of whom were familiar with the piercing glare of his steely blue eyes as well as his dry humour. Appointed to command the 9th Battalion Royal Marines in May 1943, he continued as Commanding Officer when the unit became 46 Royal Marine Commando the following August. He commanded the unit in France and Belgium from June to November 1944, receiving the DSO and bar for courage, leadership, judgment and initiative in the many actions fought following the D Day landings. He assumed command of 3 Special Service Brigade in Burma, carrying out a series of raids down the Arakan coast. He personally planned the assault phase for the combined operations on Myebon and Kangaw, where his able planning and confident leadership led to the award of a second bar to his DSO.

In Cyprus, Lt D. Shallow and a group of 40 Commando sportsmen obtained leave to attend a ski camp run by the NAAFI at Troodos. The enterprising manager had acquired the services of a few Bavarian ex prisoners of war to act as ski instructors. There were no prepared ski slopes but the young marines had great fun while experiencing numerous collisions with the fir trees. The snow-falls were particularly heavy that winter and X Troop, under command of Capt J.A.C.Uniacke, cleared a path through deep drifts to one of the mountain villages which had been cut off from the outside world for some days. The marines went to their rescue with food supplies and other essentials.

January 1949, started on a sombre note with news that British planes had been shot down by Israeli fighters. 45 Commando was immediately alerted to proceed to Egypt leaving Brigade HQ to hold the fort in Malta. Thankfully the tension evaporated as quickly as the incident had flared and at 2000 hours on 18 January (it may have been coincidence) Ernest Bevin announced the Governments intention to allow the Jews, interned in Cyprus, to proceed to Israel provided the Jewish authorities supplied transport. The announcement was greeted with a joyous demonstration by the Jews at Xylotymbou and, although their celebrations were cut short by a storm, they were all delighted to know their confinement was at an end.

While it was intended to send the Jews to their new homeland with all possible speed a massive evacuation of their race was taking place all over Europe and shipping was in short supply. Every boat that the Jewish authority could obtain was pressed into service, even the IJI boats impounded by the Royal Navy at Haifa and other Palestinian ports were made seaworthy. According to Mne A. Dawson of X Troop– "The first time we took a group of Jews to Famagusta for embarkation the ships were not ready and we had to take them back to camp. We anticipated a bit of trouble but they took it calmly."

The evacuation of the internment camps progressed steadily and by 8 February, 3,470 Jews had been moved in convoys of Commando vehicles from Xylotymbou and Caraolos to Famagusta. A further 1,595 were taken to Famagusta on 10 February. Service personnel, entering the camps as they were cleared, found them extremely filthy. Tins of food and oddments of clothing and furniture were scattered everywhere. Hundreds of dogs were seen roaming between the empty huts and most of them had to be shot.

Responsibility for guarding the camps ceased on 19 February and the Commando, unfettered once again, re-grouped as a fighting unit. Extensive use was made of local ranges. Groups of officers and NCOs turned their attention to defence TEWTs* while sub units explored the local country-side, map reading and marching, with compass and stars as guides. The Assault Engineers practised demolition work and the Signals Section made good use of their specialist training by providing a 22 Set wireless link between the ski camp at Troodos and Nicosia. Heavy snow in this area had carried away long sections of telephone wire.

There was little time for entertainment but the Commando Brigade Band, which had returned to Cyprus on 16 February, spent a week with the Commando, playing at drill parades, the mid-day meal break and in the NAAFI canteen at night, before commencing a tour of other garrison units in Cyprus.

A programme of field work and exercises spanning two weeks was carried out in the areas of Larnaca and Limassol. Even the cold wet weather could not dampen the enthusiasm of the men who were only too happy to be on the move

---

* Tactical Exercise Without Troops

177

again. Y Troop decided to keep going at the end of the final exercise and, a few minutes after 'stand down' in the early morning, set out on a 30 mile cross country trek to the base camp at Dhekelia, ostensibly to be first in line for breakfast!

In Larnaca, the main centre of Cypriot Communist activity, the unemployed paraded to celebrate the release from prison of Mr Servas, the Communist Mayor of Limassol. The Island press – reporting on the Municipal elections due in May – forecast that any opposition to the re- election of Servas would result in trouble. In the event the local situation remained reasonably calm and no Commando involvement was required.

News that the Commando would be returning to Malta was made known when the Chief of the Imperial General Staff, F M Sir William Slim*, visited the Commando on 12 March. He complimented the Guard of Honour on being the smartest he had seen on his tour of the Far East and Middle East stations. Before leaving Cyprus 40 Commando, accompanied by the Brigade Band, held a farewell parade in Larnaca which impressed the locals. The unit sportsman marked the occasion of their departure by winning the Cyprus Garrison Boxing and Shooting Trophies and on that high note the unit embarked in the *Empress of Australia*.

Looking down from the ramparts of Valletta excited family groups waved greetings as the troop-ship entered Grand Harbour and moored close to the battleship HMS *Vanguard*. The lively sound of the Brigade Band playing "Sarie Marais" drifted across the water as Maltese traders in hired boats, clustered around the *Empress of Australia* displaying lace tablecloths and pottery-ware to the men waiting to disembark. Customs officers, knowing that radios (purchased in Nicosia), duty-free cigarettes and the odd bottle of Kio brandy would be the main items in the kit bags, satisfied themselves with a cursory search and the men were free to proceed ashore.

Brigade transport moved the unit to Mtarfa Barracks, a substantial stone complex situated on the high ground in the centre of the island and remote from the main Commando Brigade locations at St Andrews, St Patricks and St George's. The advance party had everything ready and the remainder of the day was devoted to numerous administrative duties, not the least of which would have been the unpacking, checking and stowing away of troop and unit stores. By 1730 hours most of the outliers had made their way to their quarters or rented apartments. In the dining hall, some of the inliers, sipping a last mug of tea , would have been planning a "run ashore" to one of the bars in Sliema or less salubrious drinking places in Straight Street known as the "Gut", a down-town section of Valetta notorious for poor quality liqour, prostitutes and punch-ups.

In reality, the bars in the drab weathered limestone houses comprising that small section of town were little different to waterfront bars in many other sea

---

* Field Marshal Sir William Slim GCB,GBE,DSO,MC,.

ports around the world frequented by the Navy. The men who visited the dingy establishments did so mostly out of curiosity and to be able to tell their mates back home that they had seen the "red light district". Most came away with empty pockets and suffered a sore head reminder the following morning.

Although it is unlikely that Field Marshal Slim's praiseworthy remarks reached the ears of the C-in-C Malta, the unit found itself much in demand for ceremonial functions. Three Guards of Honour were paraded for Italian and British Admirals and the Commando provided the Malta Palace Guard* for a period of one month, assuming the duties on 21 May from the Malta Artillery.

Versatility is an intrinsic part of a marine's make-up and the transition from guarding illegal Jewish immigrants to guarding the Governor's Palace was undertaken with aplomb. The Palace Guard was a focal point of interest for visitors, particularly the tourists and when the marines paraded in their green berets, even the Maltese were impressed. The changing of the Guard on Saturdays, when the Commando Brigade Band was in attendance, attracted a large crowd of spectators. On these occasions the men found the guard duties not unpleasant.

In addition to the ceremonial duties the Commando's involvement in military and amphibious training kept everyone fully occupied. On any day of the week experienced cliff leaders could be seen encouraging the rifle troop personnel to emulate their skills – 'hanging-on by the eyebrows'– on the rocky outcrops of Ghain Tuffieha. HQ staff pored over tide tables and loading manifests while representative groups from all the troops took turns at exercising with the landing craft in St Paul's Bay. During this period the unit took part in an amphibious exercise demonstration for the Duke of Edinburgh.

Part of the training programme was set aside for recreational activities, in which all ranks participated. The opportunity to compete in any of the Malta Garrison sports events was always a welcome challenge and during this period a strong team of athletes, who trained on the athletics track at the race-course outside Valletta, won the Garrison Inter-Unit Athletics Rose Bowl trophy.

Behind the scenes, the unit M T Section undertook the task of the refurbishment of a fleet of Bedford vehicles. The trucks had been in a stores park in Egypt for five years but when the transport team had finished its work they were infinitely superior to the vehicles which had accompanied the unit since its days in India. The vehicle replacements could not have arrived at a more opportune time. The first intimation of an imminent move was notified to Brig Hardy by the CGRM when he visited London in early June.

Communist domination of China was growing at an alarming rate. Canton was vunerable and Hong Kong next in line. In consequence a decision was taken to send the Commando Brigade to Hong Kong as a measure of insurance against communist expansion in that region. The Brigadier initiated a number

---

* The provision of the Palace Guard was a commitment of the Malta Duty Regiment.

of arrangements relating to the move while he was in London and, on his return to Malta,the units were well advanced with the packing and marking of stores with serial numbers. This latter routine had been performed many times before but the Quartermaster personnel, ultimately responsible for items arriving at the destination readily available and in good order, gave the matter their undivided attention.

Arrangements had to be made regarding the families. A number would return to Britain either by choice or because husbands were nearing the end of their tour with the Brigade. Others would stay on in Malta with the expectation of joining the Commando units in due course. The wives had seen very little of their husbands during the tour in Malta and were now faced with another long separation. Lt Col Houghton was included in the number who were due to return to UK and 40 Commando gave their very popular CO and his wife a rousing send-off. His successor, Lt Col B.J.D.Lumsden OBE, assumed command on 9 July 1949.

The advance party sailed from Malta in HMT *Empire Windrush* on 29 June and the main body of the Brigade followed in the SS *Georgic* in 21 July. The personnel in *Georgic* were pleasantly surprised to find that four and five berth cabins were available for all ranks instead of the more usual troopship dormitories. The trooper called at Port Said, to embark Capt D.L. Roberts, with a reinforcement draft of 100 other ranks for 40 Commando. Meanwhile 45 Commando travelled overland from Akaba to join the *Georgic* at Suez. The ship made further calls at Aden and Singapore before docking, after a four weeks sea passage, at Kowloon on 21 August. The arrival was quite an occasion as the *Georgic* was the largest liner to call at the Colony since the war. On the wharf, the band of the Argyll's and Sutherland Highlanders took turns with the Commando Brigade Band to play while the ship tied up alongside. "We arrived prepared to repel a communist incursion over the border." said Col J.D Shallow, recalling memories of that occasion when he was a subaltern in the unit, "But while on route the threat had diminished. As we clambered down the gangway fully armed and equipped we were met, not only by the Argylls' Band but also small Chinese boys handing out free bottles of orange squash!"

Both Lt Gen Sir John Harding, C-in-C Land Forces and Lt Gen Festing, the GOC Hong Kong, were on the wharf to welcome the Brigade and, with formal ceremonies completed, the units deployed to their respective locations. 40 Commando was accommodated in Lye Mun Barracks, where the old Victorian buildings, perched on the hillside above Shau Kei Wan, looked down over the entrance to Kowloon Harbour. It was a pleasant site and the living quarters were cooled by refreshing light winds off the sea. In contrast, Brigade HQ, billeted in the Railway Hotel in Kowloon, found the close confines of the densely populated town uncomfortably hot and humid. In Hong Kong, 42 and 45 Commandos were accommodated in barracks similar to that occupied by 40 Commando.

Shortly after their arrival Lt Gen Festing visited 40 Commando and inspected the unit on parade. The ceremonial edge had not been lost on the sea passage and the GOC, having complimented the men on their turn-out, informed them that their operational requirements would be directed largely towards the maintenance of law and order, and the prevention of riots and insurrection in the towns of Victoria and Kowloon.

The Commando units were well acquainted with this role but it did not obviate the need for regular refresher training. The political situation in Hong Kong was reasonably quiet and it was possible to arrange for a number of exercises of unit and brigade strength to be held in the New Territories. These commenced in September and culminated with a tri-service internal security exercise at the end of October. Towards the latter stages of the final exercise, monsoon rains soaked everyone and everything but at least it helped to relieve the exhausting humidity. The weather at one point resembled typhoon conditions and the rain penetrated even the most watertight parts of Lye Mun Barracks. It was during one of these storms that QMS Bedborough unfortunately died following a fall into a monsoon ditch.

The presence of the green beret in Hong Kong may have acted as a stabilising influence and helped keep in check any overt moves by political dissidents. The general situation remained calm and the only outward sign of discontent was a tram strike which was settled peacefully. There was no requirement for the same intense level of military policing and patrolling that had been necessary in Hong Kong in 1945. While the Brigade remained vigilant it was possible for the units to settle down to a steady routine of guards and patrols, training, fatigues and sport. It was regretable that in this peaceful interlude Lt A.E. Edwards received fatal injuries in a motor cycle accident while escorting a motor convoy in the New Territories.

Two Brigade exercises were held in January 1950. The first, Ex Alabaster, was designed to test the Colony's internal security in the Commando Brigade area and the second, Ex Shopkeeper, gave Brigade HQ its first opportunity since the end of World War II to control all three Commando units simultaneously in the field. 40 Commando, acting as enemy, spent a busy three days attacking and being attacked in the hilly country and along parts of Hiram's Highway. This road was originally constructed by X Troop 42 Commando and Japanese prisoners of war, under the supervision of A/Ty Capt J.W.(Hiram J.) Potts who was serving with 40 Commando in 1950. The road now forms part of a very fine highway bearing his name.

In between exercises, a suitable occasion was found for Brig Hardy to present RSM W.Chesterton with his Long Service and Good Conduct Medal. A draft from UK included Lts R. Davidson, T. Priest and W.B.Mansell. The three officers had recently completed a Vickers MMG course and as this weapon was being re-introduced to the Commando Brigade they were given the task of training the Vickers sections for each unit.

The most notable event in March was undoubtedly the ceremonial parade

Christopher Potts on Hirams Highway, Hong Kong. Constructed by X Troop 42 Commando and Japanese prisoners of war, under the supervision of his father A/Ty Capt W. Potts (Hiram J.) in 1945. Photo: W. Potts.

Ceremonial Parade for His Excellency the Governor of Hong Kong. Sir Alexander Grantham KCMG. Photo: J. A. C. Uniacke.

for His Excellency Sir Alexander Grantham KCMG, the Governor of Hong Kong. The parade, for which 40 Commando had been chosen to represent the Brigade, took place on 10 March at the Hong Kong Cricket Club, the only flat piece of ground in the city large enough for the ceremony. The day was overcast but this did not detract from the splendid sight of the unit marching past the saluting base and advancing in review order to the accompaniment of the Brigade Band. The spectators stands, specially erected for the occasion, were filled to capacity with important dignitaries and members of the community.

This was to be the last ceremonial for some time. Rumours of a move became reality in early May when the Commando Brigade received orders to proceed to Malaya. The rain had returned to Hong Kong and it seemed a good time to leave.

The unit drivers and their transport sailed in two LSTs on 20 May 1950 and the main body followed in HMS *Jamaica* six days later. The four day voyage to Penang was filled with a lively series of sports and less physical competitions arranged by the ships company and the commandos. On the last evening before docking in Penang, the officers of 40 Commando showed their appreciation by entertaining the officers of *Jamaica* to a cocktail party on their own quarterdeck.

The unit transport was on the quay-side the next morning ready to take men and baggage to Glugnor Barracks, situated on the island outside George Town overlooking the Penang Straits. This was a temporary staging point where jungle clothing, tents, stores and other essential items were issued. All ranks were equipped with 1944 pattern webbing, rubber-soled canvas-legged boots, soft brimmed jungle hat, poncho cape, olive green clothing, hose tops, puttees and a machete. The No 4 rifle was replaced with the lighter No 5 Jungle Carbine, first introduced to the British Army in 1944. On completion the Commando was divided into sub-units and deployed in convoys of trucks to troop locations in Kedah, close to the border between Malaya and Thailand.

CHAPTER 13

1 June 1950 to 6 May 1952

3 Commando Brigade's involvement in the
Communist Insurgency War in Malaya.

A small nucleus of officers and NCOs from each Commando flew to Malaya in advance of the Brigade, to learn about the new environment at the Jungle Warfare School in Johore Bahru. The CO of the school at that time was Lt Col 'Mad Mike' Calvert, who became well known for his exploits as a leader of the Chindits in the WW II Burma campaign. In addition to learning about jungle survival the commandos were given a thorough briefing on the history of events leading up to the current problems.

Malaya occupies the greater part of the peninsula extending southwards from Thailand. It is a little over 400 miles long and broadens to roughly 200 miles wide in the central areas. The coast-lines converge to a narrow base where a causeway connects Johore Bahru to the island of Singapore. Forest and jungle extend over the greater part of the country, with the developed areas occupied by towns, villages, rubber estates and tin mines. The central part is mountainous with peaks rising to 7,000 feet, while mangrove swamps cover areas of low-lying ground along the coast-line. Due to Malaya's close proximity to the equator the temperature is mainly constant throughout the year. The climate is both tropical and humid, with an annual rainfall in excess of 90 inches.

British influence in Malaya dates back to the latter part of the 18th Century. The peninsula had by that time been divided into a number of separate states ruled by Sultans. The Malays ceded the State of Penang to Britain in 1786 and Singapore followed in 1819. Malaka and part of Perak were next to join the Empire when the Dutch exchanged these States for British possessions in Sumatra. Eventually, after the conclusion of a number of other treaties, Britain assumed the role of protecting power over Malaya.

Towards the latter part of the 19th Century the development of tin mines and rubber estates produced the need for additional manpower, but the majority of Malays were farmers and fishermen and had no inclination towards other types of work. Chinese labour was therefore imported in increasing numbers to work in the tin mines and on the estates. In due course Indian labour was introduced into the Singapore dockyard and gradually some of their number moved north to work on the estates.

By the turn of the century the number of Chinese in Malaya almost equalled that of the Malayan population, but they managed to live in reasonable harmony, preferring to reside in their own communities and to marry within their own races.

The political element was introduced to the scene when the Chinese Communist Party (CCP), started an underground cell in Singapore in 1922.

It made little progress and was replaced in 1930 by the Malayan Communist Party (MCP) which, by 1935, had become effective in the field of industrial subversion. Although the MCP was illegal, police pressure eased and by 1939 the Party had grown in strength to nearly 40,000 members. At the outbreak of WW II, the MCP agreed to co-operate with the British and Malay authorities and Chinese Nationalists.

After the fall of Singapore to the Japanese the MCP carried on alone, forming resistance groups which became known as the Malayan People's Anti-Japanese Army (MPAJA). The MCP and the MPAJA consolidated under the leadership of Lai Teck and in early 1944 South East Asia Command (SEAC), decided to provide the MPAJA with arms, money, supplies and training in return for their co-operation against the Japanese. Weapons and equipment were delivered in considerable quantity while Allied troops prepared for the amphibious invasion of the west coast of Malaya in September 1945. The landings were cancelled when the Japanese surrendered on 16 August of that year.

The MPAJA, acting quickly, disarmed the Japanese troops and Japanese sponsored Indian Nationalist Army, which melted away after the surrender. Within days the MPAJA had assumed control of most of Malaya. Suddenly alert to developments SEAC rushed in more troops to reinforce those who had landed at Penang and Singapore in early September. Pressure was then applied to the MCP to disband the MPAJA and to arrange for the handing in of weapons. This commenced on 5 December, by which time many of the weapons and a large quantity of ammunition had been cached.

The MCP continued to function openly as the People's Democratic Movement but prepared subversely for insurrection against British rule. There were signs of growing friction between the moderate Chinese and those who wanted militant action. In March 1947, Lai Teck, who pursued a moderate course of action, was required to justify his policy before the Central Executive Committee of the MCP. Aware that opposition was mounting against him he absconded with the bulk of the Party funds before he could be questioned. His deputy Chin Peng, who favoured more militant action, replaced him as Secretary General.

While these events were taking place the British Colonial Office had carried out a series of negotiations to bind the Malayan States more closely into a Malayan Union and Colony of Singapore. The new Malayan Union promised Union Citizenship to all who were born in the country as well as reasonable acquisition of citizenship for all other nationalities residing in Malaya. This did not please the Malayans who boycotted ceremonies relating to the establishment of the Union.

HMS Jamaica. *40 Commando embarked for passage to Malaya*

Lt Col Lumsden (left) receiving the Chief of the Imperial General Staff, F. M. Slim, at Kroh air strip. Brig Hardie (rear right). Photos: 40 Commando.

187

Between 1946 and 1948 the influence of the MCP intensified into outward signs of labour unrest and an increase in lawlessness. Having observed the successful militant Communist actions in other countries Chin Peng believed the time was right for similar action in Malaya. There were widespread demonstrations and acts of violence aimed at pressurising British civilians and officials into evacuating sparsely populated areas. The vacated territory would then be re-occupied by members of the Malayan People's Anti-British Army (MPABA), a force formed by Lau Yew, military adviser to Chin Peng.

In June 1948, following further acts of violence, the High Commissioner Sir Edward Grant declared an Emergency. Action was taken to strengthen the police force with ex-Palestine police and a special Malay Constabulary was formed. Chin Peng suffered two set-backs at this time. The first was the loss of Lau Yew, who was shot by a police officer within a month of the start of the emergency. The second was the introduction of National Registration for all civilians and the compulsory carrying of identity cards. The armed forces were called upon to assist but with only five British, two Malay and six Gurkha battalions in the country the infantry were spread thinly on the ground. The following month Sir Edward Grant was killed in an air crash and the MPABA seized the opportunity to strengthen their position before his successor was appointed.

On 1 February 1950, the MPABA became known as the Malayan Races Liberation Army (MRLA), with the intention of encouraging more support against British occupation from the Malays, Indians and Chinese. The MRLA numbered just over 4,000 and consisted of 10 regiments of varying strengths, organised by a Central Committee. About 10 per cent of the force were women. No 5 Regiment based at Perak, with a total of 700 comprised mostly of Chinese, was reputed to be the strongest force. The regiment had an adequate stock of weapons but in common with other MRLA regiments ammunition was in short supply. An organisation known as the Min Yuen supplied them with money, food and information and provided a means of communication between groups. The regiments or groups were well established with training camps primarily in northern Perak and on the Thailand side of the border.

Four months later 3 Commando Brigade arrived in Malaya. 40 Commando spent the first three weeks gleaning knowledge from personnel of the advance party who had attended courses at the Jungle Warfare and Jungle Cooking and Hygiene Schools. Lts Mansell and Potts were fortunate to have survived to pass on the lessons learned on the four week course. Travelling on the night train to Kuala Lumper to rejoin the unit they slept when the train was ambushed by Communist Terrorists (CTs) and only became aware of this incident on the following morning when they dressed and noticed a number of bullet holes in the side of the compartment between the bunks. Lt Potts had placed his bush shirt on a coat hanger and found it had neat perforations through the front and back! Needless to say it made a good story when they arrived in camp.

Towards the end of the settling-in period the Chief of the Imperial General Staff, on a tour of Malaya, paid 40 Commando HQ a visit. F M Sir William Slim, accompanied by Brig Hardy, flew in an Auster to an air strip at Kroh where they were met by Lt Col Lumsden. In the one hour at the disposal of the CIGS he was shown troops under training, a demonstration of a typical ambush and also found time to talk to the men. It was not long before the training was put into practice and the Commando registered its first kill. A photo of the bandit (security force jargon for CT) with the weapons and ammunition that he had been carrying were sent to Brigade HQ as confirmation. The CTs mostly wore khaki or jungle-green uniforms, puttees and rubber boots. One, two or three red cloth stars on their caps were intended to signify the dominant or main races in Malaya.

40 Commando's tactical area of responsibility (TAOR) was larger but less populated than the TAORs covered by 42 and 45 Commandos. The troops were for the most part deployed along the Lenggong-Grik road towards the Thailand border, a distance of over 70 miles with much of the road following the line of the Perak River. Troops were based at Lenggong and at Grik, each with a TAOR of some 300 square miles. The terrain consisted of rubber trees in areas close to the roads, but beyond the rubber was secondary and then primary jungle. There were a number of tracks running through the jungle. Those running north to south on the far side of the Perak River were used as the main CT transit routes to and from their training camps. Patrolling in those areas was often profitable. However, bands of CTs also operated on the eastern side of the river ambushing civilian buses, police and military vehicles on the Grik-Lenggong road. Therefore all unit vehicles moved in convoy, normally with armoured car support. To discourage CTs lying in wait at the roadside authority was given on occasions to open fire when approaching likely ambush positions.

The unit worked hard to maintain pressure on the CTs but a tremendous amount of spade work went into every successful operation. Frequently the achievement amounted to no more than the finding of a track; the remnants of a fire; a food cache or an old camp. One report from an A Troop patrol read "Went across the Perak river to a little place called Salu where bandits have frequently been reported. No contacts made but several camps found. One bandit supporter captured who had escaped from police custody". Intelligence reports were compiled from information of this nature and could be used to good advantage at a later date.

After a few weeks Commando HQ and support units moved to Kuala Kangsar – known as the Royal Capital of Perak – taking over one of the former royal palaces! This was not as opulent as it appears although the HQ Block and Sergeants Mess were well accommodated.

The commandos did not operate in isolation. Iban trackers from Sarawak – many of whom were making their acquaintance with cars and aeroplanes for the first time – proved to be excellent navigators. Not only could they point

RSM W. Chesterton at the entrance to the Sergeants Mess.

A temporary shelter in the jungle. Photos: W. Chesterton and I. Hardie.

directly at north or south but would select the best route to follow. Before their true potential was recognised one patrol leader put the Ibans – who normally worked in pairs – at the back of his patrol. Moving slowly through the thick undergrowth along the course of a jungle stream the leading commando scout emerged into a clearing and was surprised to see the two Ibans sitting on a boulder about 50 paces ahead. They had seen from looking at the bark on the trees that the stream took a large turn back on itself and had taken a short cut!

Without doubt, one of the major contributions to success in the emergency was provided by the Junior Civil Liaison Officers (JCLOs), of whom about sixty per cent were Chinese. The balance was made up of 30 per cent Malays and 10 per cent Indians. In discussing this point recently with Col Mansell, he said "They were very sincere, intelligent and brave young men who acted as interpreters and participated without hesitation in the most hazardous opera-tions. They provided a close link between the commandos, the Ibans, police, civil authority and the local people. The commandos established a marvellous rapport with them".

The RAF gave invaluable assistance with reconnaisance, tactical support, transport and supply. Tempest and Lincolns operated in direct support of the troops. Targets were not always easy to see from the air or pin-point from the ground but this type of action harrassed the terrorists and prevented them consolidating. While appreciating that there was no air opposition and little risk of injury from ground-fire, the chances of aircrew surviving a crash-landing in the jungle were small. An Auster forced down in bad weather had both wings ripped off by the trees but on that occasion the pilot and passenger emerged unscathed.

The maps produced by the Royal Engineers from RAF mosaics proved of considerable value to the ground troops. Supply drops by parachute also enabled patrols to remain in the jungle for extended periods. Aircraft were frequently used for dropping propaganda leaflets and a number of these originated from the unit Intelligence Officer. Gen Templar*, visiting 40 Com-mando towards the end of the unit's tour in Perak, read one of the leaflets and told his ADC to obtain copies for use elsewhere in Malaya. The RAF support was very much appreciated but unfortunately the distance between the forward troops and airfields prevented any social link-up between comman-dos and airforce personnel.

The commandos maintained very close co-operation with the police and late one September evening, Capt N. Cooper received information from the police that a rubber-tapper, living about half-a-mile from the troop camp, had been told by the Min Yuen to pay money to the CTs. Apparently they would collect the money from the tapper the next morning. Capt Cooper immediately organised an ambush party and, while one group lay up in the long grass near the hut, Lt Mansell and a section took up positions inside the hut. At dawn, CTs

---

* General Sir Gerald Templar

191

were seen approaching the hut, but a noise alerted them and they fled into the undergrowth. Lt Mansell set off after them with his section and, seeing a CT crawling away on the other side of a valley, shot him. Shortly afterwards Lt Mansell, finding that he was about 50 yards ahead of his group, took cover behind a tree – near the dead CT – and was himself shot. He continued to follow the CT trail with his section until contact was finally lost.

Opportunities for rest and relaxation were infrequent but periodical visits by the Commando Brigade Band to the troop locations were a welcome diversion. Football was played when possible but the on-field skill of the commandos could not match the local Malay opposition when a combined Kuala Kangsar schools' team beat them 6-0!

A few families managed to follow the Commando Brigade to Malaya but the general conditions and operational requirements prevailing left little time or opportunity for family life. The 40 Commando families were accommodated in the Runnymead Hotel in Penang, which was taken over for this purpose. During one comparitively quiet period they were invited to a families' day at Kroh, where they were given lunch and the children were taken for rides in a scout car. Towards the end of November a rest camp was established on the island of Pangkor. It was a safe area where the off-duty troops could relax and enjoy swimming, fishing and other recreational activities.

The announcement of a pay increase was favourably received and consisted of a 75 per cent rise in the basic daily rate of pay for marines and corporals and a 33 per cent increase for SNCOs. A marines pay went up to 6/6 (35P), corporals pay to 8/6 (45p) and sergeants to 10/6 (55p). A further incentive was the offer of a £100 bounty to marines and NCOs who re-engaged on completion of 12 years service.

Throughout the autumn the task of "hunting bandits" continued relentlessly. In Kedah, B Troop arrested seven men who were identified by a surrendered insurgent as "wanted persons". The troop also gathered in 31 agents and suppliers to the CTs. In Lehat, A Troop, working with the police on a screening operation, arrested eight insurgent suspects. A further 18 suspects were apprehended in the area of Puising. Close to the Grik-Lenggong road a patrol from Q Troop, climbing a steep "bandit track", came under fire from automatic weapons. After a 15 minute fire-fight the insurgents withdrew leaving a blood-stained trail. Further into the jungle a large CT camp was found. In their haste to depart the CTs had abandoned documents and medical supplies.

Groups of CTs were very active along the Grik-Lenngong road in December and commando patrols with support from the 12th Lancers combed the area. An unfortunate accident at this time led to the death of Mne (D) K. Mathieson while he was on convoy duty. A few days later a B Troop patrol was ambushed near Grik. One marine was hit by automatic fire and evacuated by helicopter to Taiping. Camps were found and destroyed and the whole area stirred up but no contacts were made with the CTs.

With the year drawing to a close Brig Hardy, in accordance with custom, circulated a message to all men in 3 Commando Brigade. He summarised the events that had taken place in the early part of 1950 in Hong Kong and then focused attention on the problems confronting the commandos in the jungle. He said "This task could be compared with big game hunting, because success comes from cunning and determination, and because the smaller the number of hunters chasing one beast, the greater the chances of success."

"During the four months July to October, we killed or captured more bandits and destroyed more camps than any other State. We are now halfway through our second four months and things are fairly quiet, but the number of successes have also decreased. There is, however, no need to be disappointed yet – these things tend to go in waves. For example, one infantry battalion has had only two major contacts in thirteen months."

"It is possible that the bandits have got used to our way of operating, and if that is so, we must use more cunning. There is always the danger too that as the novelty wears off people become inclined to lose patience in an ambush, or to give up the scent when hunting. We have not reached that stage yet. The motto for the future is–

Be cunning in every operation. Be tenacious when hunting. Be patient when ambushing."

Many of the Ibans were, at this time, completing their tour of duty with the Security Forces and preparing to return to Sarawak. They had adapted well to working with the commandos and the JCLOs, who acted as their interpreters. When the Ibans first arrived in Malaya they wore little more than head bands of bright feathers. Six months later they were returning to their homeland worldly wise but retaining their primitive dignity, proudly wearing khaki uniforms, green berets with the corps badges and glistening brass-work on their white canvas belts. There was no let-up over Christmas or the New Year for the security forces and it looked very much as if the MRLA was increasing its minor guerilla attacks. A squad of Frontier Police investigating a fire at Temingore Tin Mine on Christmas Day was ambushed by 50 insurgents. The outnumbered police put up a stout resistance but three men, including the officer in charge, were killed and four more were wounded. Two days later, Sgt M.J. Taylor, leading a B Troop patrol in the same area, was fatally wounded. Patrols from the Commando retaliated on 10 and 11 January 1951 in skirmishes with CTs, killing one of their number and arresting four suspects.

A week later a unit convoy was ambushed near Grik and two marines in a 15 cwt truck were wounded. At no time was it possible to relax. A large re-settlement programme was in progress and a number of patrols from the Commando were involved in screening and checking the identities of squatters who were being moved into a new village. A patrol led by Lt M.G.Dowling, was operating in a expanse of small dwellings on 14 January when he decided to check on the occupants of one of the huts. A shot was fired as he entered the building and the bullet hit the butt of his carbine. He ran out, called for support and re-entered the hut with the patrol sergeant close behind him. Another shot was fired killing Lt Dowling. The Sergeant then quickly located the occupant of the hut and killed him. The dead Chinese was one of the top Communists in the area who had been extracting money from the local people.

Much work had already been carried out in the re-settlement of squatters. This was part of a plan to combat the insurgency and was introduced by Lt Gen Sir Harold Briggs following his appointment as Director of Operations in Malaya in April 1950. The General, who had gained much experience of jungle fighting during his campaigning days in Burma between 1942 and 1945, planned to separate the MRLA from those who supplied the necessities for survival. The main source of supply was the Chinese squatters. The plan also included the re-grouping of labour employed in the mines and on the rubber estates.

The Chinese squatters had been vulnerable to the pressures of the Min-Yuen to provide money, food and clothing as well as recruits. By moving them into well sited areas which could be protected by the police and in due course by their own home guard contact with the MRLA could be broken. The task was enormous and required very careful planning and preparation. The MCP and the Min Yeun did everything possible to disrupt the programme and many of the squatters, who had no wish to move, employed delaying tactics. Progress was slow, but very steadily the moves that would eventually break the lifeline of the MRLA went ahead.

At the end of January, Brig Hardy relinquished command of 3 Commando Brigade and was succeeded by Brig C.F.Phillips DSO, OBE, who had commanded 47 Royal Marine Commando in the Normandy landings and at Walcheren. New arrivals to 40 Commando included Maj H.E.Johns MBE, who was to take over as second-in-command, Capt A.P Willasey-Wilsey and Lt D.Langley.

Rigorous patrolling continued and an insurgent camp was found in the Taiping area large enough to house 70 people, complete with well constructed huts and a cookhouse. Terrorist activity around Grik had receded. The squatter re-settlement in that area was completed and the rice harvest had been collected. Although the unrest in Grik had quietened down, the same could not be said of the other areas. The MRLA was still very active and there were daily reports of attacks on tin mines, trains, road transport and shops. Passengers would be turned off buses, their ration and identity cards taken and the buses burnt. There were incidents of civilians being killed and others disappearing. Rubber trees were slashed in their thousands, and pressure on the workers by the Min Yeun and Terror squads led to many of the estates being left unattended. The Government responded by increasing the armed forces until there was a brigade or its equivalent in every state.

The Commando intensified its patrolling and made a number of successful contacts. A patrol to the north-east of Grik found a supply dump containing a large quantity of rice and medical supplies. In the Lenggong area a Y Troop patrol led by Capt J. Showell-Rogers crossed the Perak River with the object of attacking a CT camp, the location of which had been reported by RAF reconnaissance. After 12 hours of forcing their way through dense jungle they found their objective. The CTs had not been alerted by any sentries and three of them could be seen sitting in the doorway of one of the huts. As daylight was fading rapidly the patrol moved quickly into the camp.

In the fire fight that developed Capt Showell-Rogers received a severe arm wound but Cpl G.R. Howe immediately took over command and pressed home the attack. One of the CTs was killed. The other two were wounded but escaped into the jungle. Knowing that other CTs could be in the locality Cpl Howe formed a defence position until first light when he followed the trail of the wounded CTs. As was expected the patrol came under fire from an ambush position but dislodged the CTs, who broke off the engagement and withdrew into the jungle.

While the benefits of re-locating the squatters in the new villages began to show results it became obvious that food supplies were still filtering through to the MRLA. In consequence Lt Gen Briggs introduced a scheme known as "Operation Starvation". This required shopkeepers to record details of all food sold. It was impossible to obtain the full co-operation of the Chinese and was never fully effective.

On 2 April a 40 Commando patrol was ambushed eight miles from Kuala Kangsar by a strong force of CTs. Lt J.B.Coop and Cpl R.T.Ryder were killed outright in the first burst of fire and a marine was wounded as the commandos moved to regain the initiative. After a short fire-fight the CTs withdrew and contact was lost. A second patrol led by Lt P.Pennell went out to follow up the trail but made no contact. Some days later a patrol led by Lt J.J.Moore with a captured CT acting as a guide, searched through the same area. With dusk approaching Lt Moore ordered the captured terrorist (through the JCLO interpreter) to point to where he would set an ambush. Acting on the information received he moved his patrol into position in time to catch the CTs approaching along the route indicated. In the subsequent shoot-out two were killed by Lt Moore. Several others were wounded but escaped into the jungle.

In between the endless "jungle bashing", guard and convoy duties,sport provided a welcome method of relaxing and keeping fit. The Brigade Sports Officer organised a inter-unit athletics meeting which the unit won comfortably. They also excelled at boxing, winning the Malayan Area Championships by outpointing the Green Howards, and then went on to win the Far East Land Forces Championships by defeating the RASC Singapore.

FM Sir William Slim emphasised the importance of keen observation in his book "Jungle Fighting", in which he stated "Survival depends on observation; learn really to see what you look at". This was put into practice by members of a Y Troop patrol on 20 May in the Lenggong area. The patrol leader approaching a rocky outcrop accurately assessed that the position provided ideal cover for an ambush and anticipated accordingly. As the patrol moved closer to the outcrop a hidden Bren gun opened fire in their direction. Immediately the patrol took the initiative and using fire and movement, overran the position killing one CT and capturing another. One CT, who was seen briefly by some of the patrol, managed to escape. On the following day a marine of the patrol watched the funeral procession of the dead CT. To the amazement of all, he dashed into the procession shouting "There he is!" and extracted the CT who had escaped from the ambush position on the previous day.

There were 606 reported incidents in Malaya in June, although in the locality of Grik the situation remained relatively quiet. A further 180 Sakai were brought into the resettlement area at Temengor without any repercussions. During this phase Lt Col Lumsden returned to UK on completion of his tour and his successor, Lt Col M. Price DSO., assumed command on 12 June 1951.

On 20 June a CT camp was found and a cache of 50 lbs rice was destroyed. The same day six suspects were arrested by a patrol near Taiping while in Kuala Kangsar, a grenade was thrown into a shop but failed to explode. On a lighter note it should be recorded that 40 Commando competed in the annual Commando Brigade Rifle Meeting and relieved 45 Commando of the Unit Championship Cup.

July started badly. Sgt M.J.Taylor and Mne D.Wells, travelling in the rear vehicle of the morning convoy to Grik, were both wounded when the column was ambushed. Mne R.A.Gough was also wounded during the subsequent fire-fight in which the insurgents were driven off. Sgt Taylor died a few days later. On 10 July, Mne J.Chadwick was killed when a 3 ton vehicle which he was driving ran off the road during the hours of darkness. The situation improved when later the same month a Troop-screening operation on the village of Redang Panjang, led to the arrest of eight suspects. In mid August an X Troop patrol successfully ambushed six insurgents, killing two of them and wounding a third. Three Lee Enfield rifles and 88 rounds of ammunition were recovered.

In August and early September S Troop and neighbouring artillery units took part in a number of search and destroy operations. The 3-inch mortar sections were particularly active and fired 792 bombs at targets between the 84th and 92nd mile markers on the Grik-Lenggong road. However, the density of the trees reduced the effectiveness of the bombing and shelling. Pinpointing a concealed CT camp to a artillery observation post by troops who were themselves deep in the jungle also had its problems. More than one patrol experienced the trauma of finding that a range correction resulted in the shells landing closer to their own position than that of the enemy!

During the first week in October a B Troop patrol, dressed to look like Chinese, attempted to penetrate into an occupied CT camp. Led by TSM D.M. Morgan, the commandos set out into the jungle hoping that the disguise would enable them to slip past any CT lookouts. The ruse failed. The patrol was

196

ambushed by 40 CTs and in the initial burst of fire Mne G.A.Dayes was killed and the TSM and a JNCO were wounded. Mne W.Lowrie displayed great courage at this critical time, providing covering fire while the TSM moved the patrol from the ambush position. Then with the skilful use of fire and movement, TSM Morgan and his men killed four CTs. The remainder of the terrorist group withdrew into the jungle. In the follow-up the patrol found and destroyed a large well-constructed camp.

The High Commissioner, Sir Henry Gurney, was killed on 6 October in an ambush to the north of Kuala Lumpur. Security Forces found and shot five of the CTs responsible but the remainder disappeared into the jungle. The leader of the ambush party was eventually found and shot eight years later after some of his own men betrayed his hide-out.

Determined efforts made by 40 Commando to cut off food supplies to the CTs in the Grik-Lenggong area were reasonably successful. A tapioca plantation and two temporary camps near Lawin and a large food dump north-east of Sumpetar were located and destroyed. On 7 November, a successful early morning attack was made on a small CT camp near Sumpetar by a Y Troop patrol led by Capt G. Roberts.

The military received much of their information about insurgent movements and activities from the police. The Federation Police consisted of a force of about 10,200 at the start of the emergency, most of whom were Malays. By 1950 the force had been considerably strengthened by a few hundred former Palestine police and the formation of a Special Constabulary of Malays. The Special Constabulary, once trained, took over the protection of static posts thereby releasing the Federation Police to work with the military in the offensive role.

The men of 40 Commando were reconciled to making the most of their second Malayan Christmas in troop locations. Although catering facilities and expertise were not consistent with Cordon Bleu standards, the Troop Quartermaster Sergeants and cooks ensured that the Christmas dinners were special. On 3 January 1952, personnel from the unit assisted the police with a large screening operation while X Troop deployed to south Perak to assist 45 Commando. The operation extended over a number of weeks during which time X Troop was required to patrol a large area of swamp jungle in which the few tracks were mostly constructed of duck-boards. On 18 January, two sub-sections led by Lt J.Langley located a CT observation post in a tree. Recent track marks led from the OP into a waist-deep stretch of mangrove swamp in the centre of which was an extensive thicket of bush and high grass. The leading scouts had commenced to wade across when Bren gun fire, from at least three CT positions, killed Cpl J.C. Ireland, one of the scouts and wounded Lt Langley and Mnes C. Alexander and R.King. Lt Langley immediately launched part of his force in a flanking movement towards the CT positions under covering fire from other members of the patrol. The CTs abandoned their slit-trench positions which were dug on the perimeter of a camp built to house up to 80 people. The casualties were evacuated as speedily as possible but Mne Alexander succumbed to his wounds on the way to hospital.

A second deployment, involving a sub-section of A Troop and 25 police led by Lt P. Pennell, took place in the extreme north-east of Perak. The detachment, under the temporary command of the Malayan Scouts Air Service Regiment, had the task of searching and investigating conditions in a remote Malay kampong at Belum, on the upper reaches of the Perak River. The inhabitants were known to be dominated by a group of CTs and it was suspected that they were being forced to produce food for them. It took seven days for Lt Pennel's patrol to reach the kampong, travelling on foot through the jungle and following the course of the river. The element of surprise was achieved by dropping a squadron of the Special Air Service Regiment by parachute into a small clearing in the forest of 200 ft trees close to the kampong to coincide with the arrival of the foot patrol. This was the first airborne operation to be carried out in Malaya. Having completed their task the commandos and SAS had to return along the same tracks taken on the outward journey, with constant risk of ambush by CTs.

In February 1952 Gen Sir Gerald Templar was appointed High Commissioner of Malaya and Director of Operations. One of his first tasks was to revitalise the directives introduced by Gen Briggs and a combination of military and civil power provided him with the opportunity to cut through much of the red tape. He merged the Federal War Council and Federal Executive Council into one central body, which helped improve liaison and general relations between the civil administration, the police and the military. He made his first visit to Commando Brigade HQ on 22 March and inspected some of 40 Commando's positions the next morning.

Rumours of a Commando Brigade move to Malta were confirmed in early March. The news coincided with the promotion of Brig Phillips to MGRM Portsmouth Group and, in his farewell message circulated in the *Commando News*, he wrote "I cannot do better than quote what the Labour member for Huddersfield, Mr J.P.W. Mallalieu, said in the house of Commons on 6 March during the debate on the Naval Estimates." 'The Royal Marines, I think, are the most remarkable body of men I know. Because they can do anything the Army can do, and do it a great deal better. I say they are a remarkable body, and indeed they are. When it comes to "spit and polish" they cannot be beaten and when it comes to the real dirty work, they cannot be beaten either.'

On 17 April, a Memorial Service, conducted by the Brigade Chaplain, the Reverend Young, was held in the church of St John the Divine, Ipoh. The small building was packed with members of the Brigade and their guests. A marine, corporal, senior NCO and officer each read a section of the Roll of Honour which contained the names of the 33 'all ranks' of 3 Commando Brigade who had lost their lives in Malaya. Of this number 14 had served with 40 Commando. An Iban then spoke aloud the names of his people who had died while serving with the Brigade. On completion of the service 40 Commando paraded a Guard of Honour, commanded by Capt G. Glossop, for the Sultan of Perak, who then took the salute at a march past of elements of the Commando Brigade.

The 1st/6th Gurkha Battalion relieved 40 Commando and the unit moved to Singapore to return Malayan stores and to enjoy a few days local leave before embarking in SS *Halladale* on 6 May.

Before leaving Malaya, 40 Commando erected a bronze plaque in the Church of the Resurrection, at Kuala Kangsar, to commemorate the 14 officers, non commissioned officers and marines who lost their lives during the tour of the Commando in Perak. The plaque, on which the following names are recorded, was dedicated on 8 March 1952 by the Right Reverend J.H. Baines, Bishop of Singapore.

RM	9324	Mne	C. ALEXANDER	RM	7792	Mne R.H.V. EAMES
PO/X	5282	Mne	(D) J. CHADWICK	PLY/X 4758	Cpl	N.S. HOWE
RM	9447	Mne	R.J. CHERRY	CH/X 4492	Cpl	J.C. IRELAND
RM	8810	Mne	R.A. CLARK	PLY/X 5721	Mne	K. MATHEISON
		Lt	J.B. COOP	PO/X 127316	Sgt	S. ORR
RM	8330	Mne	G.A. DAYES	CH/X 4147	Cpl	R.T. RYDER
		Lt	M.G. DOWLING	CH/X 1620	Sgt	M.J. TAYLOR

The following awards to 40 Commando personnel were approved for distinguished service while on operations in Malaya.

ACpl	G.R.	Howe	DCM	Lt	J.J.	Moore	MC
Lt	D.	Langley	MC	TSM	D.M.	Morgan	DCM
Mne	W.	Lowrie	DCM	Lt	J.D.	Shallow	MC
Lt	W.B.	Mansell	MC				

Mentioned in Despatches

Maj F.C.Barton, Capt F.M.Bristowe, QMS E.R. Biss, ASgt S.R.Kaysar and Lt(QM) W. Robson,

POSTSCRIPT.

In January 1990, Chin Peng, aged 67, leader of the Communist Party of Malaya, signed peace agreements with the governments of Malaysia and Thailand at a hotel in the border town of Had Yai. The arrangement allowed the remaining 1,100 fighters to leave the nearby mountainous and jungle clad Betong salient in Thai territory after giving their weapons to the Thai military. Most of them were expected to settle on plots provided by the Thai government on the outer fringe of the jungle where this remnant of the MRLA had held out since the end of the Malayan Emergency in 1960. Chin Peng had lived mostly in China since the 1960s.

CHAPTER 14

7 May 1952 to 2 August 1956

Malta-Exercise "Beehive" and "DXM"- Visits by GOC Malta,
C-in-C and the King and Queen of Sweden – Presentation of Colours to
units of 3 Commando Brigade – Training east of Suez, Exercises Longbow
and Crossbow – Training in Cyprus, Exercises Shorelark III and Snowdrop
– Malta – Internal security in the Canal Zone and anti-terrorists
duty in Cyprus.

FOLLOWING two years of dangerous and uncomfortable terrorist hunting in the Malayan jungle, the change to peace-time soldiering in Malta effected everyone. For the most part the changes were beneficial and welcome. The Commando was once again living in barracks as a unit instead of widespread troop locations and the married men were able to send to UK for their families. No time was lost in polishing-up the brass-work and drill as the Commando was committed to two visits by Maj Gen Hemming, GOC Malta, and a two weeks tour as Duty Regiment shortly after arrival on the island.

Brig J.L. Moulton DSO, OBE, who assumed command of the Commando Brigade from Brig Phillips, was well acquainted with the work of the commandos having had considerable war-time experience commanding 48 RM Commando in Normandy and Holland in 1944 and 4 Commando Brigade in 1945.

The unit took part in Ex Beehive and Ex DXM during July and August. The first was a defence exercise against a battalion of United States Marines – who landed in the north of the island – and, as the Commando transport was still on its way from Malaya, the unit footslogged into action on the hottest day – 99 degrees – of the summer. DXM was mainly a HQ exercise, in the form of a large TEWT conducted by wireless.

In addition to the aforementioned exercises all the fighting troops completed a three-week cliff assault course followed by the Commando carrying out a full-scale assault landing with supporting arms in the north of the island. In conclusion, the unit prepared a series of demonstrations for the C-in-Cs visit to the Brigade. The last event included the scaling of a cliff, the hoisting of three-inch mortars by roller haulage and various methods of roping down. The demonstrations were repeated again on 16 October for their Majesties The King and Queen of Sweden, who were visiting Malta as guests of Lord Louis Mounbatten, C-in-C Mediterranean and brother of the Queen of Sweden.

The unit participated in the various garrison sports activities and although the water-polo enthusiasts found the local opposition too strong against which to make an impression the cricket eleven remained unbeaten in the Senior

Malta. The King of Sweden accompanied by Lt Col M. Price DSC, observing a demonstration of cliff climbing and roller haulage at Ghain Tuffeha. 16 October 1952. Photos: M. Price

Recovery of the G1098 stores vehicle onto LST Messina after an unrehearsed dive into the Bitter Lake during transfer from a LCM. April 1953. Photo: Author.

League. The marksmen shot well in the Inter Unit Rifle Meeting, carrying off numerous firsts while the footballers commenced the winter season in excellent form, winning their first six matches.

The parade ground at Floriana, which is within sight of the historic city of Valletta, was itself the scene of an historic event concerning the Commando Brigade on 29 November 1952. On this clear, warm, sunlit day the three Commandos comprising 3 Commando Brigade, received for the very first time, Colours, which were presented to the units by His Royal Highness The Duke of Edinburgh. Prior to the parade the Colours were consecrated by the Chaplain of the Fleet, the Venerable Archdeacon F.N.Chamberlain, in St. Paul's Anglican Cathedral. Lt Langley carried the Queens Colour for 40 Commando and the Regimental Colour was borne by Lt P.P.B. Aldrich.

While the Colour Parties were attending the Cathedral service, 40, 42 and 45 Commandos, accompanied by the massed bands of the Commando Brigade, HMS *Glasgow*, *Tyne* and *Kenya*, formed up on the parade ground. The parade ground was lined by RM detachments from HMS *Theseus*, *Glasgow*, *Euryalus* and *Cleopatra*, the 2nd Raiding Squadron and 3 Commando Brigade HQ. Blocks of stands, constructed specially for the occasion, were filled with senior guests, dignatories, representatives of the armed forces and civic authority as well as relatives and friends of the men on parade.The varied uniforms of the service guests and summer hats and dresses of the ladies, provided a colourful back-cloth to the serried ranks of the commandos in their blue uniforms and white helmets.

Each Commando was represented by four guards, each of three Officers, four Senior NCOs and 72 JNCOs and marines. The parade formed up in line under command of Brig Moulton for the inspection by H R H The Duke of Edinburgh. His Royal Highness was accompanied by the C-in-C Mediterranean Fleet, the Earl Mountbatten of Burma; the Commandant General Royal Marines, Gen J.C.Westall CBE., the GOC Malta Forces, Gen Hemming and the Governor, Sir Gerald Creasey. Following the inspection the parade formed hollow square for the presentation of colours and on completion The Duke of Edinburgh addressed the parade and said:

"Through three centuries the Royal Marines have maintained a tradition of service and courage which are the envy of all Her Majesty's Forces. The Royal Navy in particular has ample reason for its pride and affection for its seagoing soldiers. The formation of the Royal Marines Commandos during the last war must have stirred the shades of your predecessors, for here was an opportunity for part of the Corps to return to the amphibious warfare which was its cradle."

"These Colours are a recognition of the devotion of the war-time Royal Marine Commandos and of the courage and bearing of the Brigade in all the trouble spots of the world since the end of the war. As a Brigade you are a relatively new addition to Her Majesty's Forces but you have the honourable traditions of Her Majesty's Royal Marines behind you and the good-will and

Lt D. L. S. Langley MC, receiving the Queen's Colour from HRH The Duke of Edinburgh.
Photos: A. J. Donald

Lt P. P. B. Aldrich, receiving the Regimental Colour from HRH The Duke of Edinburgh.

support of us all for the future. Guard these Colours well and remember that, whatever the problem, a Royal Marine Commando is always expected to achieve the impossible."

Brig Moulton replied:

"Your Royal Highness, as Brigade Commander, I thank you for the Colours which you have presented on behalf of Her Majesty The Queen to 40, 42 and 45 Commandos Royal Marines. I also thank you for your kindness in travelling so far to perform this cermony and for the gracious words today. The Officers and men of the Royal Marine Commandos promise to honour and guard these Colours which symbolise our duty and loyalty to Her Majesty and of the Commandos.

"Although Colours are no longer carried in battle, we can and will honour these Colours by cultivating the ancient virtues of honour, courage and loyalty. We shall always hold ourselves ready to fulfil in our time the words of Admiral Lord St. Vincent: 'In the hour of danger they will be the Country's Sheet Anchor'".

The Brigade then reformed line and formed up in column of guards for the march past, with 40 Commando leading. The parade concluded with the Brigade reforming line and advancing in review order.

The order of the parade for 40 Commando was:–

Commanding Officer
Lt Col M. Price DSO

Field Officers for handing the colours to HRH The Duke of Edinburgh
Maj H. E. Johns MBE   Maj C. J. Terry

Colour Party

Queen's Colour	*Regimental Colour*
Lt L. S. Langley MC.,	Lt P. P. B. Aldrich

QMS C. H. Barratt
CSgt O. B. Falconer, CSgt H. L. G. Harrison

Adjutant	*Quartermaster*
Capt P. J. F. Whiteley	Lt (QM) S. Boyd BEM.,

Regimental Sergeant Major
RSM L. J. Boote

No 1 Guard	*No 2 Guard*
Capt A. T. Gardner-Brown	Capt A. P. Willasey-Wilsey MBE
Lt J. E. J. Lloyd	Lt R. H. Passmore
Lt. M. J. Webb-Owen	Lt R. J. Lee

No 3 Guard	No 4 Guard
Capt B. P. Elvey	Capt W. D. Waddell
Lt P. R. Dawson	Lt J. J. Moore MC
Lt D. A. H. Collin	Lt P. M. Reed

The Commando carried out the commitments of Malta Duty Regiment over the Christmas period but leave was arranged to enable all ranks to enjoy a two day break. The arrival of a troopship on Boxing Day, bringing families from UK, was a wonderful Christmas present for many of the married men. Early in the new year vehicles and stores were prepared for a move to Suez for winter training and exercises. The Commando embarked in HMS *Tyne* on 18 February and the time on passage was spent giving the ships company a hand with spring-cleaning and repainting. Before the *Tyne* left Suez the Captain signalled the unit "Thank you very much. Hope you polish up the desert the way you polished us".

The advance party had prepared accommodation at Arroyo Camp, a semi-permanent camp of corrugated roof huts and tents close to the west bank of the Suez Canal and adjacent to a flat, sandy area used by the RAF as a dropping zone (DZ). The tents were supplied with electric light from the camp's own generators and plenty of water was available on tap. The first few days were spent drawing stores, acclimatising to hot days and cold nights and exercising formations and movement across the desert with the unit transport – similar to convoy procedure with ships at sea. During this phase many exhausting hours were devoted to recovering vehicles from the sand, practicing desert navigation with the sun compass and learning to maintain oneself and vehicle radiators on a strict water ration!

The Commando crossed to the east side of the Suez Canal to participate in two major exercises in the Sinai desert. The first, "Longbow", involved a motorised division confronting an enemy force of armoured cars but few infantry. The exercise commenced with an advance to contact starting at midnight from a location named El Shatt. This phase started slowly but gained momentum as the division moved forward across the Sinai desert throughout the day and the following night. A test of endurance for the drivers, vehicles and bone-shaken, dust-choked passengers.

Day two, commenced with a dawn attack, with the Commando leading the advance through the confinements of the Mitla Pass flanked by high barren mountains rising in some areas to well over two thousand feet. A notional minefield blocked the way and the troops took to foot-slogging and climbing the precipitous sides of the pass to avoid the obstacle. The first opportunity to pause for a quick breakfast occured at 1730 hours! The objective was still thirty five miles ahead but the umpires eventually relented and allowed the unit transport through a "cleared path". In due course the Commando was joined by its parent infantry brigade and formed a laager for the night.

Next morning, the advance continued to the objective, followed immediately by a withdrawal to the start line close to the Mitla Pass. There had been little opportunity to sleep during the previous 48 hours and the night drive proved to be bitterly cold and difficult. Drivers fell asleep at the wheel and others lost direction in the clouds of fine sand thrown up by other vehicles. By early morning the convoy of trucks was extended over five miles of desert and all ranks were thankful when the first glimmers of daylight heralded a rise in temperature and the conclusion of the exercise at El Shatt.

The CO's Orders Group set out the next morning to reconnoitre an area 100 miles to the south where the commandos would match their wits against those of the paras of the 16th Independent Parachute Brigade in Ex Crossbow. The commandos (the bad guys) were assumed to have kidnapped a scientist (Surg Lt D. D. Miller RN, the unit's black-bearded medical officer) prospecting for radio-active metals, and to have pursuaded him to work for them in his portable laboratory in the Wadi Khamila, 30 miles inland from the Gulf of Suez. The Parachute Brigade had the task of effecting his rescue.The terrain was impressive and consisted mostly of line after line of rugged, barren, rocky ridges climbing to 1,000 ft and intersected by deep tortuously shaped gorges. The preliminaries of moving to the start line gave a taster of the challenge to come with the Commando transport, showing signs of the "Longbow" pounding, spread over 70 miles of soft sand. Firm going was eventually found and, at midnight 24 March, both sides were ready to do battle.

The nature of the ground was such that while the Paras numbered 2,500 men, the Commando force of 520 were able to delay their progress indefinitely. By nightfall the following day, A, X and Y Troops, who had withdrawn steadily through the main wadi, were holding a strong defensive position behind a minefield laid by the Assault Engineers. Orders initiated by the umpires overcame this stalemate but a series of manoeuvres skillfully directed by Lt Col Price led the Paras into soft sand and the transport of two of their battalions became bogged up to the axles in Wadi Khamila. By the end of the exercise the Paras were on half rations of water and the commandos were eking out the last of the bully beef and biscuit.

Soon after returning to Arroyo Camp the Commando transport – after 1,000 odd miles of desert travel – presented a few problems when the time arrived to waterproof the vehicles in readiness for the amphibious and triphibious exercises Shorelark III and Snowdrop. These exercises were programmed to take place in Cyprus and Headquarter staff had a busy time planning the return to Malta via Cyprus while closing down the Suez camp. The Commando embarked in ships of the Amphibious Warfare Squadron at anchor in the Bitter Lakes. In the process of transferring some of the vehicles from LCMs to LST *Messina*, the G1098 stores truck took a dive to the bottom of the Bitter Lake. Excellent team work by members of the SBS, the ships company of *Messina* and the Commando transport section, had the vehicle aboard in time to sail. Capt A. Eyre wagered the unit fitters that they would not have the engine running by the time the LST docked in Famagusta harbour. He quite happily lost!

Ex Shorelark III, consisted of a landing on an enemy occupied coast (Cyprus). Advancing 20 miles inland to the mountainous Troodos area to recover the engine of a crashed enemy aircraft (a discarded RAF fuel pod) followed by re-embarkation the following night. After one rehearsal near Famagusta the landing force sailed for Morphou Bay in the north-west of the island. It was the season of the orange blossom and the fragrance was borne on the wind to the ships off-shore. The landing and recovery of the "engine" proceeded without a hitch and the Commando was able to enjoy a few days of relaxation and sightseeing in Famgusta, Nicosia and Kyrenia before commencing the final exercise "Snowdrop".

Both 40 Commando and 16th Parachute Brigade combined forces to attack a mountainous feature 25 miles inland. The parachute Brigade dropped with guns and transport on two DZs while 40 Commando made a notional landing; captured a coast gun-battery (also notional) and advanced to secure a river crossing between two DZs. After receiving an air drop of compo rations, water and petrol the Commando moved inland to secure a pass through which the paras and commandos would move the next morning. The second day commenced with a 15 mile approach to the foot of a rocky range.This was the start line for an attack which culminated on a crest of jagged rock 2,000 ft high. The exercise ended appropriately at dusk and both units lost no time in making their way to nearest road where transport returned them to their respective bases. 40 Commando embarked that night at Famagusta and sailed for Malta at 0500 hours the next morning.

Political relations between Great Britain and Egypt cooled rapidly towards the end of April when Anglo/Egyptian talks broke down. This led to a call for a Brigade HQ detachment and 42 Commando – training in Tripoli – and 45 Commando in Malta, to move at short notice by sea to the Canal Zone. If the situation in Egypt deteriorated before 7 May 40 Commando, sailing slowly westward, would be diverted to the Canal Zone. In the event the deadline passed without any trouble and on 9 May 40 Commando arrived in Valletta Harbour looking forward to a pleasant summer in Malta.

Five days later the unit was ordered to return immediately to Egypt. Stores and equipment had to be re-packed and crates remarked. Vehicles which had been stripped for maintenance had to be re-assembled and arrangements had to be made to close the barracks and lift the unit by air to the Canal Zone. The advance party received its instructions at 1100 hours on 14 May and five hours later was flying east over the Mediterranean in a Sunderland flying-boat. The main body flew from Luqa airport in five Sunderlands, four Lancasters and seven Valettas, as and when the aircraft became available. A Valletta, leaving Malta on 17 May, crashed on take off, resulting in the deaths of LCpl R.Don and Mne D.E. Burtenshaw. A further 18 personnel of S Troop received burns and other injuries. CSgt.B. Falconer was instrumental in saving the life of a marine who was trapped by his safety belt. Flames swept through the open door of the plane after it had crashed and when seconds stood between life and death he went back and released the safety belt undoubtedly saving the marine's life. For this selfless action and disregard for his own safety CSgt Falconer was awarded the George Medal.

By the time 45 Commando, sailing in HMS *Ranpura*, had arrived at Port Said the political situation had calmed down but the Commando units were retained in the area in an internal security role. In UK the media was focused on the Coronation of Queen Elizabeth and in the Canal Zone the occasion was celebrated with a Coronation Parade at Kaspfreet Airfield. Contingents from the 1st Infantry Division, 40 Commando and three RAF Stations, which stretched the length of the runway, were inspected by Lt Gen Festing.

The entire Brigade was now in the Canal Zone. Brigade HQ occupied a camp 25 miles south of Suez before making a base at Moascar. 42 Commando was accommodated at 156 Transit Camp, on the Port Fouad side of the Canal before moving south of Suez to El Hafar and then to Arroyo Camp. 45 Commando was based at Fayid, spending a short period at Abu Sultan before moving to Port Fouad. 40 Commando was initially based at Geneifa Camp, on the southern end of the Great Bitter Lake. This was the beginning of a long period of Internal Security duties. The Brigade was involved in the thankless task of patrolling pipe lines, guarding bridges, road junctions, ammunition dumps, buildings, VIPs and themselves. For reasons of security and safety it was compulsory to travel in groups or in pairs and movement after dark in most areas was restricted to duty commitments.

The Commando said farewell to Lt Col Price on 26 June prior to his return to UK to take up appointment as second in command at the Infantry Training Centre Royal Marines. Maj Johns was promoted Local Lt Col and assumed command of the unit while Maj M. Pound took over the duties of second in command. Lt Col Price received the OBE and RSM L.J.Boote the MBE in the Coronation Honours List.

About mid-June, the unit commenced a six weeks tour of duty guarding the large Middle East ammunition base of Abu Sultan. The base had been in existence for many years and the barbed wire perimeter, doubly protected by mines in some sectors, was in a poor state of repair. The mines had a tendency to move in the shifting sand and during one perimeter patrol Capt R. Bavin was severely shaken when a back wheel of his vehicle was blown off by a detonated mine!.

Dumps of ammunition which had become unstable after years in the sun were gradually removed by teams of specialists employed on this delicate task. Preventing the removal of this dangerous material and other types of ammunition by Egyptians – who were prepared to take great risks to acquire the explosives, was the units primary task. One Egyptian, attempting to remove an ammunition container from the compound in broad daylight, was shot by a marine from B Troop when he refused to stop when challenged.

The Rifle Troops returned to Geneifa Camp to find the new 3.5 in Rocket Launcher awaiting their attention. This platoon anti-tank weapon replaced the obsolete PIAT. The new rocket launcher, used to good effect by 41 Independant Commando in Korea, had a maximum range of 1,000 yds although its effective range was considerably less. Also, at this time the 9mm Patchett Machine Carbine with folding butt replaced the Sten- gun, and the anti-tank Energa Grenade fired from a standard No 4 rifle was introduced.

The Quartermaster – with five unit moves since February still fresh in mind – was not amused when he was informed that the Commando was to make another move to a disused camp at El Ballah. Although closer to Port Said it was aptly named Sandy Camp with its nearest neighbours being an Egyptian airfield on one side, a French gypsum factory on the other and the Welsh Guards to the north. One point in its favour was its proximity to the Canal – two miles west of the camp – where it was possible for the off-duty men to swim and exchange unprintable phrases with more fortunate service personnel on homeward bound ships.

The move coincided with the annual Malta Defence Exercise (DXM) in which B,P, X and S Troops, under command of Maj Pound, were selected to take part. While this force flew to Malta in 11 Valletta aircraft, A and Y Troops, who had drawn the short straws, remained behind to prepare Sandy Camp for occupation.

Ex DXM consisted of defending Malta from an invading force, provided on this occasion by marines of the USA Sixth Fleet. The commandos on Melleiha Ridge, were well positioned to observe the landing at St Paul's Bay and, after a tactical withdrawal to Wardia Ridge, made a flanking counter attack which dislodged the enemy. The senior staff, satisfied with this contribution towards the salvation of Malta, released the Commando contingent to enjoy a weekend leave before being air-lifted back to Egypt. Unintentionally the Commando officers almost sabotaged the remainder of the exercise by organising an impromptu ban-yan and bathing party in the centre of a beach where the USA Sixth Fleet marines were due to make a night landing!

On return to the Canal Zone, the Commando moved into Sandy Camp and continued with the major task of internal security. Three Troops were fully employed on location at Nefeisha Bridge, the Banyan Tree, at the northern entrance to Ismalia and the Reserve Supply Depot at El Kirsh. The Troops not engaged on I.S duties, carried out a varied programme of weapon training, tactics and other military skills while a number of NCOs took part in a series of long range desert driving and navigation courses in the Sinai desert. Sports facilities were non existent but a flat, reasonably hard expanse of ground in front of the camp served as a multi-purpose soccer, hockey pitch and cricket ground. A mixture of oil and sand was used to produce a rather fragile surfaced tennis court but volley ball, which could be played almost anywhere became a very popular game.

Following the break-down of Anglo-Egyptian talks, the Commando Brigade's tenure of stay in the Canal Zone became unpredictable. Arrangements were made to rotate rear party personnel in Malta (Turnabout) with men in the

Canal Zone. These periods were normally of about two to three weeks duration, including the time en route in whatever HM ship was passing Malta. A number of wives decided to return to UK but the majority elected to remain. The unit wives rallied to form committees which arranged social events, childrens parties and offered advice and assistance to anyone in need of help.

A temporary change of scenery was provided in October when the unit assumed guard duties at Tel-el-Kebir during the absence of 19th Infantry Brigade on exercise. In November, the major part of the unit moved south west of Suez to Wadi Hagul for Ex Walkover. Prepared by Brig Moulton and his staff the exercise entailed a night-time climb over the precipitous Gebel Ataqua, to attack the enemy (notional) at first light. When the serious work of the exercise was completed the unit organised a ban-yan party at which a large stock of NAAFI beer was consumed. The party was also a farewell occasion for Brig Moulton who returned to UK to assume the duties of MGRM Portsmouth. Brig I.H.Riches DSO, his successor, had commanded 43 RM Commando in Italy and the Adriatic during WW II, and lost no time in making his mark on the Brigade.

In the Commando Brigade Rifle Meeting held in December, 40 and 45 Commandos tied for first place. In due course the 40 Commando team, under the skilled leadership of Capt Langley, won the 3rd Infantry Divisional District Meeting. After further intensive training the team achieved the distinction of winning the British Troops in Egypt Command Rifle Meeting, on the first occasion that Royal Marines had taken part in this event.

After a very quiet Christmas and a period of intensified security, the Commando entered 1954 with two troops deployed on IS duties and the remainder of the unit committed to guards, escorts and patrols. However, planning for an amphibious exercise commenced in January, and the Commando joined the Amphibious Warfare Squadron at Port Said on 6 February for passage to Cyprus. They were accompanied by a Beach Troop party provided by the AW Squadron, three FOB parties – two from AOBRA Malta and one from 42 Commando, a Field Surgical Unit from 23rd Parachute Field Ambulance, a section of MMGs from 45 Commando and a detachment from 4 Mobile Laundry RAOC ! The first phase of the exercise consisted of a landing and withdrawal and this was followed by a series of exercises combined with naval gunfire support.

No 14 Squadron RNZAF demonstrated its capabilities at straffing the A W Squadron on the final approach to the Cypriot coast and a local defence force from H Troop advance party – which constructed the base camp in a series of rain-storms – provided stout opposition to the 0300 hours landing on 7 February. Phase I completed, the Commando spent a non-tactical 24 hours in the base camp before commencing the field exercises on the high ground overlooking Cape Arnauti. HMS *Glasgow* and HMS *Daring* provided the gun support and helped to enliven proceedings with a *Glasgow* shell landing closer to the Commando location than planned. During this period the Mortar

Her Majesty Queen Elizabeth accompanied by HRH The Duke of Edinburgh at Floriana, on the occasion of their visit to Malta, April 1954. Photo: Author.

The Palace Guard, accompanied by the Band of 3 Commando Brigade Royal Marines, marching from Floriana to the Palace in Valletta. Photo: K. W. Bundy.

211

Platoon fired 750 bombs and the MMG sections fired 8,000 rounds. The final exercise was observed by Maj Gen Daunt, GOC Malta. On conclusion the Commando re-embarked in the AW Squadron at Famgusta and shore leave was granted over a period of three days before returning to the Canal Zone. On 26 February three Rifle Troops were again deployed on IS duties, which intensified in March following an ambush by Egyptians which resulted in the death of two Army personnel near the filtration plant at Gebel Maryan.

There were two noteworthy items in April and May. The first concerned the visit of Her Majesty The Queen and His Royal Highness The Duke of Edinburgh to Malta. A composite Troop and Colour Party were flown to Malta to participate with representative Troops from 42 and 45 Commandos and detachments from the Navy, Army and Air Force, in the Royal event at Floriana. The 40 Commando Colour Party consisted of – Queen's Colour, Lt R. H. Passmore; Regimental Colour, Lt P.R.Dawson; Senior NCO Escort, QMS. S Smith, Sgt L.R.Tilbrook and Sgt W.H.Bennett. The Troop also formed a street lining party along Kingsway, Valletta, for Her Majesty's formal call on the Governor of Malta. The weather was at its best and the people turned out en masse to enjoy the ceremony. Particularly important was the fact that this was the first occasion on which all Royal Marine Colours of 3 Commando Brigade were paraded concurrently before the reigning monarch.

Within 24 hours of the Colour Party returning to El Ballah, a larger contingent of 250 men, under command of Maj Pound, proceeded to Malta for the Queen's Birthday Parade. In Valletta, one thousand men representative of all the armed forces, took part in the ceremony on Floriana Parade watched by hundreds of spectators. The detachment enjoyed an unexpected two weeks on the island before returning to the Canal Zone in company with the Brigade Band.

The second event was far less formal and consisted of converting part of Sandy Camp into a fair-ground for Easter Monday. There were many willing helpers with bright ideas, and within a short space of time coloured bunting, music, coconut-shy, hoopla stall, roll-a-penny, fortune teller and numerous items of fun were provided to entertain the men. The massive, bearded Surg Lt Miller and stocky, Quartermaster Capt J. Wall challenged each other to a boxing contest but the referee was on the receiving end of most of the punches.

In mid-May the unit said farewell to Lt Col Johns and welcomed Lt Col T. Grey DSO, MC, to the sandy wastes of El Ballah. QMS Holland moved to Trans Jordan, to take up appointment as fencing instructor to the Arab Legion, and there were a number of other changes of personnel.

A reduction of the duration of the overseas tour to eighteen months was welcomed by all ranks. Ironically the political tension disappeared with the signing of the Anglo – Egyptian Suez agreement in August and the Commando Brigade received orders to return to Malta as part of the re-deployment programme for the Middle East. Once again the Quartermasters staff rolled up their sleeves in preparation for the move. The Troops continued with IS duties and one or two small scale exercises until it was time for the main body to embark in HMS *Gambia*. The Brigade rear party, which included A Troop and MT Section, left the Canal Zone on 6 September 1954.

The return to St Patricks Barracks was coupled with preparations for six weeks of training and desert exercises in Tripoli. Not satisfied with spending the best part of 17 months in one area of desert the Commando appeared to be keen to dig into more sand! Before leaving Malta 40 Commando said farewell to 42 Commando. This unit was due to move to England on 29 September following the Chiefs of Staff decision to obtain a better balance between home and foreign service throughout the Corps. It was intended that 42 Commando would remain fully operational and available at an approved notice and slightly reduced establishment, either to rejoin the Brigade or to serve elsewhere outside the UK.

Brigade HQ with 40 and 45 Commandos sailed to Tripoli in HMS *Forth* and ships of the A W Squadron. The units established tented camps in the vicinity of Tarhuna and were soon absorbed in a rigorous training programme. The USAF base near Tarhuna provided fighter support for the exercises while J Battery RHA and A Sqdn 14/20 Hussars were incorporated into the work-up programme. The days were dry but cool and the sand, which had blown out of Tripoli during the previous six months now swept back in, penetrating the deepest recesses of clothing, equipment and weapons. The scorpions also took a dislike to the cold and found comfort in empty boots and bedding.

A unit exercise, Little Chaos, ran more smoothly than the name implied and in the short rest period that followed arrangements were made for unit personnel to visit the ancient Roman city of Leptis Magna, on the coast near Homs. Many of the stone and marble buildings have been well preserved by layers of sand that covered the forgotten city for nearly 2,000 years. A team of Italian archaeologists commenced excavations just before the start of hostilities in 1939 and the work continued after the war.

The Brigade staff had not foreseen the possibility of two days of sand storm when planning the exercise Heinz Apple but it became part of the natural hazards to be overcome when 40 and 45 Commandos battled against each other. The US Air Force performed a number of low flying sorties despite the appalling conditions, which may have accounted for a number of wireless masts being a little shorter by the end of the exercise! The weather deteriorated further towards the end of the exercise, with frequent rain storms and the area was evacuated just before the roads were made impassable by flood water. Storm-force winds prevented the carriers *Albion* and *Centaur* entering harbour and the crossing to Malta was eventually made in four destroyers.

The unit spent a busy but none-the-less pleasant Christmas as Malta Duty Regiment, and continued the momentum into the new year of 1955 with a move to St Andrews Barracks. The vacated St Patricks Barracks was occupied by the 88th LAA Regt RA, neighbours of the Commando in the Canal Zone. Farewells were said to Maj Pounds and Maj P. Matters took over as second-in-

213

command. The latter part of January was devoted to preparations for the annual administrative inspection and range courses programmed for February. A further period of Malta Duty Regiment commenced on 1 March and the following day A Troop paraded a Guard and the Colour when the Commandant General visited the unit. The combined Home and Mediterranean Fleets were in port and the Commando paraded a Royal Guard for HRH the Duke of Edinburgh at Customs House when he first stepped ashore. The Queen's Colour was carried by Lt R.F Gray and the Regimental Colour by National Service Officer ALt P.M Cope. Prince Phillip, now Captain General, paid his first visit to the Brigade in this appointment to see a demonstration of field training, and on the evening of his departure was entertained by all the Brigade Officers in 40 Commando's Officers mess.

Another form of entertainment was provided by an all-rank cast of volunteers assisted by wives who banded together to present a variety concert for the unit in Australia Hall. While in Tripoli, a camp concert produced by Capt Beadle and Lt J. McNulty had been highly successful and this attempt to go one better provided a splendid evenings entertainment for everybody.

Preparations for Ex Medflex III that would take 40 Commando to the hilly areas of the Greek islands, were at an advanced stage when earthquakes in Greece led to its postponement. Ex Pontiflex, designed to take its place, commenced on 6 June and consisted of two weeks of minor raiding operations from the A W Squadron in the local bays of Malta and Gozo. The Squadron with 40 Commando embarked then sailed for Tripoli where two landings were made at Zuara in heavy surf.

A new weapon was introduced to the Corps at this time in the form of the Belgian designed FN 30 rifle. The self-loading rifle – slightly heavier but shorter than the No 4 rifle that it replaced – was fed by a 20 round magazine and contained the characteristic feature of a pistol grip and gas-operated recoil system.

The daily routine suddenly changed when the Commando received orders to move at 48 hours notice to Cyprus to assist in anti-terrorist operations. The main body embarked on 9 September in HMS *Birmingham* and sailed for Famagusta. The following day the advance party, under command of Capt Bavin, flew to Cyprus and on arrival at Polimedhia – four miles from Limassol – slaved madly to clear scrub and obtain tents. Within hours of the mainbody arriving P and A Troops were at Limassol helping to quell a riot. B and Y Troops deployed to Troodos where they were to spend six weeks supervising the security of the district and keeping a watchful eye on the supporters of Enosis (Union with Greece) in the mining village of Amiandos. The majority of these men were members of the National Organisation of Cypriot Fighters (EOKA).

The call for Enosis was a repetition of earlier claims for a union with Greece. An abortive uprising in 1931 led to the suspension by Britain of all representation in the administration of the colony and various restrictions were imposed which continued to the end of 1945. Post war, the British Labour Party aimed to establish a more liberal and progressive regime, but this was unacceptable to the pro-enosis Cypriots. George Grivas entered the scene in 1950, contacting young student Cypriots in Athens, who were devoted to the Enosis cause. Born in Nicosia in 1898 he joined the Greek army and on his retirement from the service in 1945 dabbled unsuccesfully in politics before directing his attention to promoting the Enosis.

In July 1952, Grivas attended the first meeting of a Liberation Committee in Athens, chaired by Archbishop Makarios. Grivas returned to Cyprus and began organising recruitment and the collection of weapons for his movement. The first large shipment of arms reached Grivas in March 1954 and in November of that year he set about drawing the elements of the Pan-Agrarian Union of Cyprus (PEK) and the National Front for the Liberation of Cyprus (EMAK) into one group. On 11 January 1955 Makarios informed Grivas that Marshal Papagos of Greece supported their aims and it was at this meeting that EOKA was formed. On 29 March 1955, Makarios gave Grivas permission to commence acts of sabotage.

By the time 40 Commando arrived in Cyprus the EOKA campaign was well in its stride. The Commando helped to impose a series of curfews but the disorder continued and a serious riot developed in Limassol on 27 September. A major part of the Commando was required to disperse the unruly crowd that was led by a mob element. In one incident it became necessary to shoot one of the ringleaders.

Disturbances throughout the island were exacerbated by a general strike, followed unexpectedly by three weeks of comparative peace. This gave the unit an opportunity to consolidate before the disturbances were renewed with more intensity on 21 October. An RAF car was burned at Pano Kivides and the following day a bomb exploded in one of the many bars in Limassol. A 40 Commando marine received injuries from bomb splinters on 25 October and a similar incident occured on 27 October. Rifle troops from 45 Commando arrived to relieve B and Y Troops, who re-joined the unit in time to assist with the enforcement of a curfew at Limassol. It was 28 October, Greek National Day.

The Cypriot Turks were very much in the minority* and vunerable to terrorist attack. Between 1955 and 1958, when EOKA activities were at their height, hundreds of Turkish Cypriots were killed and injured and their property destroyed. In consequence the Turkish Cypriots retaliated against their Greek Cypriot neighbours at every opportunity. Keeping these two factions apart was a major problem confronting the commandos.

In October 1955, a new Governor of Cyprus was appointed in tandem with the change of British Government. F M Sir John Harding, who had been the Chief of Staff MELF, established a reasonable understanding with Makarios

---

* Turkish Cypriot census 1973 Turkish Cypriots 24.6% Greek Cypriots 74.7%, others 0.7%

and was able to offer the Archbishop, on behalf of the British Government, a 38 million pound economic aid programme, contingent upon a plan to introduce limited self government to Cyprus, with the possibility of self-determination at a future date. The conservative Greek Government endorsed the British offer but Makarios, under extremist pressure, rejected the proposals.

The anti terrorist programme of patrols, search and guards continued into November. Sir John Harding visited 40 Commando on 17 November and Lt Gen C.R.Hardy CB,CBE, DSO++, who had assumed the appointment of Commandant General Royal Marines on 20 August, called on the unit four days later. The day after CGRMs visit 40 Commando's camp was flattened by a severe storm which left a trail of damage in its wake!

A major round-up of leading Communists on 14 December, including the town Mayor of Limassol, led to a serious student riot. B and Y Troops, who had the task of quelling the disturbance, were met with showers of stones and a bomb which fatally wounded Sgt Routledge of Y Troop. Sgt Routledge was buried with full military honours in Nicosia Military Cemetery on 21 December.

Security duties involved every man in the unit in one form or another, day and night, in all weathers, through Christmas and well into January of 1956. The Commando was also committed as a result of redeployment, to move to a new location in the area of Paphos where they relieved the 1st Battalion Royal Scots. Commando HQ, S and Q Troops were accommodated in the base camp at Coral Bay while B, P and Y Troops assumed responsibility for the security of Katima. The townspeople, a mixed population of Greek and Turkish Cypriots, were quick to make it known that they did not like commandos. However, the British residents appreciated the presence of the green beret in their community. Awards of the BEM to QMS Farmery and Mne Goughtrey were announced at this time for their outstanding service while engaged on IS duties.

There was little opportunity for any form of relaxation during the tours of duty but leave rostors were arranged and single men had the choice of a few days skiing in Troodos or visiting Beirut. As time progressed married men with families in Malta were able to pay them a short visit and approval was given for a limited number of families of 3 Commando Brigade to move to Cyprus. This facility did not extend to 40 Commando personnel as terrorist activity in the unit locality was considerable and neither accommodation nor schooling was available.

The general situation in Cyprus deteriorated when negotiations between Sir John Harding and Archbishop Makarios collapsed at the conclusion of a meeting with the Colonial Secretary in late February. It was stated that the Archbishop was not prepared to accept the Colonial Secretary's offer as a basis for co-operation. The authority, using the power of the state of emergency, deported the Archbishop on 9 March to the island of Mahe in the Seychelles. Gen Grivas assumed command and although the number of incidents increased, there were no major riots.

The unit was employed extensively in systematic cordon and search operations in the villages during May and June and considerable quantities of weapons and ammunition were recovered. Although the bombing incidents decreased they still presented a major hazard. Lt Col D. G. Tweed assumed command from Lt Col Grey on 2 May and both narrowly escaped injury when a bomb exploded a few yards behind the champ vehicle in which they were travelling, during a hand-over visit to one of the rifle troops. Subsequently Lt Col Tweed ordered that officers would not in future travel together except in very exceptional circumstances. Such an occasion was apparantly necessary on 9 May when Maj Maude and one of his subalterns were ambushed while on their way to a meeting with the District Officer and Chief of Police in Paphos. It was an unfortunate decision. A bomb was thrown into their jeep and the explosion killed Lt T. M. Dick instantly and Maj Maude received severe injuries.

The various elements of H Troop rarely make news but without their support the fighting troops would frequently find difficulty in operating effectively. The following detail gives some idea of the distances covered by the MT Section in Cyprus and the administrative involvement during the time that the unit had been on the island. The vehicles covered a total of 357,782 miles and consumed 37,455 gallons of petrol. The 20 minor accidents were mainly the result of bad driving by Cypriots and poor road surfaces. Between September 1955 and May 1956 a total of 322 joined the unit while 308 men returned to UK, with all the resultant issuing and return of weapons, equipment, bedding and other items, About 40% of the unit strength – 244 men – were National Service. There were over 4,100 weapons transactions through the stores.

Further awards were announced in June with Capt J. Taplin receiving the MBE and RSM G. L. Bream the MBE. Both Sgt H. James and Mne K. L. Goodney received the Queen's Commendation for the capture of two armed terrorists the previous October, in Limassol. Although there had been a lull in terrorist activity in June and July a major anti-terrorist cordon search operation was mounted in the west Paphos forest area in which 40 Commando and Army units were involved. The Operation – Golden Eagle – lasted six days and although the villagers were more co-operative than in earlier months the operation revealed nothing.

Towards the end of July a troop of the Royal House Guards arrived in Coral Bay to relieve 40 Commando of all road patrols. This eased the work load immensely and the unit was just beginning to enjoy a more relaxed routine when Lt Col Tweed received orders to hand over all duties to the 21st Medium Regiment Royal Artillery. The unit was given a deadline of 24 hours to complete the task and move to Famagusta to embark on HMS *Ocean* on 14 August. While the Commando units were sailing towards Malta, Brig Madoc, Lt Col Tweed and Lt Col Tailyour, CO of 45 Commando, were on their way to London by air, for a briefing on events taking place in Egypt. Gen Nasser had decided to nationalise the Suez Canal!

CHAPTER 15

3 August to 5 December 1956

SUEZ. Events leading to the invasion of Egypt – Return of 3 Commando Brigade to Malta – Planning for Operation Musketeer and Exercises with the Amphibious Warfare Squadron – Israel attacks Egypt – 3 Commando Brigade embark – RAF bomb Egyptian airfields – French and British Parachute troops drop – Allied sea-borne assaults on Port Said and Port Fouad – 40 and 45 Commandos return to Malta and 42 Commando to UK.

THE Middle East in 1955 was the centre of a complex political power game. Rules were made and changed without prior consultation between interested parties and some of the participating nations could be said to have had a vested interest in more than one side. America, Britain, Egypt, France, Iraq, Israel, and Syria were the primary nations involved.

The USA, with a growing commercial interest in the region, wished to cultivate a defence organization in the Middle East. The USA provided economic and military aid to the Central Treaty Organisation (Baghdad Pact), comprising Turkey, Iraq, Iran, Britain and Pakistan. Relations between Egypt and the USA deteriorated when Turkey officially recognised Israel. An offer of American military aid to Egypt was rejected by Nasser.

Britain was mainly concerned with containing the activities of the EOKA organisation in Cyprus and, following the signing of a treaty with Egypt in 1954, the withdrawal of British forces from Egypt. The Anglo–Egyptian treaty gave Britain the right to maintain the supply base at Ismailia (with civilian technicians) and to have access to the base in the event of aggression against Turkey or countries in the Arab League, unless Israel was the aggressor.

Egypt was going through a period of considerable change. The withdrawal of the British forces from Cairo in 1947 and Palestine in 1948 exposed the vulnerability of the Egyptian Army to Israel forces during the conflict in 1948-49. The abdication of King Farouk in July 1952 was followed by the deposition of his son King Ahmed Fuad II and a military council headed by Gen Mohamed Neguib assumed power in 1953. A year later Lt Col G.A.Nasser replaced Gen Neguib as head of the Military Council.

France had a strong interest in Syria and was suspicious of Britain's support for an Iraqi-Syrian union. The Algerian conflict had led to increasing enmity between France and the Arab nations. Meanwhile Iraq was vying with Egypt for leadership of the Arab nations.

Israel, alienated by all the Arab countries following the defeat of the Arab forces by the Jews in 1948, remained defiant and uncompromising. Egypt was showing increasing signs of hostility along its borders with Israel and incidents of aggression were a daily occurence.

Russia concluded an arms agreement with Syria in May 1955 and arranged to provide Egypt with T-34 tanks, self-propelled guns, other arms and jet fighters. Two squadrons of MiG-15s had been supplied to Egypt from Czechoslovakia by the end of the year. This build-up of military equipment alarmed the Israelis who arranged an arms deal with France to provide them with 60 Mystere IVAs.

Talk of possible Soviet financial support for a new Aswan Dam scheme influenced Britain (Sir Anthony Eden) into promoting a joint USA-British and International Bank offer of $400 million towards the project. During these discussions a proposal was made by Turkey that Jordan should become a member of the Baghdad Pact, and in December 1955 Britain offered financial and military assistance to Jordan to expand the Arab Legion. Col Nasser, incensed by this action applied anti-British propaganda pressure on Jordan. There were riots in Amman and the Jordanian Government resigned.

During a meeting in Cairo on 1 March 1956, Mr Selwyn Lloyd, British Foreign Secretary to the Conservative Government was told by Col Nasser that there was little chance of an improvement in Anglo-Egyptian relations unless an undertaking was given that no new Arab members would be admitted to the Baghdad Pact. Within hours, Mr Lloyd received news that Gen Glubb, a British officer seconded to Jordan to command the Arab Legion, had been dismissed and ordered to leave Jordan.

On 19 July, the USA withdrew its offer of financial support for the Aswan Dam project. Britain and the World Bank were quick to follow this course of action. The British announcement by Mr Lloyd in the House of Commons stated that "The Egyptian Government would no longer be in a position to devote to the dam project the degree of priority necessary to secure its success". America's more direct statement referred to Egypt's failure to agree to various amendments to the plan and inability to provide her share of the cost.

An appeal by Col Nasser to Russia to finance the dam project met with a negative response.The only other source of revenue within his reach was provided by the Suez Canal Company. He ordered plans to be drawn up for seizing and nationalising the Canal and announced this decision in Alexandria on 25 July. The British Cabinet and Chiefs of Staff met on 27 July, followed by talks with a representative of the French Army Staff and American Secretary of State J.F.Dulles. Military action against Egypt was contemplated but, seeking a peaceful solution, arrangements were made for the 22 nations with interests in the Canal to meet with a view to the internationalisation of the Canal.

In Cyprus on 3 August, Brig R. Madoc received a preliminary brief from Gen Sir Charles Keightley, C-in-C Middle East Land Forces, and was told to prepare to move the Commando Brigade to Malta after handing over

On board HMS Reggio. The final arms inspection before landing. Photo: H. G. Bruce

IS responsibilities to 1st Army Group Royal Artillery. The following day Brig Madoc proceeded to London by air to commence planning for Operation Musketeer.

Both Brig Madoc and Lt Col Tweed arrived in Malta on 15 August where the Brigadier outlined the plan of Operation Musketeer to his two unit commanders. The Allied intention was to make an assault landing at Alexandria followed by a drive on Cairo. The Commando Brigade was now placed under command of Gen Stockell's 2nd Corps. Meanwhile 3 Commando Brigade had been withdrawn from IS duties and was on its way to Malta.

In England, Pay and Records Office Royal Marines (PRORM) received instructions at 1945 hours on 1 August to re-activate 42 Commando. The imposition of a minimum age limit of 18 years six months resulted in considerable additional checking but the formation of the unit in the Drafting Office and signals to units by teleprinter, had been completed by 0315 hours 2 August. Nearly all ranks arrived at their destination within 24 hours of the receipt of detail. 42 Commando advance party arrived in Malta by air on 20 August.

On that day the Commando Brigade commenced amphibious training from sub-unit up to Brigade level. The water-proofing of radio sets and vehicles was practised many times and wading training of vehicles perfected. This was the first amphibious training that the commandos had experienced for almost a year and the Brigade had not exercised with LVTs, tanks, naval gun support or air support during that time. 40 Commando was given the task of rehearsing landings onto a four feet high quay – similar to the quays to be found in Alexandria harbour. The obstacle was negotiated by ladder from an LCT, a slow cumbersome process which the men – especially Lt A.P. Whitehead the MTO faced with the problem of transferring the Champ vehicles to the quay – were pleased to discontinue when it became known that the unit would not be required to land on a high jetty.

For reasons best known to the Chiefs of Staff, the restriction on the "need to know" was such that Captains of HM ships involved in these preparations were excluded from the official planning and briefings. In consequence it was difficult for the Royal Marines to justify the purpose of this type of exercise.

Gen Keightley had been appointed Supreme Allied Commander on 11 August with Vice Admiral d'Escadre Barjot, C-in-C French Mediterranean Fleet, as his deputy. The naval, land and air force task commanders were British and their deputies were French. Force Headquarters was based in London and in consequence the Brigadier and COs of 40 and 45 Commandos had to return to the capital where they were joined by the CO 42 Commando for briefing and discussions. This was the situation on 22 August when the military objective was still under discussion. While it was appreciated that a landing at Alexandria would involve considerable risk an alternative objective was not seriously considered until 25 August.

The French then proposed that a landing should be made directly at Port

Said. This idea was accepted by the joint Chiefs of Staff. Cyprus was close to Port Said and would provide a suitable platform from which to launch a task force. Unfortunately the harbour and port facilities in Cyprus were too small and lacked the depth of water required by the warships and troop transports. The amphibious force would therefore have to be launched from Malta on 27 August. By this time 371st Postal Unit Royal Engineers – attached to 3 Commando Brigade – had been billeted with 40 Commando and Landing Vehicles Tracked (LVTs) from 1st Landing Vehicle Track Troop Royal Armoured Corps had been off-loaded from LCTs in Military Bay. The LVT drivers were reservists who had last seen service with their regiment in WWII.

Looking at the broad picture, a total of 25,000 British reservists were recalled to the forces. British aircraft carriers, warships and landing-craft were despatched to the Mediterranean and elements of the French Fleet were sent to Toulon. The British 16th Parachute Brigade and French 10th Airborne Division were brought to an operational state of of readiness.

Looking at the broad picture, a total of 25,000 British reservists were recalled to the forces. British aircraft carriers, warships and landing-craft were despatched to the Mediterranean and elements of the French Fleet were sent to Toulon. The British 16th Parachute Brigade and French 10th Airborne Division were brought to an operational state of readiness, also the British 3rd Infantry Division, the 10th Armoured Division and French 7th Division Mecanique Rapide. The RAF and French Air Forces commenced to assemble fighter, bomber and transport squadrons and tried to resolve the problem of inadequate facilities in Cyprus. The logistic difficulties confronting the planners and service commanders were enormous. By the beginning of August it was clear that an Anglo-French force could not be assembled in sufficient strength to make it immediately effective before the first week in September.

Brig Madoc returned to Malta on 25 September from his third trip to London to update the unit commanders. The plan involved a sea-borne assault on Port Said to land 40 Commando (left) and 42 Commando (right), either side of the Casino Pier. The assault troops were to be carried in LVTs and LCAs, to land at 0445 hours with H Hour 35 minutes after sunrise. The landing would be preceded by air strikes and Naval gun support to destroy gun and beach defences. The French sea-borne assault was to commence on Port Fouad at 0705 hours followed by a British parachute battalion descent 10 minutes later onto Gamil airfield. The French parachutists were to drop on Port Fouad and 45 Commando was to land by helicopter in the area of the interior basin.

The task of 40 and 42 Commandos was to establish a beach-head and, at H plus 20 minutes, a squadron of tanks would land to support them in the break out from the beach-head. 40 Commando would then advance along the Bund and capture the four shipping basins. On their right, 42 Commando would advance along the Shari Mohammed Ali to capture the bridge over the interior basin and water works. 45 Commando, after landing in the area to the north of the interior basin, was to relieve 42 Commando at the bridges and provide a stop at the north end of the causeway. When this phase was completed the three Commandos would each dominate an area of the city.

On 26 September, 40 Commando embarked in ships of the A W Squadron and carried out close support live firings with HMS *Duchess* at Filfla Island, off the west coast of Malta. Lt Gen Sir Hugh Stockwell, Commander Land Forces, visited the unit the following day and gave a rousing talk to the men. The intensive training of all elements of the Commando units and A W Squadron continued throughout September and into October. There was considerable emphasis on house to house fighting (firing blank ammunition) but this could only be practised in two derelict barrack blocks near Brigade HQ. There were no facilities for a tactical grenade throwing range and live grenade training was confined to one bay on the rifle range. Exercising with tanks of 'C' Squadron was hampered by a Maltese Government restriction on the movement of armoured vehicles. Nevertheless the tank crews and commandos established a good working relationship.

Brig Madoc returned from London on 13 October with details of a new Winter Plan and Lt Gen Stockwell arrived in Malta on 17 October to attend the planning conferences. Before any changes could be implemented the plan was shelved. The men were by this time fully trained, very fit and wondering whether they would ever get to Egypt. A sense of excitement swept through St Andrews Barracks on 23 October when the Brigade was brought to 24 hours notice but the order was rescinded and the situation continued as before.

In the diplomatic arena the complex discussions, postures and promises between governments of countries immediately involved with the Suez crisis, as well as recriminations between political parties, were coming to a head. France, committed to the support of Israel, had increased the delivery of fighter aircraft to 60 a month. Israel, responding to border incidents made a raid in strength across the Egyptian border. The Jordan Nationalist Socialist Party, campaigning against the Anglo-Jordan treaty was elected to power. Israel commenced to mobilise on 25 October, accusing Egypt of making incursions into Israel. At 1700 hours, 29 October, Israeli armoured units attacked Egypt.

The British and French Prime Ministers, having already decided a course of action in the event of Israel invading Egypt, delivered an ultimatum to Cairo and Tel Aviv on 30 October stating, that unless they withdrew their forces ten miles from the Suez Canal, Great Britain and France would take their own measures to enforce the decision and occupy Port Said, Ismalia and Suez. When the announcement was made in the House of Commons at 1600 hours, Labour protested that such action independent of the USA and UNO would be a risky gamble. (At the time of the ultimatum Israel's ground forces had not reached the 10 mile limit and could therefore continue to advance to this demarcation. But Egyptian ground forces would have to abandon positions still held on the east side of the canal). The ultimatum was rejected by Col Nasser.

Commando Brigade operation and administrative orders were issued to HQ staffs at 2330 hours 28 October and the following morning the Commando units received orders to prepare for a major amphibious exercise, including the waterproofing of vehicles and the issue of ammunition. This procedure took 24 hours but the embarkation of the Brigade (less 45 Commando) comprising 178 officers and 2,300 other ranks, with over 550 vehicles including 51 Centurion tanks, was completed by 2230 hours 30 October. 40 Commando was allocated to LST *Reggio,* commanded by Lt Cdr I.Stoop and LCT *Bastion* under command of Lt Cdr R. Davidson. At 2359 hours the A W Squadron, consisting of the HQ ship HMS *Meon,* 3 LST(A)s, 5 LSTs and 8 LCTs, sailed from Grand Harbour.

The landing-craft usually turned to port on leaving harbour for exercise landings in one of the bays. However, Sgt Gratrix remembers "On this occasion we turned to starboard and kept going out to sea. After half an hour a voice on the tannoy said we were heading for Suez. The convoy sailed in two lines at an average speed of six knots, the speed of the slowest vessel. At this point in proceedings Port Said seemed a long way distant". 45 Commando, who would cover the distance more quickly in the aircraft carriers HMS *Ocean* and *Theseus* sailed on 2 November. Cdr E. Bruce, in LCT *Sallyport* recorded "To get into the habit of things we had 'Action stations' from the time of sailing. Life belts were always worn and the ship was in a war cruising state."

Late evening on 31 October, Brig Madoc received a signal from the Allied Task Force Commander, ordering the cancellation of the helicopter assault by 45 Commando as the task of capturing the bridges had been allocated to a French parachute force. In consequence 45 Commando would be available to Brig Madoc as a floating reserve. This late alteration had to be notifified to personnel dispersed in 20 ships in the convoy and with the landing only a few days ahead the Brigadier decided that 40 Commando's task would remain more or less unchanged. After the break-out from the beach-head 42 Commando was to advance to the southern end of the city, to prevent infiltration from the Arab quarter and link up with 40 Commando south of the built up area. 45 Commando would remain in reserve, and when ordered by the Brigade Commander, would be carried by helicopters to the beach-head to support 40 and 42 Commandos as required. Finally, 45 Commando would proceed on foot to join up with the French parachutists at the bridges.

On 4 November new orders were received which required the Allied parachute troops to drop on 5 November, a day earlier than planned. The sea-borne landing would be made on 6 November as arranged but naval gun support, to exclude all guns of 6-in calibre and above, would only be fired in reply to Egyptian gun-fire. Only if events indicated an opposed landing would drenching fire from support ships be ordered. The change in orders relating to gun-fire support was decided at a very senior level in UK to minimise Egyptian casualties, but it left the question of whether the Commandos would have gun-support to cover the landing uncertain. Confirmation that it would be

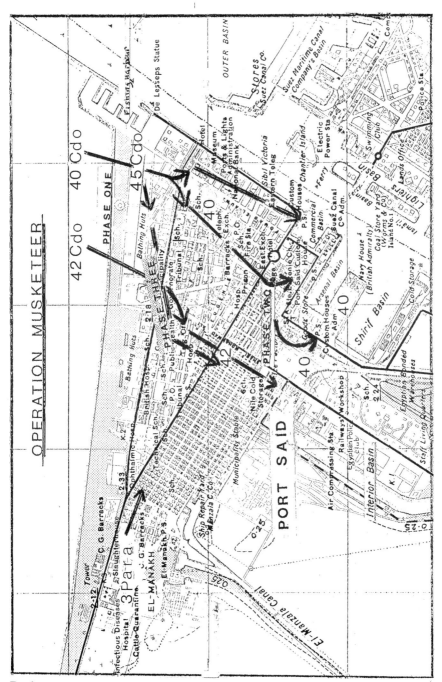

Deployment of 3 Commando Brigade at Port Said following the landings on 6 November 1956.

Approaching the beach under the cover of gun support from HMS Diamond *and* HMS Duchess. *Photo: H. G. Bruce.*

Port Said, shortly after the landing. Casino Palace Hotel in the foreground. Photo: RM Museum.

available was not made known to Brig Madoc until 60 minutes before H-hour.

Daily broadcasts received from the BBC London were not conducive to bolstering morale. The daily exchanges by MPs in the House of Commons could not be construed as supportive and statements by the Leader of the Opposition were so demoralising that on one occasion the ships broadcast system on LCT *Bastion* was turned off. The slow progress of the convoy was monitored by the USA Sixth Fleet. Boldly, in daylight on 4 November, a submarine of the US Navy surfaced and passed through the lines of British ships. No recognition colours were hoisted and no crew were to be seen. During the night of Landing Day minus two (L-2),the convoy increased speed in the direction of Port Said. On L-1 all was ready. According to Cdr Bruce in LCT *Sallyport* "The French assault element had just joined us and the place bristled with escorts. The paratroops had gone in 20 hours early, and then came news of a local armistice. Perhaps rather an anti-climax. However at 2300 hours came the news that the armistice was off and an opposed landing could be expected. The night was not so dark and I could make out the shapes of the battleship astern of us, then the carriers with the choppers. I heard their bugle call at 0200 hours. That was action stations for us also." At first light Brig Madoc could see Port Said in the distance with a dense pall of black smoke drifting over the city from a burning oil tank to the south. Lecturing to the staff of the Royal Naval Staff College in May 1957 he said "There were no lights showing and no signs of life."

40 and 42 Commandos transferred to their LVTs and LCAs and set off towards the beach. 40 Commando landed at 0447 hours, two minutes after H-hour. Their first task was to establish a small beach-head, with 42 Commando carrying out a similar assignment on their right. During the run-in there was very little shooting and the actual landing was carried out without much incident. There were no mines on the beach and it is interesting to note that there were only two beaches at Port Said where an amphibious assault could land. The other at Gamil airfield was heavily mined with anti-tank and anti-personnel mines."

The commandos in the landing craft were pleased to see that the fire support was right on time. The RAF dealt with coastal defences from H-55 to H-45 and then HMS *Diamond* and HMS *Duchess* opened up, firing nearly 1,400 rounds of 4.5-inch, in direct support of the landing force. At H-5 the Fleet Air Arm delivered a strike on the Beach area 400 yards ahead of the LVTs. The first wave of LVTs carrying A and X Troops towards the beach was fired on during the last stage of the run-in and while crossing the beach but there were no casualties. Machine-guns were found in the beach huts where they had been abandoned by their crews. Had they been more determined they could have created untold mayhem.

The first wave ashore was involved in limited fighting to capture the buildings at the back of the beach. A Troop, led by Capt R. Grant, had the task of clearing a large block of flats, about 200 yards from the beach-head.

According to Sgt Gratrix "Our 2-inch mortar-man laid smoke as near as possible to the building and we advanced a section at a time. In the process of clearing the flats two Egyptian soldiers were killed and one wounded". The 3.5-inch rocket launcher was used with great success to winkle out enemy positions in buildings. X Troop led by Maj A.P. Willasey-Wilsey, met stiffer opposition in the buildings on the right, killing 15 Egyptian soldiers and capturing three more before the area was finally cleared.

The second wave of seven LCAs carrying B, P and Y Troops, and the Commando Tac HQ, landed at 0450 hours. Y Troop, led by Capt D. Morgan, captured Liberation Barracks, to the south of De Lesseps statue while B Troop, led by Capt M. Marston, cleared the Fishing Harbour area and the breakwater before becoming reserve Troop. The HQ Troop element led by Capt C.J. Verdon, took over and established B Echelon in Liberation Barracks. The third wave, consisting of the remainder of HQ and S Troop landed at 0500 hours and the 3-inch Mortar Group set up base plates, but no calls were made by the rifle Troops for fire support.

The Fishing Harbour had been secured by 0700 hours and it was possible to call in LCT *Bastion*, carrying the Anti-Tank Platoon and first-line vehicles. A few shells passed over the ship in both directions during the run-in and on the approach along the Western Wall the commandos found themselves looking directly into the muzzles of six, 3-pounder guns. From Lt Whitehead's viewpoint on *Bastion* "It was not a pretty sight and for one moment we thought we would be lucky to go much further." Fortunately for the commandos the undamaged guns had been abandoned by the Egyptian gunners. Once ashore the 17-pounders, towed by Stuarts and crewed by gunners from 1st Battalion Royal Berkshire Regiment, deployed to cover the Rue al Gamhuriyah and Rue Vingt trois Juliet.

The Royal Navy soon discovered that the Egyptians had sunk a number of ships in the Canal entrance thereby blocking access to the Commercial Basin and quays. The superstructures of five ships were clearly visible and it was suspected that more vessels were completely submerged. Minesweepers, attempting to clear a path for the LSTs, lost their sweeps on the submerged obstructions and had to give up the task. Alternative berths for the LSTs were found alongside the Casino Hotel and in the Fishing Harbour.

The supporting armour, consisting of 11 Troop C Sqn 6 RTR, landed in the beach-head at 0535 hours to join up with the Commandos. P Troop, led by Lt J.P. Gardner, with the Centurion tanks in support, advanced along the Quai Sultan Hussein as far as the Port Police Station, completing the first leg of 40 Commando's Phase II in 15 minutes despite coming under fire at each road junction from buildings in the town. A marine was wounded while crossing these obstacles and a JNCO and marine were hit by shell splinters from a round fired by one of the tanks which exploded against the dockyard railings ahead of them. Another unfortunate casualty was caused by the back-blast of a 106mm anti-tank missile, fired from the roof of Liberation Barracks. The blast dislodged a coping stone which fell on a signaller below.

Capt Grant received orders to proceed with A Troop and one Centurion tank in support, to release the British Consul from house arrest. The approach along the Suez Canal met with some opposition and took about an hour. As Sgt Gatrix remembers it "The Consulate stood on the corner of some lovely ornamental gardens which were about 300 yds square. The buildings on this corner had to be cleared floor by floor and when cleared coloured markers – in the shape of a cross – were placed on the flat roofs to warn the Fleet Air Arm pilots that the commandos were in occupation. My section came under fire from a building on the other side of the gardens but the tank commander had spotted this and silenced the position with two HE shells". The 3.5-inch rocket launchers were also used to good effect by A Troop on enemy positions in buildings.

The Consulate square was strongly held by Egyptian infantry and A Troop had to fight hard to clear the way to the British Embassy. At the height of the engagement S Troop commander Capt Cooper, armed with his sniper rifle, went forward to see how the situation was progressing. In typical officers school playlet style his greeting to Capt Grant was "Hello Dicky, what's the form?" As he spoke a bullet flattened itself on the wall between them. "That!" replied Dicky Grant, stating the most precise assessment of the situation!

By the time the area had been cleared 23 Egyptian soldiers had been killed and a further 14 had been taken prisoner. Information provided by the prisoners indicated that eight of their number had been sent to kill the British Consul. In the clearance operation over 200 Soviet manufactured weapons and a large quantity of ammunition was found in the buildings overlooking the square.

Elsewhere the battle was progressing well. The French paratroops were in possesion of Port Fouad and the British 3rd Parachute Battalion, having captured Gamil Airfield, was fighting its way via the Coastguard Barracks and hospital towards shanty town. The British paratroops met stiff opposition and a call was made for Naval gun support to neutralise the area. At the beach-head, 42 Commando had silenced opposition on their right flank and pro-ceeded along the Shard Mohammed with amphibians and 10 Centurion tanks in support. Their progress was harassed by small arms fire and grenades thrown from buildings. The power station and cold storage depot – their objectives to the south of the built up area – were well defended by the Egyptians and there was some stiff fighting before they eventually captured these buildings.

One and a half hours after H Hour, the leading elements of 45 Commando, accompanied by the CGRM, were brought in by helicopter to land near the De Lesseps statue. The shuttle service proceeded as programmed and, accord-ing to Cdr Bruce watching the landings "It looked good, and I laughed to see the commandos so crowded that one man had to sit with his legs dangling out". While they were preparing to move along the Shard Mohammed to back

H Hour plus one hour 30 minutes. 45 Commando, accompanied by the Commandant General Royal Marines, land near De Lesseps statue.

Navy House. Scene of bitter fighting. Photos: H. G. Bruce.

up 42 Commando, a Royal Navy plane made a strike on the area, wounding 45 Commando's CO, Lt Col N.H. Tailyour, and causing 17 other casualties. Maj R. Crombie assumed command and the Commando continued the follow up to make contact with 42 Commando. Lt D. Edwards, leading a 40 Commando house-clearing team, later said "I could hardly believe my eyes when I glanced at a passing figure and recognised Gen Hardy, whose obvious intention was to have a ring-side view of the action.

By using the Fishing Harbour more extensively than planned the Navy overcame the problems of the blockaded Canal, and instead of being two hours behind schedule in bringing in the first LST, were soon ahead of programme. The beach party worked desperately hard to clear berths for the landing-craft ferrying troops and equipment from the ships. The ships blocking the Canal prevented access to the berths near Navy House, but in any event this continued to be an unhealthy area in which to remain for long.

In the meantime Y Troop, under the command of Capt Morgan, led the advance of 40 Commando with gun support from two of the four Centurion tanks allocated to the unit. Enemy resistance from the area of the huts at the north-west corner of the Commercial Basin was eliminated after one Egyptian had been taken prisoner and two had been killed. Movement along the western side was held up for a time by accurate fire from the direction of the town, resulting in the death of Mne L. Dudhill. The Centurions neutralised the enemy fire enabling the advance to continue to the Suez Canal building. Here, the opposition was quickly overrun leaving two enemy dead. During this time the tank armament and troop LMGs were used effectively against the Eyptian infantry who could be seen withdrawing southward from the town centre.

B Troop, commanded by Capt M.A. Marston, assumed the lead along the northern side of the Arsenal Basin. Almost immediately the forward sections came under intense and accurate fire from the Customs Houses on their left, killing Mne R.J. Fudge and wounding another marine. One section of the troop occupied the Police Station, where they disarmed and took custody of 12 policemen who were in the building. Wireless contact with the tanks was lost at this point and a runner was sent to X Troop with a request to secure the northern flank and neutralise enemy fire from the direction of the town and railway station.

Lt E.A.Ufton, led a section of B Troop in an attack on the Customs House. Two marines fell wounded as they raced forward but having gained an entry they cleared the area immediately in front of them and then moved to the next floor from which emanated much of the enemy fire. Two more sections led by Lt P.W.McCarthy entered the building to complete the clearance of the ground floor. The Egyptians, who had taken cover behind the customs inspection tables and in the rabbit-warren of cubicles and offices in the large hall, put up a fierce resistance and, in the process of forcing an entry into this area Lt McCarthy was killed and two marines were wounded. Lt Ufton assumed command and continued with the difficult task of clearing a determined enemy from the customs hall. His task was almost completed when he was killed by one of the enemy who had taken cover in the last office to be searched. The Egyptians had lost 17 killed. Two were wounded and another was found hiding in a cupboard.

X Troop continued with the clearance of Navy House Quay, using fire support provided by the tanks. Each of the postal and customs buildings were occupied by enemy troops and nearly all of them continued to fight until they were killed. Navy House, former HQ of the Royal Navy, was strongly defended and in order to overcome this resistance Lt Col Tweed called for an air-strike. This was delivered with great effect by Fleet Air Arm Sea Hawks just before the light faded. It did not completely silence the enemy and to minimise casualties the quay was cordoned off for the night. Two officers and six marines of X Troop were wounded in this final encounter. The Egyptians had lost a further 17 killed and four officers and six ratings of the Egyptian Navy surrendered at noon the following day.

While this local battle had been in progress P Troop, commanded by Capt P. Gardner, had been clearing small groups of enemy from the buildings along the waterfront. There were several consulates in the locality including that of the United States Embassy. Arriving at this particular building the troop commander was confronted by an irate official who said "Young man, if one of your marines steps across this threshold it will be an act of war against the United States of America". Employing considerable Royal Marine diplomacy, Capt Gardner tactfully placated the agitated embassy official while the lead section concentrated on silencing a particularly bothersome sniper hidden in an adjacent block of flats. A helpful tank gunner pierced the wall of the building with a round of armour piercing shot and followed up with a round of high explosive through the same hole for good measure.

Earlier in the day the Egyptian Garrison Commander had been taken to Brig Madoc's HQ where he asked if a cease-fire could be arranged. The Brigadier told him that he was not empowered to do so and in any case, if a cease-fire was ordered it would have to be on the same conditions as had been refused the night before when Brig Butler of the Parachute Brigade had tried to arrange a cease-fire with the Egyptian authorities. The Garrison Commander informed Brig Madoc that he was prepared to accept these conditions and the Brigadier signalled the HQ ship HMS *Tyne* accordingly. The Egyptian Commander was then taken to the house of the Italian Consul who was trying to negotiate a cease-fire.

By mid-afternoon Brig Madoc had established his HQ in a block of flats on the seafront and it was here that he first heard of the cease-fire on the BBC news broadcast at 2000 hours. By this time the 2nd Parachute Battalion and Guards Independent Parachute Company had disembarked and assembled at Raswa in readiness for the push to Ismailia. An hour later the BBC announced that the Prime Minister had informed the House of Commons that a cease-fire would take place at Port Said at midnight. The British Force was not aware at the time

HMS Reggio's White Ensign, hoisted following the capture of Navy House.
Photo: H. G. Bruce.

that the USA had threatened economic sanctions against Britain unless the action was brought to an end. The cease-fire, confirmed from HMS *Tyne* at 2315 hours, was implemented by the British and French. However, information of the cease-fire did not appear to have reached all the Egyptians. Spasmodic shooting continued from their positions during the night and an ammunition dump close to X Troop's locality exploded as fires spread in that direction.

The next morning the Commando Brigade re-organised and took control of the city with 45 Commando on the west side, 42 Commando in the centre and 40 Commando on the east side. Over 2,000 weapons were collected by 40 Commando personnel in house to house searches and guards were mounted to prevent Egyptians looting valuable stores from the dockyard.

On 9 November, Gen Stockwell informed Brig Madoc and Brig Butler that 3 Commando Brigade and the 16th Parachute Brigade were to leave Port Said. The Parachute Brigade returned to Cyprus on 12-13 November and the Commando Brigade, less 42 Commando and transport, sailed in HMT *Empire Fowey* on 14 November. 42 Commando remained in Port Said for a further 10 days and then joined the Brigade in Malta for a brief period before returning to England on 1 December.

The following casualties were sustained by 40 Commando at Port Said:-

Killed in action.

RM	15070	MNE	L. DUDHILL	LT P.W. McCARTHY
RMV	202128	MNE	R.J.FUDGE	LT E.A. UPTON

Two officers, one NCO and 15 marines received wounds.

The following awards were made to 40 Commando personnel for distinguished service while on operations at Port Said.

QMS G.D. Buttery	MM	Capt M.A.H. Marston	MC
Mne J.W. Crossland	MM	Lt Col D.G. Tweed MBE	DSO
Cpl D.E. Mant	DCM	Maj A.F. Willasey-Wilsey MBE	MC

CHAPTER 16

6 December 1956 to 6 May 1962

*Anti-terrorist duties in Cyprus – Garrison duties in Malta – Exercises in
Sardinia and North Africa. The end of the EOKA activities in Cyprus and
continuation of Malta duties and general exercises – Theft of the Regimental
Colour – Reorganisation from troops to companies. Move to Singapore*

THE Commando had no external commitments during December and with
the knowledge that the unit would be returning to Cyprus early in the new
year a bumper Christmas social programme was organised for all ranks. His
excellency The Governor of Malta, Sir Robert Laycock always ready to renew
his acquaintance with the commandos, visited the unit on 18 January 1957.
While viewing a very smooth demonstration of cliff haulage it is possible that
he remembered the more rudimentary cliff climbing drill of war-time days
and could be seen after the display discussing technicalities with the Cliff
Leaders.

At the end of the month the unit packed its bags and moved to Cyprus for
a further tour of IS duties. Lt Col Tweed assumed operational control of the
Troodos sub area on 7 February and shortly after the unit deployment had
been completed a series of three cordon and search operations were mounted,
The searches netted 23 suspect terrorists who were retained for questioning.
EOKA personnel were active at this time, laying mines at the side of roads and
in culverts. Explosion of these mines by remote control caused a number of
minor casualties and in one of the incidents Mne Godden received extensive
injuries.

On 17 February B Troop mounted an ambush in the area of Palendria and
Potanitssia. Two groups, consisting of 8 Section led by Lt Marshal, and
9 Section led by Lt Haynes, completed a successful operation which resulted
in the capture of Lenas, an explosives expert, and Christodoulo Denetraki, a
known active terrorist. Both men had £5,000 reward tags on their heads.
Denetraki, armed with an Italian rifle and grenades, was shot dead while
attempting to escape. Lt Haynes and his section made a second interception of
three armed men shortly before first light on 18 February. The terrorist group
was challenged in accordance with garrison standing orders but one of their
number immediately opened fire with a sub-machine gun, killing Lt Haynes.
The terrorist responsible was also killed in the shoot-out that followed.

The search for terrorist weapons was a time consuming but essential
exercise.During the latter part of February patrols from A and B Troops netted
two revolvers, hundred of rounds of ammunition, four 12-inch mortar bombs,

His Excellency the Governor of Malta, Sir Robert Laycock inspecting a 106mm anti-tank gun while visiting 40 Commando in January 1957. Photo: RM Museum

Lt Col D. G. Tweed MBE, DSO, discussiong tactics with US Marine Corps umpires during exercises with the US Sixth Fleet in Sardinia, July 1957. Photo: D. G. Tweed.

Members of X Troop practising cliff assault from a Dories. Photo: 40 Commando

four shot guns, a grenade, seven home-made bombs, an anti-tank mine and several sticks of dynamite. Most of the items had been concealed under floorboards, behind walls, in outhouses or buried in gardens and each find was the result of hours of painstaking work. Terrorist activity became less intense following the promulgation of an amnesty to anti government activists in Cyprus and the return of Archbishop Makarios to Athens.

While the local Cypriot population adopted a more friendly attitude towards the British service personnel the amnesty produced no positive response from terrorists and the security forces had to remain vigilant. The unit continued patrol activities and a series of cordon and search sweeps were made in Paphos Forest. Two substantial stores dumps were uncovered by B Troop personnel but no terrorists were apprehended or weapons found during these operations.

Brig Riches and the GOC Malta visited troop locations in April and the CGRM made a similar tour of the unit on 13 May. A cordon and search operation on 22/23 May in the area of Palekhori, appropriately named Final Fling, marked the end of active operations in the region following a general improvement in political relations. Arrangements were made for 40 Commando to return to Malta and prior to the unit's departure, F M Sir John Harding* visited the unit location to thank all ranks for their splendid contribution towards the suspension of operations in Cyprus. On the last Sunday before sailing, the Commando entertained neighbouring units to a

---

* Field Marshal Sir John Harding GCB, CBE, DSO, MC, ADC

237

curry lunch party and Maj Gen Kendrew, Director of Operations chose this occasion to present 40 Commando with a silver rose bowl from Cyprus District.

Once more in Malta, X Troop provided the Palace Guard and Y Troop represented 40 Commando at the Queen's Birthday Parade at Floriana. All the troops exercised with landing craft in Mellieha Bay and, on a more ambitious scale, A and Y Troops sailed with the A W Squadron to Benghazi where night landings were exercised against an enemy force provided by the 6th RTR. The unit had developed a close association with the tank crews prior to and during the Suez operation and at the conclusion of the exercise, the 6th RTR invited the Commando to their barracks at Barce where all ranks were entertained until the small hours of the morning. The amphibious exercises concluded at the end of July with 40 Commando participating in Ex Combine, a series of large-scale landings with the US Sixth Fleet and elements of the US Marine Corps in Sardinia.

Brig R. D. Houghton OBE, MC, renewed his long association with the Commando units on 20 August on assuming command of 3 Commando Brigade. Brig Madoc, who was to take command of Plymouth Group as MGRM Plymouth on his return to UK, received a rousing farewell, when he left Brigade HQ in a rickshaw, pulled appropriately by a scantily clad pseudo Chinese coolie, to remind him of his "East of Suez" service.

On 26 September, a Board of Enquiry was convened by order of Maj Gen H. Colquhoun CB, OBE, GOC Troops Malta, to enquire into the circumstance under which the Regimental Colour of 40 Commando was stolen from the unit officers mess during the night of 4/5 September 1957.

It was customary for the Colours to be displayed in a stand located in the hall of the officers mess, between the ante room and the dining room at the head of the main stairway.

The Adjutant, Capt T D Morgan was first to notice that the Regimental Colour was missing on entering the mess at 0745 hours on Thursday 5 September. The Mess Sergeant and Corporal of the duty watch, who were both in other parts of building, were alerted to the situation and it was then noted that the presentation book, normally resting in an unlocked glass panelled case, was also missing. The CO was informed and immediate full scale search and investigation activated. Later that morning the pike, Crown and Lion emblem and Colour case were retrieved from the side of the road on Pembroke Ranges.

A possible clue was revealed by the duty boilerman during the Board's investigation. He was about to enter the galley door on the first floor verandah at about 0315 hours, when a black Ford V8 entered the courtyard and five men, talking softly, left the car to enter the mess. He had assumed that they were officers returning from a late night party and turned his attention to lighting the galley boiler.

Despite days of intensive enquiries by service and civil authorities including a careful check of every car of that type on the island, there was no indication as to the whereabouts of the Colour or those responsible for its removal. The Board accepted that the location of the Colours, in the middle of a lit and occupied mess, was a justifiable risk and that the normal security measures covering the mess were sufficient safeguard and generally in accordance with the custom of the service. It was further agreed that no neglect could be imputed to anyone. In due course approval was given for a replacement Regimental Colour to be made by Messrs Hobson and Son Ltd for the sum of £106 and this was delivered to the unit by hand on February 1958.

Eight years later the Department CGRM received a letter from a Mr T.A. Wolf who gave his address as the Wisconsin State University, USA. He indicated that several years previously he had inherited a rare collection of British flags, one of them being the Regimental Colour of the 40th Commando Royal Marines. He had been asked to put the collection on display but as the Commando flag had been destroyed in a fire during transit could the Royal Marines provide a replacement? The reply was a very firm negative.

LCTs carried the Commando to North Africa in mid-October for six weeks desert training in the area of Tarhuna. The main object was to assess the reaction of a Commando unit to fighting well-armed groups of rebels in the various types of desert environment. The training period presented plenty of opportunity for live firing in the sweltering heat and dust of the day and tested the stamina of the men during the freezing nights on the rocky plateau. Finally the unit carried out an advance to contact exercise, covering 300 miles in five days. The men had been warned that WWII German mine-fields were a potential hazard and the discovery of two armed Teller-mines indicated that this was no idle caution. Towards the end of the exercise most men in the unit had cracked lips and a healthy respect for water discipline.

Returning to Malta in the latter half of November the Commando directed its attention to the Brigadiers Annual Inspection and, on a lighter note, the social programme for Christmas. One of the highlights was the children's party organised and enjoyed by the Senior NCO's and the younger generation alike. Life in general and the future of the Corps looked good. In 'The Times' of 29 October 1957, it was reported that two new Commando units were to be raised to exploit the recruiting potential of the Corps, with the first forming towards the end of 1959. The introduction of two additional Commandos would, in turn, lead to the formation of a second Commando brigade and it forecast that one of the Malta based Commando units would operate from a light fleet carrier equipped with helicopters. The article went on to say that "The expansion of Royal Marines, with its present strength of 9,000, reflects the attraction of an elite corps for the voluntary recruit and changing role of the Corps, which currently has only about 1,000 men serving in ships detachments."

The deep boom of the Royal Navy and merchant ship fog-horns reverberating across the water of Grand Harbour at midnight on 31 December,

239

announced the passing of 1957 and bid welcome to the new year. In Malta, 1958 commenced with a degree of political disharmony and the intended four month deployment of 40 Commando to Cyprus for IS duty was cancelled at the last minute. Sir Robert Laycock visited London for talks with the Colonial Secretary concerning the future of the Island. On his return the Maltese Legislative Assembly threatened to renounce agreements made with Britain and her allies. The situation eased considerably when Mr Mintoff announced that his socialist administration did not intend to implement the resolution passed by the Legislative Assembly.

No sooner had the unit stores been unpacked when a deterioration of the situation in Cyprus led to a further change of programme. The advance party flew to Cyprus and the main body followed by sea. Lt Col Hellings, who had last served with 40 Commando in 1944, arrived in Malta on 8 February to take command and, after a brief visit to Brigade HQ, continued his journey by air to Cyprus to relieve Lt Col Tweed. The unit arrived to find that the terrorist activity was less intense than expected. After a short stay in transit camp the Commando relieved the Royal Ulster Rifles in the Troodos sector where the rifle troops deployed to Platres, Pinewood and Kykko. The Commando area of responsibility covered 200 square miles, including the high ground around the 6,403-ft peak of Mount Olympus where X Troop manned outposts at Mount Olympus, Amiandos , Alona and Agros. A and Y Troops covered the more densely populated area of Platres while P and S Troops maintained security over a large sector of Paphos Forest including 15 villages.

To provide communication over this large area the Signal Platoon manned nine WS 19s, six WS B44s and 12 WS 62s over and above the normal scale of 31 and 88 sets and in addition to providing gunner-operators for the Ferret Scout cars. The MT Platoon also had a major task in this mountainous region and it was necessary for the drivers to re-accustom themselves to negotiating the narrow dirt roads and hairpin bends.

Constant patrolling, searching and vigilance earned their rewards. A patrol found a cache of pipe bombs and explosive during a house search and, on 26 March, Menelaos-Georghion, a well known terrorist and one of his associates were captured and sentenced to seven years imprisonment for carrying arms. Various other quantities of arms and ammunition were recovered in follow-up operations and, in the village of Omodhos, a cache of dynamite, too dangerous to move, was blown up *in situ*.

During April, X Troop provided a temporary relief for the Grenadiers, as Government House Guard and, having marched the 48 miles from Troodos to Nicosia, marched back again on completion. The major part of the unit spent May and June in the foothills of the Troodos Mountains, taking part in an extensive cordon and search operation (Kingfisher) with the 1st Argyll and Sutherland Highlanders. It was suspected that Gen Grivas and members of his senior staff were in the area but the search drew a blank. To provide additional manpower for operations of short duration during this period a group of personnel from HQ Troop were detached to form R Troop.

Eight Cypriots were killed in inter communal fighting in June. The Greek Cypriots of Marathasa chose this time to settle old scores with the Turkish villagers of Lefka. A unit road block established between the two locations, helped to keep the trouble makers, brandishing their knives, clubs and axes, apart until tempers cooled.

At the beginning of July 40 Commando took part in an island-wide search for EOKA sympathisers. Nearly 300 EOKA suspects were detained at Platres for questioning at the peak of the operation (Matchbox). In retaliation the terrorists ambushed a P Troop vehicle on the Platres-Troodos road but although hit by small arms fire no casualties were sustained. Mne Bostock received serious injuries as a result of an accidental discharge from his Sterling SMG, from which he subsequently died. While "Matchbox" was in progress 40 Commando was recalled to Malta. The main body sailed in HMS *Sheffield* and arrived in Grand Harbour on 25 July. Political unrest at the Jordan end of the Mediterranean had suddenly caused the alarm bells to ring in London and the Commando Brigade was alerted to stand by for any eventuality.

Brigade HQ and 45 Commando were ordered to proceed to Cyprus but were diverted to Tobruk and then moved overland to Benghazi. International tension increased. HMS *Albion* in the middle of work-up and on passage to Rosyth, was recalled to Portsmouth to embark the 19th Infantry Brigade Group, 42 Commando, transport stores and ammunition and made all possible speed to Malta. Within a few days the political storm had evaporated. The 1st Battalion Royal Sussex Regiment arrived from Gibraltar to relieve 45 Commando and by 28 July the entire Commando Brigade was united in Malta!

Earlier the same month (4 July), the unveiling and dedication of the Memorial to 3 Commando Brigade Royal Marines, took place in St. Paul's Anglican Cathedral, Valletta, attended by His Excellency the Officer Administering the Government of Malta, Mr Trafford Smith. The memorial consists of a Screen to the West Side Chapel. A Book of Remembrance, containing the names of all ranks who lost their lives while serving in the Brigade since the end of World War II, is kept in the Chapel.

The Commando Brigade now commenced an intensive period of amphibious and helicopter training culminating with an exercise at Mellieha Bay observed by Gen Laycock, the C-in-C Adm Lambe and the retiring Deputy SACEUR, F M Montgomery. Further exercises were carried out with the A W Squadron in North Africa during which time there were tests with a new type of raiding craft. The new boats (LCRs) were constructed of double marine ply and the propellers, powered by two 250hp engines, were housed in tunnels to provide protection during beaching. A Troop were first to test the LCRs on a beach regarded by the local people as dangerous. Unaware of this local knowledge the troop part-waded or swam through foam-capped waves to dry land. The only casualty appears to have been the rations carried by

Capt Wynne Potts – a curry in lieu of the 24 hour ration pack which became a congealed mass of rice, socks and rifle oil glued with salt water to the inside of his pack! The storm swept seas had not abated by the time the unit moved to Tripoli on 13 October in *Reggio* and *Striker* for the annual training and by all accounts it was a very rough passage. During this period at Tarhuna P Troop made extensive tests with the MOBAT. The anti-tank gun was a modified form of the BAT with the protective shield removed resulting in a lighter weapon with an all-round traverse. A Bren-gun mounted co-axially to fire tracer ammunition provided quick target acquisition.

Returning to Malta in mid November the unit took its turn as Duty Regiment before exercising with 848 Squadron. Technical reasons grounded the helicopters and by mutual agreement six officers and sixty men of the Squadron became commandos for a week. They tried their hands at a number of military skills including fieldcraft and unarmed combat. One enthusiastic CPO boldly attempted a strangle-hold on Lt A. P. Downton unaware that his opponent was both a PTI of many years experience and a Judo Black Belt!

Christmas followed the traditional pattern with a unit dance and church services. Officers served the mens' Christmas dinner and Boxing Day was reserved for the seniors versus officers match and children's party. Festivities concluded the Commando turned its attention to the annual range course and Brigade Commander's inspection and the Quartermaster's thoughts would have made interesting reading when he was selected to lay a kit muster!

The people of Malta entered 1959 with new resolve and a series of political meetings took place concerning the second reading of a Bill to revoke the 1947 constitution of Malta. Apart from a minor disturbance in the dockyard and despite exaggerated reporting by the UK news media, the period passed without incident. Very soon it was time to pack stores for a fifth tour of Cyprus. Prior to departure the Commando paraded for the Chief of the Imperial General Staff Gen Sir Francis Festing and a farewell visit by Gen Sir Campbell Hardy.

Once again in the Troodos area it was noticeable that the attitude of the people towards service personnel had become more friendly and relaxed. The February negotiations between Athens and Ankara, conducted on neutral ground in Zurich, had finalised in the creation of an independent Republic of Cyprus with the renouncement of Enosis and partition. It was agreed that the head of state should be Greek, the Vice-President Turkish and the minority groups were to have greater safeguards. There would be a veto on tax laws and separate Greek and Turkish municipalities. The villagers celebrated the successful outcome of a peace conference held in London and all patrolling was cancelled until further notice.

Archbishop Makarios arrived in Cyprus on 1 March. There was much rejoicing and ringing of church bells throughout the island and a national holiday was declared for all Greek Cypriots. In due course the Archbishop was selected President and Dr Fazil Kuchuk Vice-President. Dissatisfied with the outcome of events Gen Grivas returned to Athens while students of the Commercial Lyceum demonstrated.

The Commando worked particularly hard at the delicate task of maintaining peace and improving relations between Greek and Turkish Cypriots. While the number of IS commitments diminished the men were able to devote more time to sport and the skiers made full use of the Troodos snow while it lasted. As the days became warmer through March and April the process of maintaining harmony in the community continued. Incidents of violence were no longer evident and Lt Col Hellings was able to issue instructions for a reduction in the number of defence posts and the removal of sandbag and wire emplacements. Towards the end of April orders were given to pack stores and the unit returned to Malta.

The Commando was issued with the self-loading rifle (SLR) in early May. Not only was it essential to acquire mastery of the new weapon on the range and in the field but, with Malta Palace Guard duties commencing on 16 May, it was necessary to become familiar with this rifle of radically different shape and balance. B and Y Troops carried the SLR when they paraded a Royal Guard for the retiring Governor Gen Sir Robert Laycock. Capt E. Potts, who had assumed the duties of Adjutant, commanded the Guard and Lt H.B. Musgrove carried the Queen's Colour.

June found the unit practising beach landings at Mellieha Bay during the work-up for Whitebait, an amphibious exercise in which the American Sixth Fleet and Amphibious Warfare Squadron carried out joint landings in Bomba Bay, North Africa. The commandos were impressed by the Americans who approached the shore-line with an illumination of navigation lights and showers of sea water thrown up by gun-cotton charges simulating exploding shells.

Lt Col I.S. Harrison, already well known as the Second-in-Command, assumed command of the unit from Lt Col Hellings on 30 June 1959. Peter Hellings in turn relieved Brig Houghton on 22 July as Brigade Commander. July was also notable as the month the 1st Battalion Royal Fusiliers arrived in Malta after a tour of service in Kenya and the Persian Gulf, to become the third unit of the Commando Brigade. Accommodated at St Patricks Barracks the new arrivals were immediately placed on the Duty Regiment rostor and took over the Palace Guard on 25 July!

RSM W. Chisholm relieved RSM Morgan in early August and was soon fully occupied with the assimilation of the detailed activities in progress. The final scenes of a feature film depicting the Royal Marines – in which most of the unit was represented – were nearing completion and training was well advanced for the Duke of Edinburgh's Trophy and small arms meetings. There was cause for celebration when it was announced that the 40 Commando team had won the Duke of Edinburgh Trophy by a narrow margin of $1\frac{1}{2}$ points from 45 Commando.

Malta's National Day on 8 September was used by the Maltese Labour Party to stage a political rally at Hamrun where party followers were urged to boycott events organised by the Malta Imperial Government. However this did not deter the majority of the populace from following the traditional celebrations, including a regatta in Grand Harbour commemorating the end of the Great Siege in 1565. The government had just announced a five-year development plan which included the provision of a deep water port scheme and new civil orders for the dockyard.

By the end of the second week in September the Commando was camped in Derna for a period of desert training. On completion of troop training the unit commenced a four day exercise employing minimum scales of transport, rations and water. The second phase of the exercise, consisting of night movement with transport, coincided with the worst weather conditions experienced in the area since 1942. In Derna, 14 people were killed when bridges and buildings were washed away, and 300 were made homeless. The Commando's first task was to build a stone causeway across a 75 ft gap to enable the unit transport to return to camp. It then constructed a second causeway and cut a new road in the hill-side to replace bridges washed away by the flood water. Fresh water was also ferried to key points for the civilian population until such time as the water supply could be reconnected.

In much the same way as in November 1958, the unit returned to Malta and the inevitable Duty Regiment commitments which occupied most of the month. S Troop paraded guards for Gen Colquhoun on the completion of his appointment as GOC Malta and for his successor Maj Gen A.J.C. Block while A Troop provided a cliff assault demonstration for the visit of Lt Gen Sir Roger Bower, C-in-C MELF. On Remembrance Sunday the Royal Fusiliers paraded with 40 Commando on St Andrews Parade for a Drum-Head service. This marked the first occasion that the Fusiliers paraded as part of 3 Commando Brigade.

45 Commando arrived back from North Africa on 15 December and the year ended with the entire Brigade in Malta. The periodical IS tours in Cyprus and attachments to the Omman forces had also ended. Officers were able to concentrate on staff and promotion practical exams organised by Brigade HQ while a fortunate number of all ranks not involved with exams, set off for Christmas leave in UK.

The first two months of 1960 were devoted mainly to unit administration, an unusually long period for this form of activity. The subalterns training was arranged on a competitive inter-unit basis and on this occasion the honours went to 40 Commando subalterns. All rifle troops carried out trials with the Gemini inflatable raiding craft and the unit completed an air portability exercise with Hastings aircraft of RAF Transport Command.

At the end of February, 40 Commando relieved 45 Commando as Duty Regiment. The two Commandos paraded their Regimental Colours together for the first time since they were presented to the units in 1952. Lt D.G. Davis carried the Regimental Colour for 40 Commando. Garrison duties left little opportunity for other activities but the boxing team won the Malta Team Championships and another sports activity worthy of mention was initiated by a 12 man team led by Cpls B. Davies and B. Halliday. The aim was to run a 100 mile relay round the island while staying within 200 yards of the coastline. The run was divided into 18 staging posts and each man had to run 9-10 miles twice during the event. On one leg of the course Cpl Davies had to ascend a 50-foot cliff near Paradise Bay. A further challenge was provided by a 30-foot deep moat at Fort Delimara. The run was completed in 12 hours 29 minutes.

March and April were busy months for the Commandos both in UK and Malta. At Bickleigh, in Plymouth, 41 Commando reformed under the command of Lt Col J.T.O. Waters, with the aim of becoming operational by the end of October; 42 Commando embarked in HMS *Bulwark* for work-up in the Mediterranean prior to sailing to the Far East and 45 Commando sailed for Aden to relieve the 1st Battalion Royal Warwickshire Regiment. The final item of 42 Commando's work-up took place in Malta on 26 April when the unit, in company with 40 Commando, carried out a rehearsal for Ex Sky Pioneer in the presence of HRH the Duke of Edinburgh.

42 Commando was air-lifted in helicopters from HMS *Bulwark* while 40 Commando made a sea-borne assault from ships of the Amphibious Warfare Squadron. The objective was a notional enemy position a short distance inland from St Pauls Bay. Later in the day His Royal Highness had tea with the corporals, marines and their wives in the St Andrews NAAFI and then proceeded to the Sergeants Mess where he presented CSgt J. Cook with his Long Service and Good Conduct medal before meeting senior NCOs and their wives. The day concluded with The Captain General dining with the officers in their mess where a painting by Mrs Duke, commissioned by the officers to commemorate the last Malta Guard change over ceremony between 40 and 45 Commando, was on display for the first time.

The first major exercise (Sky Pioneer) to be made from the Commando Carrier, HMS *Bulwark*, took place in Libya on 29 April. Observed by the CGRM, GOC Malta and representatives of the news media 40 Commando landed at Homs and moved inland to Tarhuna while 42 Commando was heliborne 20 miles into the desert. On completion 40 Commando and Brigade HQ spent 24 hours in HMS *Bulwark* to prove that the ship could accommodate a two Commando group for short periods. 40 Commando remained in Tripoli for training throughout May in storm force winds, the most severe in 38 years, which threatened to bury everything in sand. Exactly one week after returning to Malta the unit undertook the commitments of Duty Regiment.

The sports fraternity enjoyed an excellent summer season, winning all the cricket trophies and major trophies in the Troops Malta Small Arms meeting and, in another field of entertainment, selected personnel became temporary unpaid, part-time actors for Independent Television News, who were filming a series "British Bases in the Mediterranean" Continuing the good work A Troop assisted the RAF by providing the ground support during a 20th

Anniversary Battle of Britain display and Y Troop gave a log display for the SSAFA Tattoo.

To ensure that an adequate standard of physical fitness was maintained during the summer period all ranks were required to participate in exercise Heel Tap, consisting of a 12 mile march, to be completed within four hours on three consecutive days. On the third day the march ended with a 100 yards swim in loose order.

The Commando paraded on 9 September to say farewell to Brig Hellings prior to his departure to UK to take command of ITCRM. He was received by a Quarter Guard and after speaking to the men on parade was entertained in the Officers Mess. During that day he would no doubt have recalled his earlier associations with 40 Commando as a company commander, 2 IC and commanding officer, Brig N.H. Tailyour DSO, who commanded 45 Commando at Suez, assumed command of the Brigade.

With the approach of autumn the rifle troops undertook weapons courses and seven of the unit's parachutists joined up with the 2nd Parachute Battalion to participate in a battalion group night drop in North Africa. Meanwhile all the young officers were despatched to Sicily on an initiative test. They were required to visit a number of specified places between Syracuse and Taormina on a cash limit of £5 per head. By all accounts this was achieved with a reasonable amount of enjoyment.

The winter training was carried out at Martuba, near Derna and followed very much the pattern of the previous year. A group of NCOs and marines led by Capt P. Mann and with Lt M.W. Banks as navigator, explored parts of the Rebiana Sand Sea on a long range patrol and desert navigation exercise which took them to the Cufra Oasis. A Champ vehicle overturned and a three-ton truck seized up, otherwise the 700 mile trip was completed without incident. Shortly after returning to Malta the unit bid farewell to Lt Col Harrison – who was to take command of RMFVR London – and welcomed Lt Col D.P.L. Hunter as their new CO.

Once again it was the turn of 40 Commando to assume the duties of Malta Duty Regiment. One of the first commitments was to relieve the Royal Fusiliers as Palace Guard and to some extent this took the form of a farewell ceremony as shortly afterwards the Royal Fusiliers returned to England. Both the Brigade Band and the Corps of Drums were on parade and Lt Banks carried the Regimental Colour.

The departure of the Amphibious Warfare Squadron from the Mediterranean imposed a restriction on the flexible deployment arrangements previously enjoyed by the Brigade. Alternative forms of Royal Navy transport had to be found and produced a number of logistical and administrative problems which were put to the test in January 1961. The Commando complete with transport, embarked in five destroyers of the 1st and 7th Destroyer Squadrons. The task was successfully accomplished with the aid of ramps and cranes but the embarkation process resembled the squeezing of a quart into a pint pot!

The Nautical Troop of the 22nd Special Air Service spent most of February with 40 Commando and 6th Special Boat Service, swimming, diving and canoeing around the coasts of Malta and Gozo. Their training session ended with testing their skills on an escape and evasion exercise against an enemy provided by P and X Troops. To their credit the SAS captured their objectives but the commandos captured all their canoes and took 11 prisoners of which three required hospital treatment! The following month 3 Commando Brigade HQ embarked in the TT *Oxfordshire* to join 42 Commando in Singapore.

In Malta the commando continued to maintain its lead in the field of sport. The boxing team won the Army Team Championships and the football team finished the season having lost only one game. The hockey eleven won the Troops Malta Knock-out Competition while the athletes cleared the board in the Athletics and Cross Country Championships.

On 15 May the Commando, plus vehicles sailed to North Africa in the RFA *Duquesne* and WD LST *Empire Petrel*. This was a first attempt at trooping by the ships companies and they coped well with the unusually large number of passengers. The unit proceeded to Tarhuna for training where there was a short interlude while the Commando paraded for the CGRMs visit. The parade took the form of a drive-past in the unit transport and the General Salute – fired by the MMGs, Mortars and MOBATs – culminated in a demolition explosion by the AE Section! The training period included a considerable amount of night movement. The final exercise, directed by GOC Malta, commenced with a long night drive followed by a day of continuous activity and concluded with a night attack. By the end of the training period the MT Section had recorded a total of 20,000 miles and 30 blow-outs!

Shortly before the unit returned to Malta the Admiralty confirmed that 43 Commando Royal Marines would be raised at Stonehouse Barracks, Plymouth, bringing the total number of Commando units to five. The officer to command the new unit was to be Lt Col A.P. Willasley-Wilsey MBE,MC. It was also announced that consideration was being given to the introduction of a lovat uniform and trials on the garment would be carried out in UK and Malta.

Two changes which effected training and were beneficial to the unit occurred at the end of August. The first was a modification of the Malta Duty Regiment commitments which enabled the duty unit to devote more time to its own affairs. The second change, introduced by Lt Col Hunter, took the form of a new training technique whereby one troop at a time would be built up to strength by the incoming drafts from two successive squads from CTCRM. The benefit was an immediate troop spirit derived from all marines having already served together for 15 months. It was appreciated that each troop would be at a different stage in regard to ability and experience but had the advantage of progressive training within each troop.

The 6 SBS, who shared accommodation at St Andrews, established a close liaison with the unit, and canoeing became a popular pastime.

Sgt J.H. Edmunds of B Troop and Sgt T. Shenton of 6 SBS teamed-up on the night of 1/2 September to set a new circumnavigation of Malta (canoe) record of 8 hours 55 minutes, beating the previous time by 3 hours 35 minutes. They used a new-type SBS Klepper canoe of German design and paddled by night to avoid the energy sapping heat of the day.

On 13 October, the Commando embarked in six ships of the US 6th Fleet to take part in an amphibious exercise with the 3rd Battalion 2nd Marine Division USMC. The landing took place at Bomba Bay, 70 miles west of Tobruk, and provided a valuable opportunity to work with the US forces. Despite a lack of amphibious training 40 Commando experienced no problems in carrying out the landings.

The announcement by the First Sea Lord that the strength of the Royal Marines would be increased by 500 men was the most significant item of Corps news to conclude the year of 1961. The intention was to expand the hitting power of the Commando units and provide extra administrative backing to enable the units to be less dependent on the Army for second-line support. It was not long after this announcement that a decision was taken to convert all Commando units to a new organisation of 680 men comprised of three rifle companies, a HQ company and a support company containing reconnaissance, mortar, anti-tank and assault engineer troops. It was agreed to retain association with the Commando "troop" by using that word to indicate the company sub-units.

The news that 40 Commando was to join the Brigade in Singapore became public knowledge on 26 January 1962. The Commando carried out its last Duty Regiment commitments between 6 January and 10 February, ending with a ceremonial change-over of the Palace Guard to the Fusiliers. The guard escort was formed by representatives of all the troops and the ceremony was attended by His Excellency the Governor of Malta, Adm Sir Guy Grantham GCB, CBE, DSO, and senior members of the armed services.

Between the advance party sailing on 12 February and the departure of the Commando on 29 April a major part of the reorganisation was completed. A and B Troops formed A Company. X and Y Troops combined to become C Company. The formation of B Company from V Troop plus reinforcements, was deferred until after the arrival of the unit in Singapore. The reorganisation was followed by a period of training with emphasis on helicopter operations and cliff assault. The MT Section, working under the supervision of Capt F. Robertson and QMS K.G. Smith, rejuvenated the unit transport after its North African battering and transformed the colour of the vehicles from desert fawn to jungle green.

Parading for the last time in Malta on 28 April, 40 Commando marched on to St Andrews Barracks parade to the tune of 'Her Majesty's Jollies'. His Excellency the Governor of Malta inspected the unit and presented Long Service and Good Conduct medals to Sgts R. Kinder and K.S. Eveleigh. During the afternoon of 6 May, the unit and the families embarked in HMT *Oxfordshire* and sailed from Grand Harbour at 1800 hours. The band of the Royal Highland Fusiliers paraded on the breakwater at the harbour entrance to bid them farewell, playing 'A Life on the Ocean Wave' while the Royal Navy paid its own tribute, escorting the *Oxfordshire* out of harbour with a fleet of barges, each with an Admiral at the helm. So ended the long association of the Royal Marine Commandos with Malta which began when 40 RM Commando visited the island in August 1944 to rebuild and reorganise its depleted force after the fighting in Dalmatia.

Consecration of the new Regimental Colour at Troodos Church, Cyprus 23 April 1953. Photo: RM Museum.

CHAPTER 17

22 May 1962 to 31 December 1966

Singapore – Occupation of Burma Camp, jungle training and anti-piracy patrols off Borneo – Amphibious exercise in the Persian Gulf – Anti-terrorist operations in Sarawak and Sabah.

TT *OXFORDSHIRE* secured alongside the quay in Singapore harbour on the morning of 22 May 1962. Arriving in torrential rain was disappointing for the families, however the band of 3 Commando Brigade welcomed them with lively music which dispelled the gloom. Representatives of the advance party with transport from 42 Commando attended to the move of the unit into Nee Soon Transit Camp and families were initially accommodated in hotels and guest houses in Singapore. Nine days later 40 Commando transferred to Burma Camp. Situated on a hill 14 miles north of Johore Bahru the spartan accommodation, previously occupied by the Gurkhas, was to become the unit's home base for the greater part of its tour of duty in the Far East. Across the valley, on the other side of the playing fields, the Far Eastern Jungle Warfare School – the neighbouring unit – also housed the War Dog School. A most useful liaison was soon established and maintained throughout the months ahead.

Intensive preparation for the first training exercise was organised by the second in command Maj J.F. Showell-Rogers and commenced immediately. Adapting to the change of climate, the unit's working day commenced at 0730 hours and finished at 1330 hours with a short break at 0930 hours for brunch. Night training took place on Thursdays leaving the weekend free from Friday noon. Outliers who had a considerable distance to travel would normally be collected from their billets at 0530 hours daily but the commuting problems became easier as they acquired their own cars.

Meanwhile on 14 April, V Troop Group under the command of Capt J.R.H. Walter, embarked in HMS *Bulwark* for passage to Hong Kong. The 17th/21st Lancers provided a base for the force while it carried out training in the New Territories. Rejoining *Bulwark* on 4 May, V Troop sailed to Borneo as part of an amphibious force whose task was to carry out anti-piracy patrols around North Borneo and the off-shore islands at the request of the North Borneo civil authorities. Piracy and raiding by unlawful Philippinos had become a thorn in the side of the people in the coastal region and crews of trading vessels plying between North Borneo and the Celebes. The raiders, who were quite vicious in the treatment of their victims, used power-driven outrigger canoes, capable of travelling at 40 knots and difficult to intercept. The patrols achieved the

251

purpose of deterring pirate activity although none were apprehended. On return to Burma Camp V Troop was renamed B Company.

In Johore the first post reorganisation exercises took place in heavy and continious rain which transformed the area into a sea of mud. In these swamp-like conditions vehicles and men bogged down together. WO Pollard, the new RSM, chose this moment to introduce himself to the Commando! Fortunately the weather had improved in time for the Commando's demonstration of fire power to naval officers at the Ulu Tiram Field Firing Range in August.

Further anti-piracy patrols were carried out along the North Borneo coast between 26 August and 6 September with the Commando detachment working in close co-operation with both the inshore minesweepers and the North Borneo police. Most of the time was spent in searching the off-shore islands and local trading craft but neither pirates nor raiders were found.

Lt Gen M.C. Cartwright Taylor, CB, inspected the unit at Burma Camp on 7 September. This was his first visit to the unit since assuming the appointment of Commandant General Royal Marines in January. After a tour of the camp he presented LS and GC medals to members of the unit and watched 40 Commando win the Singapore Base District Rifle Championships. Five days later the unit embarked in HMS *Bulwark* for the start of a three months deployment to the Persian Gulf. The first opportunity to land occurred on 26 September when the CGRM, accompanied by Lt Col I.S. Harrison, flew to the Trucial Oman to witness 40 Commando operating from *Bulwark* with ships of the A W Squadron. The five day exercise for which the Trucial Oman Scouts acted as enemy, was located in the area of Sharjah, centred around a lone hill in an otherwise flat featureless area of desert 20 miles south of Dubai. After a brief sojourn at Mina-al-Ahmadi to cover for the 1st Parachute Battalion while they were on exercise, the Commando moved to Aden. B Troop assisted 45 Commando with relief duties at Dhala and the Commando's operational capability was thoroughly tested while training in the extremely rough volcanic hills and deep wadis of the Jebek Kharaz 90 miles west of Aden. Using a limited scale of transport and stores a surprising degree of mobility was achieved in this area where few tracks existed and the maps were notoriously unreliable. A Brigade exercise in November was restricted by the sensitivity of the political situation which necessitated carrying live ammunition in lieu of blanks. The rifle companies spent two days on operational patrols in the sandy wasteland where occasional contact was made with local tribesmen. Contrary to intelligence reports these reputedly war-like people were not unfriendly.

HMS *Albion* with 41 Commando embarked, arrived in the Persian Gulf on 3 November to relieve HMS *Bulwark*. After a series of exercises with *Albion*, 41 Commando transferred to *Bulwark* for the return passage to UK while 40 Commando embarked in *Albion* for service east of Suez where the unit was soon to become involved in events in Borneo.

The major part of Borneo, the third largest island in the world, is part of

A Company operated as floating reserve on HMS Bulwark *during the initial development. Photo: 40 Commando.*

Indonesia and known to them as Kalimantan. To the north and west are the states of Sabah, Brunei and Sarawak, often referred to at that time as North Borneo. An ill defined border of some 1,000 miles divided North Borneo form Kalimantan, in the main running along a range which at times rises to 4,000 feet. Apart from coastal areas, where there is significant cultivation and some reasonable roads, Borneo is covered by thick rain forest with travel undertaken on foot along forest tracks or by river. The indigenous population consists of a mixture of Malays, Chinese and some Indians in the coastal areas, with Ibans, Dyaks and Murats living in the forest areas. An estimate of the population of Sabah and Sarawak at the time was just over a million.

Political elements, induced by the withdrawal of British influence from the area, proposed to set up the Federation of Malaysia, consisting of the states of Singapore, Malaya, Sabah, Brunei and Sarawak. The aim was to improve stability and to ensure the viability of the smaller members. However, the idea was not welcomed by all elements of the indigenous population, particularly the Chinese Communist Organisations (CCO), while Indonesia made it clear that they wished Sarawak, Sabah and Brunei to form part of Kalimantan. This discontent erupted into major disturbances in many coastal and river towns in North Borneo on 8 December 1962, organised primarily by Shaikh Azahari, leader of the Brunei Peoples Party.

In one incident, the British resident with his family and some other Europeans were taken hostage at Limbang in neighbouring Sarawak. L Company, as the leading element of 42 commando, flew from Singapore to Brunei and on 12 December, embarked in two river barges from which Capt J.J.Moore MC, landed his force at first light close to the police station at Limbang. The landing met with automatic fire from the rebel force which resulted in some casualties but, supported by covering fire from their own Vickers machine guns the commandos routed the rebel force and released the unharmed hostages.

HMS *Albion* proceeded to Sarawak where 40 Commando, less A Company, landed at Kuching on 14 December. Under the command of 99th Gurkhas Infantry Brigade the unit carried out intensive patrolling in the jungle and along the rivers and borders of Kalimantan with the aim of restoring the confidence of the local people. Working in close co-operation with the police and HMS *Barossa*, B and A Companies operating from *Bulwark*, patrolled as far afield as Sibu and Lundu while elements of S Company patrolled the coastal sector in minesweepers. Tac HQ was established in Jesselton and C Company was located in Tawau on the east coast. No terrorist contacts were made but the military presence did much to stabilise the situation.

On Christmas Day C Company deployed to the Lawas district to patrol the jungle and mosquito infested rivers, Nearby, 42 Commando patrolled the Tremburong district. The Indonesian terrorists, who preferred to be known as the North Borneo Liberation Army (TNKU), were first observed by the North Borneo police in the Lawas district on 24 November 1962. Although the leaders were apprehended many of their followers remained at large. The screening

254

Whirlwind helicopter landing at a forward location in the First Division.
Photo: J. D. Shallow

and interrogation process conducted by the unit and police resulted in the arrest of 137 wanted men and a considerable number of weapons. Handing over its commitments to the 1st Battalion Green Jackets on 7th January 1963, the Commando returned to Burma Camp where it took leave of Lt Col Hunter bound for UK and Lt Col J.F.Parsons MC, assumed command.

Activites during February and March were mainly functional, spiritual and physical. Visits by the Corps Paymaster, Corps Records Officer and Military Secretary preceded the CO's annual inspection. Borneo leave was given to all ranks and the Padre's uplifting spring programme boosted attendance at church. Advantage was taken of the sport facilities with soccer, rugby and hockey teams taking the field against local teams.

The Brigadier's Administrative Inspection in April involved maximum activity at all levels. On the morning of his arrival the Brigadier was greeted by a Quarter Guard and a large explosion, the latter being activated by the AEs who were preparing a mortar base plate position. HQ Company erected a command post and RAP while rifle company tasks ranged from funeral drill to preparations for prolonged jungle operations. The company tasked with jungle operations paraded fully prepared with Iban tracker, dog and a pack horse carrying Hi Fi radio equipment! The Second Quartermaster produced every conceivable form of cooking fuel for his display and showed no surprise when given a live suckling pig. It was promptly despatched by the unit butcher and charcoal grilled for the Brigadier.

Whirlwind following the course of a river in the forward area.

*Second Sea Lord accompanied by Lt Col Parsons, visiting C Company at Padawa.
Photos: J. D. Shallow.*

Towards the end of March, B Company Group, under the command of Capt Gardner, returned to Sarawak to undertake a two month period of patrol activities in the area of Kuching. While there, a CCO party crossed the border to attack a border police post at Tebedu in the Serian District of the First Division. This overt action coupled with general internal unrest and threats by CCO elements led to the decision to initiate the relevant Theatre Reinforcement Plan.

The Commando had settled down to enjoy the Easter week-end when Operation Flapjack was activated. Recall signals were sent to personnel as far apart as Penang and Singapore. By Sunday morning 90% of the unit had returned to camp and the deployment was under way with C Company flying to Kuching that afternoon. 40 Commando was given responsibility for the First Division and companies were deployed to Lundu, Bau and Serian. Meanwhile 3 Commando Brigade HQ at Kuching, with 2nd/10th Gurkha Rifles under command, had overall responsibility for 30,000 square miles of Sarawak.

Immediate action was taken to lessen the threat from the CCO with intensive night patrolling of suspect areas and the removal of shotguns and other firearms from the non indigenous population. In seven days of long working hours 2,836 guns out of a known total of 3,227 were collected.

At 0400 hours on 23 April a strong TNKU raiding party attacked a police post at Gumbang, wounding a marine in LCpl D.J.Radford's section. LCpl Radford organised a vigorous defence and eventually forced the terrorists to withdraw to the jungle. The follow up revealed a trail of blood left by one of the wounded rebels. LCpl Radford was subsequently awarded the MM for his cool leadership.

A second attack was made on Tebedu police post on 27 April with rebels crawling to within 15 yards of the building. They were out-gunned by marines from C Company and retreated into the jungle. Recalling this incident Col Shallow, who at that time commanded C Company, said "It was customary for me to talk each night to my forward locations by radio. They were quite on their own with no means of reinforcement during the hours of darkness. I remember the young officer concerned telling me that he was under attack, but of more concern to him was the fact that he had assisted that day at the birth of one of the local children!"

To deter infiltration, a night curfew was imposed along a five mile deep strip of border. Within this area night ambushes were set up with authority to open fire on sight. A Company moved from Lundu District to the Bau area while B Company maintained two troops at Lundu and one troop at Semantan. The commando had under command L Company, 42 Commando and Lloyds Company, 20th Regiment Royal Artillery. This allowed for the establishment of four company group areas each based on a town or centre of population with road communication back to Kuching. Each company established permanent troop locations close to the border, either in or adjacent to native kampongs from which patrols could be deployed forward on foot to control or lay ambush on possible border crossing points. Each of these locations or "forts" as they became known, had its own helicopter landing site for daytime re-supply or reinforcement. The landing sites were essential as some "forts" were 40 miles away from their company locations. Overall command and control was maintained by a network of 32 radio stations manned around the clock. There was plenty of scope for the employment of dogs in Sarawak and five volunteer handlers, who completed a course in June, commenced work at the border outposts.In effect, the Commando was once again committed to operations very similar to those undertaken some 12 years earlier in the jungles of Malaya. A number of officers and SNCOs had served in Malaya and their knowledge and experience were invaluable.

On 2 July, K and M companies of 42 Commando arrived to relieve B and C Companies in the Lundu and Serian areas. The in-going and out-going patrols on the border remained together overnight and during this operation a combined patrol led by Sgt Callow of B Company shot an armed terrorist. 40 Commando embarked in HMS *Albion* and returned to Singapore.

The federation of Malaya, Singapore, Sabah and Sarawak became Malaysia on 31 August 1963 and Tunku Abdul Rahman became the country's first Prime Minister. The Singapore celebrations on 16 September, to commemorate the formation of the Federation of Malaysia were well attended and ended peacefully. The CGRM made a brief informal visit to the unit on 27 September and two weeks later 40 Commando returned to Sarawak for a further tour on the border. During October and November there were various incidents of mortaring and sniping at border posts but there were no casualties.

December proved uneventful until the last day of the month, when a group of 100 Indonesian border terrorists (IBTs) crossed the border into the Bau district. Cpl M.Marriot, leading a patrol comprising three men from 6 Troop and a section of local militia, were in the area and made contact with the Indonesians in thick jungle. The leading scout, one of the local militia, opened fire and the patrol immediately engaged the IBTs in a fire fight of half an hour. The IBTs twice attempted to charge the patrol but were repelled each time. Cpl Marriot was killed and one of the militia wounded during the final terrorist attack before they withdrew into the jungle. The patrol captured several weapons, including two Armalite rifles and a quantity of ammunition. Two Indonesians were killed in the action.

There was no let-up over Christmas but a considerable effort was made to enable those men who were deep in the jungle, to celebrate festive fare and reading material flown by helicopter to the forward positions. Brig L.G.Marsh MC, who assumed command of the Brigade from Brig Barton on 5 January 1964, flew to Kuching and spent four days visiting most of 40 Commandos forward locations.

42 Commando relieved 40 commando on 30 January 1964. Returning to Burma Camp the unit commenced a varied training programme which included the study of the Malay language and courses on hygiene and jungle

warfare. Considerable emphasis was placed on fitness training, preparations for the Queen's Birthday Parade and the Brigade Commanders Inspection. A South East Atlantic Treaty Organisation (SEATO) exercise occupied most of May. The unit embarked in HMS *Bulwark*, one of 50 ships that took part, and carried out an assault landing by LCAs and helicopters on the Philippines island of Mindoro.

Shortly after the Commando had returned to North Borneo President Soekharno intimated at a summit meeting that all Indonesians within the Borneo State would be withdrawn. The security forces set up safe lanes and border check points, but soon after the political picture reverted to its former state and the military resumed patrols and the search for intruders.

At the end of July the unit moved to Sabah to relieve the 1st/10th Gurkha Rifles in the Tawau area, under the operational command of a Malasian Brigadier. With no Naval transport available, the Commando travelled in MV *Anby*, hired from the Straits Steamship Company. The situation facing the Commando in Sabah was very different to that in Sarawak. In this region the main part of the border with Indonesia ran east to west across the bottom end of the extensive Tawau Bay area and close to Nanukan Island where the Indonesian marines were based in strength. On the eastern end of the bay the border bisected Sebatik Island.

The Commando Group was deployed primarily on the west side of the bay with HQ based at a logging camp at Kalibakan. Here, the area consisted of rain forest with the rivers providing the main means of transport. To the south the land degenerated into 150 square miles of mangrove swamps, again intersected by waterways. It was clear that much of the patrolling and re-supply would be by water. Preparations were made accordingly and before the unit left for Tawau 23 drivers were given a course on boat handling and maintenance of outboard engines.

Forward locations were established at strategic points from which waterways and rivers could be controlled. One of these locations was manned by members of the attached battery of 29 Commando Regiment Royal Artillery, but single 105mm guns were also deployed in support at other locations. These added greatly to the crescendo of sound at the end of morning stand-to when once a week all weapons were tested, providing a suitable deterrent to any IBTs who might be lurking in the area!.

In addition, the Commando Group provided the main body for the Tawau Assault Group. This unique organisation was charged with observing and preventing infiltration into both the mangrove swamps and Tawau Bay itself. Small groups of marines were positioned at concealed points in the swamp area, each with their own assault boats in which to undertake patrols. A police launch, *Papa Charlie Three* manned by commandos operating powerful binoculars, was positioned in the bay close to the border to observe activity on Nanukan Island. The Group was commanded initially by Capt C.G.Bellamy and subsequently by Maj Shallow. Group HQ was established in the former

C Company Marines manning "Papa Charlie Three" a Malasia Police Launch of the Tawau Assualt Group, at anchor on the border line in Sabah, September 1964.
Photo: J. D. Shallow

Admiral Sir Varyl Begg KCB DSO DSC, C-in-C Far East, presenting CSgt A. Owen with a Bar to his Long Service and Good Conduct medal, at Burma Camp on 19 August 1963. Photo: RM Museum.

governor's yacht, SS *Petrel*, flying the White Ensign, commanded by a Sikh with a Chinese First Lieutenant, a mixed Malay/Chinese crew and Royal Marine signallers!

August proved to be a busy month for personnel at Commando HQ with a succession of visitors which included Dr K. Williams, a psychologist on the Admiralty Interview Board. During his tour of the area a subaltern, who was escorting him around, was overheard to say "Tell me Dr Williams, are you looking for a well balanced sort of chap or someone who will make a good Royal Marines Officer?"

The CGRM designate Maj Gen N.H. Tailyour CB, DSO, arrived in Sabah on 7 September 1964 and travelling by land, river and air, visited every sub-unit of 40 Commando on location. As many officers as possible dined with Maj Gen Tailyour that night, the first occasion on which they were able to exercise the new privilege that members dining would remain seated for the loyal toast, granted by Her Majesty The Queen in honour of the Corps Centenary.

There were no reported contacts with IBTs in September although considerable troop movement was observed on Nanukan Island. Elsewhere Indonesian terrorists were actively fermenting trouble and a 200 strong force landed on the Malaysian mainland in mid-October. These were rounded up by the Gurkhas and New Zealand troops and a smaller Indonesian force, landing on the Malacca-Jahore border on 28 October was dealt with swiftly by Australian troops and Malay police.

Taking advantage of a quiet interlude Lt G.B.D.Keelan with 10 men from C Company, flew to Jesselton to climb the 13,455 feet Mount Kinabalu. The team took just over a day to ascend the mountain by the normal track, but during the following December a second group, led by Lt T.Sheridan, tackled the more difficult and previously unclimbed 600 feet sheer north face. Backed by a team of female porters carrying 1,700 lbs of stores to the base camp, the six men from Recce Troop split into two teams, and using different routes made successful assaults on the summit.

Lt Col Parsons returned to UK in October on completion of his tour. His relief Lt Col J.A. Taplin MBE, was well acquainted with the Commando having already served for some months as the unit second in command. Regrettably, on 30 October, Mne M.A.Deering of A Company was drowned when swimming across a river, while on patrol in the border area. Deering had been with the unit for only a month when the accident occurred.

The unit made its first contact with Indonesians in Sabah on 2 November. Acting on information from local Ibans, a patrol led by Sgt W.G. Costley, flushed a group of IBTs from a camp, deep in the jungle north of Tawau. One of the IBTs was killed in the follow up and various weapons and ammunition were found in a cache. During November RSM G.A. Bray relieved RSM Pollard.

A month elapsed before the next contact, initiated by Lt R.A.M. Seeger and his troop, led to a skirmish on Sebatik Island on 8 December. Under cover of darkness the fighting patrol, in three Gemini inflatables, paddled their way from a motor vessel (their mother craft) to the line of the border. One Gemini remained in that vicinity to cover their return while the others proceeded a futher distance to beach about 75 yards from the OP and an adjacent hut. The boats were observed and shots were fired in their direction as the men scrambled ashore.

Sgt Costley and Mne Allen remained waist-deep in water to return fire with a GPMG, moving their position parallel to the shore-line and closer to the OP. Meanwhile Lt Seeger led his assault group across the narrow sandy strip of beach unaware that a bullet had pierced the fleshy part of his arm. Nearing the hut he threw two M 26 grenades towards the open entrance and, as they exploded, followed up firing his SMG. The assault group led by Cpl Tomlin, quickly checked that the surrounding area was clear, observing that there were three bodies in the vicinity of the hut. As mortar bombs exploded between them and the OP, Indonesian small arms fire intensified and the patrol returned to their boats to make a speedy withdrawal under diversionary fire from the guard ship. Apart from Lt Seeger's flesh wound the fighting patrol sustained no casualties.

For this action Lt Seeger was awarded the MC and both Sgt Costley and Cpl Tomlin were Mentioned in Despatches. The following personnel were also Mentioned in Despatches for distinguished service on operations in the Borneo Territories between April 1963 and June 1964:

2Lt J.N.Best, Lt C.R.Duttson, Sgt E.Foster, Maj J.P.Gardner MC, CSgt R.C.Locke and Lt Col J.F.Parsons MC.

40 Commando was relieved by 42 Commando on 13 December. The change over was completed within 37 hours with the employment of Wessex helicopters transferring the personnel of both units direct between the aircraft carrier and the shore locations. Returning to Burma Camp the Commando completed a backlog of administration and celebrated Christmas.

Throughout February a third of the unit was held at five hours notice to move to Sarawak. This restricted training but loading and landing trials were conducted with the Wessex helicopters of HMS *Bulwark*. Loading trials were also conducted with a SRN-5 hovercraft at the Naval Base Singapore and unit personnel, using the hovercraft and a fully armed Wessex, gave a display to HRH Prince Philip during his visit to the base. Observing at the completion of the display that the marines were all kneeling Prince Philip turned to them as he was leaving and said "All right chaps, prayer meeting over".

It may not be generally known that members of the Womens Royal Voluntary Service provide valuable welfare assistance to HM Forces Overseas. Miss C.E. Forrest WRVS, better known as Chad, had worked with the unit from September 1963. She organised a recreation room in Burma Camp, where the men when they were off duty, could write letters, play darts or listen to pop records. Chad accompanied the Commando when it went on operational tours in Borneo and furnished a recreation room in Sarawak. Chad visited the sick,

A section patrol on the River Seradong in Sabah, September 1964.

The SS Petrel, *Headquarter ship of the Tawau Assault Group with the White Ensign and ship's laundry flying together! Photos: J. D. Shallow.*

undertook requests from the men to send flowers to relatives, purchased birthday cards, organised weddings and in many ways contributed to the welfare of the Commando.

Mention should also be made of the invaluable work undertaken by the Unit Married Families Liaison Team, assisted by a number of wives. The unit was on trickle drafting and the majority of wives travelled out after their husbands, to find the unit deployed and no husbands to greet them. The policy was to concentrate the families in the Johore Bahru area. There were few quarters and most had to be assisted to find accommodation. The Wives Club provided a most valuable back-up and every family was visited regularly by an area representative who delivered a newsletter and was "on call" if required.

40 Commando became the first unit in the Commando Brigade to be equipped with light aircraft. On 28 April 1965, the 40 Commando Air Troop, consisting of two Sioux AH-1 helicopters, piloted by Lts N.D.J.Wise and R.H.B.Learoyd, flew to Burma Camp to join the unit. The ground crew, consisting of seven naval airmen plus driver, had joined the Commando prior to their arrival.

Leading elements of the unit flew to Kuching on 7 July and 10 days later the Commando was fully deployed in the Serian area. The increase in confrontation had necessitated reinforcing the entire sector to a strength of five battalions. The unit was located in four forward positions varying from 900 yards to three miles from the border and roughly 23 miles from Commando HQ in Serian. The first contact was made on 31 August. Local people reported that Indonesians had crossed the border and B Company mounted an ambush to cut their lines of withdrawal. Contact was made and in a brisk exchange of fire four Indonesians were killed and a member of B Company received minor wounds.

An unsuccessful coup in Java at the end of September resulted in a general feeling of uncertainty throughout Indonesia and the more militant anti-communist policy of the military junta caused widespread speculation as to the fate of Communists in Kalimantan. Previously CCP members in Sarawak in danger of arrest crossed the border into Kalimantan for refuge. Others went there for training. Continued civil and political unrest in Java and elsewhere in Indonesia led to a reduction in the cross border activity to Sarawak, but two troops of B Company surprised a party of Indonesians making camp. The Indonesians were driven back across the border having suffered a number of casualties. They in turn replied with rapid and accurate mortar fire killing Cpl P.J.G.Danells and wounding one marine.

The Hearts and Minds campaign in Borneo was considered as important as the successful conduct of ground and air operations. The men of 40 Commando built on their good relations with the civilians and developed a closer understanding with the local people by respecting their customs and traditions. When circumstances allowed, helicopters were used to take the seriously ill people from remote kampongs to hospital or to fly government

Lord Head, British High Commissioner to Malaysia, escorted by Lt Col Parsons and Capt Shallow while visiting A Company at Padawa.

Hearts and Minds. RN Medical Assistants (MAs) performing "Surgery" in one of the Dyak Kampongs. Photos: J. D. Shallow

officials to distant locations. The medical officer and SBAs supplemented the inadequate health and medical facilities by providing treatment and the sick bay in the forward areas frequently took on the appearance of a busy suburban surgery. Air Troop med-evac service was reported to have saved many lives.

With peace talks in Bangkok nearing conclusion and the military battle in Sarawak effectively over, the role of the border protection units changed to a watch and wait situation. Many of the irregulars on the other side of the border had settled in ethnic groups of which some wished to return to Sarawak under the terms and conditions of the current regime. Others, including the hard core Communists, seemed intent on continuing the struggle.

The granting of an amnesty by the Malysian goverment to all anti-Sarawak rebels was announced on 23 July 1966 and the withdrawal of some of the British troops commenced. Although 40 Commando continued its patrolling, albeit with less intensity, more time was given to the Hearts and Minds campaign.

On 1 August Maj E.G.D.Pounds was promoted and assumed command of the unit in succession to Lt Col Taplin. It is doubtful whether many officers had his unique opportunty of serving in one unit as staff officer operations, second in command and commanding officer, all in the same tour.

Unit locations were reorganised in September in preparation for the handover of operational control to the 5th Royal Malay Regiment. A farewell party, with musical accompaniment provided by 3 Commando Brigade Band, was held at Simanggang for units serving in the area. During the evening the District Officer, Mr P Tinggong, presented 40 Commando with a cannon. The well-preserved muzzle loader had been used in the anti-pirate wars of 1854-56 at a time when the Royal Marines detachment of HMS *Dido* operated in the area.

Relinquishing operational control on 20 September 1966, the unit returned to Singapore. The final months of the year were mainly taken up with leave and administration and the move from Burma Camp to Dieppe Barracks. The new accommodation formed part of the Fleet Amphibious Forces Base. Brig B.I.S.Gourlay OBE,MC, who had succeeded Brig Willasey-Wilsey, was the first visitor to 40 Commando in its new surroundings and took a keen interest in his tour of the camp while enjoying the opportunity to talk with the men about their recent experiences in Borneo.

CHAPTER 18

1 January 1967 to 22 March 1972

Dieppe Barracks, Singapore – Hong Kong 20 years on – Assault unit of Task Force 318 – Exercises in Aden and Australia, more exercises and emphasis on sport – Hong Kong again – Flood relief operation in East Pakistan – Deployment of 3 Cdo Bde RM to UK – 40 Commando Group proceeds to UK via Persian Gulf, Bay of Bengal and Gan.

A COMBINATION of the new and pleasant surroundings in Dieppe Barracks, the supercession of Commanding Officers and the preparations for an amphibious exercise in Hong Kong gave fresh impetus to the start of 1967. Lt Col Pounds, a popular leader, ended his tour with a rousing send off from all ranks in the unit and Lt Col R.B. Loudoun OBE, who assumed command on 10 January 1967, received a correspondingly warm welcome. The new CO had scarcely time to grasp the reins before Maj Gen Patterson* paid the Commando a visit to witness a demonstration of an airborne company assault. The assault, which also featured the new concept of an airborne operations post, was supported by RAF Canberra bombers, RNAS helicopter gun-ships and 105mm gun-fire from the 7th Commando Light Battery RA.

In the sports arena the unit boxers maintained their highly successful season and it came as no surprise to find the Commando team competing in the finals of the Far East Championships. The ringside seats on 3 February were mostly filled with enthusiastic spectators from 40 Commando and their rivals in the 1st Battalion Scots Guards. All were intent on cheering their respective teams to victory but, in winning eight out of the 11 bouts in splendid style, a rejoicing 40 Commando team and its supporters returned to Dieppe Camp with the trophy. Four days later a 3 Commando Brigade Group, including 40 Commando, embarked in HMS *Bulwark* for passage to Hong Kong and the New Territories. This Brigade Group comprised of 960 men, 48 vehicles, four field guns and two Sioux helicopters, was the largest force ever to have embarked in a Commando carrier.

Hong Kong, viewed from a distance by the commandos in *Bulwark*, would have appeared much the same as it had looked to their predecessors who arrived there from Malta in 1947. However the sky line had changed dramatically with densely packed high rise buildings towering over busy streets. An affluent society had evolved with a massive increase in population. It is also possible that observant colonials would have noticed changes in the method

---

* Maj Gen A.G.Patterson DSO,OBE,MC, GOC 17th Division Malayan District.

of operation of the Commando Brigade, in particular the helicopter facility which enabled 40 Commando Group to operate directly from HMS *Bulwark* with the Wessex of 845 Squadron and Whirlwinds of the RAF. In Ex Full Circle, the Commando practised a new technique which it evolved with 845 Squadron, consisting of a quick reaction, fixed payload heliborne company with facilities for airborne briefing and a predetermined drill for landing patterns specifically designed to speed up infantry/helicopter operations.

A few days after returning to Singapore on 4 March, elements of Commando HQ and Commando Brigade HQ embarked in HMS *Fearless* for the annual Far East Fleet amphibious exercise on the west coast of Malaya. While they were away Company Commanders and selected NCOs attended a short refresher course at the Jungle Warfare School prior to organising their own company jungle training courses of five weeks duration. Over 40 per cent of unit personnel had joined the Commando after the end of the Borneo conflict and the majority lacked any knowledge of jungle survival or jungle fighting. The training concluded with a unit exercise Round-Turn, in which enthusiastic Gurkhas from the 2nd/6th Battalion acted as enemy and Commando Headquarters tested a new type of command post shelter. The tent shelter could be erected and camouflaged in five minutes but proved to be extremly hot for the occupants when closed up for the night.

May and June were spent in Hong Kong, providing a security presence in the Colony during a period of communist inspired industrial disputes. Rehearsals for Trooping the Colour were well advanced when the unit received orders to embark within 24 hours. Officers 'operational equipment' included Sam Brown belts and swords and sword drill was continued on the flight deck, much to the amusement of the Navy.

The riots were initiated by a small hard core of communists. The Commando was formed into riot squads of troop strength and held at four hours notice while key personnel maintained a close liaison with the police and military organisations. However, the steadying influence and firm control of the police calmed the situation. The emergency was terminated and the Commando deployed to the New Territories for two exercises in which the local breed of mosquitos were the main enemy. During one of the exercises involving helicopters the first flight, led by the Battery Commander, himself a helicopter pilot, strayed a number of miles too far north and almost landed in Communist China. The men on the ground who ran to man the guns were recognised just in time. Red faces all round and diplomatic displeasure!

Returning to Singapore in late June the Gurkhas were again called upon to act as enemy in Ex Firm Stride, designed to test both Commando units, the 1st and 2nd SBS and Brigade Headquarters in counter-revolutionary warfare. Operating from HMS *Bulwark* and *Fearless*, the units were flown ashore near Kuantan, the capital of the State of Pahang. The emphasis was on mobility by helicopter and on foot and all re-supply and casevac was undertaken by air. The operation lasted for nine days at the end of which the Gurkhas and commandos shared the same helicopters back to base.

On return to Singapore, the unit devoted many hours to ceremonial drill under the direction of the 2IC, Maj G.Roberts, an ex Adjutant, and RSM R.Smith MM, in preparation for trooping the Regimental Colour on 19 August 1967. This was the 25th anniversary of the raid on Dieppe. The Regimental Colour was carried by Lt C.R.Gilding and the guest of honour on this special occasion was Maj Gen Hellings, Commander of Portsmouth Group Royal Marines. The Commander-in-Chief, Gen Sir Michael Carver KCB, CBE,DSO,MC, took the salute and later, in a letter to Lt Col Loudoun, commented most favourably on "the very high standard of performance by every man on parade; their impeccable turn-out, rock-like steadiness and precision of their drill movements." During the ceremony the Wilkinson Sword of Peace*, awarded to 40 Commando in recognition of the unstinting efforts of all ranks to preserve friendship and peace during the Borneo Campaign, was carried for the first time on parade by Lt Col Loudoun.

In the wake of the departure of the British Garrison from Aden, a stabilising presence in that sector of the Middle East was provided by British Naval Task Force 318. The Force consisted of the aircraft carrier HMS *Hermes*, the modified strike carrier HMS *Albion* with 42 Commando embarked as the assault unit, HMS *Phoebe* acting as escort and the RFAs *Lyness* and *Olwen* providing the supply element. After three weeks on station HMS *Albion* and 42 Commando were relieved by *Bulwark* with 40 Commando embarked as the assault unit. *Bulwark* sailed on 29 November but before leaving Malaya 40 Commando carried out a deep penetration exercise into the jungle which entailed being heliborne 75 miles inland from the carrier. The two hour turn round was extended by bad weather delays and it eventually took three days to land the entire unit!

Between November 1967 and May 1968, 40 Commando was destined to spend 115 days at sea, mostly out of sight of land, in a ship not designed to accommodate an embarked force for prolonged periods. It was necessary to devise ways to maintain fitness and incentive, both of which could easily deteriorate in the restricted space between decks. The air squadrons looked upon the flight deck as their domain and firm insistence had to be made by Lt Col Loudoun for its regular availability to the unit for training and exercise. Much thought went into the training programme and every available space in the ship was used for small classes on every conceivable subject.

Jungle orientated for most of the year the unit concentrated on revising conventional tactics and improving marksmanship. After three weeks confined in *Bulwark* the Commando landed on Masirah, an arid and sparsley populated island, situated off the coast of Oman. The southern end of the 30 mile long and 8 mile wide island is mainly flat and uninhabitable but to the north a RAF Station was located in the Jebel- like country which rises to

---

* The origin of the Wilkinson Sword of Peace is described at Appendix G

700 feet. Sub units,landing in rotation during four days before Christmas and between 6 and 17 January 1968, were able to perform section movement and minor tactics, weapon handling, marches of three hours duration and fitness training.

Fitness training was maintained by various means and on return to Singapore the boxing team, skilfully coached by CSgt Clark, won the Singapore District and Far East Land Forces Team Championships for the third time in succession. Also, the runners led by Lt Bagshaw showed the Navy a clean pair of heels to win the Navy Cross Country Championships. Extensive use of the running track and endless range work indicated company preparations for the annual athletics competition and a determination to win the COs Trophy. In due course the Unit Athletics Trophy was awarded to A Company and 40 Commando won most prizes in the Brigade Athletics Meeting. B Company won the COs Trophy but the unit team was out-pointed by 42 Commando in the Brigade Rifle Meeting.

Aircraft and hovercraft were the main topics of conversation in August when 848 Squadron assisted the unit to revise helicopter drills and B Company was introduced to the military uses of SRN Hovercraft piloted and maintained by No 200 Hovercraft Squadron RCT. On 12 August the Unit Light Aircraft Squadrons amalgamated to form the Brigade ULA Squadron, commanded by Capt T.P.T. Donkin. The celebration fly past was observed by Brig Gourlay who, following the announcement of his promotion to Major General, handed over command of 3 Commando Brigade that day to Brig P.J.F. Whiteley OBE.

After summer leave the Commando Brigade prepared to deploy to Australia for a major amphibious exercise. The force embarked in ships of the Amphibious Warfare Squadron on 20 September and joined the largest assembly of warships in the Pacific since World War II. Ex Coral Sands was based on a conventional war setting of which Phases I and II consisted of sea and air battles. Phase III, held in the arid and reputedly venomous snake infested area of Shoalwater Bay, North Queensland, was designed to exercise the units in section, troop and company tactics. During this fast moving six day phase the men were exposed to an enemy of considerable strength – provided by the Australians – and the full force of the sun.

The SBS parachuted into the beach-head to mark a landing site for a heliborne assault by 42 Commando. This was closely followed with a seaborne landing by 40 Commando. The planning was realistic and the exercise thoroughly well run. On completion the force re-embarked and sailed to Brisbane for 10 days rest and recreation. On the first night following their arrival the entertainments committee of the Amphibious Group organised a dance. After this excellent start the remainder of the visit was an outstanding success. Gen Sir Norman Tailyour KCB, DSO+, took this opportunity to visit the Brigade during a farewell tour prior to handing over command of the Royal Marines to Lt Gen P.W.C. Hellings DSC, MC., on 19 November 1968.

It is of interest to note that Coral Sands was the cause of a short verbal dual in the House of Commons on 16 November, when Mr Boyd- Carpenter asked the Secretary of State for Defence (Mr Denis Healey), if he would make a statement as to the lessons which have been learnt as a result of the exercise.

Mr Healey: "Since the exercise involved the combined Services of four nations it will be some time before the final report, from which the lessons will be drawn, is completed, but initial impressions suggest that the exercise was successful and provided valuable practice in the co-ordination of combined forces".

Mr Boyd-Carpenter: "Has the right honourable Gentleman seen the report by The Times correspondent, which brings out clearly the fact that aircraft carriers are essential to any British action to assist Australia in this area? In those circumstances will he reconsider his decision to scrap in 1972 all the carriers—"

Mr Speaker: "Order. There is another Question on aircraft carriers."

Mr Boyd-Carpenter: "All the carriers, including the *Ark Royal* on which the right hon Gentleman is at present spending £30 million?"

Mr Healey: "The right hon Gentleman will be aware that I am not responsible for the views of The Times correspondent, or any other newspaper correspondent."

On return to Singapore a number of the old hands spent their savings on presents and looked forward to a white Christmas in UK. The newcomers, most of whom had arrived direct from initial training, were introduced to the strange new world inside the jungle where they were initiated into the methods of living, fighting and surviving in the unfamiliar and frequently inhospitable terrain. Personnel with previous jungle experience were selected for specialist courses and a number were chosen for training as War Dog Handlers. Although dogs had been used by the Commando units in the fifties during anti terrorist operations, any training had been of the briefest nature and experience had been acquired by trial and error. Now, the Jungle Warfare School offered a 12 week course followed by two months "in the field" training, where the trackers and infantry patrol dogs worked with the troops. During exercise Enchanter in February 1969, trackers and their patrol dogs were lifted ashore by helicopter from HMS *Albion* to Penang Island and successfully searched out members of the opposing force.

The land phase of this amphibious exercise – part of Fotex'69 – only lasted for 36 hours but it enabled the many newcomers holding key positions to experience the planning and preparation stage of an amphibious assault and subsequent re-embarkation. Later, the Commando flew to Asahan to give a demonstration of live firing to a joint services audience. The demonstration consisted of a Commando attack, using Wessex helicopters for the troop lift and fire support from mortars, artillery, fighter aircraft and helicopter gunships. During this and other exercises it was not unusual to pick up signals from operational units in Viet Nam on the Commando net which, to some extent helped to keep in mind the true purpose of the training.

The tempo of activity increased in March when companies carried out a series of IS and jungle exercises, the Recce Troop went to Hong Kong for detachment training and 29 Cdo Light Regt RA with Support Company, gave a presentation of supporting arms. Several officers and NCOs, acting as umpires for the 28th Commonwealth Brigade's last exercise Crowning Glory, had the opportunity to observe the 8th Royal Australian Regiment and 1st Royal New Zealand Infantry Regiment using tactics and procedures learnt in Viet Nam. American and Commonwealth troops in the Viet Nam campaign made a positive attempt to implement a Hearts and Minds campaign similar to that successfully employed by British Forces in other communist influenced areas of the world. A form of Hearts and Minds programme (Concord), had been used in Malaya for some years and in Singapore each service unit undertook responsibility for a school or youth organisation. When 40 Commando took a group of school cadets to the Cameron Highlands for Adventure Training it was the first time that many of the youngsters had been out of the concrete jungle of Singapore and the train journey itself was an adventure.

Lt Col D.C. Alexander assumed command of the unit from Lt Col Loudoun at 2359 hours on 24 April 1969, and at noon next day received his first senior VIP, the C-in-C Far East, Adm Sir Peter Hill-Norton KCB. Ex Jollies Jaunt in May was a unit security exercise in Marang, a quiet backwater of the north-east coastal section of Malaya. HMS *Albion*,on her last exercise before returning to UK waters, carried the Commando Group and M Company, 42 Commando (the enemy) to the exercise area. After six days of intense activity 40 Commando, the victors, and M Company, the vanquished, emerged from the jungle well satisfied with their efforts.

In between field exercises and periods at sea the Commando boxers won the RN Novices and Open Championships and, for the third consecutive year, the FARELF Inter Unit Team Championships. A considerable amount of sport, including the Unit Rifle Championships, won by A Company, occupied the recreational activities programme between May and September. The Judo Squad visited Japan and the Fencing Team toured New South Wales, Australia. In the China Shield football competition between ships and units in the Far East, the finalist were 40 and 42 Commandos, the first time that two Royal Marine units had opposed each other in the finals since 1901. The game ended with a 3-2 win to 40 Commando. The unit athletes were not outstanding although a number of individuals showed promise. The cricketers had a mediocre season and were given a good tousing by 42 Commando's fine seam bowlers. The swimmers fared better, winning the RN Championships but were pipped at the post by the Royal Signals in the finals of the Army Championships. Not the least of the sporting efforts was made by the rowing team, who travelled 1,400 miles to honour a challenge to the Royal Hong Kong Yacht Club, and won the race which only took four minutes!

The unit had an opportunity to display its wares when it paraded as a Commando group on 29 July for the Brigade Open Day and repeated the display on a very wet "Dieppe Day" on 19 August. In early September, C Company moved to Gemas, Malaya, to act as enemy against the Gurkhas while A Company sailed to Hong Kong for a month's training in the New Territories. The officers arranged a special dinner at the Hong Kong Club on 23 September for Capt A.P. Downton MBE, the Assistant Military Secretary. Among the guests was Lt J.J.D.(Paddy) Ashdown, the current leader of the Liberal Democrats, who was then studying languages at HMS *Tamar*.

Two exercises in November were preliminaries to Square Hole, a major 3 Commando Brigade exercise programmed for December. Square Hole was designed to test the Brigade's capabilities in a jungle scenario of civil unrest and insurgency, but it developed into a 10 day test of endurance in terrible weather. An estimated 14 inches of rain fell in 12 hours and caused the worst floods in Malaya for 30 years. Lt Gen Hellings chose this occasion to spend nine days with Commando Brigade and visited 40 Commando on 20 November to observe B Company displaying the finer arts of abseiling and river crossing.

The exercise was aptly named according to one marine who said "We dug square holes, oblong holes and every other shape of hole which promptly filled with water. Every second word was...dig!" Shortly after this episode Lt F. Hughes received the Queen's Commendation for saving the lives of eight children during the storms. The children, all non-swimmers, were thrown into the fast moving flood water when an assault boat taking them to dry land capsized in a whirlpool. Fortunately they were swept into the branches of trees to which they clung. Members of the crew righted the craft while Lt Hughes swam with each of the children from the trees to the boat.

Activities during the first three months of 1970 were mainly directed towards company training and administration in the local area. Visitors included the Chief of the Defence Staff* and the unit gave a warm welcome to the 95th Commando Light Regiment. Elements of 40 Commando carried out infantry-artillery co-operation with the 79th (Kirkee) Commando Light Battery RA, the last joint service exercise before the battery returned to UK.

Preparations were made for the Brigade Open Day on Monday 9 February and the 40 Commando's sports officer took advantage of the centralised unit to organise a week of sport, whether games included in the programme were in season or not. The fencing team consisting of a young and inexperienced group of enthusiasts, surprised everyone with their achievements. Trained by CSgt Neilson and Sgt Harrison they fenced calmly and skilfully to win the FARELF Inter Unit Competiton. Four of their number were then selected for the Navy team which in turn won the Inter Service Championships. The soccer team maintained its position at the top of the league but the seven-a-side rugby team met defeat at the hands of the more experienced Australians and New Zealanders.

Ex Flying Fish, an eight day amphibious exercise which commenced on

---

* Marshal of the RAF Sir Charles Elworthy GCB,CBE,DSO,MVO,DFC,AFC,MA.

4 April, provided the unit with the first opportunity in nearly a year to work with an LPD and Joint Force Headquarters embarked in HMS *Fearless*. The unit embarked in HMS *Bulwark* and carried out an assault landing with 847 and 848 Naval Air Squadrons onto Penarak airstrip.

B Company, having spent a lively and at times sleepless two weeks in March acting as enemy to 42 Commando, became involved in another busy but more interesting exercise with HMS *Bulwark* in April. The company assisted the squadrons in a presentation given to the national press and television teams during the preliminary stages of a five nation SEATO exercise Bersatu Padu. The helicopters were used to show their capabilities for troop carrying, load lifting and acting as gun-ships. During the presentation B Company personnel fired the SS 11 wire guided missile to demonstrate the devastating effectiveness of the anti-tank weapon on an eight foot target at 2,000 yards. On completion, *Bulwark* proceeded on a show-the-flag visit to Kobe, in Japan, where EXPO 70, an international exposition set in 815 acres on the outskirts of Osaka, provided the major sight-seeing attraction.

Ex Bersatu Padu, closely followed by Ex Granada in June, were both devised to test Britain's ability to fly a viable force from UK to Malaysia, to arrive in time and in adequate physical condition to combat a rapidly developing counter insurgency threat. In addition, the exercises were designed to test joint command and co-operation between the armed services of UK, Australia, New Zealand, Malaysia and Singapore. Prior to the start of *Bersatu Padu*, in which 40 Commando joined forces with 19th Brigade (UK) and 4th Malaysian Infantry Brigade, an immense amount of trouble was taken by the planners to study Vietcong methods and to incorporate the assistance of the local people to provide the maximum realism into proceedings.

Ex Granada, held in the Penerak and Bukit Ribut areas of Malaysia, involved 25,000 service-men from the five nations. Space in HMS *Bulwark* was at a premium when the 900 men of 40 Commando Group embarked for Phase One. Disposing of the enemy forces in Penerak took three days. The Commando then re-embarked in preparation for Phase Two. During this phase 42 Commando joined forces with the Gurkhas to act as enemy. The Gurkhas constructed a very realistic communist training camp in the jungle and when this was captured on 24 June it was found to contain living and working accommodation, a vegetable garden and a mined and booby-trapped effigy of Lt Col Alexander!

It would be very difficult not to enjoy summer leave in Singapore and all ranks made the most of the sea and sunshine in July. Even the return to duty had its attractions in the form of a three month deployment to Hong Kong. The unit sailed across the South China Sea during the first week in August to occupy newly decorated quarters in Sek Kong Camp and to take over the duties of the 7th Queen Elizabeth's Own Gurkha Rifles while they carried out an amalgamation of their two battalions. A secondary commitment of the tour was to undertake the duties of "Typhoon stand-by unit" for the areas of

Lt Col D. C. Alexander during Ex Granada, in the Penerak area of Malaysia.
Photo: D. C. Alexander.

Tai Poo and Sha Tin. The first alert came when Typhoon Anita was reported heading resolutely on course for Hong Kong. The Commando made ready to go to the aid of the citizens but as the typhoon approached the coast it suddenly side-stepped the British colony before advancing into mainland China.

When the excitement had died down the companies alternated with each other in providing ceremonial guards at the official residences of the Governor and GOC, carrying out a programme of field firing and undertaking a series of raiding party exercises with the Mine-Sweeping Squadron. In due course preparations were made for the unit to take over OP and patrol duties on the Hong Kong-China border. It was the time of the Cultural Revolution and politically very sensitive. During the reconnaisance and briefing sessions it was made clear to sub-unit commanders that nothing should be done to change the established routine. In commando terminology this instruction was interpreted as "Don't rock the boat!" However, the commandos did wear their green berets, a decision that had to be approved by the Governor Sir David Trench.

There were no incidents to make headline news while 40 Commando was on the border. The major part of the time was spent observing and logging the ordinary day to day activities of members of the Chinese Communist Army and the farming community at close quarters. Patrolling the villages along the Hong Kong side of the border in a Hearts and Minds role helped to relieve the monotony of a very restricted routine.

All sub-units completed the annual range course in September in between visits by the Deputy Commander Land Forces* and an officer of the General Staff Hong Kong. Brig P.J. Ovens OBE, MC, who had assumed command of 3 Commando Brigade in June, also paid the unit a visit in early October. Although the unit was called upon to stand-by for a further period of border duty this did not materialise. Lt Col Alexander, who had almost completed his tour of command, used the opportunity to introduce a new event to the unit, designed to test the efficiency of sub-units in weapon proficiency, map reading and other military skills. Known as the Rover Trophy Competition it was intended that the event should be held annually. The trophy, presented to the unit by Lt Col Alexander, is in the form of a silver salver inset with a coin from each country visited by ranks of the commando during the CO's tour in command. On this occasion the salver was presented to the Signals Troop, the undisputed winners.

The Commando handed over the Hong Kong Garrison duties to the Gurkhas on 12 October 1970 and embarked in HMS *Intrepid* and *Triumph* in preparation for an amphibious exercise. Extreme weather conditions resulting from Typhoon Joan led to the early termination of the exercise and the ships were forced to ride out the storm at sea before returning to Singapore.

Lt Col D.L. Bailey, who assumed command from Lt Col Alexander on

* Maj Gen D.H.T. Horsford CBE,DSO.

22 October, greeted the unit on its return to Dieppe Barracks. After a few days leave the unit prepared for the Remembrance Day Parade and Spearhead Unit. During the night of 12-13 November a combination of hurricane force winds and spring tides caused the build-up of a tidal wave which swept up the Bay of Bengal swamping the land with 10 feet high waves, drowning outlying islands and causing wide-spread devastation. Hundreds of thousands of people were killed or rendered homeless. Op Burlap, the first major aid programme, was provided by a combined Naval, Military and RAF task force formed in Singapore under the command of Cdre D.W.Napper, Commodore Amphibious Forces (COMAF). Elements from Brigade Headquarters and 40 Commando embarked in HMS *Intrepid* and *Triumph* and LSL *Sir Galahad* and sailed for East Pakistan on 20 November while 9 Troop flew to Dacca the following day. On arrival the organisation and control of the shore element was placed under the command of Brig Ovens. The main role of the unit was to assist in the distribution of food supplies and clothing, the provision of medical help and re-establishing communications.

The area for which the British Task Force was responsible covered 1,600 miles of low-lying islands never more than three feet above sea level and interspersed with innumerable waterways. Shallow water prevented *Intrepid* and *Triumph* approaching closer than 35 miles to the shore-line and all stores and supplies had to be shipped or flown to the main supply dump a further 45 miles inland at Patuakhali. The eight landing craft and the helicopters from 847 NAS in *Intrepid* were well suited for this task and 2,000 tons of stores were taken ashore in these craft. Lt Col Bailey relieved Brig Ovens at Patuakhali on 29 November while Maj J.Thompson assumed command of 40 Commando. By 8 December 1970 the Pakistan Army and civilian authorities were able to control the situation on their own and the Task Force returned to Singapore.

News of the imminent return of 3 Commando Brigade to England after 28 years became public knowledge in January 1971. 42 Commando were to fly home in April followed by Brigade Headquarters, to occupy Bickleigh Barracks and Stonehouse Barracks, Plymouth respectively. 40 Commando-Group would be the last Commando to leave the Far East and, on return to UK, would take over Seaton Barracks, Plymouth. In preparation for the move to Europe Brig R.B. Loudoun and a team of officers flew out from UK to give the Brigade officers an informative presentation on NATO. Meanwhile 40 Commando pursued a busy programme of rifle meetings, company exercises, an Air Portability Parade and a week of sport, prior to taking over as Spearhead Unit in February 1971.

Ex Summer Frolic, the first amphibious exercise of 1971, preceded the annual SEATO exercise in April. The Commandant General, Gen Sir Peter Hellings visited 40 Commando in the field to observe some of the tactical movement and later, at Dieppe Barracks, was entertained by the officers and SNCOs in their respective Messes.

ON 18 March 1971, three days after the completion of Summer Frolic the

2,500 men comprising 3 Commando Brigade Royal Marines and sub units paraded for the last time in Malaya. At 1758 hours Air Chf Mshl Burnett* C-in-C Far East Command, arrived at the parade ground in HMS *Simbang* where he was met by Brig Ovens and Col D.W.Sluman, who accompanied him to the dias. At 1800 hours precisely he took the salute as the Guard of Honour came to the present and seven helicopters, representing the attached Air Squadron, flew past. After reviewing the remainder of the parade to the accompaniment of the Brigade Band, Sir Brian returned to the dias for the Sunset Ceremony. The White Ensign was lowered and the final commitment of 3 Commando Brigade Royal Marines in the Far East drew to a close.

The air trooping to UK of 42 Commando and Headquarters 3 Commando Brigade commenced the next day and was completed by the end of April. Meanwhile 40 Commando transferred to the 28th Brigade for training and operations and embarked in ships of the Amphibious Warfare Squadron for SEATO Ex Subok, in the Philippines. The task force, commanded by Rear Adm Gaddis USN in the USS *Iwo Jima*, spent two weeks performing every conceivable manoeuvre against surface, air and submarine attack. Finally 40 Commando and elements of the US Marine Corps exercised assault landings from LCVPs and helicopters. During three days ashore the Commando, aided by Royal Engineers and US Marine Corps Engineers, had an opportunity to put the Hearts and Minds philosophy to practical use by renovating a local school and constructing a culvert under a road.

The six month period following the formation of 40 Commando Group on 1 May was primarily occupied with three major exercises, leave and preparations for the units departure from the Far East. A visit by the 1st/9th Battalion Landing Team USMC to Dieppe Barracks on 6 May enabled the Commando to repay hospitality received from the Americans during exercise Subok. A week later the Wessex helicopters of 848 Squadron flew 40 Commando to HMS *Albion,* on the carriers arrival from UK, and the amphibious force proceeded to Brunei for Ex New Look II. The exercise was designed as a work-up between *Albion* and the Commando in preparation for a ship-unit deployment later in the year. Returning to Singapore at the end of May the Commando vacated Dieppe Barracks and moved across the airfield to Kangaw Barracks previously occupied by 42 Commando. While proceeding on unit leave a week later, LCpl D. Weeks was killed in a car accident. His death was a sad blow to numerous friends. He had been very much liked and respected.

Ex Round Up, the last large scale amphibious exercise off the west coast of Malaysia with HMS *Albion* before the unit's final embarkation, commenced on 19 July, with a night fly-in to Penerak Air Strip. The five days ashore were divided between operations against an enemy provided by the 7th Battery RA and acting as unpaid extras for a Ministry of Defence film about life in the Royal Navy.

* Air Chief Marshal Sir Brian Burnett GCB,DFC,AFC,BA.

Dieppe Day commemorated on 19 August, was the occasion for a commando parade and drum-head service followed by an all ranks and families buffet lunch and an afternoon of sport and games. Everyone made the most of the social occasion despite a tropical storm which threatened to turn the camp into a sea of mud. On the last Sunday in August Lt Col Bailey and a representative party of all ranks and wives attended a memorial service at the Anglican Church in Kualar Kangsar, in memory of all 40 Commando personnel who were killed on active service during the Malayan Emergency. The service was taken by the Rev J. Beech.

A final jaunt into the jungle in September for Ex Last Look, enabled the rifle companies to refresh their knowledge of jungle combat and to introduce newcomers recently joined from UK, to the leeches and other delights of nature found in the Mersing area. When this was completed all training north of the Johore Causeway was curtailed to ease commitments on the unit transport prior to embarkation. In addition to handing-over Kangaw Barracks to the Base staff, loading stores and vehicles and the embarkation of the Commando in HMS *Albion,* the unit performed two ceremonial parades. The first of these events, the march- out of 40 Commando Colours from Kangaw Barracks to HMS *Albion,* was held on the 307th birthday of the Corps. The second parade, at Kangaw, marked the closure of Far East Command.

On 28 October 1971, RSM R. Whitehouse marched-out the Colours from Commando Headquarters and presented them to the Colour Party, comprised of Lt A.H. Robinson (Queen's Colour), Lt A.J. Lane (Regimental Colour), QMS Watkins, Sgt Thomas and Sgt Dykes. The guard, under the command of Capt B.H.C. Le Mesurier, escorted the Colours to Blackham House where they were encased and driven to the dockyard. On arrival alongside HMS *Albion* the Colours were uncased, marched on board and placed in the Wardroom where a Royal Marine Officers Far East Dinner was to be held that night.

The C-in-Cs parade at HMS *Simbang* the following evening consisted of six guards and represented three services and three nationalities. While there was considerable variation in the uniforms of those on parade three weeks of preparation had produced a uniform drill of commendable standard. Air Chf Mshl Burnett took the salute and while the guns of the 7th (Sphinx) Battery RA were firing there was a fly-past of Sioux, Whirlwind, Wessex V, and Iroquois helicopters followed by a Bristol freighter, a Sunderland flying boat and six Mirage jets. After the inspection the guards marched past in column of route and as each passed the saluting base its Regimental Colour was let fly and its regimental march was played.

HMS *Albion* sailed from the Naval Base on 30 October and, after taking part in the C-in-C's Far East Fleet review, left the area the following day. The Commando's departure from the Far East coincided with the retirement of the CGRM, Gen Sir Peter Hellings KCB,DSC,MC,. In his farewell massage to the Corps he made reference to the Royal Marines becoming a predominately UK based force with important tasks within NATO on both the northern and

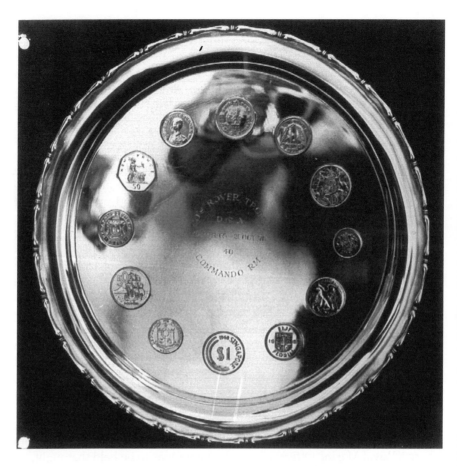

The Rover Trophy, inset with a coin from each country visited by ranks of the Commando during Lt Col Alexander's tour in command.
Photo: D. C. Alexander.

southern flanks of Europe. Tasks that would provide many opportunities for interesting and exciting service.

The immediate task of 40 Commando Group on leaving Singapore was to cover the withdrawal of British Forces from the Persian Gulf. There were two preparatory exercises. The first Curtain Call, was held at Penang Island, followed by nine days sub-unit training in Mombassa. During the latter period the Quartermaster's staff and medical team were able to provide assistance to the local people in Bamba, who were suffering from the effects of a long period of drought. Ex Gulfix, programmed to take place in the Trucial States, had to be cancelled as a result of the sensitive political situation in the Gulf preceding the formation of the Union of Arab Emirates. In the event the Iranians made premature landings on the islands in the Straits of Hormuz and in consequence the Commando Group's commitment was terminated on 8 December.

On 10 December, Capt J. Jungius RN, commanding HMS *Albion*, received instructions to proceed to the Bay of Bengal to assist in the evacuation of British Nationals from East-Pakistan. HMS *Albion*, with 40 Commando embarked and accompanied by the frigate HMS *Arethusa* sailed the next morning and while Midshipmen painted a huge Union Flag on the flight deck, to aid identification, the Royal Marines made preparations to accommodate an unknown number of Nationals. The *Albion* was still closing the distance on 13 December when an easing in international relations made it possible for RAF Hercules to air-lift the evacuees from Dacca. There being no reason to proceed further, a decision was taken to fly 40 Commando to UK. HMS *Albion* diverted to the island of Gan from where the unit was air ferried home in Hercules and Belfasts to Brize Norton and Lyneham in good time for Christmas leave. The advance party had prepared Seaton Barracks for the arrival of the main body and were ready to unload the stores and heavy baggage on the arrival of HMS *Albion* in Plymouth on 19 January 1972.

The Commandant General, Lt Gen B.I.S.Gourlay OBE, MC, visited Seaton Barracks on 8 March to welcome 40 Commando on its return to UK after 24 years continuous service overseas. He spoke to all ranks and outlined the commitments and problems that would confront the unit in the immediate future. A six weeks training period in preparation for a four months tour of duty in Northern Ireland commenced on 22 March.

CHAPTER 19

March 1972 to 16 December 1975

*Northern Ireland Tour, the Marching Season, Bloody Friday and
Community Relations – West country training – B Company visit to the
Bahamas – Second Northern Ireland Tour – Wilkinson Sword of Peace,
second award – Fitness for Role Training, Spearhead Unit and Cyprus
Emergency – Third Northern Ireland Tour.*

LT COL J.F.MOTTRAM OBE, succeeded Lt Col Bailey on 23 March 1972 and
set to work on the reorganisation of the unit for its new role in UK and
forthcoming tour in Northern Ireland. The changes included the formation of
three additional rifle troops from Support Company personnel and the dispersal of the Assault Engineers to the rifle companies. In addition, a Public
Relations Team was formed and representatives were appointed to each
company.

The CO had acquired a knowledgeable understanding of the task ahead
while in charge of the Joint Services Team at the Army Staff College Camberley.
Sharing an office with Lt Col Gray, who had commanded the 1st Parachute
Battalion on his previous tour in Belfast, they spent many hours discussing
tactics and other details which were to prove invaluable in the preparation of
operational procedures.

Inevitably other commitments, as diversified as air portability training and
ceremonial parade work, required attention during the pre- Northern Ireland
training period (NITP). The Commando was due to become operational on
1 June and from that date it had to be ready to operate:- as a landing force on
the flanks of Allied Command Europe; in an IS role world-wide or in support
of national contingency or United Nations operations world-wide. The unit
was formally at seven days notice to move, but preparations were made to
ensure that it could pack up and be ready to go in 12 hours, if required to do
so.

The Commando paraded on Plymouth Hoe on St Georges Day 23 April,
prior to marching through the city to St Andrew's Church for the Corps
Remembrance Day service. The Rev D.L Peyton-Jones DSC – who had served
as a troop commander with 3 Commando Brigade during the fifties – conducted the service attended by the Lord Mayor of Plymouth, Alderman Mrs
D.F. Innes – who had taken the salute during the march through the city – and
the heads of the Armed Services in Plymouth. Gen Sir Peter Hellings and many
other retired Royal Marines officers joined lustily in singing the well known
hymns.

40 Commando
march through
Plymouth
23 April 1972
St. Georges
Day.

*Orange Orders
march through
Belfast 12 July
1972
commemorating
the Battle of the
Boyne. Photos:
J. F. Mottram.*

*Lt. Col. J.
Mottram "on
hand" during
the marches.*

283

The following day the unit moved to Kent for 10 days intensive training at Hythe ranges and Lydd Camp where disused buildings, known as Rype Village, had been adapted to simulate conditions in Northern Ireland. Simultaneously, a reconnaisance party visited Belfast where the Company Commanders and other key personnel were able to see the locations which would become their responsibility. No one in the unit had previously served in Northern Ireland and it was essential to ensure that everyone fully understood the reasons for a military presence and its implications.

Although Northern Ireland, or Ulster as it is sometimes called, covers only one sixth of the total area of Ireland, it contains more than one third of the island's population. Nearly half a million of the one and a half million people live in the county borough and suburbs of Belfast, and Newtownabbey, while a further 56,000 live in the county borough of Londonderry. The remainder of the population is contained within the counties of Armagh, Down, Antrim, Londonderry, Fermanagh and Tyrone.

Incidents of conflict date back to early history but the problems between the descendants of the Scottish and English settlers have their roots in the 17th Century when James I colonised Ulster with English and Scottish tenants. Land was set aside for the church, with fortified castles and houses protecting estates on which the tenants, mostly Protestants were established.

An uprising by Irish and Anglo Irish against the Ulster community in 1641 was finally crushed by Cromwell after 11 years of fighting. Again, in 1688 the Catholics beseiged the Protestants in Derry (now Londonderry). The apprentices closed the city gates in the face of the beseiging army which eventually withdrew after receiving heavy casualties. The Protestants won a second victory at Enniskillen on the day the Derry siege was raised. In 1690 an international army of English, French, Netherlanders, Danish and Inniskillings led by William of Orange defeated James II at the Battle of the Boyne and surviving Catholic leaders fled to Europe. These events are now historic symbols. Members of the Orange Order march through the streets on 12 July to commemorate the Battle of the Boyne and the siege of Derry is celebrated by the Apprentice Boys March on 12 August. At the close of the 17th Century the Protestants controlled the country and Roman Catholics had lost their rights to citizenship. It was not until 1801, when the Act of Union became law, that Ireland was incorporated in the United Kingdom with Scotland and Wales, but a further 28 years passed before Roman Catholics were granted full Parliamentary rights.

Entering the 20th Century the island soon became embroiled in a movement for Irish self government but this was rejected by the Ulster Protestants. The issue led to civil war which ended in 1921 when the 26 mainly Roman Catholic Counties of Southern Ireland, were granted independence. Orignally named the Irish Free State the counties now form the Republic of Ireland.

In Northern Ireland the politics reflect the past history of the area. In the late sixties a number of clashes between Catholics and Protestants occured mainly in Belfast and Londonderry and a series of civil rights marches, held in support of claims of discrimination against Roman Catholics in housing, elections and jobs, led to further strife. A period of relative peace followed the setting up of a independent inquiry by the Northern Ireland Government with a promise of reform to remove grievances, but further violence erupted during Junior Orangemen parades in August 1969. The unsettled situation continued in much the same fashion into the seventies.

40 Commando relieved the 2nd Parachute Battalion in Belfast on 15 June. Throughout the four months operational tour the Commando Group served under the command of 39th Infantry Brigade as a city battalion with responsibility for Northern Belfast. The tactical area of responsibility (TAOR) extended from Unity Flats – a Catholic enclave in a section of the city centre – through the Catholic New Lodge and Protestant Tiger bay sectors to the northern extremities in the Newtownabbey and Monkstown district. C Company was responsible for Unity Flats, part of the city centre and the docks. Support Company maintained responsibility for the New Lodge sector while A Company were accountable for Newington, Tiger Bay and Mount Vernon. B Company covered North Belfast and an area of wooded country. In due course 29 Commando Light Regiment relieved B Company who moved to support A Company.

The main task of the Commando Group was to assist the Royal Ulster Constabulary (RUC) to maintain law and order and to deal with terrorist incidents. This involved arresting known members of the Provisional Irish Republic Army (IRA), finding and recovering arms, explosives and ammunition, preventing intersectarian strife and looting and promoting good relations with the Catholic community. The Commando commenced its tour at a time of varying levels of activity and when changes were being made to the internment policy. Interrogation centres were closed and the Security Forces were maintaining a low profile during the IRA cease fire which spanned late June to early July. The Protestants reacted by forming the Ulster Defence Army (UDA).

The conduct of operations by the Security Forces in Northern Ireland differed considerably to that experienced by commando personnel in Malaya and Borneo. In the jungle the patrol commander, whether he was a young officer, sergeant or corporal, was invariably on his own for long periods, particularly before helicopters were more extensively available. The CO of a unit was rarely directly involved in incidents in the jungle. In Belfast, where feelings between Protestants and Catholics ran high and where an incorrect action by a member of the Security Forces could spark off an incident, everyone, from the Brigadier downward was involved at all times. Maj Gen Mottram recalling his period as CO said:- "If an incident escalated – and there were hundreds of incidents in Belfast in 1972 – the Company Commander would be on the spot in minutes. If it grew more serious the CO, who spent a considerable amount of his time driving round the streets with his Rover

21 July 1972 Bloody Friday. The aftermath. Photos: J. F. Mottram.

Commando Headquarters Operations Centre Belfast.

Group, could be there as rapidly as the Company Commander".

The Commando achieved its first find on 23 June – a cache of 165 lbs of explosive – in the New Lodge area during the uneasy peace of the Provisional IRA cease fire. A gun fight broke out in Unity Flats on 26 June and peace talks ended when further gun fighting occured in Lenadoon Avenue on 9 July. Security Force vehicle and foot patrols were under constant threat from snipers but their retalitory action was restricted to firing only when gunmen had fired the first shot. In the 40 Commando sector the threat was countered by the deployment of sharpshooters around the periphery with orders to respond immediately to any gunmen who showed themselves. The Commando had several successes which in due course cut short the activities of the IRA in this area.

The marching season between mid July and mid August is the traditional time for the various Lodges to parade with banners and bands. The 12 July marked the 282nd anniversary of the Battle of the Boyne and loyalists of the Orange Order marched in their thousands across Belfast to meet on the field at Edenderry, six miles south of the town centre. The tremendous rally would seem to have been motivated more by sectarian and political encouragement than by its religious origins. The chance of a head-on confrontation between Protestants and Catholics was a real possibility, particularly in the area of Unity Flats where the Protestant columns passed close to the Catholic community. To prevent incidents while marches were in progress the commandos erected hessian screens between buildings and roads at key points and manned the route to keep the two factions apart. It was a time-absorbing task and a large manpower commitment.

The commandos incurred three casualties on 13 July, when altercations between Catholic and Protestants escalated into gun battles in the Ardoyne, Falls, Andersontown, Lenadoon and New lodge districts. The relative quiet that followed these incidents ended on 20 July when a disturbance in Crumlin Jail signalled the start of a massive IRA bombing campaign. In 40 Commando's TAOR 12 bombs exploded without warning. Two of the bombs, planted in crowded shopping areas, caused numerous casualties and extensive damage. Vehicles were used to barricade the streets and others were overturned and set on fire. The day became known as Bloody Friday!

The dismantling of all the barricades in the New Lodge area commenced in the early hours of 24 July. This difficult and sensitive task was achieved without major incident. The following day Mne D. Allen was killed by a gunshot in the back of the head while maintaining a neutral security presence at the funeral of a member of the Ulster Defence Regiment. Numerous shooting incidents between July and the end of October resulted in a further fifteen commando casualties of whom two died of gun-shot wounds. Thankfully the unit had a superb medical team led by Surg Lt P. Goodman RN. The doctor monitored the Commando radio link from his landrover-ambulance and when a casualty was reported, was able to be on the scene within minutes.

Recalling that period in a recent interview, Maj Gen Mottram said: " I visited the injured in the Royal Victoria Hospital where a number of our men were in the intensive care unit. On several occasions I saw my own ambulance arriving at the hospital and realised that something else had happened! It was a very intense period."

Action was taken to remove all the IRA "no go" areas when Operation Motorman swung into action on 31 July. Barricades were removed, patrolling was stepped-up to saturation point in Catholic areas and OPs were established in high-rise buildings. The pressure on the IRA was intensified to the extent that the commandos completely dominated the area and the Provisionals' leaders decided to leave Belfast. Maj Gen Mottram said: "The commando approach was to deal promptly and firmly with incidents of shooting or other trouble while at the same time developing the community relations spirit". To a certain extent this was achieved. Commando personnel looking after the mixed Protestant and Catholic communities built up a good relationship with the people. In the small Catholic enclaves the marines became familiar with every face and every detail, to the extent that any changes – an extra bottle of milk on the door step – were instantly noticed. Aggravation was dealt with quietly and diplomatically, more often than not by the young marines and corporals themselves.

All ranks endeavoured to foster good relations with the people of Belfast regardless of their religion or political affiliations. A constructive community programme organised by Maj J. Smith, the unit second in command, provided assistance to families whose homes had been bomb-wrecked. Pensioners were given bus outings and sports, games and camp expeditions were arranged for the children. The camps were very popular and gave many children their first glimpse of the countryside. Parents welcomed these gestures but many were concerned when the IRA issued hand bills containing warnings that a serious view would be taken of parents encouraging fraternisation with British troops through their children.

On one expedition in County Antrim, Lt J.Watkins, Sgt R Dyke and three marines went to the assistance of the Larne police who were unable to control a crowd of rioting Protestants and Catholics, one of whom had been shot. Forcing themselves between the two groups they overpowered two armed ringleaders and kept the factions apart until Army personnel arrived to take over. Lt Watkins was subsequently awarded the MC and Sgt Dyke the MM for their courageous action.

Constant 24 hour patrolling, the manning of OPs and road blocks, searching cars, buildings and screening people continued through August and September. It amounted to a lot of hard work, lack of sleep and occasionally a feeling of frustration, however the morale of the unit remained extremely high. During this busy period the unit received a number of senior visitors including Maj Gen Whiteley MGRM Commando Forces and Brig P.J. Ovens, Brigade Commander, 3 Commando Brigade.

There were long periods of diligent searching which revealed nothing, but on 6 September a substantial arms find of 12 weapons and 6,000 rounds of ammunition was found. Eight days later the Imperial Hotel was wrecked in one of the worst bomb incidents recorded. No prior warning was given, two people died and a further 40 were injured in the blast. The Protestants retaliated with two bomb attacks on the Republican Meeting Club. This extremely tense situation prevailed when the 1st Queen's arrived in Belfast on 17 October to relieve 40 Commando on the day that Mne A.P. David died from gunshot wounds.

During 40 Commando's tour in Belfast 606 shots were fired and 34 nail/petrol bombs were thrown at commando personnel. They in turn fired 602 shots and 989 baton rounds. The searching of 33,028 cars and 2,292 houses revealed 52 weapons, 4 grenades 764 lbs of explosive and 7,403 rounds of ammunition. Out of 382 arrests 335 were released 37 charged and 10 detained. Civilian casualties, mainly from bomb incidents, totalled 21 deaths and 193 injured. Recorded IRA casualties amounted to three dead and 19 wounded. The Commando Group incurred three dead, including a Royal Artillery gunner, and 17 confined in hospital.

Returning to Seaton Barracks after three weeks leave the Support Company reverted to its former role and the unit immersed itself in a training programme orientated towards the defence of NATOs flanks. B Company Group, under command of Maj Garrod, flew to the Bahamas at the end of November, in company with elements of 6 SBS and 1st RM Raiding Squadron, to familiarise themselves with jungle fighting.

After receiving a cautionary warning to keep an eye open for poisonous snakes and spiders the company group, operating with 230 Squadron RAF and 6 SBS, patrolled in the heat of the jungle and exercised with Gemini raiding craft among the coral reefs of Andros Island. The highlight of the exercise was the seizure of a large quantity of marijuana dropped from a low flying plane onto two small off-shore islands. Observant marines from 6 Troop recovered the narcotics contained in 13 canvas bags and delivered this to the police. Congratulated by the local authority on their find they were informed that the Indian hemp had a street value of half a million pounds. Even so, the marines still had to pay for their own run ashore in Nassau! In Devon, adverse weather conditions hampered training but the unit completed the annual range course, field firing and two long distance load carrying marches before Christmas.

Following the formal visit by Lt Gen Sir Ian Gourlay on 10 January 1973, attention turned to the forthcoming exercises with the United States Marine Corps in the West Indies. Nine days later the Commando was heliborne to HMS *Bulwark* from Stadden Heights and, after an uneventful 12 day sea passage, disembarked at Camp Lejeune where the self-styled "worlds most complete amphibious base" housed 60,000 men. The USMC Reservation in North Carolina extended over 68 square miles including a training area of

Exercise "Rum Punch" Vieques Island 8 February 1973 Operating with the US Marine Corps. Photos: J. F. Mottram

mostly flat woodland interspersed with swamps and creeks. Each Commando company received a five-day, training session in this area followed by a unit exercise Firm Stride, in which the Commando was supported by USMC helicopters and amphibious tractors. The American marines also proved to be excellent hosts and a number of commandos took advantage of the USMC week-end air flights to Boston, Pittsburg and Miami.

Proceeding on to the Caribbean the Commando disembarked at Vieques for five days intensive training with helicopters and landing craft. The training culminated with a UK/USA amphibious exercise Rum Punch which ended on 6 March. The hard work was rewarded with three days rest and recreation in Puerto Rico before returning to Plymouth on 21 March.

Preparations for a second tour in Northern Ireland occupied most of April and May. The unit, in company with 7th (Sphinx) Commando Light Battery RA, relieved 42 Commando in North Belfast on 14 June where joint patrols operated together during the hand-over period. Finding themselves in familiar surroundings, the marines of 40 Commando renewed their acquaintance with police colleages with whom they had worked previously. They were aware that tension had diminished and that the attitude of people was generally more friendly. Patrols renewed their "tea stops" with the local community but their raison d'etre was always foremost in mind. Within the first 24 hours of taking over the TAOR four leading Provisional IRA officers were seized with explosives in their possession!

Relentless pressure was maintained on all forms of IRA terrorist activity and similar attention was given to extremist Protestant gangs such as the Ulster Freedom Fighters. Painstaking efforts were taken to build up comprehensive intelligence information that could be used to benefit the community as a whole. "Search and arrest" operations were used to seek out arms and explosives and to remove the terrorists from the streets. In the first month of the tour a further five IRA officers and one Protestant extremist were arrested and several finds of explosives were made. However, much of the time was spent on routine foot and mobile patrols, manning operations rooms, OPs and attending to essential domestic duties.

This was a period of intense activity in which every effort was made to reduce the level of violence so that political progress could be developed. Good communication with the people was vitally important and Lt B.Brooking RN, the unit education and public relations officer (PRO), achieved excellent results in this respect. Marines on patrol engaged the local people in conversation, listened to their points of view and gradually gained their confidence. The community relations programme did much to break down barriers and promote good will. As one marine put it– "Humour plays a big part in our role in Northern Ireland. Tight discipline with good humour and a laugh sometimes has more effect than 10 rubber bullets".

The Ulster Assembly elections in June were a key event, but in the Commando's area of Belfast the day passed without incident and the summer months

Troops and vehicles heliborne ashore from HMS Bulwark *for "Firm Stride" 17 February 1973. Photos: J. F. Mottram.*

that followed, including the marching season, were mainly peaceful. Lt Col Mottram made a brief visit to London on 16 July, to receive from the Defence Secretary, Lord Carrington, the second Wilkinson Sword of Peace to be presented to 40 Commando. The citation outlined the efforts made by all ranks to foster good relations with the people of Belfast; the unit's commitment to community relations projects for the children and elderly, and assistance given to families ...to help restore some degree of normality into the daily life of this troubled area, thereby earning the respect of all sections of the community whether in the calm of routine vehicle searches or among such tragic scenes as occurred on Bloody Friday, while helping the injured and homeless.

Overall, there was a significant reduction in shooting and bombing incidents during the unit's second four month tour. Only five shots were fired at B Company, who controlled the hard core Republican sector in the Lodge and C Company's main incident was a bullet through the windscreen of a troop commander's landrover. In the latter incident fire was returned and in the follow-up, a spattering of blood and two spent cases of Armalite ammunition were found in the position occupied by the gunman.

The snipers did not fire a shot during this period. The OPs had been developed to such a high degree that nearly all the wanted men had been apprehended. A total of 47 people were held on remand for arms or explosives offenses. In comparison with the first tour the reduction in rounds fired – 40 plus 145 baton rounds – was significant. There was a marked fall in bomb explosions but a considerable increase in the number of bomb hoaxes. It had been possible to treble the number of car searches and these, coupled with other search commitments, resulted in the seizure of 40 weapons, 320 lbs of explosive and 4,228 rounds of ammunition. Civilian casualties as a result of terrorist action amounted to 5 killed and 12 injured. The unit incurred no casualties from terrorist action but regrettably Mne J.J. Shaw died from injuries received in a road traffic accident in Belfast on 26 July.

Her Majesty the Queen approved the award of the Military Medal to Mne M. Gibson and Mention in Despatches to Lt Col J. Mottram and Maj J.M.C. Garrod for distinguished service in Northern Ireland.

The Commando handed over the TAOR to 1st Queen's on 17 October and returned to Seaton Barracks for leave before starting a work up for the Administrative and Fitness for Role Inspections due in the new year. In the teeming rain and swirling mist of Devon, Support Company staged a Carl Gustav tank-hunting demonstration at Oakhampton Battle Camp for the Captain General's visit to Commando Forces on 30 November. The Dartmoor damp respected neither person or vehicle but very senior officers maintained the initiative with a "shoulders to the wheel" when Prince Philip's car, succumbing to the weather, required a push start!

For the first time since the unit's return from the Far East the entire Commando was able to spend the spring months of 1974 in Plymouth uninterrupted by major exercises or unexpected moves. While this pleased the married men it was nevertheless a busy period in which the unit re-orientated to the NATO role and carried out several Corps commitments. Considerable emphasis was placed on air portability training and each company spent a session on the moor working with the helicopters of 707 Squadron from RNAS Yeovilton. Also, there were refresher courses in fieldcraft and weapon handling interspersed with nerve gas, bacteria and chemical warfare training (NBC). The NBC training spread over eight weeks, concluded with a 24 hour defence exercise in which all ranks – assuming a robot appearance – carried out normal duties clad in respirators and full protective clothing.

The exceptionally cold weather on Dartmoor proved a new and trying experience for many marines but the snow and sleet conditions were ideal for teaching cold weather survival. Rock climbing and roping techniques on the Dewerstone, Sheeptor and Cornish cliffs were incorporated into a three day exercise which severely tested men, clothing and equipment. The DPM combat suits and DMS boots were not as waterproof as had been claimed by the manufacturers and shrunk webbing caused difficulties. In the more hospitable surroundings of the Commando Forces Education Centre in Seaton Barracks, the CEO ran special naval maths and english test (NAMET) classes, O and A level instruction and resettlement interviews.

Lt Col Mottram relinquished command to Lt Col M.C.L. Wilkins on 20 February 1974, prior to taking up appointment as Chief of Staff of the British Defence Staff, Washington DC.

The Fitness for Role inspection on 6 March – to ensure that the Commando was prepared in every respect for an air portable move to the southern flank of NATO for a limited war in winter – was the climax to a successful and well conducted start to the year. Attention then centred on other activities. Support Company had responsibility for running a series of Youth Acquaint courses for boys aged 15 to 18 years, drawn from different areas of Britain. The four day courses were designed to give them a chance to try their hands at many of the Commando activities and aimed at introducing them to the Corps' role and training.

The men of all companies gave an extra polish to their boots and parade drill for the affiliation of the Royal Marines with the Church of St Lawrence Jewry in London on 23 April. St Georges Day was chosen appropriately for the Commando to march through the City to Guildhall Yard with bayonets fixed, Colours flying and the Band of Commando Forces playing. After the service the Commando marched to the Mansion House where the salute was taken by the Right Honourable The Lord Mayor Sir Hugh Wontner in the presence of HRH Prince Philip, Captain General Royal Marines. Afterwards, all ranks on parade joined other representatives of the Corps as guests at a luncheon given by the Lord Mayor and Corporation of the City of London in the Mansion House. Seven days later, C Company provided a street lining party at Windsor for a state visit by Queen Margarethe and the Prince of Denmark. After the ceremony the company lunched at Hounslow Barracks and enjoyed a visit to the Imperial War Museum and a London musical before returning to Plymouth.

Gen Sir Ian Gourlay made his annual visit to 40 Commando on 15 May and presented the CGRM's Commendation to Mne D. Fitzmaurice, for his initiative, professional skill and sense of responsibility in saving a man's life under difficult circumstances during cold weather training. Mr F.Judd MP also visited Seaton Barracks eight days later to open the new Commando Forces swimming pool.

There was a further ceremonial commitment on 12 June when the Isle of Wight received County status resulting from changes in the Local Government Act. The Earl Mountbatten of Burma received the additional appointment of Lord Lieutenant to his office of Governor held since 1965. On arrival he was received by a Guard of Honour provided by A Company under the command of Capt J.C.R.Lee, The Guard was accompanied by the Band of FONAC.

Gen R.E.Cushman Jnr, Commandant US Marine Corps, visited the unit on 18 June and attended a demonstration of weapons at Oakhampton Range. He was invited to fire a GPMG (SF)* and after firing a series of one or two rounds was recommended by Sgt Johnson to fire longer bursts. The General replied that when he was a recruit he had always been taught to conserve ammunition! After dining with the officers that evening he presented Lt Col Wilkins with a plaque in recognition of the hard work by all ranks concerning the demonstration.

The following day the Commando carried out a recall exercise on assuming the duties of Spearhead unit and repeated the procedure eight days later. Having in mind the possibility of a quick move to Northern Ireland the CO decided that all recent arrivals to the unit were to be given a crash course to prepare them for such an emergency. In the event, the Commando deployed quickly on 20 July to reinforce the British Western Sovereign Base in Cyprus! Extremist elements of the Greek National Guard (GNG) had staged a coup d'etat on 15 July against the Makarios regime. President Makarios was flown to Britain by the RAF and Nicos Samson – a former EOKA gunman – assumed the duties of President. After the coup the Greek National Guard attacked a number of Turkish villages to the north of Famagusta and, alarmed by these actions, Turkey mounted an amphibious landing near Kyrenia coupled with an airborne assault on the plains on 20 July

Mistrust between Cypriot Greeks and Turks following the formation of the independent state of Cyprus in 1960 resulted in the immergence of irregular forces on both sides. In December 1963, rioting broke out in Nicosia and British troops from the Sovereign Bases deployed to keep both factions apart. A negotiated demarkation line drawn across a map of the city in green chinagraph became known as the "Green Line". Wide-spread fighting between the Greek

---

* Capable of sustained fire.

London Ceremonial – The Affiliation of the Royal Marines with the Church of St Lawrence Jewry. 23 April 1974. 40 Commando marching through the City of London with Band playing, bayonets fixed and Colours flying.

Malta – Ex Double Base, Lt Col M. C. L. Wilkins indicating the line of attack to Brig J. C. C. Richards. Photos: M. C. L. Wilkins

and Turkish Cypriots led to the deployment of a United Nations Force in Cyprus, comprising 6,300 troops from Austria, Denmark, Finland, Ireland and the UK. The tension increased in subsequent years forcing the minority Cypriot Turks into enclaves protected by UN troops. Armed irregulars bands continued to roam about with little control up to the time of the Turkish incursion.

Arriving at Akrotiri, 40 Commando was placed under the command of Headquarters 19 Air Portable Brigade. The units primary tasks were to maintain the integrity of the Sovereign Base Area (SBA) perimeter including movement within the Commando boundaries; to deal with any IS incidents or special tasks in the southern sector and to liaise closely with the defence commander RAF Akrotiri. The situation was potentially explosive. Mistrust and division between the Greek and Turkish Cypriot communities was exacerbated by the Turkish invasion and Greek Cypriot attempts to hold Turkish communities hostage. Before the coup, the area around the SBA had a mixed Cypriot population but the majority of the Turkish population had been forced to flee as refugees into the base where a camp was built for them at RAF Episkopi. The presence of 5,000 Turkish refugees, fed and accommodated by the British, led weight to Greek Cypriot accusations of pro Turkish sympathies by the British. This was not helped by press reports of atrocities by members of the Greek National Guard. Anti British feeling in the Limassol area was modified by the needs of the townsfolk who relied to a great extent on the trade created by the British families.

The Commando, assisted by Scorpions of B Squadron Royal Horse Guards, manned road blocks and control posts in addition to 13 OPs which provided all round surveillance of the area including the villages of Episkopi and Kollossi. In the process of manning one of A Company's positions Mne Lawless received wounds in the arm and thigh when Greek Cypriots opened fire. One shot was returned and wounded a Cypriot who died later. The incident helped to bring about a closer liaison between the Commando and GNG and subsequently the man responsible for initiating the incident was arrested. Also, working on information received from the GNG, C Company found a number of shotguns and ammunition that had been cached by Turkish Cypriots in various locations in the base area.

After three weeks the general situation appeared to have stabilised and the unit prepared to return to UK. The leading elements had already departed on 8 August when the Turkish forces attacked the Greek Cypriot forces with a series of armoured thrusts to capture Famagusta and half of Nicosia, leaving the airport just out of reach. As a result of this additional threat the advance party, reinforced by 7 (Sphinx) Commando Light Battery RA, 611 FAC Section, NGSFO* from 95 Commando FOU and Dieppe Flight 3 Commando Brigade Air Squadron, returned to Cyprus and the main body of the unit to form

---

* Naval Gun Support Forward Observer

297

40 Commando Group.

The TAOR was initially the same but the positions of OPs were changed and the number increased. To minimise any misunderstanding between the Commando, the GNG and supporters of Nicos Samson (EOKA 'B'), Lt Col Wilkins arranged liaison meetings with representatives from these groups and the Cypriot police. Elements of the Commando Group assisted in the erection of several camps to house the influx of refugees and assisted with the move of service personnel and their families from Limassol into the base. As the only RN ship capable of providing gunfire was deployed off the eastern SBA the NGSFO was deployed to that area. 40 Commando remained in the same area throughout the tour although boundaries were changed on several occasions. Elements of the unit were given specific tasks and Support Company was moved to Dehkelia in the Eastern Sovereign Base on 1 August.

By the end of August, cease-fire lines had been established and a buffer zone created between the two opposing sides by the United Nations Force (UNF). The UNF had as its aims the prevention of further fighting; to contribute to the restoration of law and order, normal conditions and humanitarian relief. Also, to carry out Red Cross functions as required by the International Committee of the Red Cross. By early September the events had stabilised sufficiently for 40 Commando Group to return to UK. The air lift from RAF Akrotiri was completed by 19 September with vehicles and heavy stores following by sea.

The following appointment and awards were approved for operations in Cyprus:

Lt Col M.C.L.Wilkins   OBE   Cpl J.W.Hall   QGM

Mention in Despatches Cpl D.J. Gormley

In the brief interlude before pre-Northern Ireland training commenced on 11 November, the unit football team won the Tunney cup and the hockey eleven the Halse Cup. The NI training followed the previous pattern with two exceptions. The unit attended the inaugural demonstration of an entirely new form of firing range designed to test troops in the location of an enemy by his fire and identification of the weapon used. The Rover Trophy competition was incorporated into the tests and Lt Col Wilkins invited Col Alexander who instituted the competition, to present the trophy to 12 Troop.

The main body arrived in Belfast on 25 February and by midday had assumed control of Andersontown. The unit was the first Commando to have operational control of this predominately Catholic area. With a large section of the 53,000 population unemployed it was the scene of numerous clashes between the security forces and IRA. Although a cease fire was in existence between the Republican and Loyalist parties, considerable friction between the official IRA and a splinter group had resulted in a series of murders within their own ranks.

The restrictions of the cease fire also imposed constraints on Security Forces operations but constant vigilance and the employment of efficient operational procedures resulted in a reduction of the level of violence in the general area. A Company's location was predominantly Catholic and although by reputation an IRA stronghold, relations between the local community and commando personnel were reasonably friendly. In contrast, the Glassmullin area occupied by B Company was the scene of various incidents including knee capping, robbery and a sectarian killing. Support Company, in the Turf Lodge district, apprehended two armed men who had taken shots at their operations room while C Company, in the green belt suburbia of south-west Belfast, experienced two or three shootings a week, but not at them!

Numerous visitors during the four month tour included Mr M. Rees MP, Under Secretary for State, the First Sea Lord, Adm Sir E. Ashmore GCB,DSC,ADC, the Commandant General, Lt Gen P.J.F. Whiteley OBE – who relieved Gen Sir Ian Gourlay KCB, OBE, MC, as CGRM on 11 April – and the Band of Commando Forces. The band performances at sub unit bases, the Suffolk Community Centre and civilian wing of Musgrave Park Hospital were all thoroughly appreciated. The cease fire held throughout the tour that ended on 25 June 1975. Even so it had not been without incident. Of the 145 suspects arrested, half of the 110 subsequently charged had committed serious offences, including attempted murder and possession of fire arms or explosives.

The following personnel received the award of Mention in Despatches for distinguished service in Northern Ireland

Maj T. Courtenay, Lt S. De'Ath and Cpl P.G.T.Moore.

The GOC Northern Ireland's Commendation was awarded to CSgt K.G.V.Gill

The unit handed over responsibilty to the 1st Battalion Black Watch and returned to Plymouth to resume sub unit training. Immediately after summer leave 40 Commando Group embarked in HMS *Bulwark* to spend the best part of September and October in the Mediterranean for a major NATO southern flank Ex Deep Express. The unit formed part of a UK Combined Amphibious Task Force operating in conjunction with land and air elements of the Allied Command Europe Mobile Force, the 32 Marine Amphibious Unit USMC, the Italian San Marco Tactical Group and Turkish Naval infantry. Brig J.C.C.Richards commanded the Combined Land Force.

After a brief stop at Gibraltar the force proceeded to Malta for work-up exercises and shore leave. 40 Commando fired their weapons on 41 Commando's ranges and the two COs, Lt Col Mike Wilkins and his brother Lt Col Keith Wilkins, were able to catch up on family news. The combined task force met up at Antalya in Southern Turkey on 18 September where Brig Richards gave his orders to the commanders of the land force units. The entire force then sailed to the Aegean Sea for an exercise in Dongaby Bay before continuing to Saros Bay in Turkish Thrace for the main four day exercise. Both A and C Companies covered about 50 miles on foot while B Company enjoyed a leasurely session of cross training in USMC Amtracs.

Realism was limited by restrictions on night movement – for reasons of safety – and the need to confine the main landing within an area viewed by a large audience of senior NATO observers. A Turkish battalion employed as enemy were much impressed by the speed of movement of the land force and, according to their liaison officer, the professionalism of the Commando attacks was a joy to watch. At the end of the exercise the amphibious force sailed for Istanbul, passing the beaches of the ill fated World War I Gallipoli landings where four battalions of the RM Brigade belonging to the Naval Division had landed. The campaign, in which LCpl W.R. Parker RMLI won his VC, proved to be one of the fiercest and bloodiest of World War I.

During November a training team ran a two week pre Junior Command Course for 45 students from the Commando Forces and C Company carried out the London Remembrance Day and Lord Mayor show commitments. A Company deployed to Salisbury Plain and B Company to Hythe. All the sub units returned to Seaton Barracks in December in time to bid farewell to Lt Col Wilkins and to welcome Lt Col J.H.A. Thompson, who assumed command on 17 December 1975.

CHAPTER 20

17 December 1975 to 21 September 1981

*West Atlantic Deployment – Presentation of New Colours – Fourth
Northern Ireland Tour – Spearhead Unit 77 – Laying up of the Old Colours
– National Firemens' Strike – Royal Tournament 78 – Amphibious
Exercises in the Shetlands and Norway – Fifth Northern Ireland Tour
(residential)*

IMMEDIATELY after leave the unit commenced the first of three important but contrasting events that would occupy most of the year. The first of the activities, the West Atlantic (Westlant) Deployment, began on 7 January 1976. The bulk of 40 Commando Group, including 145 Commando Light Battery, a Royal Netherland Marine Corps detachment, Dieppe Flight, 1st Raiding Squadron RM and elements of Brigade Headquarters and the Commando Logistic Regiment, embarked in HMS *Bulwark* at Portsmouth. The main body of 40 Commando was heliborne to the carrier by 848 Naval Air Squadron as it passed Plymouth two days later.

Training on the outward passage to Curacao was designed to promote fitness and to achieve as much military training as space and facilities permitted. The flight deck was allocated to the Commando Group for half of each day, alternating mornings and afternoons with the helicopter squadron. Fitness training was pursued on the fore part of the deck while the stern end was set apart for live firing. This was an excellent arrangement allowing both the Squadron and Commando a fair share of the main working space.

The first exercise Van Gogh, took the form of a limited, opposed amphibious landing on the north shore of the island of Aruba – 50 miles west of Curacao – where the primary vegetation on the rocky ground is cactus. The commandos soon discovered that the spikes of one variety could penetrate the sole of a SV boot or tyre of a half ton vehicle! The two day exercise involved a considerable amount of marching and included a night attack on the northern tip of the island.

The second phase consisted of cross training and field firing with the US Marines Corps on the island of Vieques. The island also provided the location for the second exercise Rum Punch – 11 to 14 February – and was ideally suitable for the live firing of all weapons. The combined Marine Corps landing extended over three days of almost non-stop troop, company and Commando attacks followed by hasty defence and terminated in a night attack. The force proceeded on to Kingston, Jamaica for a five day port visit, and then sailed to Nassau where planning and briefing for Ex Clay occupied most of the time.

The three day exercise designed to test the troop commanders, using skills and procedures for rural operations and counter revolutionary warfare, took place on South Andros, one of a series of low lying islands intersected by creeks and mangrove swamps. Extensive reefs prevented access to most of the beaches. Night movement was impossible as secondary jungle consisted of a mass of impenetrable saplings. There was also the hazard of potholes, ranging from the size of a rabbit-hole to a tennis court, some of which ran underground for hundreds of yards to the sea. In consequence most of the action took place near the coastal fringe giving an opportunity to foster community relations.

The island doctor was on leave and in the absence of any dental facilities the Commando Medical Officer, Surg Lt J. Burslem and dentist, Surg Lt M. Roberts, both held clinics. One patient was taken aboard *Bulwark* for a general anaesthetic. Continuing the sea passage *Bulwark* called at Fort Lauderdale, Florida, where the Commando Group made the most of a six day R and R visit, with trips to Disneyland and Cape Carnaveral. The return trip across the Atlantic via Gibraltar was used to remove a few pounds of excess weight acquired in Florida and to revise drills in preparation for the forthcoming tour in Northern Ireland. Arriving at Gibraltar on 18 March a large contingent from the Commando, including the commanding officer, assembled on the jetty to participate in the "Top of the Rock" race, a gruelling uphill canter won by LCpl G. Hulance with a time of 21 minutes and 43 seconds.

The Westlant Deployment ended on 23 March with 40 Commando once more in Seaton Barracks where pre-Northern Ireland training and rehearsals for the presentatation of New Colours commenced in mid-May. During the work up B Company provided ceremonial guards in London for the President of Brazil and the Commandant of the US Marine Corps. The unit also became a temporary fire brigade on the Friday before Cup Final day when all hands were mustered to extinguish a fire on the Dartmoor ranges. It was not a popular occupation and marines employed devious ways to dodge the column. A soccer fan with two Cup Final tickets, felt justified in making a Friday afternoon start to London in order to arrive at Wembley in good time. His plan unfortunately collapsed when the back of his girlfriend's car was accidentally rammed by a Landrover outside the guardroom. The boot flew open to reveal the red-faced marine!

The Old Colours of 40 Commando were trooped for the last time on 1 July 1976, before HRH The Duke of Edinburgh presented the unit with New Colours on Plymouth Hoe. Thousands of holidaymakers and local people were drawn to the Hoe on this warm sunny day to watch the presentation which commenced with a 21 Gun Salute fired by 145 (Maiwand) Commando Light Battery. The Captain General then mounted the dias to receive the Royal Salute prior to inspecting the Commando. The Old Colours, which had been presented to the unit by the Duke of Edinburgh in Malta in 1952, were then marched off parade. The consecration of the New Colours was performed by the Venerable Archdeacon B.A. O'Ferrall assisted by the Reverend J.C.Criber,

Principal Chaplain Church of Scotland and Free Churches and the Right Reverend Monsignor F.W. Walmsley, Principal Roman Catholic Chaplain. After the ceremony 40 Commando marched through Plymouth, exercising the right of the Royal Marines as Freemen of the City, accompanied by the Band of Commando Forces under the direction of Capt W.W. Shillito LRAM.

The Old Colour Party		The New Colour Party	
Queen's Colour	Lt J. Lott	Queen's Colour	Lt D.C.Dow
Regimental Colour	Lt A.I.B.Troup	Regimental Colour	2Lt R.M.Hill
Escort	WO2 E.P.B. Cooper	Escort	WO2 P. Pearce
	CSgt B. Pinder	CSgtD.Copley	
	CSgt J.N.Kidd	CSgt G. Dalgarno	

In July, the Support Company was temporarily disbanded and the Recce Troop increased in number preparatory to the third unit tour in Northern Ireland. The standard pre-NI training took place at Hythe, Lydd and Thetford (for battalions on rural deployment). The Commando, in company with 145 (Maiwand) Commando Light Battery, relieved the 3rd Battalion Parachute Regiment at Bessbrook in South Armagh on 17 August. The TAOR consisted of 400 square miles of South Armagh and 30 miles of border with Eire. There were 45 crossing points of which four were officially recognised! The country is mostly farmland similar in appearance to north Devon, and the towns – with the exception of Newry – are no larger than villages.

South Armagh was very different from anywhere else in the Province. Not for nothing was it known as Bandit country. Smuggling, cattle rustling and lawlessness were interwoven in the history and its proximity to the border with Eire allowed the free passage of gunmen, and the initiating of bombing and cross-border shoot-outs from the safety of the Republic. Cross-border co-operation by the Garda and RUC was still in its infancy.

The South Armargh Brigade PIRA was a formidable force with a record of numerous successes and few setbacks. Security forces, under close observation at all times, had quickly found that carelessness was extremely costly. In Crossmaglen market square, five men of one battalion were shot on the first day of their tour. No military vehicles, except covert vans, used the roads south of Bessbrook. Movement was on foot or by helicopter. Patrols near the border were a minimum of twelve, in three lots of four. It was therefore a professionally rewarding place, because it was considered to be nearer to proper soldiering than Belfast or Londonderry. Every man carried a full first line of small arms ammunition, M79 grenades and smoke.

Patrols went out for several days and nights with the aim of dominating the area. The work of the patrols and OPs was exacting in the cold and wet conditions of autumn and winter. In addition to the ammunition the men carried five or six days rations, one sleeping bag per two men, telescopes. camera, flares, radios etc.

Sea King gun for transit ashore during Exercise Forest Venture 15 July 1977. Photo: 40 Commando.

A dawn landing by A Company at Lulworth Cove 10 November 1978. Photo: 40 Commando.

By 1975, a wave of sectarian killings, hijackings of the Belfast-Dublin train and culvert bombings, had led to fears that control of the area was slipping from the grasp of the security forces and a firm grip had to be re-established. In 1976, the 1st Royal Scots, the 3rd Para and 40 Commando, assumed responsibilty in turn for the area, with the same uncompromising attitude on how the problem should be faced. This produced a coherent operational method which, in Maj Gen J.H.A.Thompson's opinion, marked the turning of the corner for the TAOR. It still remains a highly dangerous place, but 1976 set the pattern.

145 Commando Battery and Mortar Troop were based at the UDR Centre in Newry. They were responsible for the capture of two terrorists, of which one was wanted for a murder in Belfast. A youth was also arrested and charged with possession and use of fire arms. Gun shots were heard almost daily. B Company, who had a relatively peaceful tour, was based in Bessbrook while C Company occupied the RUC station Forkhill only 900 yards from the Eire border. A Company were based in the RUC station at Crossmaglen, a difficult location where anti-British feelings were intense. The base was hit by mortar fire on 31 August resulting in the wounding of six commandos and extensive damage to the buildings. The Provisional IRA had mounted a multi-barrelled mortar on the back of a lorry and, having placed it in a disused backyard, fired it by means of a timing device. The terrorists would have crossed the border by the time it detonated. A second mortar attack occured on 23 October when the Provisional IRA drove a lorry into Crossmaglen Square and launched 10 mortar bombs into the base. Seven landed in the base and three hit a garage outside. All the bombs exploded, wounding six commandos, a soldier from the Royal Signals and causing extensive damage.

During the tour 40 Commando Group recovered over half a ton of explosives and 17 weapons. There were 69 shooting incidents, including some protracted cross-border shoot-outs and 174 suspects were arrested, of whom 55 were later re-arrested by the police. The Commando Group suffered 13 wounded.

Maj Gen Houghton, the representative Colonel Commandant visited the unit at South Armagh and presented CSgt A. Jones with the BEM, awarded in the Queen's Birday Honours 1976, for covert operations at Crossmaglen, while serving with 45 Commando on a previous tour. A few days after CSgt Jones received the medal from Mag Gen Houghton, he participated in an operation which earned him a bar to his BEM; the only occasion since WW II that a bar to the BEM has been awarded to a member of the Royal Marines. Mne H.S. Jennings received the General Officer Commanding Northern Ireland's Commendation for operational service of a high standard during the tour.

The Reconnaissance Troop mounted a long term OP in the attic of the Sinn Fein office in Crossmaglen, working on the assumption that this would be the last place that the PIRA would expect to find a security forces post. Initial

C/Sgt A. Jones (fourth from left) at South Armagh, after receiving the BEM from Maj Gen Houghton. Photo: J. H. A. Thompson

access was made by picking the lock of the front door and change-overs, including the essential polythene bags, were made every five or six days, at night, through a side-window, when the office was empty.

The removal of a roof tile provided observation of the infamous town square and the OP party could also eavesdrop on some of the conversations in the office two floors below, the first floor being unoccupied. Considerable information was obtained until the cover was blown, when a member of the local Sinn Fein, with less than honourable intentions, invited his secretary into the loft. He led the way up the ladder and on poking his head through the trap door, must have been terrified when confronted by the muzzle of a sergeant's pistol. The OP was withdrawn, but silence was preserved by warning him that his wife would be informed if he so much as breathed a word!

The Commando handed over responsibility to the 1st Battalion Royal Highland Fusiliers on 16 December and returned to Seaton Barracks for Chrismas leave. The Support Company was reformed and the quick recall system tested in readiness for Spearhead duties between 8 February and 8 March 1977. However, there were no emergencies and during this period the Old Colours were laid up in the Royal Marines Museum at Eastney. The simple ceremony was observed by Lt Col Thompson and representatives of the unit. The Second in Command Maj S.R.C.Bemrose OBE, received the Queen's Colour from Lt A.I.B.Troop and the Regimental Colour from Lt R.M. Hill before handing them in turn to the Curator, Maj A.G.Brown.

The annual shoot to kill exercise Marksmen, took place at Lydd between 27 February and 11 March. An exceptionally high standard was attained with the SL rifles by all ranks who improved on the Small Arms Manual's recommended "six inch group at a 100 metres prone lying", by producing four inch groups! Towards the end of April the Commando moved to the Outer Hebrides for Ex Whisky Galore. The aim of the exercise was to test the concept of a Commando Group working from LSLs in the absence of LPH facilities. The unit sailed north in *Sir Bedivere* and *Sir Galahad*, but lack of shipping space precluded the inclusion of Commando Battery support. Four Wessex from 846 Squadron provided air support and the VT-2 Hovercraft was used on a trials basis.

Training for the Silver Jubilee ceremonial duties in London began on return from the Hebrides. The rifle companies and Support Company were involved in street lining along Fleet Street and Ludgate Hill while elements of B Company, travelling in rigid raiding craft from Greenwich to Westminster, formed part of the River Thames pageant. A quiet summer with few external commitments enabled the unit to make the most of the sports facilities. In mid July the unit embarked in HMS *Hermes* for a series of heliborne landings in Devon and Cornwall and, after summer leave, moved to Salisbury Plain as part of the Commando Brigade for tactical training not normally covered in major unit exercises. In October, the three rifle companies each spent a week with the Recce Troop in Cornwall, refreshing their knowledge of roping skills and boat-work with rigid raiders and ended with a moon-light landing, cliff assault, raid and withdrawal.

A Company undertook the November ceremonial duties in London and then deployed to the Strathclyde area of Scotland where 40 Commando Group assumed control of a tri-service fire fighting force. This action arose as a result of a national firemens' strike. The armed forces were called upon by the government to maintain fire cover throughout the country and at one stage almost one third of the Corps was involved, including the Band Service. Basic instruction in the use of equipment and the Green Goddess fire engines was provided by Army instructors before and after the units had moved to their appointed locations. 40 Commando Group assumed responsibilty for 5,300 square miles of the Strathclyde area embracing the City of Glasgow. A fire control base was established in the emergency operations room at Police Headquarters and a helpful police staff provided communications and pilot vehicles to lead any of the 57 Green Goddess fire engines, located at 16 bases, to the scene of a fire.

There were over 2,300 call-outs between November and the end of December. When possible Fire Officers accompanied crews to provide technical advice but there were occasional errors of judgément. Blocks of high-rise flats were fitted with hydrants that had a connection on each floor. The procedure was to attach a hose to the connection on the floor below the scene of the fire and then switch on the main hydrant. In one incident youths had tampered with the branch connections. When the main supply was switched on the water gushed onto each landing to flood stairs and lift shafts! The largest fire during the strike was thought to have been on 7 January, at the Grosvenor Hotel in Glasgow. The Commando Group had 10 appliances operating for seven hours and although the hotel was gutted the fire was prevented from spreading to the adjacent terrace of picturesque mid-Victorian houses. The service fire fighting teams, which included elements of 40 Commando, in other parts of the country also played their part in saving life and property. Mne P.W Roach showed exceptional initiative in fighting a house fire in West Bromwich for which he received the Ralph Garrett Memorial Award for 1977/78.

The Commando returned to Plymouth on 18 January 1978 for a late Christmas leave and then went to the assistance of farmers on Dartmoor who were having difficulty in recovering their sheep from deep snow drifts. The weather had improved by the end of March for the Annual Range Courses at Lydd, which incorporated the Rover Trophy Competition, won by Support Company. After Easter leave the unit shooting team commenced training at Hythe Ranges and preparations were made for Ex Dawn Patrol, that was to take the Commando to Sardinia and Greece for most of May. The LSL's *Sir Bedivere* and *Sir Geraint* made a short visit to Gibraltar to allow the Commando to challenge the Top of the Rock Race record of 19 minutes 30 seconds, but without previous training Mne Cragg's time of 21 minutes 19 seconds was a reasonable result. A further brief call was made at Sardinia for live firing before joining the NATO Fleet for an amphibious landing at Teulada. Two days of cross training were followed by a call at Crete and finally, on to Southern Greece for the final phase of the exercise in which the rifle companies were flown to the objectives in US Marine Corps helicopters. Concluding the visit with a beach banyan the Commando re-embarked and returned to Plymouth on 2 June.

C Company, strengthened by the Surveillance Troop and Assault Engineers, commenced training for the cliff climbing display that was to form part of the 1978 Royal Tournament. After four weeks on Dartmoor and a week at Culdrose they advertised their readiness for the bright lights at Earls Court with a high abseil display in Hyde Park and a death slide from Tower Bridge. In the more secluded location of Seaton Barracks, CSgt P.Brown, the Corps and National Judo coach, organised a combined service and civilian Judo course directed by Olympic medallist Brian Jacks. On 16 June the unit bid farewell to Lt Col Thompson, who was chauffeur driven in a vintage staff car to take up his new appointment as Colonel GS at Headquarters Commando Forces.

Lt Col J.M.C Garrod, assumed command on 17 June 1978. This was his fifth tour with 40 Commando, having previously served with the unit in Cyprus in the 50s, Borneo in the 60s and Northern Ireland in the 70s. In addition to the numerous administrative inspections connected with the supercession programme, Lt Col Garrod was host to Maj Gen Sir Steuart Pringle, the Lord Mayor of Plymouth and officers of HMS *Hermes* and the RN Staff College, for a presentation of the unit's operational role. C Company, having put the final touches to their cliff climbing display, proceeded to London for the Royal Tournament while B echelon and the RAP – led by Capt C.Healy and Surg Lt I.Riddell – deployed to Salisbury Plain for a logistics exercise. Towards the end of July, Recce Troop flew to Switzerland for mountain warfare experience while the Anti Tank Troop received delivery of the new Milan missiles and one-tonne land-rovers.

The unit rifle meeting and NBC instruction swiftly dispelled any soporific effects of summer leave so that the Commando was well prepared to commence amphibious training with HMS *Hermes* on 23 August. The work-up exercises on the south coast, the first undertaken between a Commando and a LPH for two years, preceeded the deployment of the UK/NL Landing Force in *Hermes*, *Fearless* and three LSLs, first to the Shetland Islands and then, in hurricane-force winds to Norway, for a major NATO exercise. All ranks of the Commando were very thankful when the time arrived for the assault landing! The exercise itself was fast moving and a variety of evolutions were sucessfully completed. Lt Gen Richards visited the unit "in the field" and presented CSgt E. Blythe with the Commandant General's Commendation for bravery for trying to rescue three children from a blazing house in Belfast during the firemens' strike.

Preparations for the first residential tour of a Royal Marine Commando to Northern Island commenced in October. Families were kept well in the picture with regular briefings and to ensure that everything ran as smoothly as possible Mrs Jill Garrod led a party of wives to Ireland on a fact finding visit. The unit sportsmen took advantage of this period in Plymouth to compete in Corps competitions. While the football eleven and rugby fifteen did well as runners-up in the Tunney Cup and Argyle Bowl, the boxing team, coached by CSgt Brown, managed to go one better by winning the Corps Boxing Championships. The MGRM Commando Forces inspection took place on 6 December followed by a continuation of pre NI training until Christmas leave.

A massive packing up programme commenced in January and at one stage Seaton Barracks had all the appearance of a transit camp. Eventually, all the stores and equipment of the unit and household effects of the families accompanying the Commando arrived in South Derry, The unit was located at Ballykelly and assumed responsibility for the southern half of the county from the 1st Battalion Gloucestershire Regiment on 5 March 1979. The Commando accommodation at Ballykelly faced north overlooking Lough Foyle with the hills of County Donegal a visible sign that Southern Ireland was very close. It was a lovely setting but the commandos' were not there to enjoy the view. In addition to a TAOR extending from Lough Neagh to the Sperrin Mountains, the unit had administrative responsibility for the former RAF airfield housing themselves and 17 lodger units. Two rifle companies were deployed in the towns of Maghera and Magherafelt rotated at six week intervals with two companies who were responsible for the security of the airfield base and the rural areas. A further commitment, the provision of a reserve element for the 8th Brigade, entailed sending a company to London-derry on various tasks, as and when required

The unit was made welcome by the local community and in turn received many visitors including the GOC Northern Ireland, Lt Gen Sir Timothy Criesey and later in the tour, the CGRM, MGRM Commando Forces and DWRNS, Commandant E.S.A. Craig-McFeeley, to see her detachment of 25 Wrens serving with the Commando. Sporting links were soon established with the people of Limavady and Coleraine and extensive use was made of the base recreational facilities by the service personnel, their families and the local schools and youth clubs.

A major re-deployment in May resulted in Support Company assuming responsibility for patrolling County Fermanagh, with its topographic prob-lems of rugged terrain and a 120 miles border with Southern Ireland. The area had previously been the domain of armoured units but it was decided to introduce an infantry element into the area in an effort to stem terrorist activity. The sub unit operated from four bases one of which had been extensively damaged by a 1,000 lb bomb shortly before their arrival. The deployment of a company to Fermanagh meant that the unit had two compa-nies permanently deployed operationally, unlike the normal Army battalion which would only have one company deployed on the ground during a residential tour. This was possible because 40 Commando's tour was for one year, as opposed to the Army's normal two year residential tour, and the Commando was therefore able to work at a higher pressure.

40 Commando also became responsible for an additional location, 100 miles from the base thereby adding to the problems of communication and supply. A consistently high level of patrolling was maintained at all times and while there was little tangible evidence in terms of weapon finds or arrests it was noticeable that the General and European Elections in South Derry were trouble free.

The low level of violence within the area enabled unit personnel to forge a friendly relationship with the people of South Derry. Schools and clubs were invited to use the base recreational facilities where commando personnel, in their off-duty hours, provided coaching and organised events. Help was also given in a variety of ways to handicapped children at a school in Magherafelt. Four months into the tour the Commando Forces Band arrived to play three concerts a day to the delight of service and civilian audiences. It was therefore with deep shock that unit personnel heard of the death of Lord Mounbatten, Life Colonel Commandant of the Royal Marines, on 27 August 1979, as the result of a terrorist bombing incident while on holiday with members of his family in Ireland.

The Commando TAOR was extended still further in August, to include a strip of land between the border and the River Foyle. Patrolling of this area of farmland, known as the Enclave, was undertaken alternately by A and C

Company from Creggan Camp and brought the total patrolling commitment of the Commando to 1,200 square miles. The reserve company was deployed to Londonderry on a number of occasions during the marching season but the period passed without any major incident. However the murder of a part-time UDR soldier at Rosslea and the attempted murder of another UDR soldier in an ambush at Swatragh gave ample evidence of terrorist activity.

Community help during the summer months extended to the loan of marqees and tents to youth clubs and Boy Scouts for fetes and camp expeditions. On one occasion a combined effort by C Company and the resident REME Recovery Team rescued an Irish excavator driver and his machine from a peat bog near Bellaghy. The recovery was made more complex when the excavator driver, once more on firm ground with his machine, selected the wrong gear and reversed back down the hole!

The Creggan Enclave was exchanged for the Belleek Security Forces Base in November. The base was only 20 yards from the border and bullet holes in the riverside walls were evidence of terrorist activity in earlier years. The commando now had one company less one troop based in the South Derry TAOR and one company plus one troop in County Fermanagh. This period of change was also the time for Lt Col Garrod to return to England to take up his new appointment at DCGRM. His successor, Lt Col R.J. Ross OBE, assumed command on 9 November 1979.

There were signs of an increase in the number of cross border incursions by the IRA in the area of Fermanagh. As a result of one of these incidents two Commando landrovers, escorting a RUC vehicle to the Kinawley Security Force Base, were ambushed and the blast of a 850 lb land mine hurled the rear landrover and its occupants 30 feet into a roadside ditch. Mne Stubbs the driver was pinned under the vehicle for an hour but Mnes Parker, who crawled out with a broken wrist, and Davies, who had a broken leg, took up fire positions as a precaution against further attack. Both the Support Company's Air Reaction Force and Quick Reaction Force were first on the scene and, it is said, the three casualties were chatting up the nurses within minutes of being admitted to Enniskillen Hospital!

In December, an alert patrol in Rosslea prevented a major fire and possible destruction of a commercial garage and adjacent houses, when two incendiary devices beside a storage tank of diesel fuel were neutralised. Other devices discovered outside supermarkets in Maghera and Draperstown received similar treatment. Patrols were unable to prevent a car bomb explosion in the centre of Enniskillen, resulting in extensive damage to shops but no casualties. Numerous hoax telephone calls throughout the area required investigation.

The relatively quiet weeks leading up to the end of the year were suddenly disrupted in January 1980 by a spate of incendiary bomb explosions in Castledown, Bellaghy, Maghera, Lisnaskea and Beleek. The incendiaries caused numerous fires and damage to property but thankfully no casualties were sustained. Support Company moved to the Security Force Base at

Rosslea on 6 January to exchange duties with B Company. Both companies and Lt Col Ross – who visited the base that day – passed a culvert on the road-side where earlier that morning an 800lb bomb had exploded under an RUC landrover, killing both occupants. The following day a part-time member of the UDR, farming in the local area was killed by shots in the back and head while driving a tractor. It is unlikely that he heard or saw his assailant. With Eire only a short distance away it was easy for members of the PIRA to slip back quickly over the border after such incidents.

Diligent observation by Cpl L.C.EW.Robertson's patrol led to the discovery and removal of an incendiary blast device in a Lisnaskea farm- house shortly before Support Company handed over its TAOR to the Grenadier Guards on 3 March. During this period A and C Companies, the Staffords, the 1st and 5th Battalions Ulster Defence Regiment and the Royal Ulster Constabulary, took part in an extensive cordon and search operation of the thickly wooded country area of Portglenone. The operation was controlled by Commando Tac HQ from the Magherafelt Police Station and the co-operation between the police and security forces proved excellent. This was the unit's final commitment of the tour in which the commando vehicles had totalled up an estimated one and a half million miles!

Although there were no outstanding sports victories during the year all ranks participated in local fixtures. The civilian teams were only too happy to play at anything from badminton to rugby, knowing they would receive a friendly reception and a sporting game. Before leaving Magharafelt C Company organised a sponsored slim and Capt J.Davis, who managed to shed 20lbs, presented a cheque for £208 to Town Park Special School.

Accommodation in Shackleton Barracks became fully stretched in February with the arrival of the Argyll's advance party and the Band of Commando Forces. The Band, under the direction of Bandmaster K. Vickers, performed 13 concerts in a week-long tour of local organisations, schools and hospitals. While preparing to vacate the barracks the unit made welcome a number of last minute visitors. They included MGRM Commando Forces Maj Gen J.J. Moore on an inspection of Commando locations in Fermanagh; the Representative Colonel Commandant Gen Sir Peter Hellings renewing acquaintance with his old unit and R Adm M, La T, Wemyss and Mr K. Speed MP, Under Secretary of State Royal Navy, who were visiting the Commando for the first time. Prior to 40 Commando's return to Plymouth, Lt Col Ross received the following message from Brig C.T.Shortis OBE commanding the 8th Infantry Brigade:

"On completion of your very successful tour as the first Royal Marines unit resident in Northern Ireland please pass on my thanks to all ranks for the skill determination and courage with which they have carried out their tasks in South Derry, Fermanagh and the Enclave. Your Commando will be remembered here for their professionalism, good humour and high morale. You have particularley impressed us by the way you have tackled routine tasks so cheerfully and efficiently despite the relatively low level of terrorist activity. In this way each Marine has made a significant contribution to improving the security situation in the Province. It has been an honour and a pleasure to have you under command. I wish you a safe return to Plymouth and best wishes for the future."

Her Majesty the Queen approved the following awards for distinguished service in Northern Ireland with 40 Commando:

Col J.M.C Garrod	OBE	Capt R.P Williams	MBE
WO2 D.A.Chisnall	BEM		

Mentioned in Despatches

RSM WO1 J.R.French, Cpl B.M.Gill, Sgt J.G.McLeman, Capt R.M. Rundle.

The following personnel received the General Officer Commanding Northern Ireland's Commendation for operational service of a high standard during the residential tour:

Sgt J.R.Fears, Sgt P.R.Kelsey, Mne A.J,Parker, Cpl L.C.E. Robertson, Sgt R.G.Smith and SNS Etherington, who served with the unit.

The main body of 40 Commando returned to Plymouth in early March and celebrated their home-coming with an all-ranks dance at Seaton Barracks. After leave, the sportsmen made the most of the end of the winter games season, fielding two teams in the inter-unit seven aside Easterbrook Cup Competition and playing three games of football before the goal posts were taken down and cricket nets erected.

Training in many of the specialist skills required revision prior to the unit's participation in the Commando Brigade Logistic exercise Rough Diamond on Salisbury Plain in June. Other activities included sending a team of officers and NCOs to Lydd, to assist 41 Commando in their pre-Northern Ireland training and the provision of officials for the Corps Small Arms Meeting at Hythe. Also, a composite troop flew to Gibraltar for a raiding exercise with submarine HMS *Olympus* while a second detachment joined 42 Commando for their deployment to the New Hebrides, South Pacific. During this work-up period Gen Sir Peter Hellings visited the unit to unveil a painting by artist Margaret Burton, commemorating the Commando's one-year tour in Northern Ireland.

Phase One of Ex Rough Diamond, consisting of company battle procedures, helicopter drills and the live firing of all weapons by day and night, concluded with a demonstration of a heliborn assault for Gen Ho Yun Jin of the South Korean Marine Corps and other overseas visitors. The second part of the exercise tested the Commando battle procedures and drills over a 24 hour period and concluded with a five- day Brigade exercise (phase three) consisting of endless marching and digging in very wet and cold conditions. The unit returned to Seaton Barracks to prepare for the 25th Anniversary of the granting of Honorary Freedom of the City of Pymouth to the Royal Marines. On 24 July the Commando, preceded by the combined Royal Marines Band from Commando Forces and Flag Officer Third Flotilla, augmented by Musicians from BRNC Dartmouth, marched through the City, along Royal Parade and Union Street, with bayonets fixed and colours flying. The salute was taken outside the Civic Centre by the Lord Mayor of Plymouth. On return to Seaton Barracks the unit paraded again while the CGRM, Lt Gen Sir John Richards KCB presented Northern Ireland awards. Also, the Commandant General presented the British Empire Medal to WO2 D.L. Jones for his services to SHAPE while serving in Brussels.

On 26 July a team of seventeen men led by Lt Cutler, set out from Condor Barracks in Arbroath, to run the 704 miles to Plymouth. Their aim was to raise money for the Jimmy Saville Appeal on behalf of the National Spinal Injuries Centre at Stoke Mandeville Hospital. The run was made in relays covering five stages of 12 miles each day and the off duty men made collections along the route. On arrival at The Hoe on 7 August – three minutes earlier than programmed – they had raised £2,500.

To fit in with other unit activities Dieppe Day (19 August) was commemorated with a Families Day at Seaton Barracks on 30 July. The programme commenced with a drum-head service on the parade,led by Rev A. Rowe and Rev I. Thompson and well fortified by an excellent buffet lunch the afternoon was devoted to a inter-company 'Its-a- Knockout' competition and families races.

After summer leave, the unit embarked in HMS *Bulwark* and LSL *Sir Bedevere* as part of a 3 Commando Brigade force for exercise Team Work 80 in Norway. This large scale maritime and amphibious exercise, in which 60,000 men, 170 ships and 400 aircraft of nine NATO countries participated, extended over wide areas of the North Atlantic, English Channel, North Sea, Norwegian Sea and Norway. 40 Commando, supported by 8 Battery 29 Cdo Regt RA and one troop of Royal Engineers, had responsibility for 800 square miles of islands and mainland in the Trondheim area where the rugged terrain, lack of roads and numerous fjords added to the problems of movement. The Sea King and Wessex helicopters helped to overcome many of the difficulties but much of the ground had to be covered by foot and vehicle patrols.

The four days of phase one were used by commanders at all levels to build up local knowledge and a little colour was provided by the Norwegian Home Guard who acted as saboteurs and fifth column. The previous military formation of any strength to occupy the area had consisted of German troops in WW II. In consequence a few local people were initially apprehensive at this re-occupation of their land but the commandos soon developed a friendly

The Commandant General in conversation with Mne Davies on the final stage of a speed march. 14 November 1980. Photo: 40 Commando.

relationship with the local residents and put them at their ease. In the interval between the first and second phase of the exercise full use was made of the excellent rock climbing, canoeing and sub-aqua facilities and at least one local fisherman provided boats for rowing and fishing.

The second phase commenced on 17 September with an amphibious assault on the main town followed by a series of attacks to secure further objectives on the islands and mainland. The exercise ended seven days later at Kyksaeterora 50 miles further north. Tired feet were soon forgotten on the return trip to UK when HMS *Bulwark* called at the port of Hamburg and the commandos were warmly welcomed by the 49th Field Regiment Royal Artillery and the 4th/7th Royal Dragoon Guards. Only one week after returning to Seaton Barracks the Commando re-embarked in HMS *Bulwark* for a night landing by helicopter on Dartmoor in the most atrocious weather conditions experienced for many years. The consolation took the form of a cross Channel trip to the port of Brest where elements of the unit received a warm welcome at the French Commando Training Centre at Roscauvel.

Although the greater part of September and October were committed to exercises the sportsmen marked up some reasonable results. The boxing team won the Corps Competition held in the new sports complex at CTCRM. The football team had a very good season but lost to CTCRM in the finals of the Tunney Cup, The hockey players were runners up in the Clark Trophy and the rugby fifteen won the Plate Competition. Although of no outstanding importance it is worth mentioning that after numerous attempts, 40 Commando managed to defeat the might of HMS *Bulwark* in the traditional Flight Deck Sports Competition. For the first time the name of 40 Commando was to be engraved upon the revered trophy. The following month it was announced that HMS *Bulwark*, as part of the Government defence cuts, would be taken out of service in March 1981, six months earlier than planned! The axe was also to terminate 41 Commando's existence and bring about a drastic pruning of the Royal Marines Band Service.

A composite company, with attached ranks from the RMR and RNLMC under the command of Capt R.J.Fletcher, flew to Brunei in early February 1981 for six weeks Commando Forces jungle warfare training. Ex Curry Trail was considered to be one of the more popular exercises and there was no shortage of volunteers to go. Preliminary training in UK, which concentrated on basic jungle skills and fitness, commenced in early January, when all ranks received dental checks and cholera, smallpox and yellow fever injections.

The four day flight by RAF Hercules, including stop-overs in Bahrain and New Delhi, was immediately followed by a full and intensive training programme. The preliminary work-up had paid dividends and the men were soon in the jungle practising compass marches, map reading, tactical moves and harbouring. The programme included a one week break in mid-March to enable the men to see something of Brunei. A diving expedition led by Capt Fletcher went to the island of Labuan and another group led by Lt A. Thomson flew to Sabah to ascend Mount Kinabalu. The final seven day search and destroy exercise took place in primary jungle where it was possible to to put into practice everything that had been taught. The return trip to UK was routed via Hong Kong where the jungle initiated enjoyed a short interlude of rest and recreation before rejoining the unit.

While the Curry Trail detachment was in Brunei the unit said farewell to the retiring CGRM, Lt Gen Sir John Richards KCB, and met the new Commando Brigade Commander Brig J.H.A. Thompson OBE. Immediately after the annual inspection by MGRM Commando Forces, Maj Gen J.J.Moore OBE, MC+,the unit engaged in a comprehensive two month adventure training programme designed to give all ranks the opportunity to try something new on courses organised within the Commando or run by other service organisations. The activities included climbing in Cornwall, skiing in Scotland, sports parachuting at Dunkerswell, gliding with the RAF in Oxfordshire or riding at the Corps Equitation Centre at Withycombe Raleigh. During other sports activities the A and B 7-a-side rugby teams carried off a double in the Easterbrook Bowl and Lt P.C.Betterton won the Corps Golf Championships.

At the dining out of the second in command in May, prior to taking up a new appointment at the Ministry of Defence, the officers presented Maj A.C.Letchford MBE with a replica of a rather unusual piece of Mess tableware. For many years the Officers' Mess had been justly proud of their Stilton cheese, but immediately following a mortar attack at Crossmaglen, when the cheese was in considerable danger, it was covered with a steel helmet inscribed with the words "In case of mortar attack cover Stilton". The replica was made in burnished steel with a brass insignia.

After a week of blizzard conditions on the Altcar ranges near Liverpool, the Commando deployed to Sennybridge in May for a week's tactical training and battle shooting. The unit Surveillance Troop was re-formed at this time. Between 22 June and 1 July the unit assisted 45 Commando with pre Northern Ireland training,took part in the annual Commando Brigade Field training Exercise on Salisbury Plain and deployed Mountain Leaders from the unit to the Mountain and Arctic Warfare Training Cadre in Southern Italy.

Unit sport made news with a 40 Commando victory in the Corps Athletics Championships and an event less known hit the headlines when the cycling team won the Inter Service Time Trial Championship at RAF Honnington. Sgt M. Parker, a key member of the team, went on to win the 150 miles International Two Day Cycle Race. The golfers achieved the best over-all results in the Corps Golf Championships and WO2 L.Gordon joined forces with Musn M.S Barfoot of the RM Band Service to land the best catch in the RN and RM Fly Fishing Competition, the first time the Royal Marines had won this event. Apparently a unit clay pigeon shooting club came into being at this time.

Unfortunately the summer sports season was curtailed for the men of 41 Commando at Deal. In the wake of the long term economic depression and swingeing cuts in the armed forces announced in the 1981 Defence Review, the flag of 41 Commando was finally hauled down on 5 August 1981. The following extracts from a letter by former Royal Marines Officer and member of the RMR, Maj Sir Patrick Wall MP, published in the Daily Telegraph, reflects the anxiety of a section of the armed forces faced with the practicality of implementing the defence of NATO while civil servants and politicians appeared to be mainly concerned with finding a way out of the recession:

"The Crown's most versatile and cost effective troops will remain but their flexibility will be much impaired by the decision to scrap the ships designed to support them... the Commandos must be capable of landing anywhere in the northern fjords, and for this they require landing craft as well as off-shore helicopter platforms...It is said that roll-on and roll-off civilian car ferries can perform a similar task. This is nonsense as these ships can only land vehicles at specially constructed hards of which there are very few in northern Norway; they cannot be beached nor can they carry helicopters... Surely we should do our utmost to preserve the flexibility of our Royal Marines and the Royal Netherlands Marine Corps which works so closely with them and so be able to reassure the Norwegians that the Commandos will land at the right place at the right time!"

40 Commando assumed the duties of Spearhead Battalion in August. Although well prepared, packed and ready to go anywhere in response to a crisis the unit was disappointed to find that it was not required to do so. In September, a detachment of 30 men – mostly under 18 years of age – under the command of Lt S. Scott and Sgt R.Evans, formed part of a composite company

from the Brigade to embark in HMS *Hermes* for a three months WESTLANT deployment to the Caribbean and USA. Training was carried out at Camp Lejeune with U S Marines and in the British Virgin Islands with the Island Police Force. They were also able to include a period of adventure training in the programme.

On 21 September 40 Commando said farewell to Lt Col Ross, who was about to commence a 12 months sabbatical as a student of Corpus Christi College, Cambridge. He was succeeded by Lt Col M.P.J.Hunt who assumed command of the unit that day.

Lt Col J. M. C. Garrod, on his fifth 40 Commando tour, with Lt Gen Sir Timothy Criesey, GOC Northern Ireland and CSgt E. Blythe BEM, Support Company. Photo: 40 Commando.

CHAPTER 21

21 September 1981 to 22 July 1983

Attempted murder of CGRM by IRA – Visit of Crown Prince Harald of Norway – MGRMs Inspection – Trials with HMS Invincible in the Amphibious Role – Stanford Training – The Falklands War – Sixth Northern Ireland Tour.

LT COL HUNT was well versed in the ways of commandos, with the hind sight and experience of two tours in both 41 and 45 Commando's and a G3 Intelligence and operations tour in Headquarters 3 Commando Brigade. Now, fresh from the directing staff of the Army Staff College, he was again on familiar ground. A keen sportsman, the new CO arrived at an opportune time to participate in the first Commando Marathon. In this event organised by CSgt Griffiths the 148 competitors ran from Moretonhampstead via Princetown to Seaton Barracks. Sgt Parker arrived home first in 2 hours 43 minutes and the CO came 23rd in a time of 3 hours 19 minutes! Many of the runners had obtained sponsors and the proceeds of £500 were donated to the Trenweath School for Spastics.

Rev G. Hilliard RN, the unit padre, conducted the Harvest Festival Service in Seaton Barracks Chapel on 4 October and, during the month hosted the annual Plymouth Chaplains' Conference. The Chaplains chose this occasion to present two wheelchairs to BLESMA*, purchased from the proceeds of various events held during the year.

Irish terrorist activity became the direct concern of the Corps on 17 October, when an attempt was made on the life of Lt Gen Sir Steuart Pringle Bt. A bomb, planted in the engine compartment of the CGRM's car, exploded as he left his home to drive to London. This resulted in serious injuries to both legs and the amputation of his right leg below the knee. Maj Gen Moore assumed temporary command of the Corps while the Commandant General was in hospital but within a week of the attack the CG appeared on television in cheerful and defiant mood to signal to his men that he was still at their head. Two thousand letters and messages of encouragement were received by the General, including an offer from CSgt Jackson, a former member of the SBS in hospital at the same time. He had lost a leg in an unrelated accident and sent the General his best wishes, suggesting that as the General had lost his right leg and Jackson his left they could share a pair of shoes!

Crown Prince Harald of Norway GCVO, paid an official visit to the Corps

* British Limbless Ex Servicemens Association.

Crown Prince Harald inspecting equipment worn by Sgt J. Hufford, during a visit to 40 Commando, 30 October 1981. Photo: 40 Commando.

on 30 October following his appointment, on 5 May 1981, as an Honorary Colonel in the Royal Marines. This was the first honorary appointment of a member of a foreign Royal Household into the Corps and symbolised the close bond which had developed between Royal Marines and the Norwegian people over a period of 40 years. During a busy programme he watched a cliff assault demonstration by C Company and 1st Raiding Squadron at Jennycliff. To make the Prince feel at home,"40 Commando Norsemen" wielding battle-axes and suitably attired in horned helmets, mounted a light hearted Viking raid from a long boat prior to the main event.

In the last quarter of the year A Company deployed to Willsworthy while B and C Companies experienced the rigours of winter training on Salisbury Plain. The Milan Anti Tank Troop carried out live firing and the Recce Troop tested their endurance on a 10 day survival exercise. During this period all personnel carried out NBC tests. One of 40 Commando's pre Christmas tasks was to carry out trials with HMS *Invincible*, employing the aircraft carrier in the subsidiary role of an amphibious ship. The entire Commando Group embarked with transport and practiced heliborne drills, landing in the Bovington training area in deep snow. Vehicles lashed to the deck restricted the operational space of helicopters and in consequence the flying-off took considerably longer than from an LPH. Adm Sir John Fieldhouse KCB, C-in-C Fleet, visited the Commando on 16 December and in the course of the day met many of the

Marching back from Tregantle to Seaton Barracks after helicopter landing from HMS Hermes, *19 February 1982. Photo: 40 Commando.*

men, fired some of the weapons and watched a troop attack.

Maj Gen Moore's formal inspection of the unit at Seaton Barracks on 14 January 1982 was conducted in icy weather conditions. On this occasion each company paraded in a different uniform. At the end of the month the Rifle Companies deployed to Stanford and Support Company to Sennybridge for field firing prior to exercising with HMS *Hermes*. While embarked the unit made heliborne attacks on coastal defences (notional) near Tregantle and Lulworth Cove. Operating in the LPH role HMS *Hermes* carried five Harriers, 29 helicopters, 72 vehicles with trailers, a battery of 105mm guns and 2,511 men. Although a third of the flight deck was taken over by Sea Kings, guns and vehicles the Harriers were able to fly the standard programme of sorties.

To provide a deviation from the standard military and administrative programme in March, the CO instituted an ambitious and varied adventure training programme which involved 23 different activities covering skiing in the Alps, white water canoeing in the Pyrenees, scuba diving in Cyprus and climbing and hang gliding in Wales. Most of the activities were financed by the individuals involved but useful subsidies were provided by the Regimental Institute and Mr Umar Shar the unit contractor.

Current international news items indicated a deteriorating situation in the long standing political dispute concerning Argentina's claim to the Falkland Islands (Malvinas). A resurgence of diplomatic activity by the Argentinians, after Gen Leopoldo Galtieri assumed power as President of Argentina in 1981, led to United Nations talks in February 1982. The UN Assembly agreed that there should be a standing Commission on the Falklands issue with monthly meetings and an end of year deadline on talks. The talks appeared to be making good progress until a provocative communique issued by the Argentinian Foreign Minister, Dr Nicanor Costa Mendes raised the tension between Argentina and Britain.

Tension heightened on 16 March when a group of Argentinians landed at Leith, on South Georgia – supposedly to demolish the old whaling station – and raised the Argentinian flag. Their right to be on the island was disputed by the British Embassy in Buenos Aires who directed the Argentine Foreign Minister to have the group officially recognised as demolition contractors or made to leave. A British Arctic Survey team was on South Georgia and, as a precautionary measure, Capt Barker commanding HMS *Endurance* was instructed to land his Royal Marines detachment, strengthened with nine ranks from NP8901, in the area of Grytviken to await orders. On 24 March a detachment of Argentininan marines landed at Leith and intelligence reports indicated that two Argentine corvettes were sailing towards South Georgia.

In UK, the First Sea Lord Sir Henry Leach held a senior staff meeting at which a decision was taken to initiate planning and preparation for a task force of war ships, RFAs and merchant ships taken from trade. The leading element of this force comprising the First Flotilla, commanded by Rear Adm J.S Woodward aboard *Antrim*, was currently exercising in the Mediterranean. On 29 March, Adm Fieldhouse, C-in-C Fleet, told Adm Woodward, to prepare to sail south. The aircraft carriers *Hermes* and *Invincible* were brought to 48 hours notice on 1 April and *Fearless* and *Intrepid* at Portsmouth, alerted to immediate readiness. Three nuclear submarines were also ordered south. 40 Commando was at this time on the ranges at Altcar, near Liverpool, 42 Commando, recently returned from Norway was on leave and 45 Commando, less one company in Brunei, was at its base in Scotland.

In the Falklands, the relief party to replace the Royal Marines detachment NP 8901 commanded by Maj G. Noott arrived at Port Stanley in the RRS *John Biscoe* and the new detachment commander Maj M. Norman assumed command of the combined 70 strong force. A further 800 miles to the east at South Georgia, the *Endurance* detachment and nine men from the old NP8901, under the command of Lt K. Mills RM, disembarked at Grytviken on Wednesday 31 March with instructions to provide a military presence, protect the British Antarctic Survey personnel and maintain surveillance over the Argentinian workers at Leith. HMS *Endurance* lacking adequate armament to protect itself against the Argentinian corvettes armed with Exocet missiles then put to sea.

Various relevant events took place on 31 March. In London, Sir Henry

LCpl R. Craig and members of C Company completing the SLR phase on the Altcar Ranges, 26 April 1891. Photo: 40 Commando.

Leach, First Sea Lord, met the Prime Minister and Secretary of State for Defence and advised Mrs Thatcher that he could provide a Task Force in the event of an Argentine invasion of the Falkland Islands (predicted for 2 April). Brig J.H.A. Thompson, commanding 3 Commando Brigade, who had been on a NATO exercise reconnaissance in Denmark, returned to Plymouth, ahead of his staff as previously planned, and not in any way connected with developments in the Falklands. On arrival he was briefed by his GSO 3 Training, that there had been a flap earlier in the week, but that all units had been stood down, and the Commando Brigade was not required. Col R.F. Preston, Chief of Staff HQ Commando Forces, telephoned Lt Col Hunt (at Altcar), instructing him to attend a meeting in Plymouth at 1430 hours, 1 April. He was also told to bring one of his companies with him. (The main body of 40 Commando returned to Plymouth on 1 April).

40 Commando was stood to earlier in the week, although how they would get to the Falklands in time to pre-empt an invasion was never made clear. The airstrip at Stanley was unsuitable for large commercial aircraft, and at that time the RAF C-130s were not equipped for air-to-air refuelling. At one point the Air Defence Troop was ordered to stand by, leading to facetious speculation that they might travel by civil airline to Argentina disguised as musicians with their blowpipe missiles in double-bass cases, for onward flight by local air service to Stanley!

On 1 April, in London, Maj Gen Moore handed command of the Corps back to Lt Gen Sir Steuart Pringle, and returned to Plymouth un-informed of further developments. Intelligence reports received in London the same day indicated that a large Argentine naval force was sailing towards the Falkland Islands. 40 Commando had returned to Plymouth before nightfall.

In Port Stanley, the Governor Mr R.W.Hunt, was made aware of the situation by telephone and immediately alerted Maj Norman commanding NP 8901 and senior members of the Falklands Islands Defence Force (FIDF).

Instructions were given for the Royal Marines to deploy to defend the air field, the road to Stanley and Government house. Mr P. Wall, Head of the Falkland Island Broadcasting Station was informed of current events by the Governor on the afternoon 1 April. Recalling this occasion during an interview nine years later he said– "I could hardly believe that they (the Argentinians) would be here the following morning. I think the shock reverberated all around the island. The people in Stanley were aghast when they heard the Governor broadcast that we could expect to be invaded".

Mr Hunt had discussed with Pat Wall how best to break the news to the people as there were Argentines on the island working on a fuel pipe line and the question of whether they should be arrested had to be resolved. He taped a message for Mr Wall to broadcast to the Falkland Islanders on the island radio network at 2015 hours, informing them of the imminent Argentinian threat and cautioning them to keep off the streets (in Stanley); not to become involved in any fights with Argentines and not to get in the way of the Royal Marines. The message was re-broadcast at intervals during the night. At 0425 hours 2 April the Governor made a further broadcast to declare a state of emergency and to say that the Argentinians could be expected by dawn.

A few minutes after first light the first Argentinian force landed at Mullett Creek and attacked the vacated Royal Marines Barracks before proceeding towards Government House. Pat Wall said "I could hear the firing but as I was not able to see anything I broadcast to say that if anyone could phone me with information I would try and tell the rest of the islanders. A Falklander phoned on the radio to say that a missile had made a gaping hole in the roof of his house and other houses were being hit by small arms fire."

"There was a hell of a bang at the Marines Barracks at the top of the harbour. The Argentines went in there with grenades so they were not fooling about. Somebody phoned to say that there was a shoot-out just across here on the green by the childrens playing field and there were Argentines killed around Government House because the Royal Marines defending the Governor retaliated. I had an Argentine officer come in here and he was very angry and upset because his best friend had been killed. The Royal Marines held the Argentinians at bay until APCs and artillery, brought ashore at 0830 hours, made further resistance futile. The Governor then gave orders for the Royal Marines and members of the FIDF to surrender. Control of the radio station and cable and wireless office was taken over by the Argentinians and communication with London ceased."

Members of the FIDF reporting for duty at the drill hall in Stanley on 1 April were given patrol and OP tasks and instructed to report back not later than 0500 hours the following morning. The majority returned to the hall before the appointed time but WO1 M. Clark and his section, manning an OP near the Stanley power station, found themselves in the line of fire between Royal Marines and Argentinians. Recalling that incident he said "There were several grenades thrown near our position and as soon as we were able, we got over a couple of fences, through a ditch and into the power station. When the firing stopped the Argentinians were all around the place. We were taken to the drill hall and told to dump our weapons on a table and to go home. Our future movements were very restricted but we tried to disrupt communications by cutting telephone wires laid by the Argentinians through Stanley and up the hill behind the town".

At Plymouth, on 2 April, Brig Thompson was alerted to the situation in the early hours of the morning. Most of his staff were in Denmark and he found himself planning the move of the Brigade with his G3 Training, G3 Intelligence and ex DAA & QMG. His staff returned to Plymouth that night.

Lt Col Hunt awoke to a telephone call at 0400 hours to hear Maj Gen Moore say "Malcolm, this is your General speaking. We have got a war on our hands. Get your men together and be ready to move". The CO held an O Group at 0830 hours and the weekend was spent packing. A Company made ready to embark in HMS *Hermes* on 3 April while the remainder of the unit, scheduled to embark in SS *Canberra*, was granted three days leave pending the return of the liner to Southampton.

News of the invasion was announced in London at mid-day 2 April (0800 hours Falklands time). During the course of that day, 42 Commando personnel (on leave) returned to their unit while 45 Commando, the 22nd Special Air Service Regiment and 3rd Battalion Parachute Regiment, commenced the issue of G1098 stores and other equipment that would be required in the wintry conditions of the southern hemisphere. Adm Leach, at a meeting with the Prime Minister later that night, informed Mrs Thatcher that a Task Force would be ready to sail on Monday 5 April.

Over 8,000 miles away on 3 April, Lt Mills and his small force of Royal Marines at South Georgia, fought a two hour battle against an Argentine corvette and heliborne Argentine marines, inflicting casualties and causing considerable damage to the ship and aircraft before surrendering to a force of vastly superior strength. At Port Stanley, later the same day, Mr Hunt and his family, with the Royal Marines of NP8901 and their families, were flown to Argentina and thence to Uruguay and Britain.

At Plymouth, Sunday 4 April, Brig Thompson held a briefing meeting for all unit commanders of the Brigade and Supporting Arms. Maj E. Southby-Tailyour, who knew the Falkland Islands well, described the conditions to be expected – the peat bogs and bare, road-less, tree-less mountainous terrain with persistent icy winds blowing from the Antarctic. Lt R. Veal RN continued with a description of the bleak, ice covered slopes of South Georgia. In his

SS Canberra. Lt Col M. P. J. Hunt and the officers of 40 Commando, on their way south. Photo: M. P. J. Hunt.

brief Brig Thompson estimated that the Argentine force in the Falklands numbered about 3,000 and indicated that the British force of 3,500 would be of insufficient strength to launch a direct attack on Port Stanley. The plan would be to secure a beach-head into which reinforcements could be fed.

In the light of changing events and new information that came to hand the Brigade staff worked overtime preparing and revising plans. Meanwhile the massive task of supplying, delivering and loading the thousand and one items essential to maintaining the Task Force continued around the clock. It is to the credit of all concerned that this seemingly impossible undertaking was completed within the time stipulated by Adm Leach.

HMS *Hermes* with A Company of 40 Commando embarked, and *Invincible* with elements of 3 Commando Brigade HQ and 42 Commando, sailed from Portsmouth on 5 April. Cdre M.Clapp, commanding the Amphibious Warfare Squadron, sailed in HMS *Fearless* the following day and Brig Thompson and his staff were heliborne to the assault ship as it passed Portland. The RFA, *Stromness* and LSLs. carrying elements of 45 Commando, put to sea on 7 April, about the same time as the SS *Canberra* returned to Southampton at the end of a Mediterranean cruise. Two days later the liner, which became known to everyone in the Task Force as the Great White Whale, sailed from Southampton, equipped with helicopter landing pads, re-stocked and provisioned and carrying the bulk of 40 and 42 Commandos and 3 Para. A large crowd gathered along the dockside to give the embarked force a rousing send-off and numerous small vessels escorted *Canberra* into the Solent.

On schedule, the Task Force commenced the 4,600 mile journey to Ascension Island, calling briefly at Freetown to refuel and take on water. The steadily rising temperature and level of humidity encouraged the men to spend as long as possible on the upper decks where most acquired deeper shades of suntan. They kept fit and mentally alert implementing training programmes adapted to gain the maximum advantage within the confines of ship-board space. According to 40 Commando Unit Training Officer Lt P. Martin "The factor that marked the training above all else was the degree of its intensity. With the possible exception of pre Northern Ireland training, 40 Commando had not undertaken a more consolidated period of professional and physical training in so short a period of time while coping with the problems of integration, co-operation and co-ordination characteristic of ship-board routine. Most of the problems were overcome by the sheer sense of purpose evident in troops preparing for war".

HMS *Antrim*, *Plymouth* and RFA *Tidespring* arrived at Ascension on 10 April, and embarked M Company of 42 Commando, 2 SBS and D Squadron SAS, who had flown to Ascension from UK, before continuing south to rendezvous with HMS *Endurance.* Their eventual task (unknown at that time) would be to re-take South Georgia. The leading ships of the Task Force arrived at Ascension on 17 April, the same day that Adm Sir John Fieldhouse, with Maj Gen Moore and their staff arrived by air for a conference with Adm Woodward, Cdre Clapp and Brig Thompson. Before the end of the day they had decided that a Carrier Battle Group would commence operations to gain control of the sea and air around the Falklands and a reconnaisance would be made of the islands with a view to landing and securing a beach-head on the Falklands not later than 24 May.

Up to this point Brig Thompson and his staff had been working on plans for re-taking South Georgia and the Falklands. Since South Georgia was no longer his problem he was able to direct his full attention to the Falkland Islands operation. The potential threat of a large Argentine air force, with mainland airfields only 300 miles away from the Falklands, continued to be a major worry. Although he had received assurance that the sea and air battles would be won before they arrived the air battle was, in the Brigadier's view crucial "It would be the quickest way of disbanding 3 Commando Brigade that had ever been thought of if we had got it wrong"!

Many days and nights were spent analysing the pros and cons of various landing sites and finally San Carlos was selected. It possessed a good anchorage which could be protected from submarine attack; was lightly defended by the enemy and low hills provided protection against Exocet missile attack. Intelligence reports indicated that the strength of the Argentine force on the Falkland Islands had increased to 11,000 men, of which 8,000 were around

Disembarking by LCU at Ascension Island SS Canberra is in the background. April 1982.

Mortar Troop, Ascension Island. Photos: 40 Commando.

Stanley and in Goose Green. In consequence action was taken to strengthen the Commando Brigade with 2nd Battalion Parachute Regiment. 2 Para and 45 Commando less two companies, sailed to Ascension in the RFAs *Norland* and *Stromness* respectively. 45 Commando's other two companies flew to Ascension and then rejoined the unit. Meanwhile J Company, comprising the two repatriated NP 8901 detachments, arrived at Ascension to join 42 Commando.

Before HMS *Hermes* sailed south with the Carrier Battle Group, A Company cross decked to the LSL *Sir Tristam* to await the arrival of 40 Commando. During the subsequent four weeks, as many as fifty warships, RFAs and chartered vessels arrived at Ascension. The period was one of intense activity. Military stores, hurriedly loaded in Britain, had to be re-distributed between ships to be readily available when required. Modifications were made to some of the vessels to prepare them for the strenuous role ahead and others had gun platforms fitted for air defence.

The *Canberra* dropped anchor at Ascension on 20 April. It was the first visit for most of the ships company to the dusty and barren volcanic island where, three generations earlier, the Royal Marines had maintained a garrison. Commandos and Paras, eager to land after three weeks at sea had to wait their turn to use helicopters and landing craft committed to cross decking stores and equipment. Eventually 40 Commando practised landing craft assault drills by day and night and completed a heliborne cross decking evolution. This was followed by a heliborne landing onto Wideawake Airfield where, in fierce heat and choking dust, all the unit weapons were fired. The Commando completed its one day ashore with an eight mile march to English Bay prior to re-embarkation by LCU. As light relief to the continual training, arrangements were made for the Commando Forces Band to play for a 40 Commando concert on *Canberra's* flight deck. Brig Thompson, a former CO of the unit attended as guest of honour.

On 14 April, Capt B.Young RN, commanding the Antrim Group, had received orders to retake South Georgia. News that the island was back in British hands was signalled to London and the Task Force on 25 April. After many difficulties and incidents in which two helicopters crash-landed in atrocious weather, a composite force of 75 men comprised of part of M Company, elements of SAS and SBS and 10 marines of Antrim's detachment under command of Maj M. Sheridan, was heliborne ashore. This force, supported by the guns of HMS *Plymouth* and *Antrim* advanced on the Argentinians at Gryviken, who surrendered without a fight.

The Argentine forces in the area of Port Stanley were also given a taste of things to come when, on 30 April-1 May, one RAF Vulcan from Ascension straddled the airport runway with bombs, scoring a hit halfway along the eastern end. The 8,000 mile trip was accomplished with the assistance of 17 refuelling operations from Victor tankers. This operation was followed by a Sea Harrier attack on Stanley airfield from HMS *Hermes*. The sinking of the battleship *General Belgrano* on 2 May, was a devastating blow to Argentina but their airforce retaliated by sinking HMS *Sheffield* two days later.

At Ascension, the long period of waiting came to an end on 6 May when the Amphibious Group received orders to commence the 4,000 mile journey to the Falklands. *Canberra* sailed at 2000 hours 8 May, escorted by HMS *Ardent* and *Elk*. The shipboard training continued much as before but was more productive in the fair weather and calm sea conditions. 40 Commando, taking their turn with other units, exercised by companies for a full hour each day, with sessions of running on the promenade deck and circuit training on the sun deck. The wearing of DMS boots gradually replaced soft shoes until eventually they were worn for all training sessions. After leaving Ascension the running period was replaced by speed marching with fighting order and rifle or load carrying. The only men excused were the few who had sustained injuries and as a result the standard of fitness was excellent.

Proficiency in weapon handling and stoppage drills was undertaken with zeal and determination while Forward Observation Officers gave instruction in the use of gun battery fire support. Training ranged from air photographic interpretration to the handling and conduct of prisoners. First aid instruction received special attention and paid dividends after the landings in the Falklands where the professional medical teams complimented the men on the high standard of first aid administered to casualties. Recreational activities alternated with the training and 40 Commando pulled their way to victory in the *Canberra* tug of war competition.

With the Amphibious Group on its way to the Falklands the British War Cabinet gave warning that all Argentinian warships more than 12 miles from the coast of Argentina would be liable to attack. Adm Woodward's Battle Group mounted a series of successful strikes against the Argentinian air force and navy. Five of their fighter aircraft were brought down and a trawler and supply ship sunk.

Orders for Operation Sutton (the landing at San Carlos) were delivered to *Canberra* on 12 May and the following day unit COs were heliborne to HMS *Fearless* for a briefing by Brig Thompson. The original outline plan required 40 Commando to land at San Carlos Settlement from *Canberra* by LCU, simultaneously with 45 Commando landing at Ajax Bay from *Stromness* by LCU. Because of the increased threat from Goose Green Brig Thompson brought forward 2 Para (landing from *Norland* by LCU) from the second wave to the first wave, and slipped 45 Commando to the second wave.

3 Para would then proceed ashore and 42 Commando would remain in reserve in *Canberra*. Prior to the Amphibious Force entering San Carlos Water, marines from 3 SBS and a FOB team would be heliborne ashore from HMS *Antrim* to silence any opposition at Fanning Head and the SAS would create a diversion at Darwin.

Lt Col Hunt held his 'O' Group in the Meridian Room aboard *Canberra* at 1715 hours 17 May. The Commando was to land at 0630 hours 21 May close to the settlement at a point referred to as Blue 2 Beach. A and B Companies had the task of clearing White Rincon and Little Rincon respectively before moving to defensive positions on Verde Mountain. C Company had responsibility for clearing San Carlos Settlement and estabishing a defensive position to the south while the Recce Troop established OPs on Verde Mountain.

The Amphibious Force linked up with the Carrier Group on the 18 May. Late that evening orders were received from London to transfer 40 Commando (less B Echelon) to HMS *Fearless* and 3 Para to HMS *Intrepid* to minimise losses in the event of *Canberra* being hit. Next morning the sea, apart from a long Atlantic swell, was unusually calm and the transfer was accomplished in LCUs. In *Fearless* the crowded compartments, particularly for B Company packed into the wardroom, contrasted starkly with the comparative luxury of *Canberra*. Tragically, a Sea King helicopter crashed into the sea during the transfer operations. Of the 30 passengers 21 SAS soldiers and the air-crewman were killed. The pilots escaped. It was thought that an albatross bird strike may have been the cause as a dead bird was found at the scene of the accident.

The mist which had helped to screen the Task Force on the final approach to the Falklands cleared during the night of 21 May. HMS *Fearless*, followed by HMS *Intrepid*, entered the narrow inlet to San Carlos Water at 2245 hours, passing between Jersy Point and Fanning Head and beyond *Antrim* before dropping anchor to the west of Chanco Point. The last ship was safely in San Carlos Water by 0010 hours. At 0052 hours HMS *Antrim* opened fire with its 4.5-inch on Fanning Head and after 30 minutes of pounding the Argentine OP the SBS moved in to secure the position. The Argentinians remaining at the OP were all casualties but others who had survived the bombardment moved inland, about 8 miles north of San Carlos.

At 0330 hours the sub units of 40 Commando embarked in the LCUs and LCVPs. There was some delay while 2 Para, with no previous experience of transferring from a ship to an assault boat in an Atlantic swell, carried out a similar operation. The assault force then proceeded towards Blue 2 Beach to make an unopposed landing at 0630 hours. A and B Companies quickly checked that the immediate ground to their front was clear before ascending Verde Mountain to establish defensive positions on the reverse slope. While C Company verified that there were no Argentinians in the area of the settlement Lt Col Hunt and Capt A. Pillar knocked on the door of Mr P. Short to announce their arrival. Anticipating a joyous welcome the two officers were somewhat surprised when Pat Short opened the door and said very calmly "Oh! you're here. We wondered when you were going to come"! The islander immediately made himself useful, passing on local information to Lt Col Hunt and helped to move stores inland on his tractor and cart. Meanwhile Capt Pillar gave instructions for the union flag to be hoisted on the pole in Pat Short's garden and then proceeded to organise defensive positions to the south of the settlement. The Recce Troop moved forward to establish OPs on Verde Mountain but found progress slow due to their heavy loads and the difficult terrain.

*East Falkland. Observation Post on The Verde Mountains, San Carlos.
Photo: 40 Commando.*

Further south 2 Para also had an unopposed landing and established their defensive positions on Sussex Mountain to cover the approaches from the direction of Darwin and Goose Green. The SAS diversion at Darwin had proved effective and the San Carlos landings continued undisturbed. 45 Commando was put ashore at Ajax Bay and 3 Para at the Port San Carlos Settlement. Darkness gave way to a clear blue sky and the amphibious ships moved into San Carlos Water. So far everything had progressed according to plan. Attention now focused on landing the 12 Rapiers comprising J Battery air defence system, the 105mm light artillery and the ferrying of men and materials from *Intrepid* and *Fearless*.

During the day the LSLs and other store ships moved into San Carlos Water followed by *Canberra*. A dawn bombardment of the Goose Green air strip by HMS *Ardent* prevented Argentine Pucarra aircraft from taking off but a lone Macchi from Port Stanley strafed HMS *Argonaut* soon after 0800 hours inflicting casualties among the men on the upper deck. Two Gazelle helicopters on a reconnaissance flight were shot down about eight miles north of San Carlos by Argentine soldiers. The Argentinians had been billeted at Port San Carlos and were retreating in front of 3 Para.

The Argentine air force started to retaliate against the Task Force in strength at 0855 hours local time, with a series of local sorties flown from Stanley and long range sorties from Rio Grande in Argentina. The *Ardent* was singled out for attack and then *Argonaut*. Both were badly damaged and there were further casualties. The *Ardent* had to be abandoned and *Argonaut* – immobilised by two 1,000 lb unexploded bombs – was towed into San Carlos Water. HMS *Antrim, Broadsword* and *Brilliant* were also hit during numerous attacks by some 80 aircraft of which 16 were believed to have been shot down. It was fairly late in the day before the Rapier battery could be brought into action but the ships anti aircraft missile systems proved effective and 40 Commando Headquarter gun teams, on the flight deck of *Canberra* contributed to the anti aircraft defence until they disembarked. By good fortune the assault ships and landing ships remained unscathed and unloading continued with only minor disruption.

On Verde Mountain 40 Commando personnel dug in or built up sangars dependent on whether their positions were sited on water-logged peat or rock. By last light nearly all the defence positions were protected by overhead cover. At 2113 hours one of A Company's OPs sighted a six man patrol moving south but it was too distant for them to take effective action.

Although 22 May dawned clear and fine over the Falklands the Argentine airforce on the mainland was grounded by stormy weather and no Argentine sorties were flown from Goose Green or Stanley. Full advantage was taken of this respite from air attack. The Brigade Support Area, established at Ajax Bay the previous day, began to take shape, with hundreds of tons of ammunition and stores ferried ashore by LCUs and helicopters. Also, a Casualty Clearing Station was set up in a disused Mutton Factory. It was uncomfortably close to the ammunition dump but there were no other buildings of suitable size available. Responsibility for the defence of the Rapier detachment on Lookout Hill was given to A Company and the day was spent on improving the defences.

Two patrols were heliborne forward of A and B Company positions before dawn on 23 May. One remained forward to observe while the other returned through A Company during the afternoon. Argentine pilots flying close to the sea through a barrage of cannon, missile and small arms fire, made five attacks in the course of the day, all of which were directed at the ships in and outside San Carlos Water. A probable eight aircraft were brought down but HMS *Antelope,* abandoned after being severely damaged by two 1,000-lb bombs, was finally torn apart when fire reached the magazines and a series of explosions illuminated the night sky.

The Argentine bombing attacks in the area of San Carlos continued on 24 May with Skyhawks, concentrating on the shipping, skimming low across the water in an effort to avoid the air defence systems. Stray bombs from Argentine aircraft and shells from the ships light anti aircraft guns thudded into the hillside around 40 Commando's positions. Also, a Rapier missile, which failed to find its target, landed in B Company's area. Undaunted by this mixed barrage a B Company GPMG post shot down a Skyhawk in the last attack of the afternoon. Although patrols were active throughout the day there was nothing of significance to report.

The Royal Navy was singled out for attention on Argentina's National Day 25 May. Super Etendard aircraft flying from mainland airfields launched Exocet missile attacks on the shipping and HMS *Coventry* and *Atlantic Conveyor*, a chartered vessel carrying much needed Chinook helicopters, were hit. Both ships had to be abandoned with the loss of 12 lives. By dawn on 26 May only the two LPDs, the LSLs *Sir Geraint, Sir Lancelot* and *Sir Galahad* and *Europic Ferry* remained in San Carlos Water. That afternoon, Lt Col Hunt received a summary of future intentions from Brigade Headquarters, which included a warning order that one company of the Commando would be required to move to Ajax Bay to relieve 45 Commando at first light on 27 May. Brig Thompson's orders indicated that as helicopter transport was not available 45 Commando would march overland to secure the settlement at Douglas, while 3 Para would move forward to occupy the settlement at Teal Inlet. 45 Commando sailed to Port San Carlos in LCUs and then commenced a 84 mile yomp across East Falkland, completing the first 17 miles carrying Bergan rucksacks. The men of 3 Para set off in similar fashion.

Meanwhile 2 Para launched successful attacks against the Argentine positions at Darwin and Goose Green. The capture of these numerically superior garrisons removed the threat of a flanking attack on the beach-head. As a result of the actions 2 Para incurred the loss of 18 all ranks, including their Commanding Officer, Lt Col H. Jones. A further 35 were wounded in the action.

During this period 42 Commando remained in reserve and 40 Commando continued in the role of beach-head defence unit. The positions vacated by C Company were taken over by the 2nd Field Squadron Royal Engineers who moved again on 28 May to occupy 45 Commando's vacated positions at Ajax Bay. Towards the end of that afternoon a member of the FOO party attached to B Company, captured an officer of the Argentine Marine Corps Special Forces. Capitan de Corveta Camiletti had been sending radio reports of activity to Stanley from a well concealed hide in an outcrop of rock overlooking San Carlos Water. A thorough search of the area was made by Sgt P.Kay's patrol before the prisoner was taken to Commando HQ.

Soon after 1935 hours Argentine Skyhawks bombed the Logistic Base at Ajax Bay destroying and setting light to sections of the stores and ammunition dumps. In the same attack two parachute retarded bombs hit the old meat factory – housing the Casualty Clearing Station (CCS) – but failed to explode. A few minutes later, two Skyhawks approaching at low altitude from the west, dropped four parachute retarded bombs into the San Carlos Settlement area. According to Lt J.P. Dutton– "The first bomb – which did not explode – landed in the water near the jetty. The other three bombs straddled the command post area". Casualties among the Brigade Logistic Regiment and 45 Commando personnel at Ajax Bay amounted to five men killed and 20 wounded. In

40 Commando's locality two trenches were hit. Mne D.G.McAndrews of the QMs department – in one of the trenches – received shrapnel wounds and died later aboard ship. Sapper Gandhi of the Royal Engineers, in the second trench, was killed by blast injuries. Ironically the second occupant in each trench escaped with no more than temporary hearing problems. All the wounded, including those in the dressing station, were evacuated to the hospital ship *Uganda* although some may have staged in HMS *Intrepid*.

The unexploded bombs in the CCS and 40 Commando's location were defused but remained where they were until the end of the campaign. Extinguishing the fires in the ammunition dumps was no easy task and explosions continued to rend the air for hours afterwards. During the night an A Company sentry fired shots at three Argentinians who, when challenged, made off into the darkness. Some days later a patrol found the bodies of two Argentine soldiers near a stream.

The 28 May was spent clearing up after the air raid and completing the move of B Company to 2 Para's former positions. The following day A Company was heliborne to Darwin to escort 1,400 Argentine prisoners to Blue Beach. C Company was made Brigade reserve and instructed to be ready to move at one hours notice. Late on the afternoon of 30 May, Lt Col Hunt received a warning order to be ready to move 40 Commando as soon as the 5th Infantry Brigade arrived on the following night. The news was greeted with satisfaction by the entire unit.

Next morning, 31 May, an Argentine Canberra bomber dropped four 1,000-lb bombs close to the Commando Headquarter positions but there were no casualties. The first elements of 5 Brigade arrived before nightfall and 40 Commando remained poised ready to move throughout the morning of the next day. During the day, J Company of 42 Commando was placed under command, B Company rejoined the unit and the Gurkhas landed and moved to Sussex Mountain. Maj Gen Moore assumed command of the land operations as soon as the main body of the 5th Infantry Brigade were ashore.

At 1500 hours the Commando Brigade SO3 called at Lt Col Hunt's HQ and handed him an Operational Order placing 40 Commando under command Headquarters Land Forces Falkland Island as divisional reserve troops. Lt Col Hunt, very concerned that his unit was being left out of the action, went to see Maj Gen Moore aboard HMS *Fearless* and asked him to reconsider 40 Commando's deployment. Maj Gen Moore listened to what he had to say but replied, quite reasonably, that he was to do as he was bid. Lt Col Hunt was unaware until some time later that intelligence sources had indicated the possibility of an Argentine airborne attack in the beach-head locality.

The period between 2 and 7 June was mainly uneventful in the San Carlos area. C Company relieved the Gurkhas on Sussex Mountain and B Company deployed to Port San Carlos. Patrols were sent to Fanning Head and Cape Dolphin while routine patrolling of Verde Mountain continued. The Welsh Guards abandoned an attempt to march to Goose Green and in company with

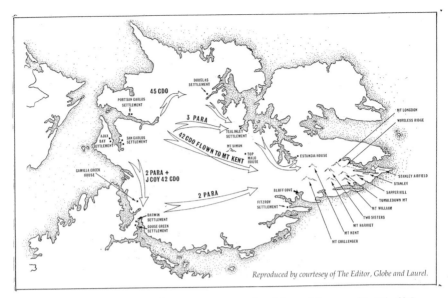

elements of the Scots Guards, were eventually shipped forward to Bluff Cove on the nights of 6 and 7 June. The remainder of the Welsh Guards followed in RFA *Sir Galahad* on the 7/8 June. They were still embarked off shore the following morning when Argentine aircraft bombed the *Sir Galahad* and *Sir Tristam*. Both ships had to be abandoned with the loss of 50 men.

During the afternoon of 8 June, B and C Companies were brought to six hours notice for possible operational tasks on Pebble Island and Mount Rosalie while A Company was ordered to stand by for a move to clear Mount Low. In the event the bombing of the *Sir Tristam* and *Sir Galahad* resulted in the cancellation of all these tasks. Survivors of the bombing arrived at San Carlos during the night.

A patrol, checking the area around Windy Gap on 9 June, made contact with a solitary Argentine infantryman who was only too happy to give himself up. On the the same day at 1825 hours Lt Col Hunt received a warning order that two of his companies were to be placed under command of the Welsh Guards, while he in turn, was required to take command of two companies of the Welsh Guards that had been depleted by casualties.

The leading elements of A Company commenced the flight to Fitzroy in Sea King helicopters soon after midday, passing the still burning hulls of the LSLs before landing on the north side of Lock Cove. OC A Company, Maj S.B. Cusack was met by the Adjutant of the Welsh Guards and taken to the command post for briefing by Lt Col J.F Rickett MBE. Meanwhile, Lt S. Buzza sighted the company positions and the troops dug in to the sound of enemy gun fire. A few shells exploded in the valley on their south side and intermittent shelling continued until nightfall. C Company, at two hours notice to clear either Pebble Island or Mount Rosalie or extract a SAS patrol from West

Falkland, found themselves airborne and – as dusk fell – were digging defence positions adjacent to A Company.

B Company, continuing the task of guarding the Port San Carlos beachhead, sent 5 Troop to clear the area at New House, to the north of the settlement. The patrol, led by Lt M. Howell found and captured six Argentinian soldiers and an officer in that location. A further three Argentine soldiers at Moss Side House, all suffering from severe frostbite, gave themselves up.

The opening phase of the battle for Port Stanley commenced on the night of 11/12 June and resulted in the capture of Two Sisters by 45 Commando, Mount Harriet by 42 Commando and Mount Longdon by 3 Para. The three units suffered a total loss of 30 killed and 98 wounded. On the same night HMS *Glamorgan* was hit by an Exocet with the loss of 13 men. The Welsh Guards, with A and C Companies of 40 Commando under command, had been given the task of securing the Start Line for 42 Commando's attack on Mount Harriet. The approach to the Start Line was made in single file with No 2 Company Welsh Guards leading followed by A and C Companies. The track went east from Fitzroy to Stanley and after a few miles this deteriorated into extensive stone runs which delayed progress. An overcast sky cleared as the companies arrived at the FUP to witness 42 Commando's attack supported by naval and army guns and mortars.

As soon as 42 Commando had consolidated on Mount Harriet the Welsh Guards and 40 Commando companies moved back into defensive positions. These positions were held during the following day with intermittent shelling from Argentine and Task Force artillery onto forward positions. At last light 13/14 June, the composite Welsh Guards/40 Commando unit moved forward to take up new positions to the east of a prominent lake. The leading Welsh Guards company took a northerly route which proved to be mined. Mne W. McGregor stepped on a mine and a short time later 2Lt P.A. Cooper, his Troop Commander also triggered an AP mine. Both suffered serious leg injuries. Although enemy shelling added to the problems LMAs Black and Kenny worked calmly to treat and extricate the wounded. An engineer section from 59 Independent Squadron RE and 40 Commando AE Section carried out mine clearance which took five hours to complete. For this action LMA Black was awarded a Mention in Despatches and LMA Kenny received a C-in-Cs Commendation. These were the only awards credited to 40 Commando during the Falklands conflict.

Shortly before 2200 hours artillery and mortar barrages accompanied by bombardments from HMS *Active* and *Avenger* pounded the Argentine positions on Wireless Ridge and Mount Tumbledown as a preliminary to 2 Para assaulting the former and the Scots Guards the latter. The Gurkhas stood by to advance on Mount William while the 40 Commando/Welsh Guards unit prepared to exploit any opportunity to follow up.

Wireless Ridge was secured by 2 Para shortly before 0200 hours. The Argentine defences on Mount Tumbledown proved to be a stiffer obstacle but

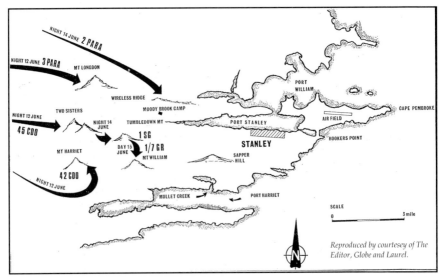

NIGHT 14 JUNE 2 PARA
NIGHT 12 JUNE 3 PARA
MT LONGDON
WIRELESS RIDGE
PORT WILLIAM
TWO SISTERS
MOODY BROOK CAMP
CAPE PEMBROKE
NIGHT 12 JUNE
45 CDO
NIGHT 14 JUNE
TUMBLEDOWN MT
AIR FIELD
PORT STANLEY
1 SG
STANLEY
HOOKERS POINT
MT HARRIET
DAY 15 JUNE
1/7 GR
MT WILLIAM
SAPPER HILL
42 CDO
NIGHT 12 JUNE
MULLET CREEK
PORT HARRIET

SCALE
0   3 mile

Reproduced by courtesey of The Editor, Globe and Laurel.

the Scots Guards had secured two thirds of the ridge by daylight and the flanking movement of the Gurkhas to take Mount William was the signal for Argentinian resistance to slacken.

A and C Companies of 40 Commando were now lifted forward in RN helicopters for a heliborne assault on Sapper Hill. No 7 Troop was put down very close to the enemy positions and during the deployment two marines were hit by Argentine fire. Almost before the troop was able to engage the enemy the Company Commander received a wireless signal ordering a cease fire. A white flag had been hoisted in Stanley.

Brig Gen M. Menedez had been instructed by the Argentine Prime Minister to continue fighting. However, he was well aware that the Task Force dominated the sea and air and that his infantry had been out-manoeuvred and out-gunned. In these circumstances he saw no alternative but to accept the terms stated by Maj Gen Moore. While 2 and 3 Para and 42 Commando moved forward into Port Stanley the composite 40 Commando and Welsh Guards unit, who were joined by 45 Commando, prepared to spend a very cold and uncomfortable night on Sapper Hill.

It was well after sundown by the time Mag Gen Moore arrived at Stanley in a Sea King helicopter of 820 Squadron. The weather had deteriorated and visibility was much reduced in snow storms that chilled the troops protected only by their combat dress on the high ground to the south and west of Stanley. In the town, Maj Gen Moore received the surrender of Brig Gen Menendez at 2100 hours. The next morning 15 June 1982, representatives of J Company had the privilege of raising the Governor's flag outside Government House while Brig Gen Menedez and his senior staff were flown to HMS *Fearless*.

News of the Argentinian surrender was received in San Carlos during early hours of 15 June. The following day, Lt Col Hunt received orders to take the

West Falkland. The Union Flag is raised at Port Howard, 16 June 1982.

Argentinian prisoners of war at Port Howard under escort to the LCVs.
Photos: 40 Commando.

surrender of the 1,000 Argentine garrison at Port Howard. A 40 Commando force embarked in LCUs but severe sea conditions forced them to return to San Carlos. A smaller force was then heliborne to Port Howard to accept the surrender and arrange the evacuation of the Argentine garrison. Preliminary instructions were passed by radio telephone to the Argentine garrison commander via Mr R. Lee, the head of the Port Howard settlement. Robin Lee had observed the build up of the Argentine force around the settlement and was able to indicate their positions to the commandos.

A large number of beach mines improvised from oil drums, with as many as three anti-tank mines attached, were found at Port Howard. The most significant event was the finding of a string of 139 anti-tank mines, connected in series and containing an estimated total of 2,500 lbs of explosive. They were located around the beach and threatened any landing from the sea. The work done by CSgt Stubbings and his team of AEs in the removal of these obstacles was magnificent since the precise location of the mines was unknown. The Argentine officer responsible for laying the mines in Port Howard was unable to provide information of any value. Tragically therefore, after completing such a difficult and dangerous task Cpl Lee lost the lower part of one leg as the result of treading on a previously unlocated AP mine. Even today, there are many areas of East and West Falkland where plastic AP mines, which cannot be traced with mine detectors, remain a lethal hazard.

The total casualty figures sustained by the Brigade for the campaign were, 69 killed and 186 wounded, plus 108 injured (frostbite/trenchfoot, broken backs, legs, arms, ankles etc).

The Argentine prisoners were ferried to San Carlos and, with a further 1,900 from Pebble Island, were transferred to the Canberra. More prisoners were embarked at Stanley and, with Argentine agreement, were taken to Puerto Madryn in Argentina. During these proceedings the news of the resignation of Gen Galtieri as C-in-C and President of Argentina was announced.

A and C Companies, feeling the effects of exposure to the elements, returned to 40 Commando on 16 June where efforts were made to provide them with shelter. Meanwhile arrangements were made to return 3 Company and Prince of Wales Company 1st Welsh Guards to their own unit. Considerable progress was made in clearing the Port Howard and Fox Bay Settlements of Argentine prisoners and warlike materials while a similar operation was set in motion at Port Stephen. An A Company advance party had already been heliborne to that location when Lt Col Hunt received orders to prepare to embark the unit. B Company was nearing the completion of its task at Port Howard and Headquarter Company had cleared the area at Fox Bay. Both these companies were lifted to San Carlos by Chinook helicopter on 23 June and 40 Commando re-embarked in the Canberra the following day.

Although the unit had found itself committed for the greater part of the campaign to an unglamourous and thankless task, it nevertheless performed all its undertakings with spirit and a commendably high morale.

The Commando Brigade with 2 and 3 Para set sail for UK on 26 June and, following a relaxed routine on the homeward bound trip via Ascension, arrived to a joyous welcome at Southampton in 11 July.

The men of 40 Commando received an equally enthusiastic reception from families, friends and members of D Company at Seaton Barracks. D Company, with considerable support from the Wives Club, had kept the home front running smoothly in their absence. The COs wife, Margaret Hunt, assisted by Cpl R.Scott and unit wives, had formed the Wives Club immediately the unit left UK. Joined by June Clark and other wives of 42 Commando the members made the Roaring Forties Club their base. Coffee mornings became a daily event and a barbecue for 250 proved the clubs popularity. Volunteers helped to keep the families up to date with information (the Commando sent a video tape of messages home from Ascension) and provided a source of encouragement and practical help for anyone in need.

Returning from summer leave, the unit set out to prove its fitness and spirit on the sports field while, at the same time, preparing for a tour in Northern Ireland. Between September and Christmas 40 Commando won the Corps Basket Ball Championships, Novices Boxing Championships and Hockey (including six-a-side), the Judo Championships, RN and RM Equitation, Devon Wednesday Soccer League and RMRA Small Bore League. They were runners up in the Corps Rugby and RN and RM Sea Angling and, to put the cherry on the cake, were placed first and second in the Corps Cookery Competition!

A detachment of 15 Wrens, who were to work with the Commando in Northern Ireland, joined the unit in October, while D Company, refreshed after a month's deployment to Cyprus, returned to undertake London ceremonial duties in November. On 29 November the Commando paraded to honour Mne Mc Andrews, the unit's one fatal casualty in the Falkland campaign. His mother planted an English oak in the grounds of Seaton Barracks in Stephen's memory.

The Commando moved to Northern Ireland on 21 January 1983, to assume command of the South Armagh TAOR from the 1st Battalion Coldstream Guards. In the eleven years that had elapsed since the unit's first Belfast tour, the military presence had remained much the same but the mode of operating had altered significantly. In 1972, the military had been the dominant force with the police providing a back up. As the years progressed, a gradual interchange of roles took place until eventually the military assumed the role of providing support to the police. The transition became evident about 1977 and by 1983 was a fact of life. Co-operation with the police was good but a sensitive approach to any situation was an essential requirement. The enthusiasm of a fresh military presence every four months had to be measured against the long term view point of the police who had to contend with the problems and danger year in and year out.

HQ and B Companies shared the Bessbrook Mill location while Support and

HMS Hermes. *Photo: 40 Commando*

A Companies looked after Forkhill and Crossmaglen respectively. C Company, under the operational control of the 2nd Battalion Ulster Defence Regiment, was based in Armagh city. In addition to the daily norm of patrolling and guard duties a major search was made for Shergar, a valuable Irish race horse, which disappeared from its stable under mysterious circumstances. Never to be found.

There were no serious incidents during the tour but it was apparent that patrols, particularly in built up areas, were under surveillance by PIRA supporters and only constant vigilance and meticulous attention to detail by the Security Forces prevented more overt terrorist action. Maj R.B.Howard-Williams, who commanded Support Company during the tour, said "We carried out a major operation at least once a week, either going out to clear a known or suspected bomb or to clear the road or railway line. The major interest in my patch was the Dublin to Belfast railway. There was considerable political pressure to keep it from being bombed and this involved intensive patrolling in order to deter PIRA operations on the line. We knew from the intelligence feedback and our own observations that we disrupted a number of PIRA attempts to place a bomb on the line."

PIRA activity increased during the final phase of the tour. In B Company's sector two RUC constables escaped injury when a large bomb exploded beneath their car. A suspected informer was murdered and a prominent terrorist was arrested. In the Crossmaglen sector a Wessex helicopter taking a search team to Bessbrook was hit by small arms fire. The co-pilot received a shoulder wound and one of the search team was hit by splinters. In Newry, Mne A.Gibbons died from injuries received as the result of an accident while on patrol.

The Commando was relieved by the 1st Battalion Duke of Edinburgh's Royal Regiment on 5 June and returned to Plymouth where D Company rejoined the unit after a four months deployment in the Falklands. Maj Gen Wilkins visited Seaton Barracks on 11 July to present South Atlantic medals and Northern Ireland General Service medals to personnel in the unit.

Towards the end of the month the Commando bid farewell to Lt Col Hunt on his departure to take up appointment as Director of Defence Commitments NATO. His successor, Lt Col T.P.T. Donkin MBE, assumed command on 22 July 1983 and a few days later led the unit on a speed march from Bickleigh to the Dewerstone on Dartmoor where he briefed the assembled personnel on an exercise that would take the unit to several Mediterranean countries. He also outlined details of the unit's new base at Norton Manor Camp, Taunton.

Lt Col Donkin checking a point of detail. Photo: 40 Commando.

CHAPTER 22

23 July 1983 to 18 July 1988

Mediterranean deployment – Norton Manor Camp, Taunton, the new unit base – Peace-keeping with the United Nations Force, Cyprus – The Wilkinson Sword of Peace, third award – Belize deployment – Ex Purple Warrior – Seventh Northern Ireland Tour

BETWEEN the end of July and early September the unit was fully occupied, preparing for the Mediterranean deployment the hand-over of Seaton Barracks to the Commando Logistic Regiment and summer leave. In mid-September, 40 Commando embarked in HMS *Hermes* to exercise with the carrier in the LPH role for the last time. After a preliminary helibourne landing on the north Cornish coast, *Hermes*, in company with RFA *Resource,* sailed to the Mediterranean. A brief call was made at Naples to embark Cdre P. G. V. Dingemans DSO, and Brig Garrod with their command staff, before proceeding eastward to commence Ex Display Determination. At the last moment the Greek government withdrew its forces from the exercise and rapid replanning was necessary to divert the force to Brindisi where three days field training filled the gap in the programme.

Continuing on a course around Crete the British amphibious unit combined with elements of the Turkish navy to make an assault landing at Saros Bay in view of a large audience of Turkish and NATO personnel. An unexpected rainstorm helped lay the clouds of dust kicked up by troops and vehicles but senior spectators were not best pleased when spots of mud spattered immaculate uniforms!

40 Commando Group and the 1st Battalion Turkish Naval Infantry exercised for five days against an enemy provided by the Turkish army and the final afternoon was allocated to international sport. After winning the football and losing the volley ball, 40 Commando retrieved the situation by taking first place in a five mile cross country team race, run in loose order. All the commando runners crossed the finishing line before the first Turkish runner came in sight of the posts!

At Istanbul, the command staffs disembarked to fly home. The ships company and embarked troops enjoyed a five day port visit before continuing to Cyprus for three days field firing with 79 Battery and armoured cars of the 1st Royal Tank Regiment. The journey continued to Alexandria where the Commando Group undertook four days cross training with the Egyptian army. Considerable publicity was given to this phase which ended with a 36 hour exercise in which a composite company from the Commando joined

Cpl Peter Robinson meets First Sea Lord, Admiral Sir John Fieldhouse at Norton Manor Camp, 14 February 1984. Photo: 40 Commando.

forces with Egyptians while two troops of the Egyptian Parachute Battalion operated with 40 Commando.

After a visit to the pyramids and souvenir shopping in the bazaars the units re-embarked to commence the return trip to UK. A call was made at Gibraltar, to allow the runners an attempt (in vain) at lowering the "Top of the Rock" record, and a stop at Sardinia, to land a bicycle team of 13 men, who intended making a sponsored pedal power ride home to Taunton!

HMS *Hermes* arrived at Devonport on 22 November, with a 750ft paying off pennant streaming astern and her decks manned, for the last time, by Navy, Marine and Army personnel. Later in the day 40 Commando marched through Taunton where the local people lined the streets to welcome the unit to its new home. The bicycle team rejoined the Commando at this point and after Mrs Rachel Haldene, the Mayor of Taunton Deane, had taken the salute, Mne J.Shaw – representing the cyclists – presented her with a cheque for £1,163 raised in sponsor money for local charities. 40 Commando, preceded by the Band of Commando Forces, then continued by march route to Norton Manor Camp, where the final weeks of 1983 were spent consolidating in the new location.

The Altcar Ranges at Merseyside were bleak and inhospitable throughout the Individual Skill at Arms Competition in January. In consequence, the subsequent move south to Salisbury Plain for company training – and inevitable digging of defensive positions – offered the welcome prospect of improved conditions. Marines, under the command of one enterprising SNCO, thought the age of miracles had arrived when he acquired a mechanical excavator to dig their trenches.

The First Sea Lord, Adm Sir John Fieldhouse, renewed his acquaintance with the unit at Norton Manor Camp in February and impressed the PW instructors with his skilful handling of infantry weapons on the 30 metre range. The Admiral toured company locations and met Cpl P. Robinson who, as one of a small element of 40 Commando personnel, yomped with 45 Commando across East Falkland during the conflict with Argentina. Cpl Robinson's back view became well known following the publication of a photograph* in the national press in which he is portrayed yomping with the Union Flag prominently displayed above his back pack.

D Company rejoined the unit mid February, on completion of eight weeks jungle warfare training in Brunei. The company personnel would eventually be called upon to impart their knowledge to other members of the unit prior to the unit's deployment to Belize in 1985. The Company had completed the commitments for which it had been formed and, after live field firing with the Commando at Sennybridge, disbanded on Friday 13 April 1984.

Various successes in the ring, gym and field during the winter season verified the unit's continued enthusiasm and determination to maintain a high

---

* Front cover of the Globe and Laurel, Sep/Oct 1982.

Cyprus. Three marines of A Company, wearing the United Nations light blue beret, return to base at the end of a patrol under a very hot sun.
Photo: 40 Commando.

sporting profile. Mne A. Ellis became the under 19's Combined Services Welterweight Boxing Champion; unit teams won the Corps Rugby and Volleyball Championships; LCpl Hawkins and Mne Beck gained first places in the Floor and Trampoline Sections of the Army Gymnastic Championships; the Karate team beat the British team and were placed fourth in the European Championships. C Company team, running in the Taunton Marathon, raised £500 for a local childrens charity.

Preparations for a six months tour with the United Nations Peace Keeping Force in Cyprus (UNFICYP) began in early May. Nearly ten years had elapsed since the unit, as Spearhead Force, had deployed to the Island on the day of the Turkish landings. The Buffer Zone (Green Line) established by the United Nations had remained comparatively quiet during the intervening years but the political gap between the two communities remained practically unchanged. In 1983 Turkish Cypriot leaders had declared the northern sector of Cyprus an independent state but the declaration is only recognised by Turkey and Greek Cypriots argue that there can be no settlement until all Turkish troops are withdrawn from the island.

The main body of the unit flew to Akrotiri on 7 June in the RAFs newly acquired troop carrying Tristars. Relieving the 2nd Battalion Anglian Regiment the unit assumed responsibility for the British Sector of UNFICYP,the boundaries of which extended from the Kyrenia District on the north coast to the Limassol District in the southern Western Sovereign Base Area (WSBA). The Commando was also responsible for the security of a major part of the Eastern Sovereign Base Area (ESBA) at Dhekelia.

Wearing the light blue beret of the United Nations, A and C Companies deployed directly to locations along the Green Line. Meanwhile, B and Support Companies moved to the ESBA . Lt Col Donkin established his Headquarters in St David's Camp – also in the Green Line close to Nicosia – and elements of Headquarter Company were deployed both at St David's Camp and the ESBA.

The peace keeping duties performed by A and C Companies along the 22 mile British Sector consisted of manning OPs, providing escorts and patrolling, at the same time building up a close link with the local community. The Commando element in the ESBA was responsible for security within the Base, the Base perimeter and outlying stations along a road forming a corridor between Greek and Turkish held territory, extending from the ESBA to Avios Nicolaos.

The aim was to maintain the cease fire agreed in 1974 between the Greek and Turkish forces. With this in mind it was vital that as representatives of the United Nations the commandos should be completely impartial in their dealings with the people, should respect local laws and customs and be absolutely trustworthy. The task required considerable patience, understanding and diplomacy.

In the British Sector, the width of the Buffer Zone and nature of the countryside varied considerably along its length. On the western side, where A Company operated from a disused box factory, the two mile wide Green Line contained some of the most productive citrus groves in Cyprus. In contrast, C Company had its base in an old school in a suburb of Nicosia where the Green Line narrowed at some points to less than 100 yards. The economy in this area was based on cereal crops and light industry.

Patrolling, manning OPs and performing a variety of duties in the sweltering summer heat, the commandos pursued the role of keeping the peace, with patience, understanding and a genuine desire to help. Working in conjunction with the United Nations High Commission, the unit located missing persons, re-housed refugees and established links between families divided by the Green Line. In their off duty moments Commando personnel organised parties and sports events for the young and concerts for the adults. All activities of this nature helped to reduce tension and promote a closer understanding between the divided communities. There were numerous problems and disputes to be resolved but the sustained efforts achieved during the Commando's commitment led to the opening up of 223 fields along the British Sector of the Green Line, making it possible for many farmers to grow crops for the first time since 1974.

Cyprus. The Duke of Edinburgh, Captain General Royal Marines, in conversation with Mne J. Conway of Recce Troop, during a tour of United Nations Headquarters Sector Two, St. David's Camp, 6 October 1984. Photo: 40 Commando.

All ranks were able to avail themselves of a period of R and R at some stage during the tour. Cricket, volleyball, swimming and sailing were the most popular recreational activities while adventure training, confined mainly to scuba diving and mountaineering, provided alternative interest and exercise. In competitive mood, the unit won the Army Athletics Trophy and the All Island Army Unit Swimming and Waterpolo Trophy. It was most regrettable that during these lighter moments both Mne M. Shand and LCpl K. Lock received fatal injuries in separate road traffic accidents.

In the latter half of the tour, ceremonial duties and visitors added to the fullness of an already busy programme. The BRITCON Medal Parade* at Nicosia Airport, with a 40 Commando representation of the Adjutant, Lt J.G. Rose, RSM Brush, two Guards, the Queen's and Regimental Colours and the whole commanded by Lt Col Donkin, was an outstanding success. The Band of Commando Forces added the finishing touch to this special occasion. Lt Gen M.C.L. Wilkins OBE, who succeeded Lt Gen Sir Steuart Pringle as Commandant General Royal Marines on 6 April 1984, attended the parade and

---

* Ranks were required to have served 90 days on the strength of UNFICYP to qualify for the United Nations Medal.

visited both Greek and Turkish controlled areas where 40 Commando had operated during the EOKA campaign.

HRH The Duke of Edinburgh made a brief stop over in Cyprus on 6 October, en route to Egypt. Heliborne to St David's Camp the Captain General was greeted by HE the High Commissioner Mr W.J.A. Wilberforce, the Force Commander Maj Gen G.G. Greindl BCE and the Commanding Officer Lt Col Donkin. After inspecting the Royal Guard provided by A, C and Headquarter Companies under the command of Capt K. De Val, he toured areas of St David's Camp and Commando positions in the British Sector of the Green Line.

As the months passed into autumn the heat became less oppressive and frequent rain was a reminder of wet November days in UK. Possibly a coincidence, it was noticeable that visitors and sunshine disappeared simultaneously. The arrival of the 1st Battalion The Duke of Edinburgh's Royal Regiment in December signalled the end of the tour and the unit returned to UK for Christmas leave.

The death of Lt T.V.Glanville the unit Imprest Officer on 11 January 1985, as a result of a heart attack after completing an 800 metre unit run, was a shock to all. Terry Glanville, who joined the Corps as a Junior Marine on 2 January 1961, was totally dedicated to the Royal Marines. He had been an active sportsman throughout his career and had served previously with 40 Commando in Borneo.

Towards the end of the month a new Recce Troop, under command of Lt M.Hekkens RNLMC, joined Support Company and selected personnel from within the unit amalgamated under the command of Capt De Val to form E Company. There was keen competition to be included in the composite force of 119 ranks which deployed to Brunei for six weeks with the aim of providing a cadre of jungle trained personnel for each company.

Meanwhile the main body of the Commando concentrated on re-training for conventional war operations anywhere in the world. The programme commenced with section, troop and company attacks at Sennybridge, a necessary preliminary to the more advanced company and unit field firing exercises, with artillery, mortar and air support that were to follow at Otterburn.

The MGRM Commando Forces, Maj Gen J.St J.Grey, made his formal inspection of the unit in March and shortly afterwards E Company, having completed the Brunei deployment, disbanded prior to the unit moving north. The predictably cold weather on the ranges a few miles south of the Scottish border, rapidly worsened to near arctic conditions and for six days and nights the commandos concentrated on fighting the elements in addition to the notional enemy.

The parading of the entire unit for Air Portability (Inspection) followed by a 10 day work-out at Hythe and Lydd, fine-tuned the unit for Spearhead duties between 29 April and 16 June. There were no emergency calls on the Commando and the COs directive that "If not deployed, the period will be used for

350

testing imaginative training and company competitions", was carried out to the letter. It should also be noted that the unit boxing team ended the season with five RN Open titles and four Combined Services winners, a record that other service units will find hard to equal.

The extended period in camp enabled the Chief Cook, CSgt P. Wakeman to revolutionise the galley service. With the assistance of the Quartermaster and RI funds he provided two lounge areas equipped with arm chairs, a continual daily service from 0645 to 1900 hours with table cloths, 40 Commando place mats, cutlery and crockery provided and no portion control. It was made clear that this service was not available on operational tours!

The eight weeks Spearhead commitment ended with a Families Day. The unit paraded in the morning; the RM freefall parachute team dropped in during the afternoon and various static displays, inter company matches and a cross country assault course event provided all round interest. The latter event was a surprise item introduced by Lt Col Donkin to mark his last day as CO of 40 Commando and the transfer of command to Lt Col R.A.Hooper MA. As a parting gesture members of Lt Col Donkins' staff arranged for a kiss-o-gram girl to give him a suitable send off to his new appointment as Director of Drafting and Records.

Lt Col Donkin returned to Taunton on 30 August to receive, on behalf of 40 Commando, the Royal Navy Wilkinson Sword of Peace for 1984. This was the third Sword of Peace to be awarded to the unit. The presentation was made by Sir Ronald Ellis, President of the Industrial Group of Wilkinson Sword, to Lt Col Donkin, who in turn handed the sword to Lt Col Hooper. The ceremony was fairly low key as half the unit was away – A Company carrying out ceremonial duties on the Isle of Man and B Company, in London, staging a Commando Raid display at the Royal Tournament. In fact, most of the unit were away at one time or another during the summer. Elements of Support Company deployed to Holland, for the Nijmegen Marches, and Scotland, to provide the enemy for 148 Commando Battery's escape and evasion exercise. Meanwhile C Company gave a Mountain and Arctic Warfare Demonstration to the Joint Services Defence College at Poole.

The initial preparations for a six months deployment to Belize commenced after summer leave with the issue of tropical kit, injections for yellow fever and other diseases, battle fitness tests, preliminary jungle training and briefings by the IO on the geographical, historical and political background of Belize.

As a result of a long standing dispute between Guatemala and Britain over the territorial rights of Belize, formerly British Honduras, Britain has continued to maintain a military Garrison in Belize after giving the country its independence in 1981. Situated on the east coast of South America, Belize, with a population of just under 180,000, is barely 170 miles long and 68 miles wide. While the border with Mexico is well defined the line of demarcation with Guatamala follows, for the most part, no natural features. Low mangrove swamp-covered ground intersected by creeks, closely spaced rivers and streams extends along most of the coastal region, while small islands and coral form a barrier reef offshore. Inland, the area north of the Belize River is mainly undulating limestone country while, to the west, the ground is broken by a series of low, east facing escarpments covered by forest or wet savannah. A central mountain range, with the 3,680ft Victoria Peak its highest point, divides the north and south. Temperatures are sub tropical and average between 79 and 90 degrees.

The origins of the dispute with Guatamala date back over three centuries when the country was initially part of the Mayan Empire. A small settlement, founded by Capt A. Wallace on the Belize river in 1638 had, by the mid 18th Century, grown into a well established community on ground that was traditionally Spanish. Spain made spasmodic attempts to capture the settlement. However, the collapse of the Spanish Empire in 1820 led to the formation of other central American republics with Mexico and Guatamala claiming rights as successor states to the territory which had become known as British Honduras. Following extensive diplomatic negotiations Gautamala signed a treaty with Britain in 1859 and eventually Mexico annulled any claim to the territory. By the end of the nineteenth century British Honduras had become a Crown Colony of Great Britain.

Guatamala renewed its claims to British Honduras in the 1930s and 1940s while accusing Britain of not developing communications between the settlement of Belize and Guatamala as agreed in the treaty of 1859. In 1950 Britain allocated £250,000 towards the development of a modern road link between British Honduras and Guatamala but political differences remained sour.

The Peoples United Party (PUP) of British Honduras won the first general election in 1954, on anti-British and anti-colonial policies. Nineteen years later the country was officially renamed Belize. Constitutional development continued with Belize concentrating on obtaining a Commonwealth Defence Guarantee as a basis for independence. The capital cost for the formation of the Belize Defence Force (BDF), formed in 1978, was borne by the British Government. The BDF was not expected to be strong enough to replace the British garrison and it was agreed that British forces would remain for an appropriate period after Belize received its independence on 21 September 1981.

The main body of 40 Commando relieved the 1st Battalion Duke of Wellington's Regiment in Belize on 29 September 1985. As resident battalion, the Commando had responsibility for assisting the BDF in the defence of Belize against external aggression, providing training assistance to the BDF and helping the civil power with disaster relief and the maintenance of public services in an emergency.

The unit deployed to four company locations with B Company and Support Company (the latter reorganised as a rifle company) in the north, forming Battle Group North while A and C Companies formed a similar Battle Group in the south. Commando Headquarters and elements of Headquarter Company were based at Airport Camp, roughly midway between the two groups.

Her Majesty The Queen with members of 40 Commando on her visit to Belize 1986. Photo: 40 Commando.

In consequence the Headquarter Company commitment was considerable. The MT Section had a particularly arduous task as the roads were in very poor condition and the wooden bridges, unsafe and treacherous at the best of times were mainly under flood-water in the wet season. The journey between north and south could take up to 12 hours by way of the dirt road or by river transport. The same distance could be covered by Puma helicopter in 45 minutes!

The Commando had not long settled to its task before Her Majesty Queen Elizabeth, arrived on her first visit to Belize. Although principally there to meet the people of the country Her Majesty spent some time at Airport Camp with members of 40 Commando Group before visiting the Sergeants mess and lunching with the officers.

Thereafter, a rapid sequence of events kept everyone on their toes. The main body of 79 (Kirkee) Commando Battery RA arrived and deployed to the company locations. The troop commanders – having completed a crash course in jungle familiarization – imparted their knowledge to their troops and patrols made their first sorties into the jungle, with the BDF providing interpreters and local knowledge. OPs were established on remote mountain tops overlooking the Guatamalan border and Adm Sir John Fieldhouse arrived; presented LS and GC medals to worthy recipients and visited the

HRH Prince Edward with his private detective, Lt J. L. Morgan and SSgt D. Sanderson RE. Photo: 40 Commando

outposts. Also, Surg Lt T. Spalding and POMA C. Lloyd had a pleasant deviation from routine when they took over from the local doctor – who was on leave – and delivered a baby girl to a local resident.

Immediately following Maj Gen Grey's three day visit to the Commando in early December HRH ALt (UCE) The Prince Edward arrived for a two week attachment to the unit. The Prince spent the first week with B Company, acclimatising to jungle routine and Commando life and the second week with A and C Companies, gaining experience with river and jungle patrols. The standard dress for patrols consisted of DPM hat, lightweight combats, jungle boots, yoke with water bottle, ammo pouch and pack.

Support Company patrols in the San Felipa and Ensalada area, where the Marijuana trade and related crime were rampart, received a mixed reception from local people who were intimidated by the drug dealers. In the southern area of Belize the local community were more receptive but tended to look upon the commandos as a mobile medical service, although patrol commanders tried to discourage the villagers from becoming too reliant on their visits. Movement in some areas was very difficult and one patrol, proceeding from Jalacte to Esprino, had the choice of wading through knee-deep mud or

Lt J Morgan leading his troop on patrol Belize. Photo: 40 Commando.

Marine Richards of G Company live firing at Baldy Beacon 1986.
Photo: 40 Commando.

hacking a path through thick secondary jungle.

Christmas Day at the outposts was little different to any other hot and humid day in the jungle but patrols and OP personnel were pleased to receive seasonal greetings from Lt Col Hooper, who visited every unit location during the day. At the end of his six hour flight in a Gazelle helicopter he cooled off by plunging fully clothed into an air sea rescue raft filled with water! The Recce Troop – patrolling the border well off the beaten track – made a rendezvous with their Troop Commander Lt J. McKinney, as instructed, and found a traditional Christmas dinner awaiting their attention. Lt McKinney had felled timber to construct a table and benches, and the Quartermaster, Capt G. Atherton and dentist, Lt J.Main had travelled mainly on four wheel drive for three hours to deliver the turkey and plum pudding.

In mid January 1986, the unit took part in a major defence exercise Mayan Sword, involving all British forces and the BDF in Belize. Designed to test the response to an armed incursion in the Toledo District, A and C Companies undertook the defence while the northern companies acted as enemy and provided the umpires. The Commander British Forces Belize, Brig D.B.W.Webb-Carter OBE,MC, was most impressed with the combat performance and fitness of the commando personnel, evident during the six days of intense activity.

A programme of training, phased into the operational commitments during February, enabled each company to spend one week in the northern territory field firing, with Harrier, artillery, mortar and Milan support. This was followed by a civil defence exercise, to test the unit's involvement in civil aid procedures prior to and in the aftermath of a hurricane or similar natural disaster. In the second half of the tour, the commando personnel manning the outpost at Salamanca and administrative staff in Airport Camp exchanged duties for two weeks to provide a contrast to their otherwise restricted routine.

Also, in contrast to its main role, the Commando provided substantial aid to the local community and took part in sponsored charities during the deployment. Two container loads of clothing collected by the Commando Wives Club and Norton Fitzwarren RN Association, were shipped to Belize and presented to the Belize Red Cross. A team of athletes, who took time off to run in a non-stop relay from Miami to Washington, raised funds for the American drug rehabilitation charity Genesis. The commandos in Belize also organised a half marathon and raised £800 towards the Taunton Guide Dogs Appeal. In another practical way, the AE Section – supervised by WO2 J.Leach – constructed a concrete and timber footbridge over the Jalacte Creek, thereby linking a village community previously divided by the river. The task was not completed without incident. In the absence of roads the concrete piers were carried to the site one at a time in a sling suspended from a helicopter. One load slipped its moorings and its whereabouts are unknown to this day!

Although a conventional sports programme was restricted by the nature of the unit's deployment and operational commitments, every opportunity was taken to involve personnel in adventure training. The facilities at the Forces Adventure Training Center at St Georges Cay were excellent and a total of 500 men attended the courses (24 per week), in diving, sailing, water-skiing and canoeing. Further north, a team of climbers from the Recce Troop scaled Victoria Peak. The unit also had the use of the Corps Yacht *Per Mare,* while it was in Belizean waters during the last six weeks of the tour.

The arrival of the advance party of the 3rd Battalion Queen's Regiment on 3 April signalled the end of the tour and a week later the main body of 40 Commando returned to UK for post deployment leave. As a result of long periods of deployment to the Falklands (1982), South Armagh (1983), Cyprus (1984) and Belize (1985), several personnel, who were in the unit for all these commitments, spent as much as 75% of their time away from home. Despite this unit morale remained very high. Shortly after returning to UK it was announced by the Commander British Forces that the Belize Personal Certificate of Commendation had been awarded to CSgt R.C. Sheppard, Sgt S.England, Cpl E.A.Conway and Cpl.A.Lee for outstanding service during the tour.

The primary task after leave consisted of implementing a number of planned changes to the Commando organisation, with the introduction of eight men / two fire team rifle sections (three sections to each rifle troop) and the amalgamation of the Recce and Surveillance Troops. The task was complicated by a major change round of personnel but the training programme was soon in full swing and included an exchange visit between A Company and the French Commandos Marine. Elements of C Company flew to Gibraltar for raiding training and two sections of the Recce Troop visited the Netherlands to work with the Dutch Marine Reservists. The remainder of the unit carried out a revised APWT at Altcar Ranges, wearing the new combat helmet and, for some of the tests, the NBC kit.

The July FTX at Otterburn was held in idyllic weather unlike the arctic conditions experienced on the units' previous visit. However, torrential rain during the withdrawal phase on the last night soaked all those present. Shortly after returning to Norton Manor Camp a signal to "stand by to move in 72 hours", caused a mild flutter but it proved to be a false alarm and unit personnel, breathing a sigh of relief, proceeded on summer leave. The latter part of August was allocated to sub unit training, sports team trials, NBC courses and preparations for two major NATO exercises involving 3 Commando Brigade.

40 Commando and elements of the supporting arms were allocated to the MV *Bolero,* a Norwegian car ferry for passage to Norway, Denmark and West Germany, where the exercises were to be held. The initial work-up landing in UK was cancelled due to poor weather but rigid raider training and scramble-net trials were carried out off Cape Rough before the Norwegian exercise Blue Fox commenced at Larvic, the first which 40 Commando had carried out under command of 3 Commando Brigade in over three years. Re-embarking on 16 September, the unit visited the Danish port of Alburg to play local teams

A Company make a heliborne assault landing on Masirah. Photo: 40 Commando.

at football and other sports before sailing to Germany for the amphibious phase of the final exercise. According to the local press it was a most convivial visit "Early risers in town can see Danish-British relations of a very friendly nature – young Danish ladies wearing military jackets and freezing British gentlemen in shirtsleeves on their way home from the pleasures of night life."

Ex Bold Guard, was primarily a corps field training exercise centred on Schleswig Holstein. After landing in LCUs and LCVPs, 40 Commando advanced inland through flat country to establish a defensive position in the rear of the enemy positions. Before the Commando defences could be tested the exercise – in so far as 40 Commando was concerned – ended. The unit returned to UK by way of Virgin Airways to make the most of an administrative interlude before the MGRM Commando Forces visited Norton Manor Camp on 16 October. On the same day the unit boxing team won the Corps Championships.

The new S80 in use for the first time during exercises on the Island of Masirah August 1986. Photo: 40 Commando.

A composite 40 Commando force of 280 all ranks embarked in HMS *Intrepid* on 23 October for the purpose of carrying out an amphibious landing in Oman. The joint Oman-UK exercise Swift Sword, involved 5,000 British service personnel and was designed to test lessons learned in the Falklands conflict and to demonstrate Britain's ability to implement the rapid deploymment of a tri-service force outside NATO.

The exercise scenario was broadly a request from the Sultan of Oman for help to repel incursion from an unfriendly neighbour. The logistics involved were considerable and complex, involving the deployment of an amphibious force and flying in airborne troops. The ability to fly attack aircraft direct from UK was tested and six Tornados accomplished the 4,200 mile journey to Masirah non stop in 10 hours, refuelling from Tristar tankers seven times. However, the troops committed to the sea passage had a longer more leisurely trip.

Acclimatisation and the importance of maintaining battle fitness received special attention. A brief stop at Gibraltar gave the marines another opportunity to break the top of the rock record and live firing of company weapons. Lectures and daily PT on the way to Cyprus – where the temperature was in the seventies – prepared the force for field training in the Western Sovereign Base Area. Continuing onward through the Suez Canal *Intrepid* stopped at Djibouti (90° plus) for a port call mid-November, before proceeding to the final destination at Masirah where the Omanis had developed a substantial air base.

The amphibious and airborne phase of the exercise was observed by the Sultan of Oman, senior military and government personnel from UK and Oman, and representatives of the international press. The Commando force made the landing in eight landing craft, two Seaking Mk IV assault helicopters from *Intrepid* and four Seaking Mk ASW Helicopters from HMS *Illustrious*. With several tons of battle simulation pyrotechnics and the support of Sea Harriers, Jaguars, RAF Tornados and Naval gun-fire from HMS *Nottingham*, the overall effect of 250 men of 40 Commando storming up the beach was quite impressive.

The four day exercise which followed, with elements of the Sultan of Oman's land forces, gave those taking part an impression of the desert in all its moods. The scorching heat of the daytime advance through the Shiya Pass and footslog up the mountainside to attack the enemy. A 20° drop in nightime temperature, torrential rain and flash-flooding of a dry wadi with B Company half way across during a night advance, were all good experience! The final low level heliborne assault by 40 Commando, observed once again by the Sultan and a large audience, was an impressive end to the exercise. The return journey commenced on 1 December and the unit was home for Christmas.

On 9 December, the Secretary of State for Defence, Mr George Younger, who had watched the amphibious landing in Oman, officially changed Government policy on the UK Amphibious Capability, by announcing in the House of Commons that it was the Governments intention to retain an amphibious capability in the longer term. He informed members that a contract had been placed with Swan Hunter for a feasibility study for extending the life of HMS *Fearless* and HMS *Intrepid* and that industry had been invited to participate in feasibility studies for a new design for their replacement by building new ships in parallel with this work. Also, consideration would be given to the provision of an Aviation Support Ship. This was welcome news throughout the Royal Navy and Royal Marines.

In the west country it seemed appropriate to match the winter training to the climate and although the snow in January 1987 was a shade thin on the ground, the mountain warfare element of snow and mountain warfare training was taken seriously. Sub units practised basic climbing techniques before travelling north to Garlochhead for two weeks progressive hill marching, climbing, abseiling and tactical exercises on mountain slopes. In contrast, B Company maintained contact with the sun by flying south-east to Brunei for five weeks jungle warfare acquaint.

Company personnel, who tested a new jungle boot, designed to drain quickly after wading through rivers or mangrove swamp, arrived in Brunei to find that the weather was abnormally dry. One unfortunate marine was badly hurt after falling head first through Mangrove tree roots which were normally well covered by swamp water. The company also found itself involved with a jungle fire that escaped their control and destroyed their Company longhouse, rations and reserve water supply. Having absorbed a few unexpected lessons of jungle survival the men relaxed on a final week of R and R. Those more adventurous travelled as far as Thailand and Australia.

The unit bid farewell to Lt Col Hooper on 24 March 1987, prior to his departure to assume the new post of Corps Colonel at the Commando Training Centre Royal Marines. His successor, Lt Col J.S.Chester OBE, barely had time to make acquaintance with his sub units before C Company was on its way to London, for the official visit of King Fahd of Saudi Arabia, and A Company were en route to the Mediterranean in RFA *Sir Percival* for Ex Dragon Hammer. This was a large NATO naval exercise in which the American Sixth Fleet played a prominent role. A Company, plus a detachment of the Anti Tank Troop, formed part of the amphibious force comprised of elements of the Netherlands Marine Corps, US Marine Corps, Foreign Legion and Italian Tactical Group. After a series of fleet manouvres – unofficially monitored by ships of the Warsaw Pact – the amphibious force carried out landings and tactical exercises on the southern tip of Sardinia. Towards the end of the exercise A Company practised Special Patrol Insertion and Extraction with Chinnook helicopters of the USMC. The 200 ft drop from the helicopters to the ground harnessed to the end of a cable, was exhilarating and increased the flow of adrenalin of even the most relaxed marines making the descent.

While A and B Companies were away, the unit ran its first triathlon meeting. The field of 31 entrants started the course with a 400 metre swim at the Wellington Sports Centre, followed by a 20 miles cycle ride around the lanes of Somerset to Norton Manor Camp where competitors completed the event with a six mile run. Although only a limited number of personnel were able to compete, the triathlon made a welcome alternative to the standard sports events and provided considerable interest for the spectators.

The unit was reunited for the Altcar APWT at the beginning of June and then deployed to various locations. The Recce Troop assisted 42 Commando with their Spearhead training. The AE Troop exercised its demolition capability on a Kent range before constructing a footbridge in the Quantock hills and a public footpath along a dangerous stretch of road between Cross Keys and Norton Manor Camp. A Company prepared for an amphibious demonstration with HMS *Intrepid* and street lining in London, for the State Visit of King Hassan II of Morocco. B Company covered the local summer display commitments and exercised on Salisbury Plain while elements of C Company visited Jersey for adventure training and a more local area for a rural OP exercise.

During the summer the new S80 personal weapon replacing the SLR was issued to the unit. The radically different shape and size of the weapon gave the drill instructors a headache but the Corps shooting squad – formed at CTCRM in March – achieved excellent results with the S80 at Bisley in June. Even so, a member of 40 Commando was heard to comment that "While the Commando Fitness Test is now fractionally easier, the eight mile speed march

Lt Col Chester firing Phase One of the Annual Platoon Weapons Test at Altcar June 1987. Photo: 40 Commando.

with 30 lb belt, plus weapon and helmet, followed by a 90 metre firemans lift, is no laughing matter!"

Headquarter staff and elements of Signals troop held two Command Post exercises between July and September and most officers and NCOs were tested in the Battle Group Trainer at Bovington. The old GPMG Troop re-formed under the new name of Sustained Fire Troop and, after a month's work-up, deployed to Sennybridge where, in a week of intense activity the Troop fired 75,000 rounds. During all these activities the MT Section provided vehicles and drivers for every conceivable task from operational commitments to the mundane fetch and carry trips without which the unit would fail to function effectively. The MTO at this time was Lt A.J. Sankey, grandson of Lt Col Sankey who commanded the unit in Albania and Italy in World War II.

Training commenced in July for the Northern European Command Infantry Competition programmed for 5-9 October 1987 in Denmark. A Corps representative team from 42 Commando won the competition in 1986 and Lt R. Hall, in charge of the 40 Commando, eight man team from C Company, accepted the challenge to better their score. The team concentrated on developing an all round knowledge of infantry skills in preparation for a wide variety of events. These included machine gun and S80 team and individual shoots, grenade

GROUP TRAINER - BOVINGTON

"Do we attack or withdraw?" The Battle Group Trainer in full swing. Bovington, June 1987. Photo: 40 Commando.

throwing, map reading, first aid, night firing and an obstacle course. The concluding 9.3 mile cross country was a timed event, with a river crossing (by inflatable), a 1,640 yds run over wet sand and a team shoot. Although the 40 Commando team was first overall until the cross country, it lost vital seconds on the river crossing and was pipped at the post by the Royal Hampshires.

A revision of the Corps and Unit Memorable Dates undertaken in 1986 resulted in a change to the WW II date commemorated by 40 Commando from 19 August – The Raid on Dieppe, to 3 October – The Landing at Termoli. The unit held the first Termoli Day Parade on 2 October 1987, in wet conditions not unlike those experienced during the actual landing at Termoli in 1943.

During the following month the unit deployed to Stanford for field training in preparation for Ex Purple Warrior. Held in south west Scotland from 3 to 21 November, it was the largest in a series of tri-service exercises held annually since the Falklands campaign and comprised the largest British amphibious force to assemble since the Korean War.

The task force successfully put ashore 6,000 men, 2,500 vehicles and 3,500 tons of equipment. 40 Commando carried out a variety of tasks including a simultaneous amphibious/airborne landing in conjunction with 42 Commando and 1 Para Battalion Group, the evacuation of civilians, provision of patrols and OPs, and a full scale Commando attack. Although the Commando could not have been made more welcome aboard HMS *Illustrious* operating in the LPH role, the lack of training spaces, adequate living facilities, including eating spaces and ablutions areas were irritating factors which, over a period of time, could have lead to a loss of efficiency.

Preparations for a Northern Ireland Tour commenced in December and, with a short pause for Christmas leave, continued through to February 1988. The Commando relieved the 2nd Battalion Scots Guards in South Armagh on 23 February and immediately became involved in the task of policing the funerals of two PIRA terrorists who had died in an explosion of their own making. The security operations at Crossmaglen and Cullyhanna were extensive and at one stage Lt Col Chester had 11 companies and 20 helicopters under command. The unit was also responsible for policing the 10 mile route from the border through Newry for the cortege of three PIRA terrorists shot in Gibraltar by SAS personnel.

Two substantial explosives finds and the arrest of a terrorist were highlights in between surveillance, extensive patrolling averaging 45 a day, the manning of 200 vehicle check points and almost as many OPs. Rarely a week passed without the appearance of one or more visitors, mostly of senior military rank but politicians, civil servants and other dignitaries were included. The Archbishop of Armagh and Primate of All Ireland, the Most Reverend R.H.A. Eames chose Good Friday for his tour of the company locations.

The unit experienced on average a major incident every other week. An Army dog handler and his dog were both killed in an explosion while operating with a Commando patrol in the Crossmaglen area and the pilot of one of the Lynx helicopters was forced to make a landing when his aircraft was hit by machine-gun fire. A continuously high threat throughout the tour kept all personnel alert and intent on their job, up to the time of hand over to the 1st Battalion Parachute Regiment on 18 July 1988.

CHAPTER 23

19 July 1988 to 14 February 1992

Termoli Day, the 45th anniversary – Inspections and exercises –
Supercession of COs – Jungle training in Brunei, Mountain training at
Garelochead and Adventure Training world wide – A multi national
amphibious exercise in Sardinia and acquaint with the Egyptian army –
Deployment to Norway – Humanitarian aid to the Kurds in Iraq.

HOME once again from Norway the Commando concentrated on the immediate task of completing all post tour administration and reorganisation before summer leave. Between 12 September and 1 October 1988 the emphasis was directed towards re-training for priority roles and preparations for Termoli Day. Unit participation in Ex Teamwork, a large scale biennial maritime exercise designed to test NATO's forward strategy in the North Norwegian Sea and to exercise elements of the 4th USMC Expeditionary Brigade and UK/Netherlands land forces, consisted mainly of the provision of directing staff and transport. The September landings were programmed in conjunction with a major Norwegian national field training exercise and involved 45,000 service personnel of seven nations, 216 ships and submarines and 570 aircraft.

Three weeks of planning and preparation ensured the success of Termoli Day at Norton Manor Camp on 1 October, the nearest appropriate Saturday to the 45th anniversary of the actual landing. Gen Sir Peter and Lady Hellings, Maj Gen Thompson and 60 members of the 40 RM Commando (1942-46) Association, accompanied by their wives, were invited by Lt Col Chester to join the unit on this occasion. A large gathering of families and friends turned out in strength to watch 40 Commando parading with the Queen's and Regimental Colours accompanied by the 40 RM Commando Association and the Band of RM Commandos. The Drum Head Service was conducted by the Rev E.W. Jones and on its conclusion Maj Gen Thompson presented Northern Ireland General Service Medals to representative personnel of the unit and Wrens who had served with the unit in Armagh. Also, he presented a new standard to the 40 RM Commando Association before taking the salute at the march past of all on parade. After a splendid buffet lunch the visitors were entertained to a full afternoon of sports activities, abseil, free fall parachute and static displays and the day ended with the ceremony of Beat Retreat.

The unit programme for the final quarter of the year was a busy mixture of MT, Medical, Dental, Church and Staff inspections, Battle Fitness Tests; exercises on the Bovington Battle Group Trainer, company field training exercises, field firing and a Soviet Week in which ranks were acquainted with

Ex Fenn Fighter II Thetford November 1988. Photos: 40 Commando.

Lt Col Chester and Maj Bruce move forward to establish Tactical Headquarters during Ex Rolling Deep 1988.

*Exercising Landing
Drills from Rigid
Raiding Craft.
Photo: 40 Commando.*

Russian army operations, tactics and equipment.

Selected officers and NCOs from A Company flew to Brunei to attend a Jungle Warfare Instructors Course and the unit deployed to Thetford for Ex Fenn Fighter II, a continuation exercise of that held the previous year. The commitments did not end with the start of Christmas leave. As a result of the Pan Am air disaster over Lockerbie 51 men of A Company under command of Lts Hall and Thorpe, were recalled on 27 December to assist at the scene of the incident. Their primary task was to recover pieces of aircraft that had been scattered through the pine forests for subsequent investigation into the cause of the explosion.

Lt Col Chester said farewell to the unit on 17 January 1989, after nearly two years as CO and Lt Col A.D. Wray – having just completed a M Phil degree at Cambridge University – assumed command of the unit. The supercession was well timed. Maj Gen N.F. Vaux DSO, had only completed his formal inspection

367

of the unit six days earlier and the entire Commando was in first class shape and prepared for all eventualities.

A Company spent the period between mid February and mid March in Brunei having completed four days acclimatisation training in Hong Kong en route. The Brunei deployment followed a similar pattern to that of previous years. The company adapted well to the different demands of tactics in the jungle and a high level of professionalism was maintained throughout. Durability of the jungle boots was tested and it was noticeable that men wearing the old UK pattern boot required four to five pairs during the deployment whereas the new boots showed little sign of deterioration in the same period.

The main body of the unit deployed to Scotland for mountain training where the MLs accomplished their task well. All ranks at Garelochead completed the final phase of the course despite periods of very poor visibility and 120mph winds which threatened to blow them off the mountainside. Mne Seabrook of C Company was trapped in his tent by a fallen tree and was fortunate not to have been impaled.

Two weeks later, an almost deserted Camp at Taunton indicated that a three week Commando Adventure Training programme was in full swing. Groups of men took off to all quarters of the globe on a wide variety of projects. Imagination, persuasion, careful planning and positive thinking all played a part in providing what would, for many, be a once in a lifetime opportunity to achieve something spectacular. Although the men dug deep into their savings the outlay for some of the projects was considerable and sponsorship was obtained from a number of service and civilan sources. One group of nine men led by Cpl F. Perry accomplished a world record, cycling – in relay – from Perth to Sydney, Australia; covering the 2,796 miles in five days, nine hours and four minutes. Lt Jones and a team of sub-aqua divers travelled to Orkney to view the remains of the German High Seas Fleet, scuttled in 1919 at their moorings in the icy waters of Scapa Flow while another group, led by Lt P. Mansell*, flew to Florida for an Accelerated Free Fall Course followed by four days with the RM Free Fall Team on the west coast of America.

Shortly after Easter Leave the unit embarked in HMS *Intrepid* and two RFAs to take part in the multi-national amphibious Ex Dragon Hammer. After a rough sea passage to Gibraltar the UK Force joined ships of the USA, Spanish and Italian navies for landings on the hot, arid coastline of southern Sardinia on 21/22 April. A and B Companies were heliborne inland while C Company with 1 ACG carried out beach assaults. After securing the target and completing the withdrawal the Commando re-embarked and sailed to Brindisi for a cross training exercise with the Italian San Marco Battalion. During the period of deployment in Italy Lt Col Wray and a representative group from the Commando visited Termoli while other groups were invited to the USAF base

* A previous OC of the RM Free Fall Team.

at San Vito. At Termoli, the 40 Commando group, in company with J. Farmer and J. Humphrey, veterans of the 1942-46 40 RM Commando, were greeted by Dr Dalla Torre, Mayor of Termoli, on the site where Gen Montgomery had congratulated the Commando after the battle for the town. The visitors were given a guided tour of the town and after lunch, provided by the Termoli Town Council, attended a memorial service at the Sangro River War Cemetery where members of 40 RM Commando are interred. Before returning to UK the amphibious force called at Civitavecchia where most Commando personnel took the opportunity to visit Rome.

C Company and elements of Support Company separated from the main body at Gibraltar and sailed to the West Indies in HMS *Intrepid* to exercise with elements of the USMC, RNLMC, and Barbados Defence Force. Their tour took them to Florida, Vieques, Curacao and Aruba, then on to Grenada and Barbados. At the conclusion of the tour the detachment had, in three months, exercised in eight countries with 13 nationalties.

B Company flew by commercial airline to Holland to exercise with a company of the RNLMC while a RNLMC company spent a similar period with 40 Commando in Taunton. Meanwhile A Company drilled at the RN shore establishment HMS *Excellent,* Portsmouth, for London Ceremonial duties and B Company, on its return, prepared for duties at the Royal Tournament. During this period Lt M.J.Fountaine, who was appointed Second-in-Command of Headquarter Company on joining the unit in September 1987 and later commanded 2 Troop A Company, died at Portsmouth, on 5 June 1989, as a result of a regrettable diving accident. At the beginning of September, 3 Commando Brigade assembled on Salisbury Plain for field training, with the object of exercising all elements of the Brigade in the all arms battle. The training period culminated with a mighty demonstration of strength and fire power, with the Brigade exercising withdrawal in contact, defence and a breakout to attack an enemy armour and infantry concentration. At the Royal Marines School of Music, Deal, 11 Band Corporals and Musicians became the victims of a PIRA bomb attack, on the morning of 22 September.

In the 20th Northern European Command Infantry Competition in West Germany on 11/12 October 1989 the B Company team led by Lt G Beeson was placed second, while on the sports scene unit teams won the Corps Fencing, Rugby and Hockey Championships and were runners up in the Corps Boxing and Volleyball.

The Brecon Beacons were chosen as the location for a counter revolutionary warfare exercise – Fenn Fighter – in November, with personnel of Support Company dressed realistically for their part as the enemy and members of the local community. On return to Taunton the unit made ready for a visit by the Representative Colonel Commandant, Lt Gen Sir John Richards, a seminar on 'The Soviet Threat' and the Formal Inspection by Maj Gen Vaux.

Storm force winds sweeping across England in January 1990, caused extensive damage in the west country but surprisingly little in Norton Manor Camp.

Abseil demonstration by Recce Troop at Norton Manor Camp 1989.
Photo: 40 Commando.

The unit responded quickly to calls for help and working parties were employed in the clearance of storm debris and trees from overhead power lines and blocked roads. A fortunate few were able to turn their backs on the winter weather. Headquarter staff reconnoitred future exercise locations in the Mediterranean and B Company personnel were happy to pack their bags for Brunei, knowing that conditions would have improved by the time they returned in March.

Travelling northwards, A, C and Support Companies renewed their acquaintance with the Scottish mountains while a composite group of 50 corporals and marines crossed the North Sea to Norway to complete the first Novice Ski and Survival and Infantry Winter Warfare courses organised by 45 Commando. A smaller group of six PWs on a three weeks attachment to the survey vessel HMS *Herald,* coped with the task of familiarising the ships company in the use of the S80 and other small arms on a heaving deck in the North Atlantic. With this wide and varied start to the year the unit was well prepared for all eventualities.

Before the main body deployed to the Mediterranean in April, selected personnel were tasked to put their Advanced First Aid qualifications (FA2) to practical use in London during the National Ambulance Strike. Closer to home Cpl. K Davidson (FA1), found himself called upon to act as assistant midwife at the delivery of his daughter, a situation that provided him with the incentive to upgrade to FA2 as soon as possible! Mne G. R. Simmons was also in the news following the announcement that he had received the Royal Humane Society Bravery Award in recognition of saving a man from drowning off Bridgewater on 29 July 1989.

HMS *Intrepid* and the RFAs *Sir Percivale* and *Sir Tristram,* with 40 Commando Group embarked, joined forces with amphibious elements of the Italian, French, Spanish, Dutch and USA navies off Sicily at the end of April. The combined NATO group carried out landings in the mountainous region of Sardinina, taking turns at providing the opposition. Unfettered by preconceived plans or restrictions the force commanders enjoyed a free hand in planning their movements. 40 Commando, with W Company RNLMC, a troop of the Blues and Royals, elements of 59 Independent Commando Squadron RE and 29 Commando Regiment RA plus the San Marco Tactical Group, all under command of Lt Col Wray, carried out a successful landing and advance before they in turn became the defenders against a larger force of American, French and Italian troops.

After a period of cross training and a 48 hour port call at Crete the UK force moved on to Egypt where it was joined by C Company Group, 3rd Battalion Queen's Regiment. A further session of cross training and a field exercise with the Egyptian forces followed. The final phase consisted of a Commando attack and night defence with the unit and supporting arms, firing live ammunition. All in all, a spectacular ending to proceedings viewed by Maj Gen R.J. Ross OBE, who had succeeded Maj Gen Vaux as MGRM Commando Forces.

On the homeward leg through the Mediterranean, 3 Troop A Company received orders to join HMS *Phoebe* at Gibraltar and proceeded to Liberia – in the wake of the Liberian National Patriotic Front's uprising – to be ready to take off British nationals if this became necessary. After four weeks of cruising up and down with 3 Troop at two hours notice to land, the political situation in Liberia stabilised sufficiently to allow HMS *Phoebe* and 3 Troop to return to their normal duties. In the meantime the unit was involved in security commitments for the Navy, street lining ceremonial, the Royal Tournament, recruiting for the Corps and annual inspections. Cpl R. Stenhouse and Mne Chambers cycled 1,400 miles from Gibraltar to Taunton, to raise £1,050 for the childrens ward of a local hospital. Sports representatives of the unit also made their mark in the Corps Tennis Championships and John Munnings Memorial Triathlon.

Families Day was held on 1 September 1990, a month earlier than usual, to slot into the programme before the unit took part in a 3 Commando Brigade amphibious exercise, in the area of Namsos in October. Ex Teamwork provided all unit personnel with an excellent introduction to arctic warfare in Norway and preparations for 40 Commando's first Norwegian deployment continued on their return to Taunton. Various members of the unit departed to or returned from duties in sunnier regions but the majority were more concerned with the imminent move north. In addition to the acquisition of Mountain and Arctic Warfare equipment and other items essential for living and fighting in close proximity to the arctic circle, the Quartermasters department was also involved in supercession musters. Lt Col Wray, having commanded the unit for 22 months, handed over the helm to Lt Col C.G.H. Dunlop on 1 November 1990, before taking up his new appointment as Chief of Staff, Commando Forces.

Although 3 Commando Brigade was not involved in the war with Iraq the Corps was committed to numerous activities in the campaign. Detachments served aboard HM ships in the Gulf and personnel were deployed in support of the Joint Headquarters in High Wycombe and Joint Force Headquarters in Riyadh. During this period 40 Commando, lean in manpower, deployed to Norway on 13 January 1991 for its first prolonged contact with the arctic. The three rifle companies based at Ose and the Support Company at Malselvfossen, were soon immersed in the Novices Ski and Survival Course, learning the essentials of staying upright on skis and avoiding trees, experiencing their first plunge into icy water, and sleeping in snow holes. Although these preliminaries are well known to personnel who have served in 42 and 45 Commandos they were a comparatively new experience to nearly 50 per cent of the personnel in 40 Commando, sometimes referred to as the "Sunshine Commando".

Training progressed to the Winter Warfare Course and sub unit exercises, before the entire unit – with HMS *Fearless* and 539 Assault Squadron – tested the ability of the 3rd Norwegian Battalion and a French Alpine company to defend Harstad. Well before the winter deployment ended, the enthusiasts were extolling the advantages of uninterrupted training on the Northern Flank of NATO and comparing notes on the use of skis or snow shoes in tactical situations. Jungle boots and tropical diseases were no longer a topic of conversation.

Returning to Somerset and an English spring, preparations were made to provide a Street Lining Party at Windsor for the State Visit of His Excellency the President of the Republic of Poland. However, the unit swiftly adapted to new plans when, on 18 April, Lt Col Dunlop informed all ranks that they were about to deploy to North Iraq.*

A Combined Allied Task Force of 5,000, consisting of 40 and 45 Commandos with Naval helicopter support, Army and RAF personnel and a further 1,000 from the Dutch army and RNLMC, were to deploy under a Combined Force Headquarters commanded by Maj Gen Ross. The object of Operation Haven was to provide humanitarian aid and security to thousands of Kurdish refugees who fled to the mountains on the Turkish – Iraq border to escape reprisals from Iraq forces following the failure of the Kurdish uprising at the end of the Gulf War. Television coverage portrayed severe weather conditions, with snow and slush in many areas and freezing temperatures at night. The refugees lacked warm clothing and many were barefeet. Shelter was non existent and food and water scarce.

The advance party comprising the COs of 40 and 45 Cdos and key members of their HQ staff flew to Diyabakir in Eastern Turkey on 20 April where they were briefed on arrival by members of 3 Commando Brigade Staff. Lt Col Dunlop received instructions to join forces with Task Force Alpha, comprised mainly of the US Army 10th Special Forces Group (SFG). The SFG had established itself along the border early in the crisis after Operation Granby to organise refugee encampments in close co-operation with the Turkish authorities and the RAF and USAF who were dropping supplies. They had managed to gather the quarter million people into six identifiable but very squalid camps high in the mountains and although providing food distribution, basic sanitation and health care they were fighting a losing battle against loss of life from starvation and disease.

The CO of 45 Commando was instructed to team up with Task Force Bravo. This force was based on the American 24 Marine Expeditionary Unit (MEU) who had landed from the US Sixth Fleet and crossed the border into Zacho on the day the Commando advance party arrived. Their mission was to establish a zone clear of all Iraqi military personnel in which the refugees could be re-established.

The RAF carried the main body of 40 Commando to Diyabakir in Eastern Turkey and American Chinooks lifted the unit to Silopi, close to the Iraqi and Syrian borders. They arrived to find this lower region dry and dusty and the

---

* A Company completed the ceremonial commitment and flew to Iraq three days later.

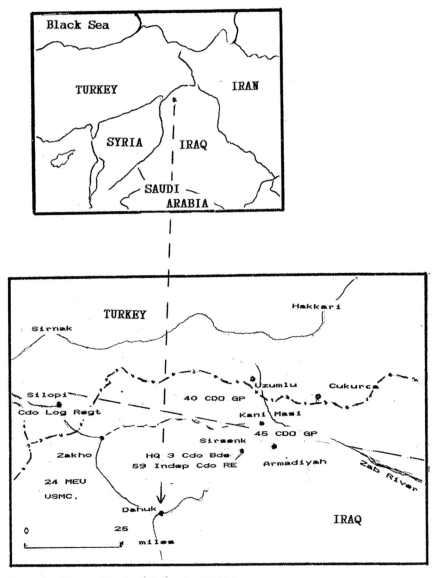

Operation Haven, Northern Iraq, April 1991

374

temperature in the seventies. Initially Lt Col Dunlop was instructed to extend his operations along the border to look after any refugees in the mountains as far east as Iran but aerial reconnaissance showed this area to be clear. At the same time the plan to extend the safe zone east of Zakho had been developing. Task Force A was directed to exploit southwards from the border (see map) and when this was completed Task Force B were to move eastwards across the front of Task Force A.

40 Commando commenced the exploitation on Tue 30 April. B Company completed a helicopter assault landing into Balokah to secure the river bridge thereby opening up the route to the mountain camp at Cukurca. C Company moved by road, previously cleared by 45 Commando, to Begova and A Company with Commando HQ were heliborne to Kani Balav to establish a blocking position. Support Company then moved into Kani Masi. Two days later 45 Commando exploited across the front of Task Force Alpha as far as Al Amadiyah. A French Battalion and 3rd Battalion US Special Forces then established positions to the east and south.

In the first few days of early May, 40 Commando's task was to move the people down from the mountains into areas where they could be either sent home or looked after with reasonable care and attention. The unit had until mid-March to accomplish the task as it was estimated that the local water resources would have dried up beyond this time.

B Company established a camp on the banks of the Great Zab River at the eastern end of the valley and then commenced to help the 130,000 Kurdish refugees from Cukurka Camp down the mountains to the road head,where they were put into trucks and moved on to Support Company.

The OC Support Company, Capt D.McKinney MBE, established a Refugee Movement Camp in the almost totally destroyed mountain village of Kani Masi, in North Iraq 10 miles from the Turkish border. The camp was the equivalent of an enormous bus terminus, with medical, sanitation and feeding facilities. Capt McKinney had charge of an international force of service and civilian personnel, medical teams and engineers who administered to thousands of refugees funnelled through the camp. When they were fit to continue the journey they were taken by truck in family groups to their homes in 45 Commando's area. During a six weeks period in that location 210,000 passed through the Centre. Of this number 100,000 were supplied with food and water and moved by trucks (3,000 truckloads) to their homes. Surg Lt F.O'Kelly, the unit medical officer, established a hospital centre in which 10,000 refugees, mostly children under four years of age, received treatment for everything from malnutrition to gunshot wounds.

Meanwhile C Company and Reservists from RMR Scotland, deployed initially to Begova, a town which apart from myriads of mosquitos, was only partially inhabited as most of the 4,500 population had fled to the hills and mountains. A few days were spent organising the distribution of food and water and providing medical aid to the community before the company moved further north to Nadzur. The mountain village was a burnt out shell in which exhausted and hungry women and children huddled together for warmth after walking across the mountains from a camp on the Turkish side of the border. The company had the task of establishing a safe route for the refugees returning south.

A Company maintained the route over the hills to the south – little more than a track winding along and down the mountainside – and worked hard to maintain this line of communication while assisting the refugees towards the safe havens.

Almost as soon as the unit arrived, Ardil ad Rasheed Beg, the leader of the Bawari tribe, made contact with 40 Commando. The tribe had originally lived in the valley now occupied by the unit but had been move out when Iraq and Turkey, by mutual agreement carried out a process of de-population along their border. Ardil ad Rasheed looked upon the arrival of the Commando as an ideal opportunity to resettle his people in the valley and regain some degree of the old power base. However, many Kurds had become better educated and more sophisticated after their resettlement further south and only a fairly small number wished to return to the more traditional tribal life of the hills. Nevertheless, their numbers provided a counter flow into the valley and A Company moved to Mosoka, the centre of a large area of villages destroyed in the de-population process, to help with the major "hearts and minds" programme of resettlement.

From mid-May until the end of July the unit was involved in a concurrent and entirely national operation searching for three missing BBC journalists. They were reported to have hired the services of a Turkish Kurd in late March to take them across the border from Turkey into Iraq to cover the uprising. Nothing further was heard of them.

An Iraq Kurd arrived at Brigade HQ in mid-May with information of their whereabouts. Thought initially to be alive and in an area inhabited by members of the PKK*, who operate inside Iraq against the Turks Lt Col Dunlop despatched a company group to find them. It was soon established that they were no longer alive and two bodies were recovered on 23 May. The search for the third body was undertaken by members of the Kurdish Democratic Party and was still continuing when the unit returned to UK.

The evacuation of Kurds from the mountains was completed sooner than expected. Lt T Cook and his troop from B Company supervised the helicopter lift of the last 1,000 people – who were public figures and feared retribution – from Cukurca to Silopi on 31 May. Once it became known that Dahuk, a town the size of Taunton, built to rehouse some of the de-populated people, had been cleared of Iraqi troops, the flow of refugees southward increased rapidly. By mid-June elements of 3 Commando Brigade including 45 Commando and C Company, 40 Commando were able to return to UK.

---

* Kurdish Revolutionary Working Party.

Lt Tim Cook helping with the repatriation of Kurdish refugees from the hills – Iraq 1991. Photo: 40 Commando.

40 Commando now assumed responsibility for a major part of the area previously occupied by Task Force B. Support Company moved to Daudiya, B Company was relocated at Al Amadiyah, alongside the French and A Company, based at Savaratuka, was responsible for patrolling some 300 miles to the south. Commando HQ was based on an Iraqi military airfield at Sirsenk. During this period the Commando was primarily involved with security and rebuilding the confidence of the people. The programme of resettlement, assisting with the building of clinics, reorganising the police, helping to re-establish churches, refurbishing schools and road improvements continued until the main body, less B Company, was recalled to UK on 15 July 1991. B Company moved to Silopi as the British representative force of a multi-national "Rainbow" battalion under command of 3/325 US Airborne, providing an air/land deterrent to any further aggression towards the Kurds by Iraqi forces. C Company relieved B Company in early August and returned to England at the end of September.

On discussing Operation Haven with Lt Col Dunlop he was able to make the following observations "Our role in Safe Haven was a living advertisement for the need for amphibious ships. In the first 10 days our re-supply was provided by American helicopters but once the troops were on the ground this facility could not maintain our requirements. Initially the only transport in our valley was my vehicle Fitted for Radio, used primarily for water supply. Everything else was accomplished on foot and we were dependent on the Americans, who were supplied by sea, until the RFA *Resource* docked in Iskinderen. Thereafter we became logistically self sufficient.

"Our doctor Surg Lt Kelly was instrumental in welding together the military and civil medical organisations from Britain, France, Canada, America, Korea and Australia and it worked superbly. In addition to looking after our own unit and attached personnel he found himself caring for many more civilians and American service personnel. At one stage we had in the unit 24 cases of suspected cholera and many cases of severe vomiting and diarrhoea resulting from contaminated water. There were also a number of American service personnel who required treatment for wounds resulting from mine explosions.

"The Commando had to be brought up to peace time establishment before we left UK. The two hundred men came from all over the Corps including RM Reservists who signed on special short service engagements. It is very much to the credit of the Reservists that they slotted into the companies so well that initially I was unable to distinguish between them and the regulars. After a while many of them were identified as builders, plumbers, plant operators and carpenters and proved very useful. We also received considerable support from British civilians recruited from the Overseas Development Admininstration, all very keen to help."

The unit is now at Norton Manor Camp preparing for the second Norway deployment and will celebrate its 50th anniversary on 14 February 1992 while deployed in the arctic region. Further tours in Northern Ireland may be expected but the rapidly changing situation in world affairs makes it almost impossible to predict the future. It is evident that there will be a new role for the NATO alliance following the collapse of Communism in Europe.

The Royal Marines escaped the swingeing cuts imposed on the armed services in the Options for Change. The ability of sub units of the Corps to respond rapidly to a call for help close to home or half way round the world is well recognised and 3 Commando Brigade is ideally suited for this purpose. The provision of amphibious ships, while guaranteed for the immediate future, is essential to out of area operations but provided the Royal Navy pursues the growing strategic view of the increasing value of fire brigade forces, the need for Royal Marines Commandos, and 40 Commando Royal Marines, is assured.

APPENDIX A

Royal Marine Commando
Provisional War Establishment 7 February 1942

H Q Personnel	Offr	WO	SNCO	JNCO	Mnes	Total	Weapon	Remarks
CO Lieut Col	1					1	revolver	
2I/C Maj	1					1	"	
Adj Capt	1					1	"	
RSM		1				1	TSMG	i/c HQ
NCO i/c clerks			1			1	"	Fighting
HQ TM Gnrs/clerks				1	3	4	"	Troop
/butcher					1	1	"	
/armourer/snipers			1		4	5	rifles	C/Sgt i/c
/carpenters					2	2	"	SniperSec
Batmen/orderlies				1	2	3	TSMG	HQ offrs
Storemen/AA defence/							LMG&	protect'n
Stretcher Bearers				1	10	11		
Total	**3**	**1**	**2**	**3**	**22**	**31**		
Signal Platoon								
NCO i/c C/Sgt			1			1	TSMG	No 11 set
Cpl signaller				4		4	"	No 18 sets
Mne signallers					17	17	revolver	No 38 sets
Total			**1**	**4**	**17**	**22**		
Demolition Platoon								
Subaltern i/c	1					1	revolver	
Pl Sgt			1			1	TSMG	
3 Secs of Cpl&7 Mnes				3	21	24	"	
Batman/orderly					1	1	"	
Total	**1**		**1**	**3**	**22**	**27**		
Close Support Pl								
NCO i/c C/Sgt			1			1	TSMG	6x3" Mor's
3 Secs of Cpl&6 Mnes				3	18	21	TSMG/	6 BoysA/Tk
Batman/orderly					1	1	revolvers rifles	
Total			**1**	**3**	**19**	**23**		
Total HQ's	**4**	**1**	**5**	**13**	**78**	**103**		

APPENDIX A1

Royal Marine Commando
Provisional War Establishment 7 February 1942

Personnel	Offr	WO	SNCO	JNCO	Mnes	Total	Weapons	Remarks
Three Companies each :-								
Company HQ								
Capt i/c	1					1	revolver	
CSM			1			1	TSMG	
CQMS (C/Sgt)			1			1	TSMG	
Clerk					1	1	rifle	HQ
Storeman					1	1	TSMG	fighting
Batmen/Orderly					1	1	"	sec
Total Coy HQ	1		2		3	6		
Three Platoons each Company								
Subaltern i/c	1					1	revolver	
Pl Sgt			1			1	TSMG	
Batman/orderly					1	1	revolver	
Three Secs								
each 1Cpl & 9Mnes				3	27	30	revolvers 3 LMG3 TSMG3 rifles 24	
Total Platoon	1		1	3	28	33		
Total Company	4		5	9	87	105		
Total Cdo HQ	4	1	5	13	78	103		
Total 3 Coys	12		15	27	261	315		
Total RM Cdo	16	1	20	40	339	418		
Medical Section								
MO	1					1		
SBPO*			1			1		
SBA*					2	2		
Total	1		1		2	4		
Camp Staff required in UK								
QM*Lt	1					1	revolver	
Cooks	1			1	6	8	rifles	
Fitter & drivers				1	4	7	"	
Pioneers					8	8	"	
Total	1		1	2	18	24		
Grand Total	18	1	22	42	359	446		

APPENDIX B

OPERATION "HUSKY"

40 ROYAL MARINE COMMANDO.

Operation Order No.1.

REFERENCE.

1. Maps 1/25000 Sheets   277 III   N.E. - S.E. - S.W - N.W.
                          276 II   N.E. - S.E.

INFORMATION.

2. Enemy
     As per HQ.S.S.Bde.Intelligence Summary No.1.

3. Own Tps.
     (a) Order of Battle - General.

         (i) "Husky" is being assaulted by two Divns. on the EAST., two Divs. on the S.E., and two Divs, on the S.W.
        (ii) 30 Corps(1 Cdn.Div.:51 Div.) is making the S.E. assault in the PACHINO PENINSULAR; S.S.Bde.being under cmd.1 Cdn.Div.
       (iii) 1 Cdn.Div.is assaulting on a two-Bde. front with,

                RIGHT ----- 1 Cdn. Inf. Bde.

                LEFT ----- 2 Cdn. Inf. Bde.(supported by S.S.Bde.)

        (iv) 1 A/Tk Bty.will support S.S.Bde during D.1.

     (b) Order of Battle - S.S.Bde.
         (i) S.S.Bde.(HQ S.S.Bde.,40 and 41 R.M.Cdos.)are making an assault on the Left flank of 1 Cdn.Div.
        (ii) This operation is divided into three phases;-

            PHASE I -- The landing and assault on C.D.Bty's and enemy defences 886893-855891.

            PHASE II - The re-organisation on the high ground all incl.rd.junc. 878912 - Pt.26. 878905 (to protect left flank of 1 Cdn.Div.)

            PHASE III- Advance to the high ground 856930 - 845925.

     (c) Plans - S.S.Bde.
         (i) Outline Plan "A".
            41 and 40 R.M.Commandos in that order will land in two successive waves at COVE 880893.41 R.M.Cdo.will establish Beach Head to the EAST. 40 R.M.Cdo.will pass through Beach Head and roll up enemy defences to the WEST. HQ S.S.Bde.will land in centre immediately in rear of 40 R.M Cdo.(Note. 41 R.M.Cdos. tasks are numbered 1 - 6 incl.,40 R.M.Cdos. tasks are numbered 7,8,9. see para.7 below.)
        (ii) Alternative Plan "B".
            If 41 R.M.Cdo.find it impossible to proceed inland,they will re-embark and land at BEACH 871889. In this case,40 R.M.Cdo.will land first followed by 41 R.M.Cdo. 40 R.M.Cdo.will establish the beach head and roll up the enemy defences to the WEST, 41 R.M.Cdo.passing through beach head and destroying enemy defences to the EAST.
       (iii) Alternative Plan "C".
            In the event of either M.V."Derbyshire" or "Durban Castle" being sunk, and troops being unable to land,the remaining Cdo.will land at COVE 880893 and roll up enemy defences to the WEST.

APPENDIX C

Capt JDLaidlaw. RM.

"Y"Tp, 40 RM Commando.

C.M.F.

~ 5th April.

Dear Chapman,

I was extremely sorry that I was unable to come & visit you. Capt Bradley told me that you were in a fairly good state and very shortly I suppose you will be on your way home. You will have heard by now about Wallace & Mr Longland. They both died in Hospital. It was just bloody awful luck

You & Wallace will always be a vivid memory for me. If ever I require a "definition for discipline & devotion to duty" I shall picture two marines getting a stretcher at the double after being told to do so under fire. Fate plays some lousy tricks & that was a mean one if ever there was one. You & he by your courage & selfishness certainly bolstered up morale that morning.

As you know Selfridge is in your Hospital C, Ward Ibelive. He is still in one piece but a bit shaky I hear. I was sorry to hear you had lost a foot. You & Frost will have to go into partnership. He is in blighty now

Bristol. He had a fitting for a new leg the other week & then went out to the nearby pub on his crutches and got merry on four black & tans.

Well I better get on with some news. The Sgt Mjr is now R.S.M. Mr Garbutt and he is doing very well at it too. We have Sgt Major Gordon now esc @ Troop. I think he will fit the bill nicely. Most of the lads are back except Bate & Hopley whose wounds are not quite better. I got back about a week ago. I have also got a stump. I lost my right ring finger. It has very nearly healed over now & will soon be O.K. for some "all In".

Mr Beadle wishes to be remembered to you. He did some great work at Anzio. Mr Dutton is the new officer & he has got 11 Platoon now. He is just the type we want too.

How is the stump getting on? I hope the "Hell" did'nt last too long. I would'nt be very surprised if you should soon run into Frost.

Well Chapman dont be afraid to ask if you think I can help you. I'll be glad to hear from you when you have a few spare minutes. Cheerio for Now!

Yours sincerely

Ian Hawilaw.

384

APPENDIX D

Honours and Awards 1942 -1945

ATySgt	J.R.	Odendaal	30– 4–43	UK	MBE
AMaj	R.D.	Houghton	14–12–45	Dieppe	MC
Lt	K.W.R.	Smale	14–12–45	Dieppe	MC
Mne	G.R.	Bevan	2–10–42	Dieppe	MM
Mne	L.C.	Bradsahw	2–10–42	Dieppe	MM
Mne	T.E.	Breen	2–10–42	Dieppe	MM
Cpl	W.	Ainsworth	23–11–43	Augusta	BEM
Capt	M.J.	Ephraums	2–11–43	Sicily	MC
Lt	T.D.	Morgan	11– 1–44	Pizzo	MC
Lt Col	J.C.	Manners	4– 2–44	Termoli	DSO
Maj	P.W.C.	Hellings	4– 2–44	Termoli	MC
Capt	L.G.B.	Marshall	4– 2–44	Termoli	MC
Capt	J.W.E.	Bradley	4– 2–44	Termoli	MC
CSM	J.J.	Convery	4– 2–44	Termoli	DSM
Cpl	F.G.	Usher	4– 2–44	Termoli	MM
Mne	F.P.	Tyman	4– 2–44	Termoli	MM
Capt	L.G.B.	Marshall	18– 4–44	Garigliano	Bar to MC
Capt	E. W.	Ecrepont	27– 6–44	Italy	MC
Capt	J.P.	O'Brien	18– 4–44	Garigliano	MC
CSM	G.	Malcom	18– 2–44	Garigiano	MM
CSM	K.S	Hawkins	27– 6–44	Italy	MM
CSM	G.A.T.	Johnson	27– 6–44	Italy	MM
Mne	N.	Patrick	18– 4–44	Garigliano	MM
Cpl	J.J.	Gorman	18– 4–44	Garigliano	MM
Lt	J.C.	Beadle	14–12–45	Adriatic	MC
Maj	J.D.	Wakeling	3– 3–44	Adriatic	MC
Lt Col	R. W.	Sankey	21–11–44	Sarande	DSO
Capt	D.G.	Angus	3– 4–45	Sarande	MC
Capt	P.	Delap	3– 4–45	Sarande	MC
Cpl	E.E.	Palmer	3– 4–45	Sarande	MM
RQMS	K.G.	Frost	14–12–45	Corfu	BEM
Sgt	C.	Cooper	14– 8–45	Reno	MM

Mentioned in Despatches

25– 8–44 Italy

Maj	N.S.E.	Maude	Lt	R.	Neale
Lt	J.A.	Smith	CSM	G.	Malcom MM
CSM	K.S.	Hawkins MM	Sgt	H.W.	Hill
Sgt	E.A.	Kinnear	Cpl	C.	Cooper MM
Mne	C.G.	Strong	Mne	F.C.H.	Jockham

3–11–44 Adriatic	19– 1–45 Italy	9– 3–45 Mediterranean
Lt. D. Copsey	Lt. M.C.M. Brockbank	Capt D.T.M. Thomson
	Cpl E.O. Hamstead	LCpl A.W. Stewart
	Mne G.A. Evans	Cpl G. McKenna

Awards published in the London Gazette on the dates listed

APPENDIX E

40 RM Commando Casualties

Between 19 August 1942 and the end of hostilities in Italy on 2 May 1945, 203 Officers, Non Commissioned Officers and Royal Marines serving in 40 Royal Marine Commando lost their lives as a result of enemy action.

A total of 421 all ranks required hospital treatment for wounds.

> *"Eternal Lord God, who, through many generations, hast united and inspired the members of our Corps; grant thy blessing, we beseech thee, on Royal Marines serving all round the Globe, Bestow thy crown of righteousness upon all our efforts and endeavours and may our Laurel be that of gallantry and honour, loyalty and courage. We ask this in the name of him whose courage never failed, our Redeemer, Jesus Christ."*

ALEXANDER	J.M.	Po/X	4237	Mne	19. 8.42	Dieppe
ALTRINGHAM	R.L.	Ch/X	112202	Mne	11. 4.45	Italy
BAIN	J.S.	Ply/x	746	CSM	9.10.44	Albania
BARRINGTON	W.H.	Ply/x	109107	Mne	9.10.43	Italy
BATES	G.H.	Ex	962	Mne	3. 6.44	Yugoslavia
BEESLEY	J.	Ch/x	844	Sgt	19. 8.42	Dieppe
BISHOP	A.	Po/x	114618	Mne	17. 7.43	Sicily
BLAKE	A.H.	Po/x	4970	Cpl	30. 7.44	Italy
BLUCK	J.A.	Po/x	117494	Mne	6. 3.44	Italy
BONE	P.J.	Po/x	101277	Cpl	3. 6.44	Yugoslavia
BREMNER	A.	Ch/x	104278	Mne	11. 4.45	Italy
BROWN	J.	Ply/x	109374	Mne	8. 3.44	Italy
BROWN	S.T.F.	Ply/x	111140	Mne	24. 7.43	Tunisia
BRYCE	W.	Ply/x	107517	Mne	10. 6.44	Yugoslavia
BURFITT	H.T.	Ch/x	110667	Mne	3.10.43	Italy
BURGESS	F.E.G.	Ch/x	110357	Mne	4. 3.44	Italy
BUSTARD	L.M.	Po/x	113418	Mne	11. 4.45	Italy
CALLOW	A.J.	Ply/x	3413	Mne	19. 8.42	Dieppe
CAPES	E.A.	Ch/x	103413	LCpl	22.12.44	Italy
CATTERALL	J.	Po/x	108069	Mne	19. 8.42	Dieppe
CHIVERALL	R.S.			Lt	8. 9.43	Italy
COCKITT	H.	Ply/x	104331	Mne	10. 3.44	Italy
COLBY	G.D.	Ch/X	112755	LCpl	11. 4.45	Italy
COMYN	A.D.			Capt	19. 8.42	Dieppe
COOMBER	A.D.	Ch/x	113202	Mne	11. 4.45	Italy

COOMBES	P.L.	Ch/x	110269	Mne	2. 4.45	Italy
COOPER	B.A.			Lt	6.10.43	Italy
COPE	H.J.	Po/x	108789	Mne	1.12.44	Italy
CORCORAN	J.E.B.	Ch/x	1679	Cpl	11. 4.45	Italy
CORNISH	A.H.	Ch/x	1013	CSgt	12. 7.43	At sea
CRADDOCK	W.H.C.	Ply/	108062	Cpl	27. 3.45	Italy
CRAIG	J.H.	Ch/x	110791	Mne	5. 3.44	Italy
CROSS	L.			Lt	3. 6.44	Yugoslavia
DAY	A.E.	Ply/x	6	Mne	8. 1.44	Italy
DAY	R.	Po/x	106905	Mne	12. 4.45	Italy
DENMARK	R.McL.	Po/x	109616	Mne	1. 9.43	Italy
DOWSON	H.	Ex	5685	Mne	19. 7.43	Sicily
DUERDEN	A.	Ply/x	108143	Cpl	19. 8.42	Dieppe
DUTTON	C.L.			Lt	3. 6.44	Yugoslavia
EPHRAUMS	M.J.			Capt MC	3.10.43	Italy
EVANS	G.A.	Po/x	108140	Mne	15. 3.44	Italy
EVERALL	H.J.	Ply/x	2081	Cpl	19. 8.42	Dieppe
FALLAS	R.S.	Po/x	4043	LCpl	17. 7.43	At sea
FANTHAM	M.	Po/x	114817	Mne	13.10.44	Italy
FINCH	E.E.	Ply/x	106278	Sgt	27. 3.45	Italy
FISHER	J.	Ch/x	105359	Sgt	19. 1.44	Italy
FOSTER	R.T.	Ch/x	2825	LCpl	11. 4.45	Italy
FRANKLIN	L.H.	Po/x	115045	Mne	19. 8.43	Sicily
GANNER	J.M.	Po/x		Mne	10. 3.44	Italy
GEE	D.P.	Ex	1172	Mne	3. 6.44	Yugoslavia
GORRIE	W.Y.	Ch/x	105950	Mne	2. 4.45	Italy
GOTTS	E.W.	Po/x	2274	Mne	19. 8.42	Dieppe
GREY	T.P.	Ex	3408	Cpl	21. 1.44	Italy
GRIFFEN	P.	Ch/x	112180	Mne	2. 4.45	Italy
GUINAN	H.W.	Ch/x	353	Mne	24. 4.43	UK
HADFIELD	R.W.	Ply/x	4097	Mne	22.12.44	Italy
HAMSTEAD	E.C.	Ch/x	104537	Mne	11. 4.45	Italy
HARVEY	L.G.	Pl/x	3864	LCpl	3. 6.44	Yugoslavia
HARWOOD	F.C.W.	Pl/x	2685	CSgt	19. 8.42	Dieppe
HASTINGS	F.R.	Pl/x	100676	LCpl	10. 1.44	Italy
HAYS	R.	Po/x	113795	Mne	11. 4.45	Italy
HEATH	A.S.	Ch/	1967	Cpl	20. 8.42	Dieppe
HERMAN	D.A.	Po/x	2835	Mne	9. 3.44	Italy
HERYET	G.W.	Ch/x	2855	Cpl	18. 1.44	Italy
HILES	W.J.			Capt	9.10.44	Albania
HILL	B.P.			Lt	28. 5.44	Yugoslavia
HILL	H.W.	Ex	5515	Sgt	11. 4.45	Italy
HOBBS	V.F.	Ch/x	112644	Mne	11. 4.45	Italy
HOPPER	N.C.	Po/x	117193	Mne	3. 6.44	Italy
HUBBARD	G.R.	Po/x	116193	Mne	8. 9.43	Italy
HUMPHRIES	J.	Ch/x	103795	Mne	16. 2.45	(POW)Germany
HURST	J.	Ch/x	112964	Mne	22. 1.44	Italy
JACKSON	T.	Ch/x	100733	LCpl	21. 3.44	Italy

JAGGARD	P.	Ch/x	111786	Mne	8. 9.43	Italy
JAMES	G.H.	Ch/x	110924	LCpl	12. 4.44	Italy
JONES	J.	Ch/x	2429	Mne	18. 7.43	Sicily
KENDRICK	R.	Ch/x	111228	Mne	24.12.44	Italy
KENNY	H.	Ply/x	101997	Mne	25.12.44	Italy
KILBRIDE	J.	Ex	3726	Cpl	12. 7.43	Italy
KLINCKE	E.S.	Ch/x	3417	Mne	22. 1.44	Italy
LAIDLAW	I.D.			Capt	3. 6.44	Yugoslavia
LEONARD	T.	Ex	3720	Mne	9.11.44	Corfu
LITTLE	W.A.	Ch/x	113276	Mne	11. 4.44	Italy
LONLAND	N.H.			Lt	20. 3.44	Italy
McGLASHON	D.P.	Ch/x	111797	Mne	11. 4.45	Italy
MCKENNA	G.	Ex	3363	Cpl	26.10.44	Corfu
MacKINISTRY	J.	Ex	4156	Mne	19. 8.42	Dieppe
Mac	PHERSON	M.S.		Capt	9.10.44	Yugoslavia
MALCOLM	G.	Pl/x	639	CSM	23. 1.44	Italy
MANNERS	J.C.	Lt	Col	DSO	3. 6.44	Yugoslavia
MANT	F.H.G.	Po/x	1227	CSM	21. 1.44	Italy
MARCO	P.D.	Po/x	107388	CSgt	11. 4.45	Italy
MARSHALL	L.G.B.		Capt	MC*	3. 2.45	Albania
MATTHEWS	F.G.	Po/x	112579	Cpl	19. 1 44	Italy
MOODY	E.J.	Ch/x	112355	Mne	11. 4.45	Italy
MORGAN	H.W.	Ch/x	1618	LCpl	19. 8.42	Dieppe
MORGAN	K.W.	Ch/x	110478	Mne	11. 6.44	UK
MULVEY	T.	Po/x	105260	Mne	1. 9.43	Italy
MUSGROVE	D.J.	Po/x	4732	Mne	19. 3.44	Italy
NASH	A.	Ply/	109509	Mne	11. 4.45	Italy
NIGHTINGALE	J.	Po/x	105298	Mne	4.10.43	Italy
O'CALLAGHAN	F.J.	Ch/x	111626	Mne	25. 6.44	Yugoslavia
OCKWELL	C.T.	Po/x	104971	Mne	18. 1.44	Italy
ORMAN	P.W.	Po/x	107304	Mne	19. 8.42	Dieppe
OVER	D.G.			Lt	19. 8.42	Dieppe
PAIN	L.J.	Ch/x	110765	Mne	11. 4.45	Italy
PEGRUM	J.D.J.			Lt	11. 4.45	Italy
PHILLIPPS	J.P.			Lt Col	19. 8.42	Dieppe
PICKERING	A.G.	Ch/x	111702	Mne	3. 6.44	Yugoslavia
PINCHER	R.	Pl/x	113394	Mne	10.10.44	Albania
PITT	E.A.	Ch/x	1257	Cpl	12. 5.45	Italy
PLATT	J.H.	Ex	1240	Mne	7. 3.44	Italy
PORTER	E.W.	Ply/x	104940	Mne	1. 9.43	Sicily
PORTER	N.M.			Maj	11. 4.45	Italy
POWELL	W.W.A.	Ch/x	3243	Mne	19. 8.42	Dieppe
PRATT	G.S.	Ch/x	3203	Mne	9.10.44	Albania
RHODES	W.H.	Po/x	21781	Mne	19. 8.42	Dieppe
RIDDLE	A.H.I.	Po/x	3021	Mne	19. 8.42	Dieppe
TUTTER	R.	Ply/x	111427	Mne	12. 4.45	Italy
SALT	J.V.	Po/x	114584	Mne	9.10.44	Albania
SCOTT	W.J.	Ch/x	1327	Sgt	11. 4.45	Italy

SHORT	D.L.W.N.	Ply/x	111155	LCpl	3. 6.44	Yugoslavia
SIMMONS	H.A.W.	Ex	4534	Mne	22. 8.42	UK
SIMPSON	S.	Po/x	3619	Mne	11. 4.45.	Italy
SINGLETON	R.B.	Po/x	107025	Mne	19. 8.42	Dieppe
SPENCER	F.	Pl/x	109442	Mne	1. 9.43	Sicily
ST ANGE	W.J.	Po/x	114352	Mne	9.10.44	Albania
STIEBEL	J.E.			Capt	17. 7.43	Sicily
SUTCLIFFE	K.G.	Ch/x	111640	LCpl	11. 4.45	Italy
SWAN	I.V.	Ch/x	2532	Sgt	14. 2.44	Italy
SWIFT	H.	Pl/x	112407	Mne	11. 4.45	Italy
TACK	R.E.	Ch/x	105806	Mne	7. 3.44	Italy
TARRANT	K.A.	Po/x	116686	Mne	3. 6.44	Yugoslavia
THOMSON	I.H.	Po/x	112654	Mne	17. 6.43	Sicily
THORPE	T.E.	Pl/x	1309	Cpl	19. 8.42	Dieppe
TOES	F.	Pl/x	2843	Cpl	3.10.43	Italy
TOWERS	J.	Pl/x	105669	Mne	7. 3.44	Italy
TURNER	A.J.	Ply/x	109504	Mne	17. 7.43	Sicily
TURRELL	J.E.	Po/x	103787	Mne	3.10.43	Italy
WALKER	P.E.	Po/x	2542	Mne	19. 8.42	Dieppe
WALLACE	G.P.	Ply/x	105075	Mne	7. 3.44	Italy
WARD	G.	Po/x	108397	Mne	24. 1.44	Italy
WEBSTER	T.H.	Po/x	3183	Mne	17. 7.43	Sicily
WEDGEWOOD	P.			Lt	11. 4.45	Italy
WHITE	C.H.P.	Ch/x	2124	Cpl	10.10.44	Italy
WIGMORE	H.A.	Po/x	886	Mne	19. 8.42	Dieppe
WISE	A.	Ch/x	111182	Mne	1. 9.43	Sicily
WOOD	R.F.	Ch/x	3476	Mne	3. 6.44	Yugoslavia
WOODALL	J.W.	Ch/x	2684	Cpl	11. 4.43	Italy
WRIGHTSON	A.J.	Po/x	114495	Mne	10. 8.43	N Africa

T Company personnel lost in HMS *Fidelity*   1. 1.43   **At sea**

ANDREWS	C.	Ply/x	1674	Mne
ANSON	H.R.J.	Po/x	100156	Mne
APPLEBY	W.T.	Ply/x	2597	Mne
BASHAM	C.E.	Ply/x	3085	Mne
BOOTHROYD	G.	Po/x	3189	Mne
BRADLEY	W.J.	Ply/x	3580	Mne
BROWNBRIDGE	R.W.	Ch/x	1085	Mne
CHAPMAN	C.C.	Ex	1169	Mne
DIXON	D.G.	Ply/x	2699	Cpl
EDWARDS	M.A.	Po/x	4386	Mne
FARRELL	R.	Po/x	2501	Mne
FISK	G.E.	Po/x	315	Mne
GOODYEAR-KETTLEY				
	F.R.	Ply/x	3095	Mne
GRANT-DALTON	H.W.F.			Capt
HEBDEN	R.	Po/x	4047	Mne
HENDERSON	A.W.	Ch/x	1123	Sgt

HERD	A.F.	Ex	3189	Mne
HEWSON	W.B.	Po/x	2397	Mne
HILDRETH	H.L	Po/x	104141	Mne
HILL	R.H.	Ply/x	3235	Mne
HUMPHRIES	H.	Ply/x	2458	Mne
HUTCHINSON	J.	Ch/x	2331	Mne
JAMES	R.K.	Po/x	108891	Mne
JEFFERS	M.	Po/x	105426	Mne
KELLEY	J.F.	Ch/x	2555	Mne
LAGOR	R.A.	Ply/	3859	Mne
LEDBURY	D.R.N.	Po/x	5001	Mne
MCDOWELL	E.	Po/x	3758	Mne
MCGEE	J.C.	Ply/x	3027	Mne
MILO	F.C.	Ply/x	2430	Mne
NASH	T.	Ch/x	2218	Mne
O'BRIEN	E.S	Po/x	1309	Mne
OBORN	A.R.	Po/x	2308	Mne
PALMER	J.	Pl/x	3323	Mne
PANTAR	H.D.	Po/x	107976	Mne
PARKER	R.S.	Pl/x	2254	Mne
PAYNE	G.T.	Po/x	4374	Mne
PEMBER	H.D.H.A.	Ex	3500	Mne
RICHMOND	J.A.	Ex	3778	Mne
SALAMAN	H.L.	Ply/x	104581	Mne
SAUNDERS	R.T.C.	Ch/x	1276	Mne
SEABROOK	J.J.L	Ch/x	1934	Mne
SHOCKLEY	H.W.	Po/x	101827	Mne
SIMMONDS	J.F.	Po/x	3601	Cpl
SWATTON	V. DSM	Po/x	2317	Cpl
THOMSON	R.	Ex	3948	Cpl
TRASK	W.A.N.			Lt
TRUMP	W.C.	Ch/x	104658	Mne
TURNER	R.C.	Ch/x	2632	Mne
TWIDALE	T.	Ex	3870	Mne
WAKEFIELD	J.H.	Ch/x	1417	Mne
WILSON	D.J.	Ch/x	2546	Mne

APPENDIX F

TERMS OF THE HAGANAH COMMAND FOR
A TRUCE IN HAIFA

1. Complete disarming of all ARAB arms, including weapons of all kinds, all explosives, military vehicles and other military equipment without exception.

2. All arms within the above description must be delivered within three hours at the following places of assembly:

    (i)   Near the RUSHMIYA BRIDGE opposite the offices of the EASTERN MOSLEM COUNCIL;

    (ii) Corner od STANTON STREET and BOURJ;

   (iii) Entrance to OLD BUSINESS CENTRE;

    (iv) Egged Station, CARMEL AVENUE.

            These will be held by the military in trust to the HAGANAH till 15 May.

3. Removal forthwith of ARAB roadblocks and freedom of traffic undisturbed will commence forthwith under military supervision

4. All foreign ARAB males will concentrate at places of assembly to be fixed by HAGANAH and will leave PALESTINE within twenty-four hours under military control.

5. European NAZIS will be delivered to the military.

6. A twenty-four hours curfew will be imposed on ARAB quarters and houses to assure complete disarming.

7. Non-delivery of arms within the time specified will be treated as an offence and will be punishable.

8. After the house curfew each person in HAIFA will be free to carry on his normal business and way of life.

9. ARABS will carry on their work as equals and free citizens of HAIFA and will enjoy all services with the other members of the community.

10. Any joint meeting will take place in the TOWN HALL.

APPENDIX G

The Wilkinson Sword of Peace

In 1799 a sword was made in London for presentation to Lt S. Snook of the Bombay Marine. Lt Snook had been so outstanding in his humanity to refugee women from the Pelew Islands in the Philippines that his brother officers and the East India Company presented him with this specially inscribed sword.

The refugees had been stranded in Bombay from 1793 to 1797 without friends or means of support. Lt Snook provided for them out of his own meagre pay until, in 1797, the East India Company made provision for the refugees to sail to Macao under his charge in the merchant ship Warley. On arrival Lt Snook was authorised to purchase a small vessel at Government expense to take them to their homes in the Pelew Islands.

Wilkinson Sword Ltd aquired Lt Snook's sword and presented it to the National Army Museum on 10 March 1965. Field Marshal the Viscount Slim, receiving the sword on behalf of the museum said "Lt Snook's unselfish behaviour typified the help the Services gave the civilians in many countries in time of war, famine and disaster."

The following year Wilkinson Sword Ltd, in co-operation with the Ministry of Defence, sponsored a special award to be known as the Sword of Peace for presentation annually to a unit from each of the three Armed Forces. The units receiving the Sword of Peace are selected each year by the Ministry of Defence on recommendation made by the Admiralty, Army and RAF Boards. The objective is to recognise outstanding efforts by British units in fostering good relations in the territories and areas in which they are stationed. The Swords of Peace are of standard service pattern, inscribed with the name of the unit concerned and the area in which it qualified for the award.

The first Royal Navy Sword of Peace was awarded to 40 Commando Royal Marines in 1967 for humanitarian services to people in Sarawak. The Sword of Peace was again awarded to the Commando in 1972 for outstanding community relations in Northern Ireland under particularly difficult circumstances. The unit received its third award in 1985, for humanitarian assistance to the people of Cyprus while serving with the United Nations Forces, the only unit in the service at that time to have won the award three times in the 19 years since its inception.

APPENDIX H

Commanding Officers

Lieutenant Colonel	J.P.	Phillipps	14-2-42	19-8-42	Killed in action
Lieutenant Colonel	J.C.	Manners DSO.	20-8-42	3-6-44	Killed in action
Major	N.S.E.	Maude	4-6-44	30- 6-44	
Lieutenant Colonel	R.W.	Sankey DSO,DSC.	1-7-44	20- 4-45	
Major	I.	De'Ath DSO,MBE.	21-4-45	14- 7-45	
Major	W.D.	Read	15-7-45	9- 9-45	
Lieutenant Colonel	C.L.	Price	10-9-45	26-11-45	
Lieutenant Colonel	R.D.	Houghton OBE,MC.	16-3-47	8- 7-49	
Lieutenant Colonel	B.J.D.	Lumsden OBE.	9-7-49	11- 6-51	
Lieutenant Colonel	M.	Price DSO,OBE.	12-6-51	29- 7-53	
Lieutenant Colonel	H.E.	Johns MBE.	30-7-53	14- 5-54	
Lieutenant Colonel	T.M.	Grey DSO,MC.	15-5-54	2- 5-56	
Lieutenant Colonel	D.G.	Tweed DSO,MBE.	3-5-56	18- 2-58	
Lieutenant Colonel	P.W.C.	Hellings DSC,MC.	19-2-58	29- 6-59	
Lieutenant Colonel	I.S.	Harrison	30-6-59	8- 1-61	
Lieutenant Colonel	D.P.L.	Hunter MC	9-1-61	11- 1-63	
Lieutenant Colonel	J.F.	Parsons MC	12-1-63	21- 9-64	
Lieutenant Colonel	J.A.	Taplin MBE	22-9-64	31- 7-66	
Lieutenant Colonel	C.B.D.	Pounds	1-8-66	8- 1-67	
Lieutenant Colonel	R.B.	Loudoun OBE	9-1-67	24- 4-69	
Lieutenant Colonel	D.C.	Alexander	24-4-69	21-10-70	
Lieutenant Colonel	D.L.	Bailey OBE.	22-10-70	22- 3-72	
Lieutenant Colonel	J.F.	Mottram OBE.	23-3-72	20- 2-74	
Lieutenant Colonel	M.C.L.	Wilkins OBE.	21- 2-74	16-12-75	
Lieutenant Colonel	J.H.A.	Thompson OBE.	17-12-75	16- 6-78	
Lieutenant Colonel	J.M.C.	Garrod OBE.	17- 6-78	9-11-79	
Lieutenant Colonel	R.J.	Ross OBE.	9-11-79	21- 9-81	
Lieutenant Colonel	M.P.J.	Hunt	21- 9-83	22- 7-83	
Lieutenant Colonel	T.P.T.	Donkin MBE.	22- 7-83	17- 6-85	
Lieutenant Colonel	R.A.	Hooper MA.	17- 6-85	24- 3-87	
Lieutenant Colonel	J.S.	Chester OBE.	25- 3-87	17- 1-88	
Lieutenant Colonel	A.D.	Wray	18- 1-88	16-11-90	
Lieutenant Colonel	C.G.H.	Dunlop	17-11-90		

APPENDIX I

Sources of Reference

Bibliography
Barzilay, D.   *The British Army in Ulster Vol. 3*   Century Books
Brown, D.   *The Royal Navy and the Falklands War*   Leo Cooper
Churchill, Maj Gen T. B. L.   *Commando Crusade*   William Kimber
Churchill, Sir Winston   *Closing the Ring*   Cassell & Co Ltd
Clark, Gen M. W.   *Calculated Risk*   George G. Harrop & Co Ltd
Durnford-Slater, J.   *Commando*   William Kimber
Giesler, P.   *Dieppe*   Public Affairs Division Canada
Halliday, J.   *The Artful Albanians, Memiors of E. Hoxha*   Chatto and Windus
Hastings, M. & Jenkins S.   *The Battle for the Falklands*   Michael Joseph Ltd
Heikal, M. H.   *Suez. Cutting the Lion's Tail*   Andre Deutsh
Jelavitch, B.   *History of the Balkans*   Twentieth Century Cambridge Press
Jackson, R.   *Suez 1956: Operation Musketter*   Ian Allan Ltd
Ladd, J. D.   *Commandos and Rangers of World War II*   Macdonald & Jane's
Lloyd, S.   *Suez 1956 – A Personal Account*   Jonathan Cape Ltd
Montgomery, FM B. L.   *Montgomery of Alamein KG*   Collins
Moulton, Maj Gen J. L.   *The Royal Marines*   Leo Cooper
Saunders, H. St G,   *The Green Beret*   Michael Joseph Ltd
Thompson, Maj Gen J. H. A.   *No Picnic*   Leo Cooper/Secker & Warburg
Yugoslavia Stravuost   *Facts about Yugoslavia*   FSI, Belgade
Kigswell, P.   *Fidelity will Haunt Me Till I Die*   RM Historical Society
O'Ballance, E.   *Malaya, The Communist Insurgent War 1948-60*   Faber & Faber
Ricklefs, M. C.   *A History of Modern Indonesia*   MacMillan
Smith, C. D.   *Palestine and the Arab Israeli Conflict*   MacMillan
Smith, J.   *74 Days. An Insiders Diary of the Falklands Occupation*

Official Reports and Papers
Dieppe Summary, 3 Oct 194 and Italian Objectives, 14 April 1945, The Army Bureau of
Current Affairs.
History of Commandos in the Mediterranean Sep 1943 to May 1945, HQ 2 SS Bde.
Report on the Crossing of the River Garigliano, Lt Col J. C. Manners
Report on the Reconnaissance of the Island of Pelagosa, Capt. I. C. McKellar.
Report on Anzio, Lt Col J. C. Manners
Correspondence to Ct Col R. W. Sankey from HQ 2 Commando Bde, Feb and April 1945.
White Paper The Falklands Campaign, The Lessons, HM Stationery Office.
Unit War Diaries and Newsletters in the Public Records Office, Kew and at Hayes.
Papers and records in the Royal Marines Museum at Eastney.

Journal
The Globe and Laurel, The Journal of the Royal Marines.

Personal Interviews
Officers, non commissioned officers, marines and privates who served in the Royal Marine
Commando, Royal Marine 'A' Commando, 40 Royal Marine Commando and 40 Com-
mando Royal Marines, including personnel currently serving in the Royal Marines. Also,
personnel of the Royal Navy, the Army, the Royal Air Force, the Coastal Forces Veterans
Association and SUBNOR, the Yugoslav Partisan Forces Veterans Association.

APPENDIX J

General Abbreviations

Adjutant	Adjt	Landing Platform Helicopter	LPH
Administrative Officer	adminO	Landing Ship Logisitics	LSL
Admiral/Vice/Rear Admiral	Adm/V/R Adm	Tank	LST
Airbourne	AB	Vehicle Tracked	LVT
Ammunition	ammo	Lieutenant Commander	Lr Cdr
Amphibious	amph	Lieutenant/Second Lieutenant	Lt/2Lt
Anti-Aircraft	AA	Major General Royal Marines	MGRM
Armoured Personnel Carrier	APC	Major	Maj
Battalion	Bn	Marine	Mne
Battery	bty	Mechanical/Motor Transport	MT
Brigade	bde	Medical/Medium	med
Brigadier	Brig	Medical Officer	MO
Captain	Capt	Mobile/Mortar Fire Controller	MFC
Casualty Evacuation	CASEVAC	Motor Gun/Torpedo/Boat	MGB/MTB
Chief Petty Officer/Petty Officer	CPO/PO	Motor Launch	ML
Colonel/Lieutenant Colonel	Col/Lt Col	Musician	Musn
Colour Sergeant/Sergeant	CSgt/Sgt	Non Commissioned Officer	NCO
Commandant General Royal Marines	CGRM	Nuclear Biological & Chemical	NBC
Commander-in-Chief	C-in-C	Observation Post	OP
Commander	Cdr	Parachute/paragraph	para
Commanding Officer	CO	Petroleum, oil and lubricants	POL
Commando	Cdo	Physical training	PT
Commodore	Cdre	Platoon	pl
Corporal/Lance Corporal	Cpl/LCpl	Private	Pte
Defensive Fire	DF	Quartermaster General	QMG
Deputy Assistant Adjutant	DAA	Quartermaster Sergeant	QMS
Dropping Zone	DZ	Royal Fleet Auxiliary	RFA
Enemy	en	Reconnaissance, reconnoitre	recce
Field Dressing Station	FDS	Regimental Sergeant Major	RSM
Field Marshal	FM	Quartermaster Sergeant	RQMS
Forming-up Place	FUP	Rendezvous	RV
Forward Observation Officer	FOO	Section	sec
General/Lieutenant General	Gen/Lt Gen	Self Propelled, Start Point	SP
Major General	Maj Gen	Senior Naval Officer	SNO
General Officer Commanding	GOC	Senior Nursing Sister	SNS
General Purpose Machine Gun		Small Arms Ammunition	SAA
(sustained fire)	GPMG (SF)	Special Air Services	SAS
Helicopter Aircraft Carrier	CVH	Special Boat Services	SBS
Her Majesty's Ship	HMS	Squadron Leader	Sqn Ldr
High Explosive	HE	Tactic(s), tactical	tac
In command, In charge	IC	Tactical Exercise Without Troops	TEWT
Intelligence Officer	IO	Temporary	temp
Landing Craft Assault	LCA	United States Ship	USS
Mechanized/Medium	LCM	Warrant Officer Class One	WO1
Tank	LCT	Wing Commander	Wg Cdr
Landing Platform Dock (Assault Ship)	LPD	Wireless Telegraphy	WT

INDEX

Ranks shown in the index are those held at the latest point of reference in the narrative.
Appendix E contains a nominal list of 40 RM Commando casualties 1942–45.

Belgium Air Force 17.
Belize S, America 344, 346, 351, 353.
Bellamy C.G. Capt 259.
Bellocchio Canal, Italy 137.
Bembridge Harbour 35.
Benghazi, Libya 2, 238.
Ben Resipol, Scotland 9.
Bennett W.H. Sgt 212.
Berck, France 11.
Bernadotte F. Count 171.
Berneval, France 16, 18.
Berriff A.M. Lt 12.
Bessbrook Mill, N.Ireland 342, 343.
Best J.N. 2Lt 262.
Bevin Ernest 159, 177.
Bibibic V. 99.
Bifurno River 56, 59, 67.
Biss E.R. QMS 199.
Bissendon D.Pte 108
Bitter Lakes, Egypt 208.
Black LMA 337.
Blake A.Capt 109.
Block A.J.C. Maj Gen 244.
Blythe E. CSgt 309.
Bol, Dalmatia 105, 106.
Bologna, Italy 134, 135.
Bomba Bay, N.Africa 243.
Bone P.J.Cpl 36, 108, 110.
Boote L.J.RSM 204, 208.
Borneo 250, (map) 251, 254, 266.
Borsh, Albania 114, 115.
Bosnia, Yugoslavia 111.
Bostock Mne 241
Bothe Mne 112.
Bovington 320, 362, 363.
Bower Lt Gen Sir Roger 244.
Boyd Carpenter 271.
Boyd VAdm Sir Denis 152.
Boyd S. Lt(QM) 204.
Brac, Dalmatia 94, 95, 97, 102, 103, 104, 105,
        110, 111.
Bradley J.W.E. Capt 29, 62, 72.
Bray G.A.RSM 261.
Bream G.L. RSM 217.
Breen T.Mne 22.
Bridgewater 371.
Briggs Lt Gen Sir Harold 194, 195, 198.
Briggs R.Rev 94.
Brindisi, Italy 49, 76, 368.
Brisbane, Australia 270.
Bristowe F.M. Capt 137, 199.
Britain 159, 184, 218, 223, 234, 328, 352, 378.
Brockbank Lt 89.
Brockman E. Lt Col 11.
Brooks R.A.D Lt Gen 155.
Brooking B. Lt RN 291.
Brown P. CSgt 309.
Bruce E.Cdr 224, 227, 233.
Bruce H.G.Maj 220, 226, 229, 230, 366.

Brucoli, Sicily 47.
Brunei, Borneo 254, 322, 346, 350, 360, 365,
        371.
Brush RSM 349.
Broz J. see Tito 95.
Bryce W. Mne 112.
Bolwell B. 28.
Bolougne, France 3, 11.
Buenos Aires 322.
Bundy K.W. 211.
Bukit Ribut, Malasia 274.
Burma 176, 194.
Burma Camp, Malaya 252, 255, 26.
Burnett Air Chf Mshl Sir Brian 278, 27.
Burslem J. Surg Lt 302.
Burtenshaw D.E. Mne 20.
Butler Brig 232, 234.
Butler Lt Col 69.
Buttery G.D.QMS 234.
Buzzer S. Lt 336.

Cairo, Egypt 219, 223.
Cameron Highlands, Malaya 272.
Camp Lejeune, USA 289.
Canada 378.
Calais, France 3.
Calbourne 13.
Calder Pte 143.
Calvert M. Lt Col 184.
Camberley 3.
Carrington Lord 293.
Carson D. Lt Cdr 111.
Cartwright Taylor M.C Lt Gen 252.
Carisbrooke 13.
Carlan Mne 22.
Carver Gen Sir Michael 269.
Castelforte, Italy 78, 81, 82, 83, 86.
Castelmare, Italy 77, 81.
Casualties 40 RM Cdo 386.
Catania, Sicily 46, 47, 56.
Canal Zone 200, 207, 208, 209, 210, 212, 213.
Canton 179.
Cape Arnauti 210.
Cape Loviste, Dalmatia 100.
Cape Andreas, Cyprus 174.
Caraolos 176.
Castel Benito, N Africa 157.
Castle Peak, Hong Kong 152, 153.
Cerni Cdr 97, 103, 107.
Cesena, Italy 135.
Chadwick Mne 196, 199.
Chale 11.
Chamberlain F.N.Ven Arch 202.
Chambers Mne 372.
Chapman Mne 90.
Charles, HRH The Prince 174.
Cherry R.H.Mne 199.
Cherbourg, France 33, 34.
Chesterton W. RSM 181, 190.

398

Woodward J.C. RAdm 322, 327, 330.
Wray A.D. Lt Col 367, 371, 372.
Wright D. Capt 11.

Xylotymbou, Cyprus 173, 174, 177.

Yarmouth Roads, Isle of Wight 17.
Yoke Beach, Albania 119.
Young B. Capt 329.
Young Rev 198.
Young P. Lt Col 18, 56.
Younger George 360.
Yugoslavia 2, 74, 95, 114, 151.

Zab River, Iraq 375.
Zakho, Iraq 375
Zeebrugge, Belgium 34.
Zebra Beach, Albania 118, 119.
Zervas Gen 121, 124, 125, 126, 129, 130, 131, 132.
Zuwarah, (Zuara), Libya 214

Army Formations and units:

British Army
8th Army 46, 49, 73, 79, 86, 134, 135.
15th Army Gp 73, 87.
5 Corps 49, 73.
10 Corps 49, 54, 86.
13 Corps 46, 49.
1 Armd Div 134.
10 Armd Div 222.
1 Inf Div 86, 91.
1 Airborne Div 46.
3 Inf Div 222.
5 Inf Div 54, 85.
6 Inf Div 85.
56 (London) Div 87, 89.
1 Guards Bde 170, 172.
13 Inf Bde 85.
15 Inf Bde 49.
16 Para Bde 206, 207, 222, 229, 232, 234, 246, 252.
17 Inf Bde 45.
18 Inf Bde 91.
19 Inf Bde 210, 241, 274.
28 Commonwealth Bde 272.
167 (London) Bde 79, 85, 88.
168 (London) Bde
169 Inf Bde 79, 187, 141.
231 Inf Bde 49.

SS Bde 5, 12, 34..
1 SS Bde 73, 74.
2 SS/Cdo Bde 73, 74, 75, 103, 107, 110, 114, 132, 134, 136.
3 SS/Cdo Bde 150, 176.
4 SS/Cdo Bde 73, 74, 200.
Royal Horse Gds 217.

4/7 Dragoon Gds 172.
14/20 Hussars 213.
17/21 Lancers 171, 250.
6 R Tank Regt 228, 238, 334.
Yorkshire Dragoons 93,
20 Fd Regt RA 257.
111 Fd Regt RA 105, 115.
21 Regt RA 217.,
29 Cdo Lt Regt RA 259, 272, 371,
88 LAA Regt RA 214.
95 Cdo Lt Regt RA 273.
7 (Sphinx) Cdo Lt Bty RA 267, 279.
79 (Kirkee) Cdo Lt Bty RA 273, 353.
Raiding Support Regt 105, 114, 115, 117.
Royal Engineers 7, 191.
2 FD Sqn RE 334.
59 Cdo Sqn RE 337, 371.
371 Postal Unit RE 222.

Grenadier Gds 170, 172.
Coldstream Gds 166, 172, 341.
Scots Gds 216, 335, 336, 337, 338, 364.
Irish Gds 170.
Welsh Gds 209, 337, 338, 340.
Gds Indep Para Coy 232.

R Scots 267.
Queen's 79, 88, 89, 141, 144, 357, 371.
Buffs 93,
R Warwickshire Regt 245.
Royal Fusiliers 81, 243, 244, 246, 248.
Devonshire Regt 50.
Green Howards 195.
Duke of Cornwall's L I 28.
Duke of Wellington's Regt 89, 352.
R Sussex Regt 241.
Hampshire Regt 50, 363,
Dorset Regt 50.
Oxfordshire & Buckinghamshire L I &
1 Green Jackets/ 1 R Green Jackets 84, 255.
Anglian Regt 347.
Sherwood Foresters 89, 91,
R Berkshire Regt 84, 228.
King's Own Yorkshire L I 82,
Duke of Edinburgh's Royal Regt 343.
Highland L I 102,
Argyll & Sutherland Highlanders 4, 5, 30, 180, 240.
Parachute Regt 160, 325, 327, 329, 330, 331, 332, 334, 335, 337, 338, 341, 363
Special Air Service 198, 247, 325, 328, 329, 330, 332.
6 Gurkha Rifles 199, 268,
7 Gurkha Rifles 274.
10 Gurkha Rifles 257, 259.
99 Gurkha Rifles 254.
Ulster Defence Regt 3423.
Army Commandos 1.
1 Cdo 150.

2 Cdo 13, 54, 73, 84, 87, 105, 110, 114, 115,
122, 132, 135, 139.
3 Cdo 17, 18, 31, 33, 46, 50, 73, 74.
4 Cdo 17, 18, 31.
5 Cdo 150.
9 Cdo 73, 87, 88, 114, 132, 139.
Special Raiding Sqn 49.
Cdo Basic Trng Depot 8, 10.

RASC 88, 195.
11261 Docks Op Sqn 168.
1 LVT Tp RASC
20 Hovercraft Sqn RCT 270.
23 Para Fd Amb RAMC 210.
RAOC 210.

Empire and Commonwealth
Australian Regt 272
Barbados Defence Force 369

Canadian Army Formations and Units:
2 Canadian Div 12, 16.
214 Canadian Inf Div 12.
Calgary Regt(Tank)16, 20, 26.
Black Watch of Canada 20.
R Regt of Canada 16, 20.
R Hamilton L I 16, 20, 26.
South Saskatchewan Regt 16, 20, 26.
Queen's Own Cameron Highlanders of
Canada 16, 20 26.
Essex Scottish 20, 21, 16, 26.
Fusiliers Mount Royal 16, 18, 21, 26.

Falkland Islands Defence Force 324.

New Zealand Army
272 Corps of NZ Engineers 118.
NZ Base Hospital 94.

Malaysia
4 Malaysian Inf Bde 274.
5 R Malay Regt 266.
Malayan Scouts 198.

Other Nationalities
Alabanian Partisans 118.
12 Bde 123.
3/40 Regt 123.

American 5th Army 49, 54, 86, 134, 135.
American 2nd Corps 86.
American 3rd Div 86.
American Rangers 1, 13.
1 Rangers 86, 87.
3 Rangers 86, 87, 375.
4 Rangers 86.
36 US Combat Engineers 88.
USMC 13.
21 Landing Unit 173.

3 Bn 2 Marine Div 248.
1/9 Bn Landing Team 278.
USMC Engineers 278.
Egyptian Army 344, 361.
French Commandos Marine 357.
French Foreign Legion 361.
Greek National Guard 132.
65 regt (Andarte) 125, 126, 127.
Italian San Marco Bn 361, 368, 371.
Netherlands Marine Corps 361, 371.
UN Peace Keeping Force Cyprus 347.
Yugoslav National Liberation Army 96.
1 Proletarian Bde 96.
26 Dalmatian Udarna Div 98, 103.
1/11/12/13/ Dalmatian Bde 98.
1/3 Overseas Bde 98, 105.
SUBNOR 112.

German units:
Afrika Corps 2.
118 Jaeger Div 103.
738 Regt 103.
1 Bn, 236 Regt 135.
162 Div Turcomans 135.

Royal Marines Formations and Units-
Royal Marine Office 3, 29, 34.
Chatham Division 2, 4, 151.
Plymouth Division 4.
Portsmouth Division 2, 4.
Eastney Barracks 2.
Depot, Deal 2, 3, 4 7.
Depot, Lympstone 2.

RM Div 2, 5.

RM Bde 1.
101 RM Bde 4.
102 RM Bde 4, 5.
103 RM Bde 5.
104 RM Trg Bde 5.
3 SS/Cdo Bde 3, 150, 151, 155, 160, 168, 184,
193, 194, 202, 207, 216, 218, 221, 222,
234, 238, 241.250, 266, 267, 270, 276,
278, 357, 369, 372, 373, 376, 379.

Siege Regt 2.4.
1 AA Regt 2.
2 Coast Regt 4.
11 SL Regt 2.
Logistic regt 160, 334.

2 Bn RM 12.
3 Bn RM 3.
4 Bn RM 34.
8 Bn RM 29.
9 Bn RM 4, 176.
12 Bn RM 4, 5.
15 Machine Gun Bn 3.

18 Mobile Bn 4.
Royal Marines Formations and Units
    continued:
RM Cdo/RM 'A' Cdo/40 RM Cdo/40 Cdo
    RM 1, 3, 8, 18, 26, 29, 29, 31, 32, 33, 34,
    38, 41, 46, 47, 50.73, 77, 78, 79, 85, 87,
    89.90.91, 93, 94, 99, 102, 105, 108, 110,
    111, 113, 115, 119, 120, 121, 127, 134,
    135, 141, 144, 152, 153, 154, 155, 159,
    160, 165, 166, 168, 173, 174, 1275, 176,
    178, 180, 183, 187, 189, 194, 196, 197,
    199, 202, 204, 207, 208, 210, 212, 213,
    215, 216, 217, 218, 221, 222, 223, 224,
    227, 231, 236, 238, 239, 240, 241, 243,
    244, 246, 248, 249, 250, 252, 254, 257,
    258, 264, 266, 267, 268, 269, 270, 272,
    273, 274, 276, 277, 278, 281, 319, 320,
    321, 322, 323, 324, 326, 327, 328, 329,
    330, 331, 333, 334, 335, 337, 338, 339,
    340, 344, 345, 346, 349, 352, 354, 355,
    357, 358, 360, 363, 365, 366, 367, 369,
    370, 371, 372, 373, 375, 376, 378.
40 Cdo Air Troop 264.
RM 'B' Cdo/41 Cdo RM 31, 34, 38, 41, 46, 74,
    245, 252,
41 Ind Cdo 209.
42 RM Cdo/ 42 Cdo RM 150, 155, 160, 168,
    176, 180, 189, 202, 204, 207, 208, 210,
    212, 213, 218, 221, 222, 223, 224, 227,
    229, 231, 241, 247, 250, 254, 257, 258,
    269, 272, 277, 278, 322, 325, 326, 327,
    328, 329, 330, 334, 335, 337, 338, 363,
    372, 373,
43 Cdo RM 74, 77, 87, 97, 102, 105, 108, 110,
    139, 210, 247.
44 RM Cdo, 44 Cdo RM 150, 151, 152, 153.
45 RM Cdo, 45 Cdo RM 150, 153, 155, 160,
    176, 177, 180, 189, 196, 197, 202, 204,
    207, 208, 210, 212, 213, 215, 217, 218,
    221, 222, 224, 229, 230, 241, 243, 244,
    246, 252, 319, 322, 325, 326, 328, 329,
    330, 334, 337, 338, 372, 375, 376,
46 RM Cdo 12, 176.
47 RM Cdo 194.
48 RM Cdo 200.
1 Raiding Sqn 320.
3 SBS 329, 330.
6 SBS 247.

3 Cdo Bde Air Sqn 264, 270.
3 Cdo Bde Band 174, 177, 178, 179, 180, 192,
    202, 346,

NCOs School 2.
Tech Trg Wing 4.
RMR Scotland 375.

H M SHIPS

Aircraft Carriers
Ark Royal 271.
Centaur 213.
Hermes 269, 321, 325, 326, 329, 342, 344.
Illustrious 360, 363.
Invincible 319, 320, 326.
Theseus 202.
Triumph 277.

Battleships
Nelson 4.

Cruisers
Birmingham 214.
Cleopatra 202.
Cumberland 4.
Dido 266.
Gambia 213.
Glasgow 202.
Jamaica 183, 186.
Kenya 202.

Destroyers
Barossa 254.
Coventry 334.
Duchess 226, 227.
Nottingham 360.
Plymouth 327, 329.
Sheffield 241, 330.

Frigates
Active 337.
Albert 18.
Antelope 333.
Antrim 327, 328, 329, 330, 331.
Arethusa 281.
Ardent 330, 332, 333.
Argonaut 332, 333.
Avenger 337.
Berkley 25, 27.
Brilliant 333.
Broadsword 333.
Brocklesby 25.
Diamond 226, 227.
Elk 330.
Euryalus 170, 202.
Glamorgan 337.
Herald 371.
Kelpy 18, 21.
Ocean 224.
Meon 224.
Phoebe 172, 269, 372.

Coastal Forces
MTB-105 35, 36.
MGB-647 112.
166 101. 658 101.

667 100. 651 100.

Converted French Merchant Ship
Fidelity 11, 35, 36.

Submarine Depot Ship
Tyne 202, 205, 232, 234.

Ice Patrol Ship
Endurance 322, 327.

Commando Carriers
Albion 213, 252, 254, 258, 269, 271, 278, 279, 281.
Bulwark 245, 250, 252, 253, 254, 259, 262, 267,
    268, 269, 274, 276.

Amphibious Ships
Fearless 268, 274, 322, 326, 329, 330, 331, 332,
    335, 338, 360, 372.
Intrepid 276, 277, 322, 331, 332, 335, 359, 360,
    361, 368, 371.

Landing Ships Infantry
Locust 13, 16, 17, 18, 19, 20, 21, 23, 27.
Messina (HQ ship) 201, 206.
Prince Albert 41, 46.
Princess Beatrix 12, 33, 39, 46.
Princess Emma 46.

Landing Craft
Bastion 224, 227.
Reggio 220, 224, 233, 242.
Sallyport 227.
Striker 172, 242.

Royal Fleet Auxiliaries
Sir Galahad 277, 334, 336,
Sir Geriant 334.
Sir Lancelot 334.
Sir Percival 361, 371.
Sir Tristam 329, 336, 371.
Dusquesne 247.

Lyness 269.
Norland 330, 398.
Olwen 269.
Resource 344, 378.
Stromness 326, 329, 330.
Tidespring 327.

Admiralty Tug and other vessels
Eminent 35.
Petrel 259, 263.
Papa Charlie Three 259, 260.

Transports and Merchant Ships
SS Derbyshire (with LCAs) 38, 39, 40, 41, 42, 43.
Durban Castle (with LCAs) 38, 41, 43.
Empire Woodrush 180, 234.
Empress of Australia 178.
Georgic 180.
Halladale 199.
Oxforshire 247, 248, 250.
Strathnaver 153.
John Biscoe 322.

Ships Taken Up From Trade
SS Atlantic Conveyor 334.
Canberra 325, 326, 327, 330, 331, 333, 340.
Europic Ferry 334.
Uganda 335.
Bolero 357.
Anby 259.

Other Nationalities
HMCS Woodstock 36.
US Sixth Fleet 209, 227, 236, 238, 243, 248, 373.
USS Iwo Jima 278.
French Mediterranean Fleet 221.
Cyrenia (Greek) 164.
Flying Arrow 164.
General Belgrano (Argentine) 329.

U Boats
U-225, U-435 and U-615 35.